D1757802

TP12008161
KSS/SSR

CLASS AND STRATIFICATION ANALYSIS

COMPARATIVE SOCIAL RESEARCH

Series Editor: Fredrik Engelstad

Recent Volumes:

Volume 18: Family Change: Practices, Policies, and Values, 1999

Volume 19: Comparative Perspectives on Universities, 2000

Volume 20: The Comparative Study of Conscription in the Armed Forces, 2002

Volume 21: Comparative Studies of Culture and Power, 2003

Volume 22: The Multicultural Challenge, 2003

Volume 23: Comparative Studies of Social and Political Elites, 2007

Volume 24: Capitalisms Compared, 2007

Volume 25: Childhood: Changing Contexts, 2008

Volume 26: Civil Society in Comparative Perspective, 2009

Volume 27: Troubled Regions and Failing States: The Clustering and Contagion of Armed Conflicts, 2010

Volume 28: The Nordic Varieties of Capitalism, 2011

Volume 29: Firms, Boards and Gender Quotas: Comparative Perspectives, 2012

COMPARATIVE SOCIAL RESEARCH   VOLUME 30

CLASS AND STRATIFICATION ANALYSIS

EDITED BY

GUNN ELISABETH BIRKELUND
University of Oslo, Oslo, Norway

United Kingdom – North America – Japan
India – Malaysia – China

Emerald Group Publishing Limited
Howard House, Wagon Lane, Bingley BD16 1WA, UK

First edition 2013

British Library Cataloguing in Publication Data
A catalogue record for this book is available from the British Library

ISBN: 978-1-78190-537-1
ISSN: 0195-6310 (Series)

Printed and bound by CPI Group (UK) Ltd, Croydon, CR0 4YY

ISOQAR certified
Management System,
awarded to Emerald
for adherence to
Environmental
standard
ISO 14001:2004.

ISOQAR
REGISTERED
Certificate Number 1985
ISO 14001

INVESTOR IN PEOPLE

CONTENTS

LIST OF CONTRIBUTORS

Gunn Elisabeth Birkelund	Department of Sociology and Human Geography, University of Oslo, Oslo, Norway
Delma Byrne	Departments of Sociology and Education, National University of Ireland Maynooth (NUIM), Maynooth, Ireland
Carl le Grand	Department of Sociology, Stockholm University, Stockholm, Sweden
Ottar Hellevik	Department of Political Science, University of Oslo, Oslo, Norway
Steffen Hillmert	Department of Sociology, University of Tübingen, Tübingen, Germany
Min-Hsiung Huang	Institute of European and American Studies, Academia Sinica, Taipei, Taiwan
Yannick Lemel	Fondation Maison des sciences de l'homme (FMSH), GEMASS, CNRS and University of Paris – Sorbonne, Paris, France
Yaojun Li	Institute for Social Change, Manchester University, Manchester, UK
Gianluca Manzo	GEMASS – Centre National de la Recherche Scientifique (CNRS) and University of Paris – Sorbonne, Paris, France
Gary N. Marks	Melbourne Institute of Applied Economic and Social Research, University of Melbourne, Melbourne, Australia
Selina McCoy	The Economic and Social Research Institute (ESRI), Dublin, Ireland
Martin D. Munk	Department of Political Science, Aalborg University, Copenhagen, Denmark

Liza Reisel	Institute for Social Research, Oslo, Norway
Silke L. Schneider	GESIS – Leibniz Institute for the Social Sciences, Mannheim, Germany
Michael Tåhlin	Swedish Institute for Social Research (SOFI), Stockholm University, Stockholm, Sweden

LIST OF REVIEWERS

The Editor would like to thank the following reviewers (in alphabetical order):

Nicolai Borgen
University of Oslo, Oslo, Norway

Idunn Brekke
Institute for Social Research, Oslo, Norway

Silje Bringsrud Fekjær
The Norwegian Police University College, Oslo, Norway

Jennifer Flashman
Yale University, New Haven, CT, USA

Carl le Grand
University of Stockholm, Stockholm, Sweden

Hans-Tore Hansen
University of Bergen, Bergen, Norway

Are Skeie Hermansen
University of Oslo, Oslo, Norway

Steffen Hillmert
University of Tübingen, Tübingen, Germany

Min-Hsiung Huang
Academia Sinica, Taipei, Taiwan

Trude Lappegård
Statistics Norway, Oslo, Norway

Yaojun Li
University of Manchester, Manchester, UK

Torkild H. Lyngstad
University of Oslo, Oslo, Norway

Arne Mastekaasa
University of Oslo, Oslo, Norway

Anne-May Melsom
University of Oslo, Oslo, Norway

Ferdinand A. Mohn
University of Oslo, Oslo, Norway

Lisa Putman
University of Amsterdam, Amsterdam, The Netherlands

Oddbjørn Raaum
Ragnar Frisch Centre for Economic Research, Oslo, Norway

Liza Reisel
Institute for Social Research, Oslo, Norway

Michael Tåhlin
University of Stockholm,
Stockholm, Sweden

Herman van de Werfhorst
University of Amsterdam,
Amsterdam, The Netherlands

Kenneth Wiik
Statistics Norway, Oslo, Norway

Ståle Østhus
SIRUS, Norwegian Institute
for Alcohol and Drug Research,
Oslo, Norway

In addition, we greatly appreciate excellent administrative support from Julia Orupabo and Marjan Nadim, both at Institute for Social Research, Oslo, Norway.

EDITORIAL BOARD

INTRODUCTION

Tracing the roots back to Plato and Aristotle, it can be argued that "Differences among men have been the subject of speculation and investigation for thousands of years" (Bendix & Lipset 1964 [1953], p. 7). All known societies have been characterized by inequality in the distribution of resources, and social stratification analysis aims to describe and explain these differences. There are several ways in which this topic can be analyzed (see Grusky, Ku, and Szelényi, 2008). Theoretically, one may argue that social and economic inequality is produced by two types of matching processes in the labor market: Employers match social positions (jobs, occupations) with unequal rewards (earnings); and, looking for jobs, individuals are matched with these positions, thereby receiving unequal rewards (Sørensen & Kalleberg, 1994). The degree of inequality in access to resources such as earnings varies across time and place, and comparative analyses have revealed cross-national differentiation in stratification processes, partly related to welfare state arrangements and national policies (Birkelund, 2006).

Social stratification research has occupied a prominent place in sociology for a long time, and as new groups have entered the labor market (such as women and immigrants), their outcomes of the matching process, in particular their access to prestigious and awarding positions, have also been important topics for modern stratification research (Birkelund, 1992; Heath et al., 2007). Thus today, social stratification analysis comprises a range of topics, including social mobility, economic inequality, labor market inequalities, ethnic stratification, gender inequality, family patterns, educational attainment, health inequality, the stratification of cultural consumption, lifestyles, values and attitudes.

This volume of Comparative Social Research includes 12 papers discussing unsolved issues and new developments within class and stratification analysis. One section addresses theoretical and conceptual definitions of social class, another section includes papers elaborating different research designs, a third section contributes by decomposing social class and empirically looking at co-variates, and the last section includes discussions on methods and measurements.

THEORETICAL AND CONCEPTUAL DISCUSSIONS

The three papers in this section include theoretical and conceptual discussions, such as the definition of social class, how social mechanisms can be elaborated and tested, and a discussion on occupational segregation by cognitive ability.

Theoretical Definition of Social Class

Carl le Grand and Michael Tåhlin provide a theoretical discussion of contemporary class theory, followed by empirical investigations and constructive suggestions to improve our understanding of social class in modern capitalist societies. Using data from 11 European countries they find tight links in the labor market between social class, occupational prestige, and wages which are strongly associated with skill requirements of jobs, and only weakly tied to other positional assets, such as power relations at work. The authors therefore argue that the "iron law of inequality" in modern labor markets contradicts the usual theoretical definitions of social class, be it Goldthorpe or Wright's. Contemporary class theory might improve, they suggest, by reforming the theoretical and operational definition of social class, emphasizing skill requirements of jobs, economic efficiency, and social equilibrium.

Social Mechanisms: Agent-Based Modeling

Inspired by his former teacher, Raymond Boudon, Gianluca Manzo develops an agent-based model to test social mechanisms involved in educational attainment. Instead of just describing these patterns, Manzo wants to come closer to a theoretical understanding of stability and changes in the social reproduction of educational inequality. Using French data, the paper starts by describing the strength of the origin effect on educational attainment. Manzo then develops a micro-founded formal model of the observed macro-level educational outcomes in which educational choices are modeled as a result of subjective ability/benefit evaluations and peer-group pressures.

Occupational Stratification by Cognitive Ability

A central psychometric thesis argues that occupations are cognitively stratified because some occupations require higher intelligence than others for successful performance. Therefore, the argument goes, occupations are increasingly stratified over time by cognitive abilities. Using cross-sectional and longitudinal data containing information on IQ tests of individuals and their occupations, Min-Hsiung Huang explores the correlations of occupational mean IQ scores, occupational minimum IQ scores, and occupational prestige, arguing that occupational segregation by cognitive ability is less intensive than the psychometric argument suggests.

RESEARCH DESIGNS

The papers in this section in various ways discuss alternative research designs, looking at the impact of demography, selection processes and utilizing an explorative design.

Intergenerational Mobility: The Importance of Demography

There is a long tradition in sociology describing intergenerational patterns of social mobility. Studies of social origin effects on educational attainment as well as studies of origin effects on social destination are usually based on data comprising families with at least one parent alive and at least one child. Thus, mobility is seen from the children's generation, asking where they come from and where do they arrive. An alternative approach, discussed by Steffen Hillmert, starts with the parent's generation, including partner choice and fertility in addition to the status attainment (educational attainment, occupational attainment, as well as family formation) of their children, thereby turning mobility analysis up-side-down.

Modeling Selection Processes: Including Minorities into Class Analysis

Comparing the United States and the United Kingdom, Yaojin Li analyzes the assimilation of immigrants and second generation immigrants into labor market positions. Using long-term illness as an instrument variable to condition labor market position on access to work, she includes five minority groups in the United Kingdom and seven in the United States. The study documents interesting group differences over time in labor market positions in the two countries, leading to new topics of investigations, such as why are the outcomes so different for the Pakistani/Bangladeshi in the

United Kingdom compared to the United States. Overall, the findings are more supportive to a revised straight-line perspective than the segmented assimilation theory.

The Dimensionality of Social Stratification and Lifestyles

Comparing France and Norway, Birkelund and Lemel design an explorative study to empirically measure if social stratification is best conceptualized as a one- or a two-dimensional social space. The analyses reveal a strong first latent dimension of social stratification, supporting a gradational stratification perspective rather than a two-dimensional approach. Mapping lifestyles clusters onto social space; separate for each country, the analysis reveals a more common pattern than might be expected, and the authors discuss the relevance of these analyses for the way we conceptualize lifestyles and social stratification.

OPENING BLACK BOXES

Opponents to class analysis have argued that class analysis can be compared to botanic, a descriptive classifying exercise where items (people) are grouped by a classification device, presumably because they belong to similar categories. The papers in this section open the "black box" of social class, by decomposing social class and/or including co-variates to social class.

Decomposing Social Origin Effects

Comparing the United States and Norway, with different educational institutions and financial risks associated with higher education, Liza Reisel analyses social origin effects on the likelihood of dropping out of higher education. By decomposing aggregated occupational class categories into measurements on parent's educational and income resources, Reisel comes closer to a theoretical and empirical understanding of which aspects of socioeconomic origin matters most, in different national contexts.

Educational Attainment: Co-variates

Martin D. Munk analyses social origin effects on completion of upper secondary education, including more variables than usually found in educational attainment analysis. The Danish PISA data comprises a rich set of family background variables in addition to information on cognitive and non-cognitive skills. Including these variables, Munk argues that in addition to parents' education and occupation, non-cognitive capacities, such as having drive and strong beliefs, are important for educational outcome.

Hidden Disadvantage: Non-Manual Workers

Classification schemes are vital for the outcomes of social research, and Delma Byrne and Selina McCoy critically discuss the implications of a new Irish classification of socioeconomic groups. Studying social origin effects on access to higher education in the Republic of Ireland, they show that the new classification scheme has leveled out the disadvantage of a specific group of children, namely those who grow up in the "other non-manual" occupational group.

MODELING TECHNIQUES AND MEASUREMENTS

This part includes three papers addressing modeling techniques and measurement problems.

Measuring Social Inequality

Ottar Hellevik has criticized the use of log-linear methods in social stratification and mobility analyses, arguing in favor of other measures of inequality, such as the Gini coefficient. In his paper, Hellevik summarizes his critique, claiming that methodological choices also have political implications, as when researchers using log-linear models conclude that egalitarian reforms have proven ineffective, whereas other measures of inequality would conclude opposite.

Measurements of Income Inequalities

Gary N. Marks discusses measures of income elasticity's across countries. Income elasticity seems generally to be higher in the United States and United Kingdom than other so-called Western countries, and Marks discusses these figures critically. Comparing economic and sociological research, Marks asks if the estimates of intergenerational income elasticity and correlations for the United States and United Kingdom are too high.

A New Educational Classification

Silke L. Schneider introduces the International Standard Classification of Education (ISCED) 2011, covering almost all countries worldwide, maintained and documented by the UNESCO Institute for Statistics. We may expect this classification to be particularly important in future comparative analysis of educational attainment, and Schneider also explains how the new classification can be adapted to existing data and cross-national surveys.

Gunn Elisabeth Birkelund
Editor

REFERENCES

Bendix, R., & Lipset, S. M. (1964 [1953]). *Class, status and power. A reader in social stratification*. Glencoe: The Free Press.

Birkelund, G. E. (1992). Stratification and segregation. *Acta Sociologica, 35*, 47–62.

Birkelund, G. E. (2006). Welfare states and social inequality: Key issues in contemporary cross-national research on social stratification and mobility. *Research in Social Stratification and Mobility, 24*, 333–351.

Grusky, D., Ku, M. C., & Szelényi, S. (Eds). (2008). *Race, and gender in sociological perspective* (3rd ed.). Boulder, CO: Westview Press.

Heath, A. F., & Cheung, S. Y. (2007). *Unequal chances. Ethnic minorities in Western labour markets*. Oxford: Oxford University Press.

Sørensen, A. B., & Kalleberg, A. L. (1994). An outline of a theory of the matching of persons to jobs. In Grusky (Ed.), *Social stratification: Class, race, and gender in sociological perspective*. Boulder, CO: Westview Press.

PART I
THEORETICAL AND CONCEPTUAL
DISCUSSIONS

CLASS, OCCUPATION, WAGES, AND SKILLS: THE IRON LAW OF LABOR MARKET INEQUALITY

Carl le Grand and Michael Tåhlin

ABSTRACT

Economic inequality in contemporary advanced societies is strongly tied to the variation in wages across occupations. We examine the extent to which this variation is captured by social class and occupational prestige and ask how the associations between class, prestige, and wages can be explained. On the basis of data from 11 countries in the European Social Survey (ESS) 2004, we find (a) that class and prestige account for a very large proportion of the occupational variation in wages; (b) that the tight links between class, prestige, and wages are strongly associated with the skill requirements of jobs but only weakly tied to other positional traits, including authority, autonomy, and scarcity; and (c) that these findings are highly similar in all countries examined. We conclude that the rank order of positions in the labor market is a social constant driven by efficiency requirements of work organizations rather than by the exercise of power. This iron law of labor market inequality clearly contradicts major class theoretical models, including Wright's and Goldthorpe's. In addition to empirically refuting contemporary class theory, we offer a number of more conceptual arguments to the same effect. At a macro

Class and Stratification Analysis
Comparative Social Research, Volume 30, 3–46
ISSN: 0195-6310/doi:10.1108/S0195-6310(2013)0000030006

level, however, power relations arguably affect the rate of economic inequality by determining the reward distance between positions in the constant rank order, as indicated by the large cross-national variation in wage dispersion.

Keywords: Class; skill; power; efficiency

INTRODUCTION

For the centennial of the *Communist Manifesto* in 1948, Joseph Schumpeter, then president of the American Economic Association, initiated a symposium at the association's annual meeting. The contributions to the symposium, under the title "The sociology and economics of class conflict," were published in the *American Economic Review* in the following year. Talcott Parsons was invited to represent sociology. In his remarks, he claimed that Marx' perspective on classes had become outdated due to its focus on the distinction between capitalists and workers. Instead, a more general differentiation among occupations had grown in importance as industrialization and modernization had progressed. This is an early formulation of the "middle class issue" that a few decades later would come to dominate the theoretical discussion of class. In the differentiation between occupations, Parsons distinguished two aspects of the organization of work that he saw as especially important drivers of social and economic stratification. One is the division of skill requirements that is inherent in functional role specialization. The skill dimension in part concerns innate ability, and in part competences that are costly and difficult to acquire. The other important aspect of work organization is the increasing centralization and differentiation of leadership and authority in large establishments, whereby individuals who are responsible for coordinating the actions of others necessarily acquire another status in crucial respects than those who mainly carry out tasks designed by others (Parsons, 1949, pp. 17–20).

Parsons' functionalist perspective, developed since the 1930s, was an important influence for his students Davis and Moore (1945) in the *American Sociological Review* on the causes of social stratification is one of the discipline's most controversial texts. The perspective eventually culminated in Donald Treiman's book *Occupational Prestige in Comparative Perspective*, published 1977, at a time point when theoretical work on the sociology of inequality had already been redirected to issues of power and control rather than efficiency. Although Treiman ties his theoretical model to the concept of power, it is evident that he sees efficiency requirements as the ultimate cause of inequality: "Analysis of the universally shared occupational prestige hierarchy suggests that high prestige is allocated to those occupations which require a high degree of skill or which entail authority over other individuals or control over capital. ... These are the fundamental aspects of power. ... But the more powerful an occupation, the more important it is that it be performed well/and thus/the greater the incentive to attract competent personnel to it. /Hence,/the most powerful positions will also be the most highly rewarded." (Treiman, 1976, pp. 287–288).

This functionalist perspective on inequality came to be heavily criticized in the wake of the social and political turbulence in the late 1960s. By the mid-1970s, the earlier emphasis on efficiency and social equilibrium had given way to a focus on power, exploitation, and conflict. Two main intellectual figures in the research on social class that was established during this period are Erik Olin Wright and John Goldthorpe, initially labeled as followers of Marx and Weber, respectively, but eventually converging toward a common stance on many (but not all) issues. Wright's work has been highly influential concerning analyses of the class position of the middle class. He sees class-related inequality within the category of employees as determined by two factors: (a) authority within production processes and (b) skills and expert knowledge. Authority is a class dimension because managers and supervisors make use of delegated class power. Skill is a class dimension because professionals and other experts (as well as managers) receive "loyalty rents," that is, they are offered privileged locations within exploitation relations. There are two causes of such rents. First, qualifications and expertise are often scarce, not only due to natural supply limitations but also – and primarily – due to strategically created and reproduced obstacles to supply increases. Second, the performance of qualified tasks is difficult for the employer to monitor, who therefore has to rely on the motivation and loyalty of employees rather than on external control in order to maintain high levels of effort. In sum, the employer buys commitment from selected categories of employees by giving them a high level of rewards (Wright, 1997, pp. 19–22).[1]

The other central figure in class research during recent decades is John Goldthorpe. He originally developed a continuous occupational scale measuring prestige (or "social standing"; see Hope & Goldthorpe, 1974). In the course of the 1970s, he abandoned this scale for a class model with distinct categories for the purpose of studying social mobility across generations. In the class schema – which, however, builds on and correlates strongly with the original prestige scale (see Goldthorpe & Llewellyn, 1977) – occupations were grouped according to their typical "market and work situations." The most important source of inspiration here was Lockwood (1958) doctoral dissertation *The Blackcoated Worker* (1958), in turn based on Weber's discussion of how classes should be defined and distinguished. Goldthorpe divided employees into classes by "combining occupational categories whose members would appear ... to be typically comparable, on the one hand, in terms of their sources and levels of income, their degree of economic security and chances of advancement [market situation]; and, on the other, in their location within systems of authority and control governing the process of production in which they are engaged, and hence their degree of autonomy in performing their work-tasks and roles [work situation]" (Goldthorpe, 1980, p. 39).

On the basis of this definition, skills may be seen as tied to the "market situation" and authority as tied to the "work situation." But the class model in this guise is close to being completely descriptive – a more elaborate analysis of the mechanisms involved in the connections between class and inequality is missing in these early formulations. With the paper on the "service class" Goldthorpe (1982) embarks on the theoretical journey that ends with the article (2000) on dependence and control as the bases of inequality between groups of employees. In essence, class differences in reward levels (among employees) are explained by arguing that members of the privileged class (the "salariat") (a) are difficult for the employer to replace and (b) carry out work tasks that are difficult for the employer to monitor. The employer solves these two problems by creating a specific structure of incentives (the "service relation") with the purpose of fostering loyalty, commitment, and work effort. Goldthorpe's theory has thereby largely coincided with Wright's. Meanwhile, Wright – in his corner – has modified his operational class definition such that it essentially has coincided with Goldthorpe's (see, e.g., Wright, 1997, p. 37). This synthesis may have pleased many class analysts, since it apparently combines the best of two worlds: theoretical clarity and empirical predictive validity.

The literature survey above shows that skills and authority, on both sides of the theoretical chasm between power and efficiency, are seen as the main operational criteria of class. But the two theoretical perspectives suggest fundamentally different mechanisms for why skills and authority are important for inequality. According to the "efficiency" perspective, the driving mechanism is productivity, while the "power" model seeks to avoid workers' productive resources as a central mechanism. In the power perspective, the distribution of labor market rewards is a *zero-sum game*, with one party's gain being another party's loss. Rewards tied to skill and authority are thus seen as acquired *at the expense of* other workers' rewards. In the efficiency perspective, by contrast, wage premia for skill and authority reflect high productivity assumed to contribute positively to the value of the entire work organization; that is, inequality is driven by *growth* rather than exploitation.

This division between power and efficiency is the topic of the present paper. We attempt to assess which of the two theoretical perspectives that best explains the empirically observed hierarchical order among employees in the labor markets of modern capitalism. Our conclusions are primarily based on empirical analyses, in which we use data from 11 countries in the European Social Survey (ESS) 2004 (see further below). In addition, we outline some arguments of a more conceptual kind that – independent of our empirical results – point rather clearly in one direction.

The paper is organized as follows. We begin by formulating in more detail the two theoretical perspectives that we see as the main contenders for explaining labor market inequality. We then discuss a few questions of principle with regard to the validity of the power-based model. After describing the data and methods we use, we turn to the empirical analyses and report results in two steps. In a first step, analyses of variance are carried out where we show how wages differ between classes, between occupations within classes, and between individuals within occupations, in the 11 different countries. In a second step, on the basis of factor analysis, we examine how four different determinants of inequality (skills, authority, autonomy, and scarcity) are related to the hierarchical structure of labor market rewards (class, occupational prestige, and wages) among employees. We conclude with a summary and discussion of our main findings.

TWO THEORETICAL PERSPECTIVES ON LABOR MARKET INEQUALITY

Skills and authority are the two central dimensions of the hierarchical structure of labor market rewards among employees. But what are the underlying explanatory mechanisms? According to one model, workers are rewarded in proportion to their productivity. In economic theory, productivity is typically seen as residing in individuals. In human capital theory (Becker, 1962), for example, individuals increase their productivity by spending resources (time and money) on education and training of various kinds, in school, on the job, or elsewhere (in the family, in civil society, at the gym, etc.). But productivity can also be seen as tied to positions, that is, jobs (as in Thurow, 1975). Different jobs have different skill requirements, which not only means that individuals with varying amounts and types of abilities and qualifications are selected into them but also that individual skills develop more in some jobs than in others (see, e.g., Farkas, 2003; Kohn & Schooler, 1983). Further, differences in technology or work tasks across jobs give different structural opportunities for realizing the productive potential of any given individual. Both individuals and jobs thus differ in productivity-related skill levels, and both sides of this coin need to be taken into account, including the degree of match between them (see, e.g., Duncan & Hoffman, 1981). The connection between authority and rewards can also, in principle, be explained within the framework of the efficiency model. The performances of managerial or supervisory tasks are obviously tied to certain skills, on both the individual and job side. The link between these skills and productivity may thus – fully or partly – explain the correlation between authority and rewards.

According to an alternative theoretical model, the importance of skills and authority for labor market rewards is explained by factors related to power and control. In this line of reasoning, workers in some positions are harder to replace than others (either because their tasks are especially important for the firm's activity or require scarce competence) and are more difficult to control than others (because their work tasks cannot be monitored or directed in any simple way). The main agent in this explanation is the employer who must find a way of generating loyalty and work effort among employees who are difficult to replace or to control. One strategy to achieve this is to offer prospective rewards, that is, opportunities for promotion and wage growth that materialize as a reward for appropriate behavior. This type of solution is particularly emphasized by Goldthorpe (2000). Another solution is to offer bonuses or other kinds of performance pay to managers and experts. In this case, the reward level of the worker is tied to the firm's profit level (or some similar criterion), a scheme that provides incentives for employees to internalize the goals of the employer. This strategy need not involve long tenure or prospective rewards as in well-developed firm–internal labor markets. On the contrary, a highly skilled employee or high-level manager who fails to deliver can be fired on short notice (like the coach of a football team). Hence, employer choices of how to deal with problems of control can vary significantly over time and space.

CONCEPTUAL CRITIQUE OF THE POWER MODEL

The power model, both in Wright's and Goldthorpe's version, is thus based on two main mechanisms for explaining why workers with skilled or managerial tasks are more highly rewarded than others: (a) that these employees are difficult for the employer to replace and (b) that they are difficult for the employer to control. In our opinion, both these explanatory mechanisms are theoretically weak.

Concerning replaceability, we disregard cyclical scarcity, that is, temporal deficits of labor supply of any given category, which by definition cannot contribute significantly to class inequality and other kinds of structural differentiation. Structural scarcity, that is, permanent or long-term labor supply deficits, are of two main types. The first type concerns assets – or skills – that are specific to the firm. This is the kind of scarcity that Goldthorpe bases his theoretical model on. In our view, strong arguments indicate that this particular type is not well suited as an element in class theory. To begin with, if workers' skills are firm specific, not only does the employer face difficulties in replacing the worker but the worker has difficulties finding alternative jobs and employers. Hence, both parties are dependent on each other. This kind of reciprocal dependence (Goldthorpe uses the term "bilateral") is analyzed formally by Becker (1962), when examining the distinction between general and firm-specific on-the-job training. It is also an important theme in Williamson's (1975) model for explaining the choice between the firm and the market for minimizing transaction costs, where "firm" (or "hierarchy") is the equivalent of Goldthorpe's notion of "service relation" and "market" is the counterpart of the "labor contract." The reciprocal nature of the dependence involved means that firm-specific skills are highly equivocal as power resources of employees and, therefore, unlikely to explain much of service class privileges.

There is a further theoretical reason that asset specificity with respect to firms is unlikely to be an important mechanism in the class context. Consider the skill formation of professionals and skilled manual workers, respectively. The former type of skill is typically school based, while the latter is often firm based. In schools, the skills learnt tend to be significantly more general and standardized than in the case of skills developed on the job. Therefore, the skills of manual workers should be much more firm specific than the skills of professionals, so skilled workers should be more difficult for the employer to replace than are professionals. To the extent that this argument is valid, it is a further reason to strongly doubt that firm-specific skills are a useful mechanism to explain service class privilege, since the service class largely consists of professionals.

The second form of structural scarcity of labor supply is skill specificity with respect to occupation rather than to the firm. This type of scarcity is structural on the basis of power, for example, of the kind that Weber calls closure, and thus reflects asymmetrical rather than reciprocal dependence. The argument, which has a prominent place in Wright's theoretical model, is that the supply of skills of a certain kind is artificially restricted based on strategically maintained limits on entry into certain occupations.[2] Many of these strategies are based on occupational licensing and limits on educational admission (see Weeden, 2002, for a large-scale empirical analysis of the U.S. labor market from this perspective). Since most (though not all) such strategies create shortages of labor supply in professional rather than working class occupations, the closure mechanism is in principle a promising feature of an explanation of class inequality. Still, there are strong arguments against the view that occupational closure is a major causal factor in this regard.

One important argument is that explicit closure (or similar strategies) is far from pervasive, and in many cases actually reversed. Labor supply of professional skills, that is, the fraction of the population with a degree from tertiary education, has been larger than labor demand for these skills for extended periods of time in several countries. Thus, rates of over-education are high in most OECD countries and have been rising in several cases during recent decades (see, e.g., Büchel et al., 2003; Korpi & Tåhlin, 2009). In fact, governments in many countries, especially in the European Union, have had strong educational expansion high on their agenda for a long time. These policies have, to a large extent, been successful, in the sense that a large expansion has in fact occurred, and have met little resistance from the interest organizations of professionals. Further, to the extent that explicit closure strategies are adopted, the variation in their implementation and degree of success is very large, across occupational categories as well as across countries and over time. For example, rules of admission to higher education are very different from one country to the other; significantly, to the extent that commonality exists, the most frequent rule seems to be free (unlimited) admission, hardly a sign of closure. The combination of widespread open admission and large variation in closure where it exists makes it unlikely, we think, that closure could be a major driver of class inequality. After all, the basic structure of class-reward gradients is close to being a social constant (as shown below), and should therefore be explained by highly pervasive and invariant features of

stratification. Closure does not appear to be a phenomenon that meets those requirements.

There is a further important argument against strategic closure as a major driver of inequality. Even if the extent of closure were large and stable, it needs to be shown that a major part of it is due to simple self-interest on the part of privileged educational and occupational groups rather than motivated by the common interest of citizens in having access to reliable high-quality services. Medical services are the clearest example. Are professional licenses in this field required mainly because of strategic power resources held and used by doctors, nurses, and other medical occupational groups? Or is the major motive for medical licensing that the general population typically desires public control over medical practice to minimize risks of maltreatment? We believe that the latter, rather than the former, is most often the case. It would be absurd to argue that medical skills are a mere façade or social construction, without any basis in real competence. Of course, this is not to say that medical professional associations never act on the basis of simple and strategic self-interest. It seems clear, for example, that the highly restricted access to medical education in most countries can at least in part be explained by strategic insider action. But such strategies would hardly succeed if medical skills had no real basis. Power in this case (and in many others of the same kind) would appear to be endogenous to the possession of socially valuable resources – such as skills – rather than an exogenous force.

Note that these remarks concern closure as a strategy, that is, the intentional raising of formal barriers to entry into educational tracks and occupational positions. Obviously, there are countless examples of implicit, unintended closure, in the sense of cultural and motivational hurdles, jointly raised by members of all classes, which reduce access to privileged places in the educational and occupational structure. Such implicit borders are what most of the vast literature on intergenerational social mobility is about, and given the strong reproduction of classes across generations, it is clear that this kind of mechanism operates forcefully in all societies. But as explanations of inequality, closure as a strategy with formal rules as an instrument and closure as an unintended consequence of everyday life are very different. Certainly, Wright, for one, draws a sharp dividing line between them, and claims that class theory would hardly be identifiable as a distinct perspective on inequality if implicit, nonstrategic closure was all there is to the picture (see, e.g., Wright, 2009). Class would in that case, according to Wright, not add anything of theoretical significance to a general and rather uncontroversial perspective focusing on individuals' command over resources and human capital.

That concludes our conceptual discussion of skill scarcity in the class context. With regard to the second main mechanism of class models – employers' problems of labor control as a source of structural inequality – the theoretical weakness is of a different, more formal kind. Assume that the productivity (P) of a certain individual in a certain job[3] is the product of effort (E) and capacity (C), that is,

$$P = E \times C$$

and, further, that the employer is rational and aims at maximizing the rate of employment contract profitability (R), expressed as the difference between productivity (P) and the wage (W), that is,

$$R = P - W$$

The employer's maximization function can then be expressed as

$$R = (E \times C) - W$$

The hypothesis of class theory (in both Wright's and Goldthorpe's version) is that the worker's reward (W) is set relatively high in jobs that are difficult to monitor as an incentive for the worker to supply a high level of effort in the absence of external control (such as direct supervision or machine pacing). The effort level is thus high by definition in easily monitored jobs, but needs to be upheld by internal control, that is, incentive-based motivation, in jobs that are difficult to monitor. But in that case, the effort level of the high-reward category will, at most (if the employer's incentive strategy works optimally), be *equal* to the effort level of the low-reward group. Assume that the supply of effort can vary from zero to one, where workers in easily monitored jobs by definition (through external control) reach the maximum value, and, further, that the control system is optimally designed so that the effort supply of workers in jobs that are difficult to monitor is also maximized. The employer's maximization function can then be reduced to

$$R = C - W$$

since $E = 1$.

In order to explain the higher wage level of the group with jobs that are difficult to monitor, that is, to explain how R (the employer's rate of profitability) can be maintained despite paying high wages to the workers, the only remaining part of the productivity equation is capacity (C).

The conclusion is that monitoring difficulties at most can explain why the wage level for workers in jobs that are hard to control is *not lower* than for workers in easily controlled jobs. To explain why their wages are not merely equal to, but significantly *higher*, than other workers' wages, the capacity component of productivity rather than the effort component is of decisive importance. Since the effort level in jobs that are difficult to monitor cannot (by definition) exceed the effort level in easily controlled jobs, the entire advantage in productivity – that in turn motivates the employer to pay a higher wage – must (by definition) come from capacity rather than effort. The whole idea that wage inequality is driven by the variation in employers' control problems rather than the variation in workers' productive capacities (or skills) thus fails.

In sum, strong theoretical arguments speak against the view that factors related to power and control rather than to productive resources explain labor market inequality at the micro level. But while conceptual considerations of this kind are important, they cannot, by themselves, settle the issue. A careful empirical analysis is also needed, to which we now turn.

ANALYTIC STRATEGY

Inequality in modern societies tends to be shaped by three processes (see, e.g., Weeden, 2002, p. 55). First, the division of labor in society produces a set of jobs or positions (such as occupations); second, these positions are differentially rewarded; and third, individuals are allocated to these differentially rewarded positions. Our main purpose here is to analyze the second of these processes. We thus take an existing set of positions – as well as the allocation of individuals to them – for granted, and direct our attention to the question why rewards across these positions are unequal. The hierarchical structure of working life can be described in many ways, of which we here distinguish three: class, occupational prestige, and economic rewards (wages). We begin our analysis by showing how these three are empirically related to each other. Previous research has documented strong correlations between them (see, e.g., Ganzeboom et al., 1992), but we give a contribution here by analyzing them within a common framework and with comparable data from 11 countries in Europe. We show that class, prestige, and wages form a single, common dimension that expresses the hierarchical order in the social structure of positions among employees. The relations between this dimension and four distinct, theoretically determined criteria of class (skills, authority, autonomy, and scarcity) are then examined in order to assess which of these factors "explain" (i.e., are most strongly correlated with) the hierarchical structure of rewards.

The first section of empirical analyses shows the extent to which the variation in wages across individuals can be accounted for by the occupations of employees, and the degree to which the variation in wages across occupations, in turn, can be accounted for by the class position of employees, that is, by occupations aggregated into classes. We use Goldthorpe's class schema, which nowadays is operationally very similar to Wright's class model (see, e.g., Wright, 1997, p. 37; Chan & Goldthorpe, 2007, p. 513) as well as to other class schemas, such as the Swedish SEI classification (see Tåhlin, 2007) and the new European socioeconomic classification (Rose & Harrison, 2007). A first conclusion is that the economic rank order (wages) between occupations and classes is very similar in all the countries we study, that is, the *character* of inequality appears to be internationally constant. The other conclusion is that the size of the wage differentials differs markedly across countries; that is, the *degree* of inequality is internationally highly variable.

In a second empirical section, the different explanations of the hierarchical structure of positions in the labor market are evaluated. We conclude that the major alternative to the efficiency model is thoroughly falsified by our data, with a high degree of concordance across countries. Until a reasonable theoretical alternative has been presented, we thus assume that the model based on efficiency as the driving mechanism is the most accurate explanation of labor market inequality.

DATA AND VARIABLE CONSTRUCTIONS

The empirical analyses are based on data from the ESS 2004, with representative samples of the adult population in 21 countries. In the analyses presented below, employees in the following 11 countries are included: Austria, Denmark, Finland, France, Germany, Great Britain, the Netherlands, Norway, Spain, Sweden, and Switzerland. For the remaining 10 countries, the wage data are of insufficient quality for our purposes (e.g., with very high internal nonresponse rates).

In order to facilitate inferences to the population of adult employees in each country, we have combined (by multiplication) two weights. The first is the design weight (DWEIGHT), included as a variable in the ESS data file with the purpose of correcting for differential sample selection probability. The second weight corrects for female over- or underrepresentation for the subsample we use: employed persons with available information on all included variables. The latter weight has been constructed by dividing the proportion of women in each of our country samples with the proportion employed women in each country according to OECD statistics. As Birkelund (1992) and others have shown, the variation in job characteristics across classes differs significantly by gender. We would have preferred to estimate and report results separately for women and men, but given the very limited number of cases in our data, such a separation is not feasible. Gender–class interactions are an important issue for future research.

Below we give an overview of our variable constructions. A more detailed description of operationalizations is provided in Appendix A. Appendix B contains descriptive and supplementary statistics, with means and standard deviations of all variables used reported in Table B.1.

Wage is estimated as hourly earnings before tax. The variable is measured with three questions. First, "What is your usual gross pay before deductions for tax and insurance?" Second, "How long a period does that pay cover?" Third, "Regardless of your basic or contracted hours, how many hours do you normally work a week (in your main job), including any paid or unpaid overtime." We have devoted substantial effort to improve the reliability of the variable. For example, a number of respondents replied that they received pay per hour, and then stated the pay they received per month. Obviously, however, some undetected measurement errors remain. Another problem with the wage measure is a high rate of internal non-response for certain countries, which may result in unstable estimates. Still, we believe that the quality of the cleaned wage data is reasonably high and certainly sufficient for the analyses we present below. According to established practice, hourly wage has been transformed into logarithmic units; that is, wage differentials can be interpreted as proportional rather than absolute (Table B.2).

Occupation is operationalized as ISCO-88, and *social class* consists of five occupational categories – service class I (high level white collar), service class II (middle level white collar), class IIIa (routine nonmanual), class VI (skilled manual workers), and class VII/IIIb (unskilled manual and service workers) – according to the EGP class schema (Erikson & Goldthorpe, 1992).[4] We also use a continuous version of the class variable (see subsection "Determinants of the hierarchical structure of working life"), constructed on the basis of a regression (specific for each country) with wage (in percentile form) as outcome and four class category dummies (for classes I, II, IIIa, and VI, with class VII/IIIb as the reference category) as predictors. The B coefficients from these regressions are then used as values on the class scale.

Skill is measured by five variables: (a) *The respondent's education* (number of years above compulsory school); (b) *Educational requirements for the job* (number of years above compulsory school); (c) *The work experience of the respondent* (number of years of labor force participation); (d) *Initial on-the-job training* (number of months, after being employed, before being able to do the job reasonably well); (e) *Continuing on-the-job training* (opportunities to learn new things in daily work). These five indicators of various dimensions of skill are combined into an index by including them as predictors in a regression analysis (OLS) with log hourly wage as the dependent variable:

$$\log(\text{wage}) = a + bx_1 + bx_2 + bx_3 + bx_4 + bx_5 + bx_6 + bx_7 + r, \quad (1)$$

where x_1 is the worker's work experience, x_2 is the experience squared, x_3 is the excess educational job requirements, x_4 is the matched educational job requirements, x_5 is the excess schooling, x_6 is the initial on-the-job training, x_7 is the continuing on-the-job training, a is the intercept, r is the residual error term, and b is the regression coefficients. The quadratic experience term captures the curve-linear association between experience and wage (Mincer, 1974). The terms x_3, x_4, and x_5 are based on combined information on the worker's schooling and the educational requirements of the job such that

$$R = S + XR - XS, \quad (2)$$

where S is the worker's schooling, R is the educational job requirements, XR is the excess job requirements, and XS is the excess schooling. Thus, $x_3 = XR$, $x_4 = S-XS = R-XR$, and $x_5 = XS$. This matching equation is based on the so-called ORU model (Over, Required, Under) developed by Duncan and Hoffman (1981), which is a highly robust specification for estimating the associations between schooling, educational job requirements, and job rewards (such as earnings); see Rubb (2003) for an overview of a large number of empirical studies.

We have performed separate regression analyses based on Eq. (1) for each of the 11 countries. The index values are the predicted values from these wage regressions. Hence, the relative weights of the five components are determined by their respective regression coefficients (i.e., b in Eq. (1)). The wage variable is consequently used in order to provide weights for the five variables that form the skill index, but wage is not a part of the index. Further analyses show that it is of no substantial importance which stratification variable that is used as the outcome for this weighting procedure; if, for example, occupational prestige is used instead of wage, the index values become very similar. Finally, the index values are rescaled into wage rank (percentile) units by an additional regression (wage rank regressed on skill).

Authority is measured with an indicator of the number of persons who the respondent is supervising. Logarithmic units are used for this variable (with a constant of 1 added) so that workers with no subordinates have zero value, and individuals with supervisory responsibility are distinguished with regard to their relative (proportional rather than absolute) number of subordinates. Several different specifications of this variable have been tried, for instance, by distinguishing individuals with no subordinates as a separate category (a dummy variable), but the results across specifications are almost identical. The logged supervision variable has been rescaled to similar units as the skill variable by entering it as a predictor of wage rank (percentiles), and using the predicted values as the scale of authority.

Autonomy is measured with two indicators: (a) the degree of supervision that the respondent is subjected to and (b) the degree of freedom to decide how one's own daily work is organized. In this case as well, the variables need to be weighted in order to be combined into an index. As with skill, this has been accomplished with regression analyses, separate for each country, with (log) wage as the dependent variable and the two autonomy indicators as independent variables. The predicted values from these regressions make up the index values.

Scarcity is measured with an indicator of how difficult it would be for the employer to replace the respondent if s/he left. (For a validation of this kind of indicator, see Tåhlin, 2007.) As in the cases of skill, authority, and autonomy, the scarcity variable has been scaled by using the original scale (see Appendix A) as a predictor in a regression with wage rank (percentiles) as outcome, and using the predicted values from this regression as scale values.

In the analyses presented below, the four class criteria are used both in what is called a *gross* version based on zero-order correlations, that is, using the observed values of the variables disregarding the covariation between the criteria, and in a *net* version based on partial correlations. In the net version, the covariation among the four criteria has been empirically removed for each variable via the following four regression analyses:

$$\text{Skill} = \text{authority} + \text{autonomy} + \text{scarcity} + r_1$$
$$\text{Authority} = \text{skill} + \text{autonomy} + \text{scarcity} + r_2$$
$$\text{Autonomy} = \text{skill} + \text{authority} + \text{scarcity} + r_3$$
$$\text{Scarcity} = \text{skill} + \text{authority} + \text{autonomy} + r_4$$

where r_1, r_2, r_3, and r_4 are residuals, used as net indicators for each criterion.[5]

The test of which model – power or efficiency – that is the most valid explanation for inequality is based on the distinction between gross and net in the above sense. According to the power model, the association between skill and rewards is fully explained by the correlations between skill and the other three criteria. In this view, skilled jobs are not better paid because they require higher capacity, that is, are positively related to productivity, but because they are difficult to control and/or because the supply of appropriate labor is scarce. The same kind of argument goes for authority, but in this case with a difference between Wright and Goldthorpe. Wright explicitly claims that authority has a direct effect on rewards because of relations of domination within the firm, whereas Goldthorpe at least implicitly explains the connection between authority and rewards with factors related to control (monitoring difficulties) and scarcity (asset specificity).

It is important to emphasize that the empirical examination of the two models – power and control versus efficiency – is asymmetrical. We cannot directly measure efficiency or productivity but only the mechanisms that are assumed to lie behind the power and control model. Hence, the test has an indirect element: To the extent that the power and control model receives support, the efficiency model can be rejected. If, however, the power and control model is rejected, due to lack of empirical support, we cannot interpret the outcome as unequivocally supporting the efficiency model. In the latter case, the outcome is consistent with the efficiency model but without direct indicators of efficiency we cannot reach any further.

EMPIRICAL RESULTS

The Impact of Social Class and Occupation on Workers' Earnings

Figs. 1 and 2 show the results of an analysis of variance of (log) hourly wage with class and occupation dummies as independent variables. Since class for employed persons has been operationalized as categories of occupations, occupation has been specified as "nested within" the class. The total wage dispersion is divided into three components. First, wage differentials between class categories; second, wage differentials between occupations within the same class; and third, the remaining wage differentials, that is, between employees working in the same occupation. Fig. 1 shows wage differentials measured as the variance of (log) hourly wage in the

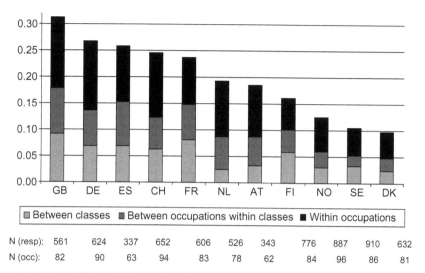

N (resp): 561   624   337   652   606   526   343   776   887   910   632

N (occ):   82   90   63   94   83   78   62   84   96   86   81

Fig. 1. Total Wage Differentials (Variance of Log Hourly Wage) Divided into Differentials between Classes, between Occupations within Classes and within Occupations among Employees in 11 European Countries.

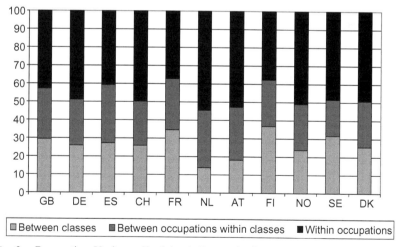

Fig. 2. Proportion Variance Explained (Percent) of Log of Hourly Wage Divided into Differentials between Classes, between Occupations Within Classes and Within Occupations Among Employees in 11 European Countries.

11 countries and Fig. 2 shows the shares of total wage inequality accounted for by the three components.

From Fig. 1, it can be seen that the total wage dispersion as measured by the variance of (log) hourly earnings differs strongly across these 11 European countries – from around 0.10 in Denmark and Sweden to more than 0.30, around three times more, in Great Britain. It is worth noticing that wage inequality between persons with the same occupation is larger in Great Britain than the total wage inequality among all workers in Denmark and Sweden. Wage inequality is also relatively large in Germany, Switzerland, Spain, and France, ranging from 0.24 to 0.27. Between these extreme groups are Norway, Finland, the Netherlands, and Austria with a more moderate wage dispersion ranging from 0.13 to 0.19.

Fig. 2 shows that class and occupation taken together explain a very large part of the total wage dispersion in most of the countries. R^2 – the proportion of variance explained by class position and occupation – varies from 46 percent in the Netherlands to 63 percent in Finland and France. Class alone (see the lower part of the bars) explains between 24 and 29 percent of the wage differentials in most of the countries. Exceptions to this are, on one side, the Netherlands and Austria with only 14 and 18 percent, respectively, and, on the other side, Finland, France, and Sweden where class explains between 32 and 37 percent of the total wage variance. We have no explanation for the low explanatory power of class in the Netherlands and Austria other than perhaps measurement errors in the class variable.

The occupation of the employee explains a considerable share of wage inequality, in addition to wage differences across classes. In most countries, wage differentials between occupations within classes explain between 24 and 29 percent of the total wage inequality. Exceptions are Sweden with only around 20 percent, and, on the other side, the Netherlands and Spain with about 32 percent.

The third and last component in the variance analysis is the wage differences that cannot be explained by class and occupation, that is, wage differentials among employees active in the same occupation. According to our results, these wage differences constitute around half of the total wage dispersion. Finland and France are exceptions, where this type of wage inequality is relatively small – about 37 percent. These conclusions must, however, be taken with caution, since it is reasonable to believe that there are measurement errors in both the dependent and the independent variables that vary among countries. The implication is that the within-occupational wage inequality in reality is smaller and the inequality between classes and occupations is larger than what these results show.

To sum up the results so far, Figs. 1 and 2 show that the 11 European countries differ strongly in terms of the size of the wage differentials between classes and occupations. These country differences are largely due to the fact that the size of the *total* wage dispersion is very different among countries. By contrast, in regard to the *relative* class and occupational differences (i.e., the proportion that class and occupation explain of the total variation in wages), the patterns are quite similar across countries. If we were to make the intellectual experiment that all countries had the same total wage dispersion, then we would find that the differences between countries regarding wage inequality by class and occupation are relatively small.

These conclusions are visualized in linear form in Figs. 3 and 4. Fig. 3 shows the large differences across countries in absolute wage dispersion, both in total variance (the solid line) and in variance between classes (the dashed line). There is a very strong, in fact almost perfect, correlation between these two lines: class variance in wages is thus a strictly increasing function of total wage variance (or *vice versa*). In sharp contrast, Fig. 4 shows the relation between cross-national differences in total wage variance (the same line as in Fig. 3) and the proportion of this variance that is explained by class (i.e., the squared correlation between class and wages). These two lines are almost perfectly *un*correlated. The reason is that the correlation between class and wages is essentially an international constant. In other words, while the unstandardized class-wage association closely follows the amount of total wage dispersion, the standardized class-wage

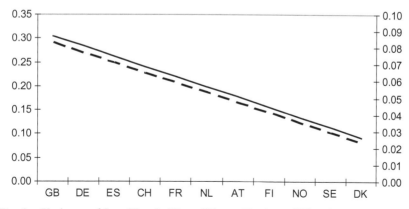

Fig. 3. Variance of Log Hourly Wage (Linear Version of Fig. 1). Total Variance (Solid Line, Left Scale) and Class Variance (Dashed Line, Right Scale), by Country.

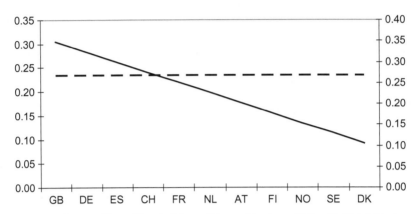

Fig. 4. Variance of Log Hourly Wage (Linear Version of Fig. 2). Total Variance (Solid Line, Left Scale) and Proportion Variance Explained (R^2) by Class (Dashed Line, Right Scale), by Country.

association is close to being completely unrelated to the amount of total wage dispersion. We interpret this clear pattern of empirical regularities as strongly indicating that macro-level factors – such as institutions, which differ greatly across countries – are powerful determinants of the *degree* of class inequality, but that micro-level factors – such as occupational variations in work tasks and requirements, which differ very little across countries – decisively shape the *character* of class inequality. It is to explain the latter that we turn in the next section, leaving explanations of the former to future work (but see, e.g., Pontusson et al., 2002, for a useful macro-level analysis).

Before then, in Figs. 5 and 6, we repeat the same type of analyses as in Figs. 1 and 2, but now with continuous occupational prestige instead of class and occupation categories as the indicator of the hierarchical order in the labor market. Fig. 5 shows wage differentials (in logarithmic units) when occupational prestige goes from low to high values in 11 eleven countries. For the sake of clarity, the prestige scale has been transformed to mean = zero for each country. Fig. 6 also shows wage differentials by occupational prestige, but now with standardized values (mean is zero and standard deviation is one) for both variables. Thus, the difference between Figs. 5 and 6 is that the former shows the observed wage differentials by prestige, whereas the latter shows the country differences that remain when wage and prestige are measured with the same units (standard deviations) in all countries. In other words, Fig. 6 indicates how large the international

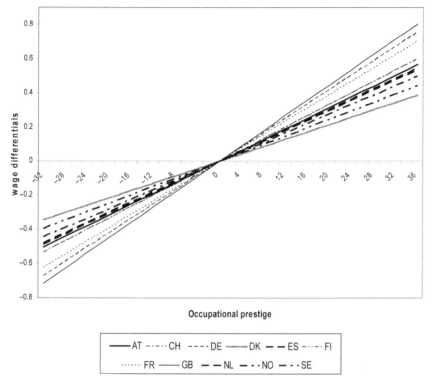

Occupational prestige

Fig. 5. Wage Differentials by Occupational Prestige in 11 European Countries. Log Hourly Wage, Mean = 0.

variation in wage inequality by prestige would be if the distribution of wages and prestige were the same in all countries.

As expected, the "fan" is more spread out in Fig. 5 than in Fig. 6; in other words, the country variation is much smaller in the standardized case (Fig. 6). In addition, it is likely that the remaining (poststandardization) country variance is even smaller than indicated here, since measurement errors (especially in the wage variable) ought to result in larger country differences than would be the case if the variables were measured more precisely.

To sum up, there are two main results of the analyses in this section. First, the hierarchical order among occupations and classes with regard to earnings is very similar in the countries we examine. This result supports the well-known finding of Treiman (1977) that prestige ratings of occupations show very little international variability, and indicates that the basic

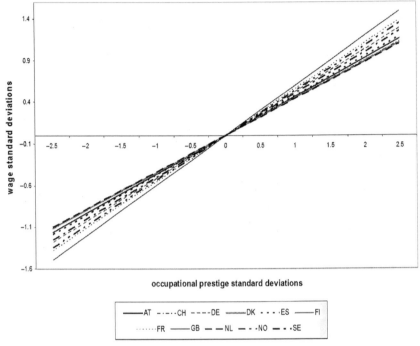

Fig. 6. Wage Differentials by Occupational Prestige in 11 European Countries:
Standardized Values (Mean = 0, Standard Deviation = 1).

principles of the division of labor are the same in all modern industrialized
countries with common mechanisms accounting for reward differences
across positions. Second, given the invariant rank order of positions, the
economic distance between ranks differs greatly across countries. As pointed
out above, a plausible explanation for these international differences is
cross-national variation in institutional traits, such as the prevalence
and scope of collective bargaining, labor market legislation, and so on.
However, further analysis of this macro-level issue is beyond the scope of
the present paper.

Determinants of the Hierarchical Structure of Working Life

We now proceed to analyzing the covariation between the hierarchical
structure of working life and the job characteristics that can be assumed to

be tied to this hierarchy. On the basis of the earlier discussion, the analysis contains three hierarchical indicators – class, prestige, and wages – and four hierarchical criteria – skill, authority, autonomy, and scarcity. The causal order between these seven variables is complex; a full model of their interrelations appears difficult to specify. However, it seems reasonable to view skill, authority, autonomy, and scarcity on the one hand and class, prestige, and wages on the other as two causally ordered categories of variables, with the former category as determinants and the latter as outcomes. A possible method in this case – in which we thus want to analyze several outcomes and determinants simultaneously – is to simply estimate correlations between the seven variables, a procedure which makes it easier than in a regression framework to treat the variables group-wise. We have chosen to follow this route by using factor analysis, in order to examine whether the pattern of correlations can be reduced to a smaller number of underlying dimensions. It should be stressed, however, that the main results presented below do not depend on the particular method used. Conventional regression analyses show the same overall picture, but in a less compact and visually accessible way.

In the following overview of empirical results, we consistently report combined analyses for the 11 countries rather than separate analyses by country. The reason is that the results are almost identical across countries, which is a significant finding in itself. This contributes to motivating the title of the paper: the iron law of labor market inequality. It also further corroborates an important conclusion of the wage variance analyses above: that the micro-level processes related to the occupational division of labor are strongly similar across countries, which in turn leads to an internationally invariable character of class inequality.

Fig. 7 shows the first factor (principal component) in the analysis, that is, the factor that best summarizes the pattern of correlations between the seven variables (three outcomes and four determinants). Four variants of this factor are shown in the figure where we gradually (from variant 1 to 4) purify the associations between class, prestige, and wages on the one hand and skill, authority, autonomy, and scarcity on the other. (For detailed numbers and country-specific results, see Appendix B, Table B.3.) The first variant (the left-most group of bars) is based on the gross version of the four determinants; that is, they overlap each other so that the correlation between authority and wages, for example, partly reflects that both authority and wages are associated with skill, and so on. Further, this variant is based on the unrotated factor solution, that is, the raw (unadjusted) outcome of the analysis.[6] This first variant is thus the simplest, least polished solution.

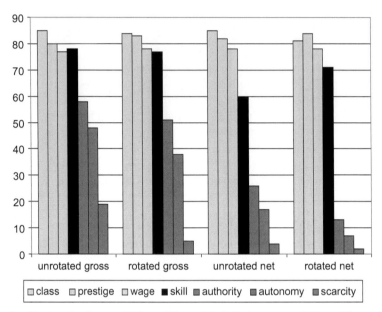

Fig. 7. Factor Analyses of Three Hierarchical Outcomes and Four Hierarchical Determinants among Employees in 11 European Countries. Factor Loadings × 100. *Notes*: All factors are extracted as principal components, rotated by varimax, and common for all 11 countries. Loadings are unweighted averages across countries.

It is evident, first, that class, prestige, and wages are closely connected to each other in a common dimension of rewards. Second, three of the determinants – skill, authority, and autonomy – are relatively strongly tied to the primary reward factor, while the fourth determinant – scarcity – appears to be out of place. Third, skill is apparently the determinant that is most closely connected to the primary factor, but the difference relative to authority and autonomy is rather moderate in size.

The second variant (the second group of bars from the left) shows the first factor in a rotated solution, but still based on the gross version (zero-order correlations) of the four determinants. The difference in outcome relative to the first (unrotated) variant is small, but indicates that the relative importance of skill (compared to the other determinants) grows when the pattern of correlations is purified.

The third variant (the third group of bars from the left) implies a larger change. Here, we show an unrotated solution based on the *net* version of the four determinants; that is, the empirical overlap (covariation) between skill, authority, autonomy, and scarcity has been eliminated from the analysis by estimating partial correlations. As expected, the loadings of all four determinants are thereby somewhat reduced, since none of them can free-ride on the others. But this loss in loading is clearly smaller for skill than for authority and autonomy (while the loading of scarcity was already low). The interpretation of this result is obvious: the correlation between skill and the three hierarchical outcomes (class, prestige, and wages) to a relatively *small* extent reflects that both skill and rewards covary with authority and autonomy, while the correlation between authority (or autonomy) and the three outcomes to a relatively *large* extent reflects that both authority (or autonomy) and rewards covary with skill. In other words, authority and autonomy appear to be secondary hierarchical determinants, while skill seems to be the primary determinant. This result is the opposite from what would be expected on the basis of Goldthorpe's as well as Wright's class theories, but is clearly compatible with theoretical models based on efficiency and productive capacity (rather than power and control) as mediating mechanism between skills and rewards.

In the fourth variant (the right-most group of bars in Fig. 7), the rotated solution of the analysis based on the net version (partial correlations) of the four hierarchical determinants is shown. The previous conclusion is reinforced: when the analysis is purified, the relative weights of the four determinants are polarized, so that the large importance of skill for work life rewards, and the relatively limited importance of authority, autonomy, and scarcity becomes even more evident.

Fig. 8 shows a four-factor solution of the last (right-most) analysis in Fig. 7, that is, the rotated factors based on net (partial) associations among the determinants. (For detailed numbers and country-specific results, see Appendix B, Table B.4.) The four factors in Fig. 8 are dominated by one hierarchical determinant each – skill, authority, autonomy, and scarcity, respectively – and the bars in the figure indicate the loadings of class, prestige, and wages on these four factors. In other words, each determinant loads strongly on one factor but only weakly on the three others. (These loadings are not shown in the figure; see Table B.4 for full results.) The group of three bars to the left (skill) is identical to the first three bars in the right-most group in Fig. 7, and shows (to repeat) that skill is closely connected to all three hierarchical outcomes (class, prestige, and wages). These bars are shown here again in order to give a reference point for the three other groups of bars in Fig. 8. From the second group of three bars, it is evident that class and authority are associated to some, but clearly limited, extent. Aside from this, association, authority, as well as autonomy and

CARL LE GRAND AND MICHAEL TÅHLIN

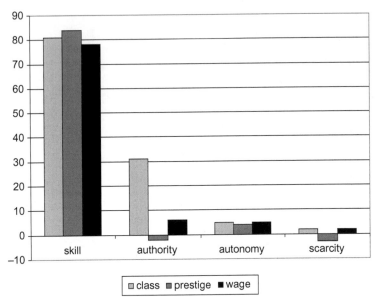

Fig. 8. Factor Analysis of Three Hierarchical Outcomes (Class, Prestige, and Wages) and Four Hierarchical Determinants among Employees in 11 European Countries. Factor Loadings × 100. *Notes*: All Factors Are Extracted as Principal Components, Rotated by Varimax, and Common for All 11 Countries. Loadings Are Unweighted Averages Across Countries.

scarcity (see the third and fourth group of bars) are – in their net versions – almost completely disconnected from the hierarchical structure of the labor market. In other words, while class, prestige, and wages all load strongly on the skill factor, they hardly load at all on the three factors associated with authority, autonomy, and scarcity, respectively. The associations between the three latter determinants and the three hierarchical outcomes are apparently spurious, driven by their correlations with skill. Holding skill constant in the analysis (by estimating partial correlations) essentially breaks the links between authority, autonomy, and scarcity on the one hand and class, prestige, and wages on the other. Once the skill story is told, there is not much more to say about labor market inequality.

In Fig. 9, we give a more detailed picture of how class is tied to the four determinants by dissolving the continuous form of the class variable into five class categories. (For detailed numbers and country-specific results, see Appendix B, Table B.5). The four factors reported are in all other respects

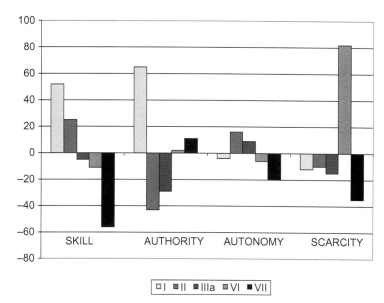

Fig. 9. Factor Analysis of the Relation between Five Class Categories and Four Hierarchical Determinants among Employees in 11 European countries. Factor Loadings × 100. *Notes*: All factors are extracted as principal components and rotated by varimax. Factor 1 (skill) and Factor 2 (authority) are common for all 11 countries, Factor 3 (autonomy) is common for 10 countries (Spain is excluded), and Factor 4 (scarcity) is common for 6 countries (Germany, France, Great Britain, Finland, Norway, and Sweden) with 5 countries excluded (Austria, Switzerland, Denmark, Spain, and the Netherlands). Loadings are unweighted averages across all included countries.

the same as in Fig. 8. We can see that skill is the only determinant that has a clearly hierarchical relation to class, that is, that service class I has the highest value (loading) on the factor and that unskilled workers have the lowest value, while the three other categories are placed in between. Authority identifies the top class (service class I) but aside from this tends to be inversely hierarchical (net of the skill factor). Autonomy is conspicuously weakly tied to class, but has – with the important exception of service class I – a weak hierarchical form across class categories. Scarcity, finally, has a completely deviant shape, with skilled manual workers in a clear top position and unskilled workers at the other end, with all three white-collar categories below zero, that is, with a negative association to the factor.[7]

An important reason for the high position of skilled workers on the scarcity factor is, we believe, that their skills to a relatively large extent are developed on the job rather than in school, which is the converse situation relative to high-level white-collar employees. (Due to lack of space, we do not show these results in detail here.) It is therefore reasonable to assume that skilled workers are comparatively difficult for the employer to replace, more difficult than service class employees. We think the reason is that school-based education is typically more standardized, that is, creates skills of a more general kind, and is therefore more replaceable than work-based training is. This is a completely different picture than the one expected from Goldthorpe's or Wright's class theories, according to which high-level white-collar employees are the most difficult to replace for the employer, either because they have a large amount of firm-specific skills (Goldthorpe's favored mechanism) or a large amount of permanently scarce occupational skills (Wright's favored mechanism).

CONCLUSIONS

The *Communist Manifesto* appeared in a time of social and political upheaval across Europe. Similarly, the class models examined above, which still dominate sociological thinking on inequality, were conceived in a politically and culturally turbulent period. During this time – the late 1960s and early 1970s – functionalist perspectives in the Parsonsian vein gave way to theoretical models with an emphasis on power, control, and conflict rather than on efficiency and social equilibrium.[8] We think that a crucial mistake made by the class theorists of that era, which through path dependency still heavily affects research on inequality, was to use factors related to macro-level social conflict as explanatory mechanisms in the analysis of micro-level stratification processes.

Power-related factors, important as they obviously are at the macro level, do not explain the structure of micro-level labor market inequality. This is true whether we measure inequality by class, occupational prestige, or wage differentials. Instead, efficiency-related factors are the fundamental driving forces behind the hierarchical order of positions in the labor market, at least in modern capitalist societies. Employers' efficiency requirements and workers' productive resources – not employers' control strategies and workers' closure strategies – determine the rank order of positions in working life. This is the picture painted by our findings, a picture that is remarkably similar in all the European countries we have examined despite the considerable institutional variation between them. The strength of the associations involved and their low degree of international variability justify the label "the iron law of labor market inequality." Hernes and Knudsen (1991) use the expression "the iron law of inequality" to describe the similarity in stratification patterns between socialist Lithuania and capitalist Norway. More generally, our results echo the strong stability in prestige ratings by occupation across time and space (Treiman, 1977). Our contribution here is to expand Treiman's generalization by (a) bringing class and wages into the analysis and (b) testing the theoretical mechanisms involved.

However, we are not claiming that power relations in the labor market are nonexistent or unimportant. First, as our results have shown, there are large international differences in the degree of earnings inequality across positions in the otherwise invariant hierarchical order. If non-European countries were included in our comparison, these cross-country differences in inequality would surely be even more apparent. Such macro-level effects can, in our view, be explained by collective action in distributional struggles over (temporarily) finite resources and rewards. But such macro-level mechanisms need to be analytically distinguished from the division and performance of labor that bring those resources about. Power is a crucial aspect of the former kind of process, but not – according to our results – of the latter.

Second, our aim has been to explain why positions are differentially rewarded, that is, to understand the nature of the hierarchical order of positions within the division of labor in society. Thus, our analyses do not concern the allocation of individuals to these positions. While skilled workers are typically allocated to skilled jobs, the matching process is far from perfect. A large amount of empirical research testifies to the importance of ethnic, gender, and racial discrimination – as well as of factors like class background, social capital, and homo-social reproduction – in the allocation of workers with equal productive characteristics to unequal positions in the educational system and in the labor market. Moreover, inequality of opportunity in early phases of school and work careers – due to discrimination, social capital, homo-social reproduction, and so on – will have long-term effects. There are vicious and virtuous circles in regard to skill formation: skills beget skills. Children of well-educated parents attain relatively high levels of schooling; in turn, this increases their chances of acquiring jobs with relatively large opportunities for on-the-job training. Such processes of cumulative advantage pull the skill distribution apart, with far-reaching consequences for social inequality, but have not been of concern to us here.

Within the scope of our chosen task – explaining the variation in rewards between positions held by employees in the labor market – a number of objections may, of course, be raised against our analyses and findings. To begin with, the methods we use (analysis of variance and factor analysis) are useful instruments for analyzing the total amount of inequality among employees, but not for examining the large reward gaps that may obtain between numerically small categories and the large majority of workers. If, for example, a small group of top-level managers receive very large economic rewards, and have very large amounts of power and authority, compared to other employees, this will only have a marginal impact on inequality estimates based on analyses of variance precisely because the elite category contains such a small share of all individuals. We realize that this objection may be warranted, but our goal here has been to explain the general structure of inequality among all employees rather than the reward gaps at extreme points of the distribution.

A possible objection to the results of the factor analyses is that the measures of autonomy and scarcity, and to some degree authority, are weaker than the measure of skill, and that this difference in measurement quality across indicators may bias the results in favor of finding relatively strong skill effects. We have several answers to this kind of argument: (a) If skill is easier to measure accurately than autonomy and scarcity are, one important reason may be that skill is in fact a more salient and fundamental aspect of work content and work situation than are the others. (b) Even if measurement error should weaken the observed impact of authority, autonomy, and scarcity, relative to the impact of skill, why should the *shape* of the impact be affected? In other words, the hierarchical class *order* should still come through, despite the attenuated *magnitude*; however, all dimensions except skill conspicuously fail to meet the rank-order test. (c) The results are highly similar across all 11 countries, despite probable cross-national differences in the degree of measurement error. (d) A result not shown here (available upon request) is that a strongly simplified skill measure (years of education required in the job) is sufficient to reach results that are very similar to those found when using the more elaborate skill measure; in this sense (as in many others), our findings are robust. (e) Finally, a good theory must be falsifiable; if all negative empirical results are rejected with reference to measurement error, the theory does not fulfill the falsifiability condition (at least not in practice).

An additional objection concerns the type of explanation used. The sociological version of the efficiency model typically assumes that social hierarchies emerge out of functional necessity. Such explanatory accounts are obviously very problematic if feedback mechanisms, based on individuals' actions, are not specified. In this regard, sociological functionalism is often vague and hence theoretically weak. Functional explanation in sociology is therefore nowadays seen as flawed, almost by definition. In contrast, functional explanation in economics is much clearer when it comes to specifying how labor market inequality emerges and is maintained. The point of departure is the neoclassical axiom of perfect competition in markets under capitalism, that is, that firms and other organizations exposed to competition are forced to seek and adopt efficient ways of carrying out their tasks in order to survive. Competition is the mechanism that explains why most work organizations operate efficiently: those who do not have been killed (or marginalized) by the market success of those who do. In this way, we can understand why a certain division of labor is created and reinforced, and why "more productive" workers receive larger rewards than the "less productive." While employers are obviously not always completely rational profit maximizers, it is reasonable to assume that markets in capitalist societies provide enough economic incentives for most work organizations to achieve at least moderate levels of efficiency. Even such a weak assumption of market efficiency would, in our view, appear sufficient to justify our theoretical interpretation of the empirical findings above.

Class is a crucial concept in research on inequality, and will continue to illuminate efforts at explaining the distribution of labor market rewards, as well as other important social outcomes. Our findings strongly support the view that class – as conventionally operationalized – plays a central role in accounting for social and economic inequality. But the mechanisms involved at the micro level seem to be very different from the ones emphasized in current theoretical models. The main conclusion of the present article is that efficiency mechanisms are much more important than power mechanisms in determining the rank order of positions in the labor market. This conclusion is well corroborated, we believe, both conceptually and empirically.

Our findings are devastating for currently dominant sociological perspectives on inequality. The negative empirical results for standard class theory cannot be brushed aside as minor anomalies, since they go straight to the heart of the whole class theoretical enterprise. The major postulated mechanisms assumed to explain class inequality are apparently very weak, if at all operative. Consequently, research on class and stratification needs to be fundamentally reoriented in the years ahead. Employers' efficiency requirements and workers' productive skills must be placed at center stage theoretically, rather than pushed to the sidelines of explanatory accounts.

Sociologists tend to dislike concepts like efficiency and productivity, partly because explanations based on them are seen as legitimating inequality, but such ideological concerns should not stand in the way of analytical progress. Avoiding serious theoretical and empirical consideration of potentially central causes of inequality does little service to anyone, least of all to the disadvantaged groups of society that supposedly are the ultimate beneficiaries of sound research on class and stratification. Theory, policy, and social change are closely connected: If we do not understand how the world works, how can we contribute effectively to improving it?

ACKNOWLEDGMENTS

Earlier versions of this paper were presented at the Equalsoc network conferences in Berlin, May 2009, and Tallinn, June 2009, and at the Social Policy and Welfare Research network conference, Stockholm, October 2009. Thanks to the participants at these occasions and to Göran Ahrne, Gunn Birkelund, Robert Erikson, Martin Hällsten, Christine Roman, Stefan Svallfors, Ryszard Szulkin, Donald Tomaskovic-Devey, Lars Udéhn, Erik Olin Wright, and two anonymous reviewers for helpful comments.

NOTES

1. In his early work on class and income determination, Wright (1979) grants that efficiency is an important mechanism for income determination *within the working class*. His argument is close to that of human capital theory. "Skills cost something to produce and maintain and unless the wages of skilled workers more or less cover these costs, the skill will cease to be produced" (*ibid.*: 81–83). However, income differences *between* classes (including "classes" of employees) are seen as power driven.

2. In recent formulations, Wright (see, e.g., Wright, 2009) calls this kind of mechanism opportunity hoarding with reference to Tilly (1999).

3. Productivity is neither a pure individual trait nor a pure job trait, but depends on the match between individuals and jobs. For example, the productive utility of education (an individual trait) depends on the complexity of to-be-carried-out tasks (a job trait), and vice versa. The link between productivity and matching is reflected in our measure of skill; see below.

4. It is sometimes believed that occupation and skill are necessarily linked, since occupations are partly defined with reference to required education and/or training. For example, the ISCO classification at the one-digit level is explicitly (though not entirely) based on considerations of occupational skill requirements. But

occupational categories reflect a wide range of different characteristics inherent in the job tasks, working conditions, employment relations, and other properties of the positions concerned. Class schemas, even when operationally based on occupational categories, typically avoid – indeed resist – class definitions with reference to skill, in preference of other criteria.

5. In addition, we distinguish a fifth variable on the basis of this set of regressions: a measure of the common (overlapping) variance among the four class criteria. This variable, labeled "common" in Appendix B (Tables B.1, B.3, B.4, and B.5), is included in the analyses below wherever we use the net indicators.

6. In factor analysis, unrotated factors are estimated in a first step, with the goal of maximizing the proportion explained variance in the underlying data (the input variables). In order to ease interpretation of the factor pattern, the initial factors can then be moved ("rotated") in the data space according to some criterion. The most common rotation criterion ("varimax"), which is also the one we use here, is to maximize the variance in loadings (factor-variable associations) within factors, subject to the constraint that the factors be uncorrelated with each other.

7. The reported loadings for the third factor (autonomy) are based on results for all countries except Spain, which shows a slightly deviant pattern. The fourth factor (scarcity) is relatively heterogeneous across countries. The reported loadings in this case are based on the results for six countries. In addition to Spain (as in the third factor), Austria, Switzerland, Denmark, and the Netherlands are excluded from the reported averages here. However, none of the deviant country cases provides any support for the hypotheses derived from either Goldthorpe's or Wright's class theory. (See Appendix B, Table B.5, for country-specific detailed results.)

8. An illustrative case in point is Goldthorpe's transformation of his scale of social standing (Hope & Goldthorpe, 1974) to the first version of his class schema (Goldthorpe & Llewellyn, 1977). One crucial factor involved in this conceptual shift appears to have been Goldthorpe's perception of worker strikes, economic recession, and other macro-level events at the time (Marshall, 1990, p. 56).

REFERENCES

Becker, G. S. (1962). Investment in human capital: A theoretical analysis. *Journal of Political Economy, 70*, 9–49.

Birkelund, G. E. (1992). Stratification and segregation. *Acta Sociologica, 35*, 47–62.

Büchel, F., de Grip, A., & Mertens, A. (Eds.). (2003). *Overeducation in Europe: Current issues in theory and policy.* Cheltenham, UK: Edward Elgar.

Chan, T. W., & Goldthorpe, J. H. (2007). Class and status: The conceptual distinction and its empirical relevance. *American Sociological Review, 72*, 512–532.

Davis, K., & Moore, W. E. (1945). Some principles of stratification. *American Sociological Review, 10*, 242–249.

Duncan, G. J., & Hoffman, S. D. (1981). The incidence and wage effects of overeducation. *Economics of Education Review, 1*, 75–86.

Erikson, R., & Goldthorpe, J. H. (1992). *The constant flux. A study of class mobility in industrial societies*. Oxford: Clarendon Press.

Farkas, G. (2003). Cognitive skills and non-cognitive traits and behaviors in stratification processes. *Annual Review of Sociology, 29*, 541–562.

Ganzeboom, H. B. G., de Graaf, P. M., & Treiman, D. J. (1992). A standard international socio-economic index of occupational status. *Social Science Research, 21*, 1–56.

Goldthorpe, J. H. (1980). *Social mobility and class structure in modern Britain*. Oxford: Clarendon Press.

Goldthorpe, J. H. (1982). On the service class, its formation and future. In A. Giddens & G. MacKenzie (Eds.), *Social class and the division of labour* (pp. 162–185). Cambridge: Cambridge University Press.

Goldthorpe, J. H. (2000). Social class and the differentiation of employment contracts. In J. H. Goldthorpe (Ed.), *On sociology: Numbers, narratives, and the integration of research and theory* (pp. 206–229). Oxford: Oxford University Press.

Goldthorpe, J. H., & Llewellyn, C. (1977). Class mobility in modern Britain: Three theses examined. *Sociology, 11*, 257–287.

Hernes, G., & Knudsen, K. (1991). The iron law of inequality: Different paths, but same results? Some comparisons between Lithuania and Norway. *European Sociological Review, 7*, 195–211.

Hope, K., & Goldthorpe, J. H. (1974). *The social grading of occupations: A new approach and scale*. Oxford: Oxford University Press.

Kohn, M. L., & Schooler, C. (1983). *Work and personality*. Norwood, NJ: Ablex.

Korpi, T., & Tåhlin, M. (2009). Educational mismatch, wages and wage growth: Overeducation in Sweden, 1974–2000. *Labour Economics, 16*, 183–193.

Lockwood, D. (1958). *The blackcoated worker*. Oxford: Oxford University Press.

Marshall, G. (1990). John Goldthorpe and class analysis. In J. Clark, C. Modgil & S. Modgil (Eds.), *John H. Goldthorpe: Consensus and controversy* (pp. 51–62). London: Falmer Press.

Mincer, J. (1974). *Schooling, experience, and earnings*. New York, NY: Columbia University Press.

Parsons, T. (1949). Social classes and class conflict in the light of recent sociological theory. *American Economic Review, 39*, 16–26.

Pontusson, J., Rueda, D., & Way, C. R. (2002). Comparative political economy of wage distribution: The role of partisanship and labour market institutions. *British Journal of Political Science, 32*, 281–308.

Rose, D., & Harrison, E. (2007). The European socio-economic classification: A new social class schema for comparative European research. *European Societies, 9*, 459–490.

Rubb, S. (2003). Overeducation in the labor market: A comment and re-analysis of a meta-analysis. *Economics of Education Review, 22*, 621–629.

Tåhlin, M. (2007). Class clues. *European Sociological Review, 23*, 557–572.

Thurow, L. C. (1975). *Generating inequality*. New York: Basic Books.

Tilly, C. (1999). *Durable inequality*. Berkeley, CA: University of California Press.

Treiman, D. J. (1976). A standard occupational prestige scale for use with historical data. *Journal of Interdisciplinary History, 7*, 283–304.

Treiman, D. J. (1977). *Occupational prestige in comparative perspective*. New York: Academic Press.

Weeden, K. (2002). Why do some occupations pay more than others? Social closure and earnings inequality in the United States. *American Journal of Sociology, 108*, 55–101.

Williamson, O. E. (1975). *Markets and hierarchies.* New York: Free Press.

Wright, E. O. (1979). *Class structure and income determination.* New York: Academic Press.

Wright, E. O. (1997). *Class counts. Comparative studies in class analysis.* Cambridge: Cambridge University Press.

Wright, E. O. (2009). Understanding class. Towards an integrated analytical approach. *New Left Review, 60*(November–December), 101–116.

APPENDIX A: VARIABLE OPERATIONALIZATIONS

(Variable numbers from ESS 2004, code book)

Wage is measured with three questions: G91 "What is your usual gross pay before deductions for tax and insurance?" [To be recorded in country's own currency and later converted into Euros.] G93 "How long a period does that pay cover?" The variable categories are one hour, one day, one week, two weeks, four weeks, calendar month, and year. F21 "Regardless of your basic or contracted hours, how many hours do you normally work a week (in your main job), including any paid or unpaid overtime."

Occupation is operationalized as ISCO-88.

Class (employees only) consists of five occupational categories – service class I, service class II, routine nonmanual workers (IIIa), skilled manual workers (VI), and unskilled manual and service workers (VII, IIIb) – according to the EGP class scheme (Erikson & Goldthorpe, 1992). A continuous version of the class variable (see subsection "Determinants of the hierarchical structure of working life") is constructed on the basis of a regression (specific for each country) with wage (in percentile form) as outcome and four class category dummies (for classes I, II, IIIa, and VI, with class VII/IIIb as the reference category) as predictors. The *B* coefficients from these regressions are then used as values on the class scale.

Education (number of years above compulsory school). F7 "How many years of full-time education have you completed?" The length of compulsory school is subtracted from this number of years, separately for each country and year of birth, in order to calculate the number of years of schooling beyond compulsory school.

Educational requirements for the job (number of years above compulsory school). G61 "If someone was applying nowadays for the job you do now, would they need any education or vocational schooling beyond compulsory education?" If yes: G62 "About how many years of education or vocational schooling beyond compulsory education would they need?" The answers are grouped into eight categories, from 1 (less than 1 year) to 8 (10 years or more).

Work experience (number of years): G118 "In total, how many years have you been in paid work?"

Initial on-the-job training (number of months in current job before being able to do the job reasonably well). G63 "If somebody with the right education and qualifications replaced you in your job, how long would it take for them to learn to do the job reasonably well?" The answers are grouped into eight categories, from 1 (one day or less) to 8 (more than five years).

Continuing on-the-job training (opportunities to learn new things in daily work). "Please tell me how true the following statement is about your current job: My job requires that I keep learning new things," measured with a scale ranging from 1 ("Not at all true") to 4 ("Very true").

Authority is measured with an indicator of the number of persons who the respondent is supervising. F16 "In your main job, do you have any responsibility for supervising the work of other employees?" If yes: F17 "How many people are you responsible for?" Logarithmic units of the number of subordinates $+1$ are used for this variable.

The degree of supervision that the respondent is subjected to: G78 "My work is closely supervised," inversely coded to reflect freedom from control; the answers range from 1 ("Strongly agree") to 5 ("Strongly disagree").

The degree of freedom to decide how one's own daily work is organized. F18 "Please say how much the management at your work allows you to decide how your own daily work is organized"; the answers range from 0 ("I have no influence") to 10 ("I have complete control").

Scarcity. G80 "In your opinion, how difficult or easy would it be for your employer to replace you if you left?" The answers range from 0 ("Extremely difficult") to 10 ("Extremely easy").

APPENDIX B: DESCRIPTIVE AND SUPPLEMENTARY STATISTICS

Tables B.1–B.5.

Table B.1. Means (Upper Row) and Standard Deviations (Lower Row) of All Variables Used, by Country (N Based on List-Wise Deletion of Cases with Missing Data).

	AT	CH	DE	DK	ES	FI	FR	GB	NL	NO	SE	AVG	SD
Class	49.4	50.4	52.3	50.9	49.3	50.4	50.1	50.4	48.4	49.9	50.2	50.2	1.0
	12.7	16.2	15.4	14.7	15.0	17.0	18.2	15.8	10.7	15.4	16.6	15.3	2.1
Prestige	42.6	45.4	43.9	46.0	40.8	43.7	43.6	42.7	47.5	43.2	43.0	43.9	1.8
	12.6	12.3	12.5	12.8	15.8	14.2	13.5	14.8	12.0	12.8	14.2	13.4	1.2
Wage (log)	2.48	3.05	2.58	3.06	2.01	2.58	2.40	2.59	2.73	2.98	2.69	2.65	0.31
	0.42	0.46	0.51	0.31	0.51	0.40	0.48	0.55	0.42	0.35	0.32	0.43	0.08
Wage (percentile)	49.3	50.5	50.6	50.5	48.4	50.2	50.4	50.3	50.3	50.4	50.8	50.1	0.7
	28.8	28.7	28.9	28.8	28.6	28.9	28.6	29.0	28.8	28.9	28.7	28.8	0.1
Skill	49.4	50.1	52.8	51.0	49.1	50.9	50.0	51.0	49.2	50.3	50.4	50.4	1.0
	16.1	17.4	17.9	15.7	18.3	17.5	18.6	19.5	16.4	17.0	17.1	17.4	1.1
Authority	49.4	50.0	52.2	50.5	49.1	50.5	50.1	50.5	48.5	49.8	50.0	50.0	0.9
	9.4	10.4	11.5	8.2	10.2	11.4	11.4	11.7	8.8	9.7	9.2	10.2	1.2
Autonomy	49.6	50.1	51.4	50.7	50.1	50.8	50.2	50.6	48.2	50.0	50.0	50.2	0.8
	10.1	9.3	11.2	6.6	7.9	7.1	8.1	9.8	6.7	6.4	7.3	8.2	1.6
Scarcity	49.3	50.1	52.1	50.8	50.3	50.8	50.1	50.4	48.4	50.0	50.1	50.2	0.9
	2.1	2.6	3.9	1.0	0.5	1.7	0.2	4.9	1.8	4.4	5.0	2.6	1.8
Skill net	0.7	-0.3	0.6	0.1	-0.1	0.0	-0.3	0.3	0.6	0.0	-0.1	0.1	0.4
	14.8	16.1	15.6	14.3	16.8	15.8	16.7	17.6	15.5	15.7	16.1	15.9	0.9
Authority net	0.1	0.1	0.1	-0.1	-0.3	-0.2	0.0	0.0	0.0	-0.1	0.1	0.0	0.1
	8.6	9.9	10.4	7.7	9.5	10.7	10.4	10.7	8.3	9.0	8.9	9.5	1.0
Autonomy net	0.0	0.2	-0.7	0.0	0.1	0.0	0.1	0.1	-0.1	0.0	0.0	0.0	0.2
	9.3	8.8	9.9	6.1	7.5	6.6	7.7	9.3	6.4	6.1	7.0	7.7	1.4

Scarcity net	0.0	−0.1	0.0	0.0	0.0	0.0	0.0	0.1	0.0	0.0	0.0	0.0	0.0
	2.0	2.5	3.8	1.0	0.5	1.6	0.2	4.8	1.8	4.4	4.9	2.5	1.7
Common	0.0	0.0	0.0	0.0	0.0	0.0	0.0	0.0	0.0	0.0	0.0	0.0	0.0
	1.0	1.0	1.0	1.0	1.0	1.0	1.0	1.0	1.0	1.0	1.0	1.0	0.0
Class I	0.13	0.18	0.17	0.22	0.17	0.20	0.19	0.22	0.28	0.20	0.19	0.20	0.04
Class II	0.31	0.35	0.28	0.33	0.25	0.23	0.32	0.27	0.37	0.28	0.28	0.30	0.04
Class IIIa	0.32	0.19	0.20	0.11	0.14	0.19	0.18	0.18	0.13	0.19	0.14	0.18	0.05
Class VI	0.11	0.16	0.22	0.11	0.11	0.13	0.12	0.11	0.10	0.14	0.13	0.13	0.03
Class VII/IIIb	0.13	0.12	0.14	0.23	0.32	0.25	0.18	0.21	0.11	0.20	0.25	0.19	0.07
N	284	625	588	590	287	749	579	532	502	868	861	588	193

Class I, high-level white-collar employees; class II, middle-level white-collar employees; class IIIa, routine nonmanual employees; class VI, skilled manual workers; class VII/IIIb, unskilled manual and service workers.

Table B.2. Wages (Log and Percentile) and Prestige by Class, by Country.

Wage (log)	AT	CH	DE	DK	ES	FI	FR	GB	NL	NO	SE	AVG	SD
Class I	76	101	108	56	96	89	110	117	57	62	62	85	23
Class II	46	56	63	24	49	35	51	59	29	35	30	43	13
Class IIIa	12	18	15	7	−7	0	−3	1	−1	6	0	4	8
Class VI	3	19	14	11	27	17	18	19	15	15	9	15	6
Class VII/IIIb (ref.)	0	0	0	0	0	0	0	0	0	0	0		

Wage (percentile)	AT	CH	DE	DK	ES	FI	FR	GB	NL	NO	SE	AVG	SD
Class I	72	76	78	73	75	79	78	73	61	73	76	74	5
Class II	59	58	62	55	58	58	60	59	51	59	60	58	3
Class IIIa	41	36	41	38	32	35	31	34	32	37	33	35	4
Class VI	36	40	43	45	50	47	43	43	42	46	44	44	4
Class VII/IIIb	35	27	32	33	37	34	29	34	32	30	33	32	3

Prestige	AT	CH	DE	DK	ES	FI	FR	GB	NL	NO	SE	AVG	SD
Class I	56	59	60	58	63	61	59	60	56	56	60	59	2
Class II	49	49	50	51	50	52	49	48	52	48	50	50	1
Class IIIa	40	43	40	43	34	37	38	37	38	41	38	39	3
Class VI	38	38	38	37	36	37	37	35	38	36	37	37	1
Class VII/IIIb	26	28	26	31	26	30	27	27	29	30	28	28	2

Class I, high-level white-collar employees; class II, middle-level white-collar employees; class IIIa, routine nonmanual employees; class VI, skilled manual workers; class VII/IIIb, unskilled manual and service workers.

Table B.3. Factor Analyses Summarized in Fig. 7, by Country (Factor Loadings × 100).

F1 gross unrot.	AT	CH	DE	DK	ES	FI	FR	GB	NL	NO	SE	AVG	SD
Class	81	83	86	86	84	87	88	87	82	85	86	85	2
Prestige	69	78	83	79	79	86	83	85	79	79	84	80	5
Wage	76	77	77	73	78	79	81	80	72	77	79	77	3
Skill	74	73	79	80	79	81	82	78	73	81	80	78	3
Authority	57	55	64	57	55	60	61	67	56	59	44	58	6
Autonomy	54	51	59	42	45	48	48	48	45	40	44	48	5
Scarcity	32	29	30	25	3	12	19	29	−15	20	28	19	14

F1 gross rot.	AT	CH	DE	DK	ES	FI	FR	GB	NL	NO	SE	AVG	SD
Class	78	82	86	88	86	86	86	87	78	85	86	84	3
Prestige	84	81	87	83	82	85	84	85	81	79	84	83	2
Wage	74	79	77	75	75	80	83	80	76	77	79	78	3
Skill	69	72	80	75	79	80	83	78	75	81	80	77	4
Authority	26	45	56	52	51	61	52	67	44	59	44	51	11
Autonomy	34	38	46	21	37	43	40	48	28	40	44	38	8
Scarcity	−7	−4	−1	0	−13	−3	−5	29	14	20	28	5	15

F1 net unrot.	AT	CH	DE	DK	ES	FI	FR	GB	NL	NO	SE	AVG	SD
Class	82	83	88	85	83	86	89	86	82	84	85	85	2
Prestige	72	79	86	82	81	87	84	86	79	81	85	82	4
Wage	77	78	78	75	78	80	81	82	72	78	79	78	3
Skill	54	51	52	68	65	64	57	59	50	67	71	60	8
Authority	30	30	32	22	15	22	27	29	31	25	19	26	6
Autonomy	23	23	14	5	19	16	18	14	29	13	17	17	6
Scarcity	4	5	4	0	4	5	6	2	−6	8	7	4	4
Common	79	83	83	78	81	83	84	89	80	85	84	83	3

F1 net rot.	AT	CH	DE	DK	ES	FI	FR	GB	NL	NO	SE	AVG	SD
Class	72	80	85	83	83	84	85	87	74	76	83	81	5
Prestige	79	80	87	83	82	88	86	86	81	86	87	84	3
Wage	76	79	80	74	78	80	83	82	76	77	78	78	3
Skill	76	62	61	76	74	71	69	58	74	81	80	71	8
Authority	−3	20	21	13	8	16	14	32	6	6	10	13	9
Autonomy	8	17	12	−3	4	8	10	12	1	3	5	7	6
Scarcity	−3	2	2	−3	−1	6	2	3	2	3	3	1	3
Common	53	79	79	73	71	79	76	89	55	74	78	73	11

CARL LE GRAND AND MICHAEL TÅHLIN

Table B.4. Factor Analyses Summarized in Fig. 8, by Country (Factor Loadings × 100).

F1 net rot.	AT	CH	DE	DK	ES	FI	FR	GB	NL	NO	SE	AVG	SD
Class	72	80	85	83	83	84	85	85	74	76	83	81	5
Prestige	79	80	87	83	82	88	86	86	81	86	87	84	3
Wage	76	79	80	74	78	81	83	82	76	77	78	79	3
Skill	76	62	61	76	74	72	69	63	74	81	80	72	7
Authority	−3	20	21	13	8	19	14	25	6	6	10	13	8
Autonomy	8	17	12	−3	4	2	10	11	1	3	5	6	6
Scarcity	−3	2	2	−3	−1	2	2	3	2	3	3	1	2
Common	53	79	79	73	71	76	76	89	55	74	78	73	10

F2 net rot.	AT	CH	DE	DK	ES	FI	FR	GB	NL	NO	SE	AVG	SD
Class	42	30	28	33	15	27	28	32	42	42	22	31	9
Prestige	−4	−4	3	−2	−12	0	−9	11	9	−7	−9	−2	7
Wage	17	0	−5	8	14	8	1	−7	0	11	16	6	8
Skill	−24	−52	−50	−47	−41	−54	−54	−65	−44	−40	−32	−46	11
Authority	97	95	95	96	99	95	97	92	96	98	98	96	2
Autonomy	−5	−7	−9	−6	−8	−5	−3	−5	−6	−7	−6	−6	2
Scarcity	−9	−6	−7	0	0	1	−7	5	1	−2	−2	−2	4
Common	59	17	18	11	33	4	43	−3	36	40	17	25	19

F3 net rot.	AT	CH	DE	DK	ES	FI	FR	GB	NL	NO	SE	AVG	SD
Class	8	4	−2	−4	7	7	4	0	11	9	8	5	5
Prestige	11	8	−6	−3	11	5	5	−1	11	−2	4	4	6
Wage	14	0	5	9	−1	−2	4	6	8	5	3	5	5
Skill	−33	−46	−51	−22	−30	−30	−31	−31	−21	−21	−29	−31	10
Authority	−11	−8	−8	−7	−8	−9	−9	−13	−3	−9	−5	−8	3
Autonomy	99	97	98	99	99	99	99	99	99	100	99	99	1
Scarcity	0	−5	−11	−6	−2	−5	−2	−2	5	−3	−4	−3	4
Common	29	20	38	50	45	53	26	16	59	36	40	37	14

F4 net rot.	AT	CH	DE	DK	ES	FI	FR	GB	NL	NO	SE	AVG	SD
Class	4	3	1	4	−16	7	5	−2	−2	4	0	1	6
Prestige	−3	−3	−6	0	−14	0	1	−6	5	−4	−2	−3	5
Wage	−1	−9	−2	−10	16	−1	−7	2	2	9	6	0	8
Skill	1	−12	−4	−9	15	−5	−1	−21	−12	−9	−16	−7	10
Authority	−17	−8	−8	0	1	0	−9	0	0	−4	−2	−4	6
Autonomy	1	−6	−15	−9	−4	−6	−3	−2	11	−3	−6	−4	6
Scarcity	98	99	99	99	95	100	99	100	98	100	100	99	1
Common	38	30	24	27	20	7	18	13	−29	11	23	17	18

Table B.5. Factor Analyses Summarized in Fig. 9, by Country (Factor Loadings × 100).

F1 net rot.	AT	CH	DE	DK	ES	FI	FR	GB	NL	NO	SE	AVG	SD
Class I	35	56	56	51	71	63	51	56	26	51	57	52	12
Class II	25	16	36	32	23	23	32	31	-1	22	35	25	11
Class IIIa	8	-11	-14	-2	16	-3	-7	-15	-18	4	-8	-5	10
Class VI	0	-14	-22	-10	-4	-10	-21	-7	-6	-11	-12	-11	7
Class VII/IIIb	-80	-61	-66	-77	-64	-70	-65	-71	-12	-70	-72	-64	18
Prestige	83	80	88	83	85	85	87	86	43	85	89	81	13
Wage	56	75	75	67	73	73	73	77	76	71	72	72	6
Skill	58	67	54	78	74	77	79	69	89	80	79	73	10
Authority	-16	9	16	0	2	4	-11	13	-24	-4	4	-1	12
Autonomy	13	16	17	-5	5	4	4	8	-5	0	3	5	8
Scarcity	-2	2	6	-5	3	6	13	1	2	7	5	3	5

F2 net rot.	AT	CH	DE	DK	ES	FI	FR	GB	NL	NO	SE	AVG	SD
Class I	80	48	69	76	9	64	76	74	85	64	70	65	21
Class II	-25	-5	-65	-73	-6	-37	-53	-67	-60	-12	-72	-43	27
Class IIIa	-40	-71	-10	-10	-13	-47	-24	-7	-20	-67	-6	-29	24
Class VI	1	9	8	2	25	-16	5	-7	-6	0	0	2	10
Class VII/IIIb	8	25	10	13	-9	31	7	9	-2	16	15	11	11
Prestige	15	0	7	5	-12	14	11	20	21	7	2	8	10
Wage	29	18	5	23	23	26	22	5	20	26	17	19	8
Skill	-6	-27	-26	-16	-32	-27	-24	-39	-15	-18	-17	-22	9
Authority	85	83	80	73	93	77	84	70	80	84	67	80	7
Autonomy	-1	0	-16	-9	-2	-1	4	-8	2	-1	-5	-3	6
Scarcity	-8	-5	-13	2	23	14	-8	4	-7	5	1	1	11

CARL LE GRAND AND MICHAEL TÅHLIN

Table B.5. (*Continued*)

F3 net rot.	AT	CH	DE	DK	ES	FI	FR	GB	NL	NO	SE	AAVG	SD
Class I	-15	-4	-18	-3	12	-1	-9	4	5	0	-1	-4	8
Class II	19	12	23	8	13	10	30	27	-1	12	22	16	10
Class IIIa	19	-1	7	5	4	9	11	7	-4	2	6	6	6
Class VI	-8	-1	-1	-4	-25	11	3	-61	7	7	-15	-6	21
Class VII/IIIb	-30	-43	-17	-7	-8	-26	-42	5	-8	-22	-15	-21	15
Prestige	0	14	-8	0	17	4	13	11	10	-2	5	5	7
Wage	2	-4	-4	11	-8	-3	4	7	14	3	6	4	6
Skill	-50	-59	-65	-24	-36	-38	-39	-35	-17	-24	-34	-39	16
Authority	5	13	18	2	-2	4	10	4	-5	-2	10	6	7
Autonomy	89	83	87	97	94	95	86	80	95	96	94	90	6
Scarcity	1	-6	-37	-6	-24	-15	-9	7	42	-15	7	-3	20

F4 net rot.	AT	CH	DE	DK	ES	FI	FR	GB	NL	NO	SE	AAVG	SD
Class I	2	1	-16	2	9	-2	-8	-12	19	-19	-12	-12	6
Class II	-1	5	-17	13	6	-22	-16	10	29	-5	-10	-10	11
Class IIIa	1	-2	-16	1	14	-26	-12	-6	9	-19	-12	-15	7
Class VI	2	2	89	-4	-80	89	86	56	-90	88	84	82	13
Class VII/IIIb	-4	-9	-49	-14	30	-24	-33	-35	6	-33	-34	-35	8
Prestige	-3	1	-8	4	-4	-8	-5	-4	34	-17	-7	-8	5
Wage	2	-10	-12	-14	5	4	-4	-7	4	5	-2	-3	7
Skill	7	-14	-16	-17	8	-11	-5	-39	4	-10	-18	-17	12
Authority	-21	-6	1	9	-5	1	-5	20	-2	2	3	4	8
Autonomy	4	-10	-10	-11	2	-8	-10	12	-4	-7	-6	-5	8
Scarcity	97	99	42	97	72	55	57	76	42	53	61	57	11

EDUCATIONAL CHOICES AND SOCIAL INTERACTIONS: A FORMAL MODEL AND A COMPUTATIONAL TEST

Gianluca Manzo

ABSTRACT

In their authoritative literature review, Breen and Jonsson (2005) claim that 'one of the most significant trends in the study of inequalities in educational attainment in the past decade has been the resurgence of rational-choice models focusing on educational decision making'. The starting point of the present contribution is that these models have largely ignored the explanatory relevance of social interactions. To remedy this shortcoming, this paper introduces a micro-founded formal model of the macro-level structure of educational inequality, which frames educational choices as the result of both subjective ability/benefit evaluations and peer-group pressures. As acknowledged by Durlauf (2002, 2006) and Akerlof (1997), however, while the social psychology and ethnographic literature provides abundant empirical evidence of the explanatory relevance of social interactions, statistical evidence on their causal effect is still flawed by identification and selection bias problems. To assess the relative explanatory contribution of the micro-level and network-based mechanisms hypothesised, the paper opts for agent-based computational

Class and Stratification Analysis
Comparative Social Research, Volume 30, 47–100
ISSN: 0195-6310/doi:10.1108/S0195-6310(2013)0000030007

simulations. In particular, the technique is used to deduce the macro-level consequences of each mechanism (sequentially introduced) and to test these consequences against French aggregate individual-level survey data. The paper's main result is that ability and subjective perceptions of education benefits, no matter how intensely differentiated across agent groups, are not sufficient on their own *to generate the actual stratification of educational choices across educational backgrounds existing in France at the beginning of the twenty-first century. By computational counter-factual manipulations, the paper proves that network-based interdependencies among educational choices are instead necessary, and that they contribute,* over and above *the differentiation of ability and of benefit perceptions, to the genesis of educational stratification by amplifying the segregation of the educational choices that agents make on the basis of purely private ability/benefit calculations.*

Keywords: Intergenerational educational mobility; educational choices; social interactions; social networks; agent-based models; analytical sociology

INTRODUCTION

By themselves, quantities just aid assessments, but when parameters marshal them into an array of numbers, then they can trigger alternative thinking. (White, 2000, p. 505)

About 15 years ago, Goldthorpe (1996) and Breen and Goldthorpe (1997) considered the large temporal stability of class differentials in educational attainment as one of the *explananda* that 'pose(s) an evident theoretical challenge'. While recent comparative empirical analyses (see Breen, Luijkx, Müller, & Pollak, 2009; Breen, Luijkx, Muller, & Pollak, 2010) have demonstrated that the change-resistance of inequality of educational opportunity is less pronounced than previous studies suggested (see, mainly, Shavit & Blossfeld, 1993), it is indisputable that, despite the generalised improvement of living standards and the variety of educational policies aimed at counteracting the partly social constructed ability gaps across social groups, the socioeconomic status of the family in which individuals live still exerts a substantial influence on their educational outcomes. In France, the country on which this paper focuses, while the equalising trend in educational opportunity is extremely clear (see Thélot & Vallet, 2000), although quantitatively modest (see Vallet & Selz, 2007, p. 69), individuals' social backgrounds continue pervasively to impact on the highest educational level that they reach (see Selz & Vallet, 2006), on the kind of upper secondary tracks that they choose (see Duru-Bellat, Kieffer, & Reimer, 2011; Ichou & Vallet, 2011) as well as on their chances of entering the most prestigious tertiary level educational institutions (see Albouy & Wanecq, 2003). In light of this empirical evidence, therefore, it still seems justified to consider the stratification of educational outcomes across social backgrounds as a puzzling macro-level *explanandum*.

In order to advance understanding of why the socioeconomic status of the family in which individuals live continues to exert such a pervasive influence on their educational choices, this paper introduces a new formal model of how individuals' educational preferences form. On a theoretical level, the model's novelty is that it frames educational preference formation as the result of both individual ability/benefit evaluations and peer-group pressures, thus cross-fertilising the sociological rational-choice approach to educational choices (Breen & Goldthorpe, 1997) with recent heterodox theoretical perspectives in economics regarding inequality (see, in particular, Durlauf, 1999a, 2002, 2006) and education (see, in particular, Akerlof, 1997; Akerlof & Kranton, 2002). On a methodological level, the paper's originality resides in its deduction of the macro-level consequences of the formal model by means of agent-based computational simulations (see Shoam & Leyton-Brown, 2009; Wooldridge, 2009). These computational regularities will, however, be systematically compared to French empirical survey data. An interface will thus be created between the regression-based approach that dominates quantitative studies of educational stratification and new advances in simulation methodology. Both the theoretical and the methodological development proposed can be justified in light of the current state of the literature on the explanation of educational stratification.

Since Boudon's (1974, see, in particular, pp. 29–31) pioneering study, rational-choice oriented explanations of the aggregate association between individuals' social backgrounds and their educational achievements have been regularly refined (see, in particular, Breen & Goldthorpe, 1997; Gambetta, 1987; Goldthorpe, 1996; Jonsson & Erikson, 2000). According to this analytical schema, class differentials in educational attainment arise from the composition of the strategies of rational actors who, as they proceed through the educational system, systematically evaluate their cognitive abilities, their probability of success (as a function of their ability), the benefits that they can obtain from education, and the direct and indirect education costs. The basic assumption is that the higher the social status of the actor's family, the higher the actor's ability; consequently, the better the actor's perception of his/her probability of success, the higher his/ her educational aspiration, and the lower the perceived costs of education. As a consequence, the members of higher social groups should succeed at a higher rate at each educational transition, thereby ending up with higher educational credentials.

However, after around two decades of statistical-based empirical tests (see, among others, Ballarino & Bernardi, 2001; Becker, 2003; Breen & Yaish, 2006; Cobalti, 1992; Davies, Heinesen, & Holm, 2002; Gabay-Egozi, Shavit, & Yaish, 2010; Hillmert & Jacob, 2003; Holm & Jaeger, 2008; Manzo, 2006; Mastekaasa, 2006; Need & de Jong, 2000; Raftery & Hout, 1993; Schizzerotto, 1997; Stocké, 2007; Van de Werfhorst & Hofstede, 2007), while several pieces of the theoretical framework have received empirical support – such as the systematic variation of ability, of perception of success probability and of educational aspirations across social groups (see, for instance, Becker, 2003; Need & de Jong, 2000; Stocké, 2007) – still unclear is the extent to which these micro-level factors really impact on individuals' educational decisions (see, for instance, Stocké, 2007; Van de Werfhorst & Hofstede, 2007; Gabay-Egozi et al., 2010). As recently acknowledged by Kronenberg and Kalter (2012), when one inspects the published empirical results, one of the most striking findings is that no matter what indicator of ability and perceived benefits and costs is adopted, the effect of social background on educational choices and attainment is still substantial. This is especially puzzling at the highest educational transitions, where student heterogeneity is lower because of selection at previous transitions (see, for instance, Mastekaasa, 2006).

While this might be related to inappropriate statistical model specifications and/or poor measures of the theoretical constructs of interest, one might also think, more radically, that the rational-choice approach to educational stratification does not take account of certain mechanisms which potentially mediate the link between social background and educational choices/outcomes. On this reasoning, a few empirical analyses have started to study two types of mechanism under-conceptualised within this research tradition: genetic hereditability (see Lucchini, Della Stella, & Pisati, 2010) and social interactions in the form of peer effects (see, in particular, Jaeger, 2007; Morgan, 2005).

As announced, this paper focuses on social interactions. In particular, it computationally tests the hypothesis that the (French) empirical stratification of educational choices cannot be generated without assuming that homophilic dyadic interactions taking place within friendship networks sustain self-reinforcing mimetic educational behaviours that progressively accentuate the existing social differentiation in ability and perception of education benefits.

This accounts for the methodology chosen in what follows to prove this statement, that is, agent-based computational simulations. The empirical quantification of the net effect of neighbourhood- and network-based social influences on individual outcomes has proved extremely difficult (see, respectively, Mouw, 2006; Sobel, 2006; Sampson, Morenoff, & Gannon-Rowley, 2002; Shalizi & Thomas, 2011; and VanderWeele, 2011). If two actors are related by a friendship tie and end up with a similar (educational) outcome, then this correlation may actually arise from three distinct phenomena: (1) the two actors are exposed to certain common factors, like school or teaching quality (see the concept of 'ecological effect'; Manski, 1993b, p. 31); (2) the two actors share some common social background characteristics, like parental income (see the concept of 'contextual effect'; Manski, 1993a, p. 532, 1993b, p. 31); (3) the two actors share some common individual characteristics, like an interest in school (see the concept of 'correlated effect'; Manski, 1993a, p. 533, 1993b, p. 31). If so, the similar (educational) outcome may arise not from the influence that the two actors exert on each other, which would constitute the interaction-based 'endogenous effect' in which one is interested, but from the potentially unmeasured shared factors that modify the probability of being friends and that of experiencing a certain (educational) outcome. Unfortunately, unless very restrictive conditions are introduced, the four effects cannot be empirically distinguished on the basis of nonexperimental observational data (for an overview, see Durlauf & Loannides, 2010), and, because of the pervasive problem of unmeasured heterogeneity, empirical estimations tend to be 'biased' (Harding, Gennetian, Winship, Sanbonmatsu, & Kling, 2011). Moreover, an additional complication concerns the direction of the causality. Does the average (educational) outcome among a given subset of friends truly affect their (educational) behaviour, or does the group-level factor simply reflect this behaviour? Again, as Manski's pioneering contribution demonstrated, there is no simple econometric solution to 'reflection problem' – which becomes all the more difficult to solve when the aim is to estimate the several potential sources of the overall researched 'endogenous effect' (see Cohen-Cole & Zanella, 2008).

Agent-based computational modelling cannot help solve these estimation and identification problems on empirical grounds. At the theoretical level, however, they offer a unique opportunity for rigorous study of formal models containing neighbourhood- and/or network-based interdependences among individual behaviours. First of all, there is no unobserved

heterogeneity within an agent-based model. By construction, since the
modeller defines them, all group- and individual-level variables defining
agents' attributes are perfectly known. Similarly, because agents' spatial and
network locations are defined by the modeller, the way in which agents are
linked together and the composition of their local neighbourhood is also
completely transparent. 'Ecological', 'contextual' and 'correlated' effects are
thus completely controlled for. Moreover, they can be easily separated from
'endogenous' effects. By means of appropriate procedures to control for
model stochasticity, it is in fact possible to re-run exactly the same
simulation with and without the network-based social influence mechanisms
(this counterfactual manipulation will be performed in section 'Computational results, empirical data and model dynamic'). The net effect of being in
contact with a given set of agents *over and above* the effect associated with
the distribution of individual-level characteristics can thus be isolated.
Finally, the 'reflection' problem can be efficiently handled. Within an agent-
based model, the sequence of events, the model scheduling, is defined by the
modeller so that, although sometimes complicated, it is possible to establish
what causes what. There is an additional attractiveness in using agent-based
simulations to study the effect of social interaction on individuals'
behaviour. As acknowledged by Goux and Maurin (2007), empirical data
usually do not allow for study of individuals' closest neighbours, which
represent the neighbourhoods that really matter for individuals' outcomes.
Existing studies typically proxy interaction-based mechanisms with school-
and/or neighbourhood-level aggregate variables (among analyses specifically addressing individual educational outcomes, see, for instance, Agirgad,
2011; Brännström, 2008; Fekjær & Birkelund, 2007). Agent-based models
make it possible to overcome this limitation by enabling the creation of any
sort of actor-to-actor network topology.

For these reasons, given the aim of the paper, that is, to test the
hypothesis that the actual (French) distribution of educational choices
across social groups cannot be generated unless one assumes that some
network-based social influence mechanism is at work, agent-based modelling represents the best methodological choice. Instead of inferring the effect
of social interactions from observation of their outcomes (for this criticism
within economics, see Manski, 2000), agent-based computation simulations
will enable me deductively to generate aggregate structures of numerical
data that can be compared to empirical data structures, *given* an entirely
specified set of behavioural rules and interacting patterns – the formal model
proposed provides this set of elements. On the other hand, the counterfactual possibilities offered by the technique will make it possible to isolate

the specific contribution of the interaction-based mechanism postulated. The paper thus contains a 'computational test' of the formal model proposed, in that it proves, by growing educational stratification *in silico*, the conditions under which the actual (French) educational stratification can be best approximated (on the deductive nature of agent-based models, a point often poorly understood, see Epstein, 2006, ch. 1, pp. 10–12; on the concept of 'constructive proofs', see Borrill & Tesfatsion, 2010).

The article is organised as follows. The first section provides a description of the empirical data and sets out the research strategy underlying the paper. Second section presents the formal model aimed at explaining the empirical observations – a generalisation of this model is briefly discussed in Appendix B. Third section reports the simulation results and compares them to the empirical data. Fourth section evaluates the robustness of the simulation results concerning the network-based social mechanism postulated and comments on some counterintuitive results generated by the model with respect to the link between 'weak ties' and educational inequality. Fifth section discusses the major limitations of the analysis, and is followed by a short general conclusion.[1]

DATA, VARIABLES AND RESEARCH STRATEGY

The empirical data on which I draw come from a large national survey, representative of the French population aged 18–65, carried out in 2003 by the INSEE, the French national bureau of statistics. In order to ensure that all individuals have attained their highest educational level, I consider here only male and female respondents aged 27–65 at the time of the interview for whom complete information on their own and at least one of their parents' education achievements was available.

As regards variables, the dependent variable on which the paper focuses is the respondents' highest educational level, whereas the independent variable is the highest educational level attained by respondents' parents, which is measured as the highest educational level between the respondent's father and mother (for the 'dominance principle' applied here, see Erikson & Goldthorpe, 1992, p. 238). In order to make the analysis more directly readable within the international literature, both variables have been recoded into the Casmin educational schema (see Brauns & Steinman, 1997; Müller, Lüttinger, König, & Karle, 1989; Müller & Karle, 1993; and, more recently, Breen, 2004, pp. 14–16). However, in order not to excessively increase the number of groups of artificial agents to be represented in the formal model, I have adopted the following five-category version of the original schema: (1a) inadequately completed general education; (1bc) elementary education; (2ab) lower-secondary education; (2c) upper-secondary education and (3ab) tertiary education (for a similar five-category classification, see Breen et al., 2010).

Concerning the method, as argued in the introduction, the paper combines statistics and simulation. More precisely, the analysis follows the five-step research strategy recently summarised by Hedström and Bearman (2009, p. 16) according to which: '(1) we start with a clearly delineated social fact that is to be explained; (2) we formulate different hypotheses about relevant micro-level mechanisms; (3) we translate the theoretical hypotheses into computational models; (4) we simulate the models to derive the type of social facts that each micro-level mechanism brings about; (5) we compare the social facts generated by each model with the actually observed outcomes' (for a similar, but three-step based, strategy, see also Goldthorpe, 2001, p. 10; for an overall critical assessment of these developments, see Manzo, 2007, 2010).

In the following analysis, given the way in which independent and dependent variables are coded, the 'delineated social fact to be explained' consists of the aggregate patterns contained in Table 1, which cross-classifies the highest educational destinations attained by French men and women aged 27–65 in 2003 (columns) by the highest educational level reached by their parents (rows).

In order to describe both the absolute and the relative dimension of these patterns – that is to say, the amount of education that the members of a given educational background obtain and, on the other hand, their relative position, that is, their educational opportunity, within the educational hierarchy (see Breen, 2004, ch. 2) – the following statistics have been computed, the first three referring to the absolute aspect, the others to the relative one: the percentage of cases who are educationally immobile ('ip'); the percentage of cases who are upwardly mobile ('ump'); the ratio between the percentage of cases attaining the highest educational level within the highest and the lowest educational backgrounds ('hlgr'); the generalised odds ratios of obtaining the highest educational level for the members of the highest educational background ('hggor'); the generalised odds ratios of obtaining any educational credential for the members of the lowest educational background ('lggor') and the average of generalised odds ratios computed for each group ('agor').[2]

The statistical values reported in the bottom part of Table 1 thus show that educational inequality was substantial in France at the beginning of the

Table 1. Respondents' Highest Educational Level (Columns) by Their Parents' Highest Educational Level (Rows) – Row Percentages, Absolute Frequency (in Parenthesis) and Generalised Odds Ratios; France (2003), men and women aged 27–65.

	1a	1bc	2ab	2c	3ab	N
1a	44.22 (4,175) 8.98	29.00 (2,738) 4.02	15.48 (1,462) 0.81	5.61 (530) 0.27	5.69 (537) 0.13	(9,442)
1bc	16.23 (2,527) 1.22	28.03 (4,363) 2.47	26.98 (4,200) 1.25	13.93 (2,169) 0.73	14.83 (2,309) 0.36	(15,568)
2ab	9.51 (284) 0.58	11.38 (340) 0.66	26.01 (777) 1.30	20.96 (626) 1.52	32.14 (960) 1.33	(2,987)
2c	6.84 (147) 0.40	9.78 (210) 0.60	21.32 (458) 1.10	19.51 (419) 1.57	42.55 (914) 2.39	(2,148)
3ab	5.02 (169) 0.40	4.13 (139) 0.25	11.69 (394) 0.69	17.30 (583) 2.10	61.86 (2,084) 6.90	(3,369)

Absolute (1–3) and Relative (4–6) Educational Mobility Statistics

IP (1)	UMP (2)	HLGR (3)	AGOR (4)	HGGOR (5)	LGGOR (6)
35.26	49.07	10.87	1.68	6.9	8.98

twenty-first century. More than one-third of the French respondents were indeed educationally immobile (see ip's value); the offspring of the highest educational group reached the highest educational level about 10 times more frequently than did individuals from the lowest educational origin (see hlgr's value); the overall competitive educational advantage for highest educational origin to obtain the highest educational level was about 7 (see hggor's value), whereas the likelihood of respondents of lowest educational origin falling in the less desirable educational destination was about 9 (see lggor's value), the two values thus express a quite intense polarisation of educational opportunity across social groups.

To explain these statistical facts, several hypotheses about the main explanatory factors that the literature on educational choices usually focuses on – that is, abilities, cost/preference trade-offs, subjective perceptions of success probability and peer-based social influences – will be formulated (Hedström and Bearman's step 2). These hypotheses about the relevant micro-level mechanisms will then be translated into a computational model (Hedström and Bearman's step 3) that will take the form of an agent-based model: that is to say, a computer program in which the decision of each numerical entity in the system about whether or not to make a given educational transition is driven by a set of entirely specified rules and interaction patterns (see section 'Computational modelling of educational preference formation'; Eqs. (1)–(4)). By iterating these rules until each agent reaches a stable educational level, the simulation of the model (Hedström and Bearman's step 4) makes it possible to trigger the process potentially associated with the hypothesised mechanisms so as to enable bottom-up deduction of the aggregate pattern that these mechanisms are able to generate (for the simulation algorithm, see section 'Computational modelling of educational preference formation'; Fig. 1). In this paper, the comparison of the simulated aggregate pattern with 'the actually observed fact' (Hedström and Bearman's step 5) takes the following form.

On the one hand, the formal model is evaluated on the basis of its capacity to reproduce the variety of features of the observed contingency table that I have just described, rather than a single aspect of the actual cross-tabulation (for a similar multi-statistics test, see, for instance, Burke & Heiland, 2006, tab. 1). On the other hand, the formal model is evaluated on the basis of its capacity to reproduce a distribution of contingency tables rather than one single cross-tabulation. As often recommended, but less often done, distributions of outcomes matter more than single outcomes when assessing the explanatory and predictive power of a stochastic simulation model (see, for instance, Stonedahl & Wilensky, 2010).

To meet both requirements, I implemented the following procedure. As regards empirical data, I bootstrapped 100 samples of 5,000 cases from the original French sample and, for each sample, I computed the table, cross-classifying the highest educational destinations attained by French respondents with the highest educational level reached by their parents, and I computed the statistics described above on this cross-tabulation. As regards simulated data, for a given parameter structure, the simulation of the formal model was replicated 100 times and, for each replication, a simulated cross-tabulation was created. On each of them, I then computed the same statistics as computed on the empirical data. Thus, the comparison between empirical and simulation data finally took the form of an assessment of how overlap the nonparametric 95% confidence interval computed over the empirical/simulated series of values (for this approach, see Law, 2007, pp. 269–271; on bootstrapped percentile confidence intervals, see Davison & Hinkley, 1997, ch. 5).

As advised by step 5 of Hedström and Bearman's research strategy, the mechanisms formalised by the model presented in the next section will be introduced sequentially. For each model variant, the comparison strategy that I have just described will be applied so that it is possible to assess the extent to which each (combination of) mechanism(s) is able to reproduce the qualitative structure of the empirical contingency table. As argued in the introduction, the fundamental goal of this incremental procedure is to establish in a deductive manner whether or not the structure and the level of educational inequality observed in France across educational backgrounds can be generated without assuming that some interaction-related mechanisms are at work.[3]

COMPUTATIONAL MODELLING OF EDUCATIONAL PREFERENCE FORMATION

To test the generative power of several mechanisms potentially underlying the macro-level regularities described in the previous section (see Table 1), a population of numerical entities (hereafter called 'artificial agents' or, simply, 'agents') was programmed to make four sequential binary choices. In the present thematic context, each choice represents a decision about whether or not to enrol in a given educational level L (indexed from 1, the first educational transition, to 4, the last one), the sequential nature of these levels requiring that an agent can only move to the next choice if the previous choice was positive. Since the formal model is intended to explain the relation between the group to which an actor belongs and his/her educational outcome, the artificial agents assumed to mimic the real actors are exogenously attributed to one of five groups g (indexed from 1, the highest group, to 5, the lowest one). In the present thematic context, the group to which the agent belongs represents his/her educational background. Each artificial group contains as many agents as respondents belonging to a given group in the French empirical sample.

As expressed by Eq. (1), the choice that an agent i belonging to group g is supposed to perform at each transition is assumed to be a monotonically but nonlinear increasing probabilistic function of the strength of the agent's preference P_{igL} for educational level L (with c being the centre parameter of the logistic curve set here to 1.5), so that the larger is P_{igL}, the higher the probability of the agent choosing educational level L – if not, s/he is given the opportunity to evaluate it again (the maximum number of permitted trials being three, see Fig. 1, step 2.2). Framing each decision as a stochastic choice means that the mechanisms relating agents' group to agents' educational preference that I shall postulate are not assumed to give full account of how individuals' educational preferences form.[4]

$$\Pr_{ig}(L = 1 | L-1 = 1) = \frac{\exp(P_{igl}-c)}{1 + \exp(P_{igL}-c)}, \text{ with } P_{igL} = \text{Eq. (2)} \qquad (1)$$

The analytical core of the formal model is the formation of P_{igL}, that is, the preference of agent i belonging to group g for educational level L. As expressed by Eq. (2), this preference is assumed to depend additively on four basic elements: (1) the agent's ability (A term); (2) the agent's perception of the pay-offs from the educational level compared with the perceived costs of obtaining it (B term); (3) the agent's perception of this benefit/cost balance as a function of his/her ability (φ (A) term); (4) the social influence exerted on the agent by the educational decisions of the agents with which s/he is in contact (SI term) (see Appendix B for a possible generalisation of the model).

$$P_{igL} = A_{ig} + \phi(A) \times B_{ig} + SI_{igL}, \text{with } \phi(A) = \text{Eq. [3] and } SI_{igL} = \text{Eq. [4]} \quad (2)$$

Thus, formally, the way in which I have modelled the agent's educational behaviour belongs to the family of binary choice models with social interactions as deeply analysed by Durlauf (1999b, 2001; for a less formal review, see also Rolfe, 2009). The main difference concerns the absence, in my formalisation, of any maximising functions at the agent level, which makes the model analytically less tractable but increases its realism.

Pioneering applications of this class of model can be found in Schelling (1971, 1973), Granovetter (1978), and Granovetter and Soong (1983, 1988).

The Ability Term (A)

In psychology (see Herrnstein and Murray's (1994) controversial analysis; but, among others, see also Fischer et al.'s (1996) reaction), in economics (see Gintis, Bowles, & Osborne, 2001, 2002) and in sociology (see Sewell, Hauser, Springer, & Hauser, 2003), the social, biological-based differentiation among individuals' abilities has often been mobilised to account for the relationship between individuals' social backgrounds and their educational outcomes. Empirical evidence suggests that ability systematically varies across social groups, and that this differentiation arises and stabilises very early in an individual's cognitive development (see Duncan & Murnane, 2011, chs. 2–5). No matter how ability is measured, empirical studies show that it powerfully affects educational decisions (see, for instance, Breen & Yaish, 2006; Cheadle, 2008; Need & de Jong, 2000; Jonsson & Erikson, 2000, p. 350; Mastekaasa, 2006; Stocké, 2007, pp. 512, 515).

In the present model, agent's ability A_{ig} is assumed to represent any cognitive and personality traits that might matter during an individual's educational career. In order to take account of the above-mentioned empirical evidence about the social differentiation of ability, I follow Breen and Goldthorpe (1997) and assume that the distribution of agents' ability A_{ig} has common variance σ_A^2 across groups of agents but different mean A_g. Different from Breen and Goldthorpe, however, here this distribution is taken to be log-normal rather than normal (for an overview of log-normal distribution, see Limpert, Stahel, & Abbt, 2001).[5] It is finally assumed that agents' ability is static across the four educational transitions that they must make within the artificial society (on the basis of the empirical evidence available, it is not easy to establish whether ability changes during schooling can reduce the ability gap between social groups: see, for instance, Falch & Massih, 2011; Winship & Korenman, 1997).

The Benefit Term (B)

According to Eq. (2), the second main factor driving the formation of agents' educational preferences for a given educational level is B_{ig}, that is, the estimation that agent i belonging to group g makes the net benefit of the education investment.

Since Keller and Zavalloni's (1964) seminal article, rational-choice explanations of educational decisions have introduced the assumption that individuals' education evaluations depend on their relative positions on the social ladder in order to interpret the puzzling empirical observation that individuals from different social backgrounds tend to make different educational choices even when they have similar abilities (see Boudon, 1974, p. 28). Within this tradition, the quantitative analysis of educational inequalities is now framed in terms of primary ability-driven and secondary choice-driven effects (see Jackson, Erikson, Goldthorpe, & Yaish, 2007; Jackson, 2012). The latter are also supposed to depend on actors' perceptions of the costs of education, perceptions that are assumed to follow equally systematic social variations (see Boudon, 1974, p. 29; Breen & Goldthorpe, 1997).

From an empirical point of view, while still unclear the extent to which the social differentiation of education benefits is due to status-maintenance concerns, as Breen and Goldthorpe (1997) assume, and how intensely these concerns and cost perceptions only drive secondary effects (see Gabay-Egozi et al., 2010, and Stocké, 2007), it is empirically proven that both benefit and cost subjective perceptions of education tend to be more favourable, the higher the group to which the agent belongs (see, for instance, Becker, 2003, pp. 19–21; Need & de Jong, 2000, p. 88; Stocké, 2007, p. 512).

In order to take this empirical regularity into account, agents' perceived benefits of education B_{ig} are taken to be log-normally distributed with common variance σ_B^2 across groups of agents, but with different mean B_g. For modelling parsimony, however, I do not follow the rational-choice approach in representing benefit and cost perceptions as two distinct quantities to be subtracted from each other (for an explicit representation of this kind, see, for instance, Jonsson & Erikson, 2000, p. 359). In the present model, the parameter B_{ig} must instead be interpreted as the final ratio established by the agent between his/her benefit and cost perceptions, with a value higher than 1 indicating that the agent's perceived benefits of education outweigh his/her perceived costs.

The Multiplicative Term between Ability and Benefit

The φ (A) term of Eq. (2) shows that the role performed by the agent's benefit perceptions of education in the process of educational preference formation is assumed to be more subtle than its simple additive contribution *over and above* the effect of ability. Agents' abilities and perceived benefits are supposed to interact with each other. This assumption comes from Jonsson and Erikson (2000, p. 359), who explicitly hypothesise that actors weigh their perception of the benefits of a given educational level against an estimation of their probability of success at that level (see also Breen, 1999). For the sake of simplicity, I follow Breen and Goldthorpe (1997) in assuming that this estimation can be represented directly in terms of ability (it should be noted, however, that Breen and Goldthorpe posit that 'benefits' and 'ability' affect choices only independently). Stocké's (2008) empirical results suggest that this interaction may play a role in educational decisions.

Eq. (3) provides the specific way in which the present model represents this interaction. In particular, it is assumed that, when an agent's ability is lower/higher than 0.5 (as clarified later, all agents' variables are rescaled to vary between 0 and 1), his/her perception of education benefit is *reduced/ increased* by an amount inversely proportional to this perception but (nonlinearly) directly proportional to his/her ability. Basically, the functional form thus states that, taking 0.5 as the threshold, the lower/ higher the agent's ability, the lower/higher the sanction/prize that modifies his/her initial benefit perception; however, at the same time, that the more positive the initial perception of benefits, the less the agent is sensitive to ability (the specific form also makes it possible to keep the term between 0 and 1, which, for reasons that will be clearer later, is desirable).

$$\text{if } A_{ig} \leq 0.5, \text{ then } \phi(A) = B_{ig} \times (B_{ig})^{A_{ig}}$$
$$\text{if } A_{ig} > 0.5, \text{ then } \phi(A) = B_{ig}^{(1-A_{ig})} \tag{3}$$

Andrew and Hauser (2011) have recently cautioned against exaggerating the intensity of the interaction between actors' ability and expectations, their data suggesting that, while students do indeed modify their educational expectations during their school careers as a function of their academically proven ability, they do so only in response to large changes in the latter. Despite its complexity, the functional form of the term $\varphi(A)$ is able to represent this empirical fact (numerical examples that prove this statement are available upon request).

The Social Influence Term (SI)

Eq. (2) shows that there is a third major factor supposed here to drive the formation of an agent's educational preference for a given educational level L: the amount of social influence (SI) exerted on the agent by the artificial agents with whom s/he has direct relationships (hereafter, agent's neighbours, N). In the present context, the agent's neighbours are assumed to be his/her closest friends, those persons who really matter for his/his attitude toward schooling. In particular, as expressed by Eq. (4), this influence is quantified in fractional terms as the number of the agent's direct neighbours who have chosen at instant $t-1$ the educational level L that the agent is evaluating at time t *divided* by the agent's total number of neighbours.

$$SI_{igL} = \frac{N_i(L = 1)_{t-1}}{N_i} \qquad (4)$$

This term puts an important theoretical element back into a reason-based explanation of educational inequalities. Indeed, while Breen and Goldthorpe's (1997) seminal paper makes no mention of network-based social influence as a potential mechanism generating class differentials in educational choices, Boudon's original model explicitly admitted it, even though he did not formalise it – 'not choosing a prestigious curriculum may represent a high social cost for a youngster from a middle-class family if most of his friends have chosen it; but choosing the same course may represent a high cost for a lower-class youngster if most of his friends have not', – wrote Boudon (1974, p. 30). Discarding *a priori* interaction-based reasons of this kind seems unwise because, as actors' (and their parents') networks tend to be socially segregated (see DiPrete, Gelman, McCormick, Teitler, & Zheng, 2011, for a recent survey-based study), higher- and lower-group actors are likely to obtain systematically different feedbacks with respect to schooling from their contacts – a fact that the Wisconsin research tradition has acknowledged since the 1960s (see Haller & Woelfel, 1972; Sewell et al., 2003). To the best of my knowledge, only Morgan (2005, ch. 6) and Jaeger (2007, p. 474) have recently overtly suggested that network-based imitative behaviours should be (re)introduced into a rational-choice explanation of educational choices.

Eq. (4) generalises and formalises this idea. The SI term implies that the higher the proportion of choices for educational level L within the agent's close relational neighbourhood, the larger the impact on his/her probability of also choosing L. Hence, the SI term explicitly states that social interactions with closest friends matter for educational choices because they trigger 'educational conformism'.

Why should this be so? The basic hypothesis underlying Eq. (4) is that of 'mimetic interactions' (for this concept in economics, see Orléan, 1995): that is to say, interactions in which actors have good reasons to imitate each other (for the concept of 'rational imitation', see Hedström, 1998). Cognitive- and normative-belief changes, as well as opportunity changes, may be at work here. On a cognitive level, the larger the proportion of *ego*'s contacts that choose educational level *L*, the more cognitive salient educational level *L* can become for *ego*, thus increasing the probability that *ego* will also choose educational level *L* (see Harding et al., 2011).[6] On a normative level, the larger the proportion of *ego*'s contacts choosing educational level *L*, the higher the probability that *ego* will have to pay psychological costs in terms of individual and social identity if s/he makes a different choice (for a theory of educational choices entirely relying on this mechanism, see, in economics, Akerlof, 1997, and Akerlof & Kranton, 2002). With respect to opportunity, finally, the larger the proportion of *ego*'s contacts that choose educational level *L*, the higher the probability that *ego* will gain access to resources – information about the organisation of education, course notes, or material resources like transportation and housing – exploitable during school life if s/he makes a similar choice.

In economics, the basic intuition at the core of the so-called membership theory of inequalities (see Durlauf, 1999a, 2002, 2006) is that when mimetic interactions of this kind are at work among individuals with similar characteristics, individual outcomes depending on these characteristics will be reinforced, thus spreading more quickly and becoming even more resistant to change. In the analysis of economic inequality, the concept of 'poverty trap' refers to this self-reinforcing interaction-based dynamic (see Durlauf & Cohen-Cole, 2004).

To study the extent to which this process may matter for the genesis of educational inequalities, the term SI of Eq. (2), and hence the computation of Eq. (4), will rely on a specific network structure. In particular, each agent of the artificial population that I simulate is embedded in a network of artificial dyadic links whose proportion of in-group links – that is, links with agents belonging to the same group (and therefore with the same educational background) – is a network parameter that can be manipulated. Technically, I build on the structural properties of a 'small-world' topology (see Watts, 2004) to create varying degrees of educational homophily and heterophily within agents' ego-centred networks.[7]

The Simulation Algorithm and the Model Calibration Procedure

Fig. 1 summarises the basic set of algorithms that I programmed to deduce by simulation the aggregate distribution of agents' educational choices as a function of the group to which they belong when the educational behaviour of each of them is driven by the formal model expressed by Eqs. (1)–(4).[8]

The computational sequence depicted in Fig. 1 shows that, after the initialisation stage (steps 1.1–1.3), the simulation enters a double-step loop in which agents are allowed for 52 iterations to change their mind about whether or not to choose educational level L (see step 2.1). On the basis of the identity one iteration = one week, this lapse of time was chosen to roughly mimic the year which usually lasts between two enrolling dates in the real educational system. At the end of this intermediate decision time, during which, when the social influence term of Eq. (2) is activated, agents continuously influence each other (see Eq. (4)), the educational choice of each agent is fixed (step 2.2). Only once all the agents have reached a stable educational destination, then, is computation made of the simulated cross-tabulation which expresses agents' highest educational choice as a function of the educational group to which they were attributed at the beginning of the simulation (step 2.3).

As said in section 'Data, variables and research strategy', for any specific set of parameter values, steps 1.1–2.3 are replicated 100 times (with 100 different seeds), each of these replications generating a slightly different simulated cross-tabulation. The statistics described in section 'Data, variables and research strategy' were computed on each simulated cross-tabulation and compared with the same statistics computed on each of the 100 French empirical cross-tabulations (bootstrapped, it will be recalled, from the French original sample). It should thus be clear that, except for the size of agent groups, the simulation algorithm does not contain any empirical information from the empirical data whose structure the formal model is intended to reproduce. Each simulated cross-tabulation is a purely numerical construction deduced from the behavioural rules contained in Eqs. (1)–(4) under a specific set of parameter values.

As regards determination of these parameter values, I followed the procedure usually referred to in simulation studies as 'model calibration' (see, for instance, Railsback & Grimm, 2012, ch. 20; Stonedahl & Wilensky, 2010). For each specific combination of mechanisms introduced in the simulation, model parameters are stretched to minimise the 'distance' between simulated and empirical cross-tabulations – the 'distance' being quantified here by means of the dissimilarity index, which will be computed as half of the sum of the absolute difference between the simulated value and the observed value in every cell of the table divided by the sum of the frequencies in the table (see Breen, 2004, p. 24). This tuning operation will concern only the means A_g and B_g of the log-normal distributions from which agents' ability and perceived benefits are drawn, that is, 10 out of the 16 independent parameters that may be manipulated (see Appendix A,

BEGIN
1-INITIALIZATION
    1.1-Initialization of the population
        CREATE 5000 Agents;
        ATTRIBUTE agents randomly to one of the following *g* groups:
        g1=3ab=990, g2=2c=380, g3=2ab=524, g4=1bc=1769, g5=1a=1418;
    1.2-Initialization of agent's attributes
        SET agent's state "IN the educational race";
        SET current educational transition "1=first transition=1bc";
        SET choice for the current educational transition "not chosen";
        SET number of failures at the current educational transition 0;
        IF ability term (A) "on" (see Eq. 2).
           SET agent's $A_{ig} \sim$ Log-normal with mean = A_g and variance = σ_A^2;
        IF benefit term (B) "on" (see Eq. 2).
           SET agent's $B_{ig} \sim$ Log-normal with mean = B_g and variance = σ_B^2;
    1.3-Initialization of agent's network
        IF social influence term (SI) "on" (see Eqs. 2 and 4).
           CREATE a "small-world" network with:
                1/ average degree = K;
                2/ probability of out-group links = p;
                3/ probability of being linked to an agent belonging to a specific group:
                    $P_{GSD=1} > P_{GSD=2} > P_{GSD=3} > P_{GSD=4}$ (GSD= group social distance);
2-MODEL DYNAMIC
SET iteration 0;
UNTIL any agent with state "IN the educational race":
    2.1-Intermediary Choices
        REPEAT 52 times:
           For each agent with state "IN the educational race", sequentially but randomly invoked:
                COMPUTE educational preference according to equation [2];
                    DETERMINE choice for the current educational transition according to equation [1];
                        SET iteration + 1;
    2.2-Final Choice
        IF iteration/ 52 = integer,
           DETERMINE choice for the current educational transition according to equation [1] ;
                IF choice for the current educational transition "not chosen",
                    SET number of failures at the current educational transition + 1;
                IF number of failures at the current educational transition > 3,
                    SET agent's state "OUT of the educational race" ;
                IF choice for the current educational transition "chosen",
                    IF current educational transition "4=last transition=3ab,
                      SET agent's state "OUT of the educational race";
                  OTHERWISE,
                    SET current educational transition "current educational transition + 1" ;

    2.3-Choice Aggregation
        IF iteration / 52 = integer,
           For each educational transition, COMPUTE the number of agents with choice = "chosen";
           CROSS-TABULATE agents' education choices by agents' educational group *g*
END

Fig. 1.   Basic Steps in the Simulation Algorithm.

Table A.1). It should be pointed out that the result of this parameter stretching operation is not predetermined. Nothing ensures that one will end up with a good match between simulated and empirical data under a qualitatively realistic parameterisation. As stressed by Railsback and Grimm (2012, p. 256), the purpose of such a model calibration procedure is precisely to establish if 'there is something wrong with the model so that it cannot be forced to match observations closely'. Thus, it would be inappropriate to consider the model calibration strategy adopted as tautological.[9]

COMPUTATIONAL RESULTS, EMPIRICAL DATA AND MODEL DYNAMIC

As anticipated in section 'Data, variables and research strategy', in order to assess the specific explanatory contribution of the micro- and network-based mechanisms formalised by Eq. (2), the agent-based model was simulated by introducing these mechanisms sequentially. To be noted in this regard is that, before the agent's educational preference was computed according to Eq. (2), each term entering the equation was rescaled to range between 0 and 1. This procedure ensures that the differences that might be observed between the simulations of two model variants reflect the net effect of the mechanism introduced rather than the differences in the range of values taken by the numerical variables used to express the mechanisms. As regards the order of mechanism introduction, quantitative studies on educational inequalities suggest the following (see, in particular, Stocké, 2008):

1. In order to assess how intensely ability distribution across agent groups segregates their educational choices, the model was first simulated with agents' educational choices driven by ability only (i.e. term A of Eq. (2));
2. In order to establish whether the distribution of subjectively perceived benefits of education segregates educational choices across agent groups *over and above* ability distribution, the model was then simulated with agents' educational choices driven by ability coupled with perceived benefits (i.e. terms A and B of Eq. (2));
3. In order to determine the extent to which the interaction between ability and perceived benefits contributes to segregating educational choices more than when these two factors work independently, the model was simulated thirdly with agents' educational choices driven by ability, perceived benefits and the multiplicative term between the two (i.e. when the term $\varphi(A)$, see Eq. (3), is present);

4. In order to evaluate whether or not dyadic interactions between agents have any specific inequality effect *over and above* the three previous mechanisms, the model was finally simulated in its complete form, that is to say with agents' educational choices driven by ability, perceived benefits, the multiplicative term between the two and the term expressing the network-based social influences as formalised by Eq. (4).

Table 2 reports the set of statistics (see section 'Data, variables and research strategy') computed on the distribution of simulated cross-tabulations (whose average is reported in Appendix A, Table A.2) generated under the four model variants (the last row in Table 2 refers to the model discussed in Appendix B).

As a benchmark, let us first consider a model in which none of the mechanisms postulated is at work (see Table 2b). Unsurprisingly, since no source of inequalities across agent groups is present, no educational stratification arises. For instance, the average generalised odds ratio ('agor') expressing the overall level of educational fluidity fluctuates around 1 across replications, meaning that no agent group has a competitive educational advantage at any educational level. The specific numerical structure of the simulated educational outflows is also easy to explain (see Appendix A, Table A.2b). When none of the mechanisms postulated is at work, by construction the educational preference of each agent, no matter what group s/he belongs to, amounts to 0, which implies that each agent has a very low probability of choosing a given educational level (namely, about 0.18). The sequential nature of the four educational choices to be made, coupled with the fact that the agent can go through each educational transition no more than three times (see Fig. 1, step 2.2), automatically explains that, on average, about 55% of each agent group is not able to make the first transition. As testified by the value of the dissimilarity index ('di'), this simulated distribution is extremely far from the distribution observed in the empirical data.

When the agent's educational choices are driven only by his/her ability, a substantial improvement towards realism is accomplished (see Table 2c). If agents' abilities are differentiated across agent groups – in particular, the higher the group, the higher, on average, the agents' ability (see Appendix A, Fig. A.1, solid line) – ability differentiation is sufficient to generate some amount of stratification of educational choices across agents' educational backgrounds. For instance, agents belonging to the highest group attain the highest educational level between two and three times more frequently than do agents belonging to the lowest group (see Table 2c, column 'hlgr').

Table 2. Non-Parametric (0.025–0.975) Percentile Intervals of Absolute/Relative Educational Mobility Statistics (See Section 'Data, Variables and Research Strategy') Computed on Each of the 100 Empirical Bootstrapped Cross-Tabulations and, on the Other Hand, on Each of the 100 Simulated Cross-Tabulations Generated by the Simulation of Several Model Variants.

IP	UMP	HLGR	AGOR	HGGOR	LGGOR	DI
(a) Empirical French Data (bootstrapped cross-tabulations)						
37.46–40.44	44.44–47.21	6.38–8.86	1.61–1.79	5.38–8.13	8.23–12.00	NA
(b) 'Straw Man' Model: All Mechanisms Are Absent						
25.56–27.65	20.18–22.43	0.63–1.51	1–1.02	0.7–1.36	0.83–1.15	42–44.18
(c) Model Variant 1: Ability						
26.45–28.18	35.39–37.44	2.07–3.05	1.03–1.05	1.17–1.56	1.64–2.08	24.57–26.72
(d) Model Variant 2: 'Model Variant 1' + Perceived Benefits						
32.09–34.14	38.51–41.75	5.14–7.81	1.17–1.25	2.76–3.89	2.69–3.53	15.89–18.17
(e) Model Variant 3: 'Model Variant 2' + Ability/Benefits Interaction						
33.68–35.6	38.23–41.34	5.97–8.96	1.22–1.32	3.42–5.4	2.77–3.74	14.81–17.17
(f) Model Variant 4: 'Model Variant 3' + Social Influence						
34.22–36.32	43.09–46.65	6.86–9	1.3–1.48	5.44–10.09	3.27–4.28	11.04–13.28
(g) Model Variant 5: 'Model Variant 4' + Inflation Spiral Mechanisms (see Appendix B)						
31.89–34.37	50.44–54.28	5.17–6.54	1.28–1.44	5.22–9.53	3.16–4.15	13.89–16.38

This value, like those of all other statistics computed on the simulated data, however, is far lower than the value computed for the empirical data. As testified by the value of the dissimilarity index ('di'), the overall distribution of educational choices across group of agents is still quite distant from the French actual distribution.

The model variant containing both ability and perceived benefits makes it possible to get closer to the empirical data. When both ability and benefit perceptions are systematically differentiated across agent groups – in particular, the higher the group, the higher, on average, the agent's ability/ benefit perceptions (see Appendix A, Fig. A.1, dotted lines) – the simulation of the model produces a deeper stratification of educational choices compared to that generated by the model with agents' behaviour driven by ability only. The percentage of agents undertaking the highest education transition within the highest group compared to the lowest group is now considerable larger (compare Tables 2c and 2d, column 'hlgr'). Statistics expressing the relative positions of the highest and lowest groups of agents ('hggor' and 'lggor', respectively) also present higher values than in the previous scenario, indicating that systematic differentiation of benefit perceptions across agent groups contributes to deeply segregating educational choices among these groups.

This is an important theoretical result. Indeed, in line with Breen and Goldthorpe's (1997) hypothesis, the simulation demonstrates in a rigorously deductive way that a bottom-up dynamic in which educational choices are driven by socially differentiated perceptions of education benefits is able to accentuate group differentials in educational choices *over and above* 'primary effects' – controlled for here by including the differentiation of agents' ability in the simulation. As a meaningful numerical example – if one extracts agent-level data from the simulation being commented on here, and if one considers agents from the highest and the lowest groups with strictly comparable ability, namely, those whose ability ranges between 0.2 and 0.4 – it would appear that, when differentiated benefit perceptions are present, despite the same level of ability, the median educational level attained by agents from the highest group is the second or the third one (in 71 out of the 100 replications of the simulation), whereas the median educational level reached by agents belonging to the lowest educational level is the first one (in 94 out of 100 replications).

That said, the simulation of the model variant including ability and benefit perceptions also shows that, given the effect of ability, the inequality effect of socially differentiated perceptions of educational benefits is not sufficient to differentiate agents' educational choices as much as they are differentiated within the French empirical data. Indeed, the dissimilarity index ('di') tells us that between about 16% and 18% of cases are still misclassified by the simulated model.

This gap is not substantially reduced when, given the ability and benefit differentiation across agent groups allowed in the previous model variant, the model is simulated by including the multiplicative term between agents' ability and perceptions of education benefits (see Eq. (3)). The Mathieu effect implied by this term – on average, agents with higher ability will also tend to have more positive perceptions of education benefit so that the two factors tend to reinforce each other – accentuates the stratification of educational choices among groups a little bit more. For instance, the overall competitive advantage of the highest agent group is larger than in the model in which ability and benefit perception act as independent mechanisms (see Table 2e, column 'hggor'). However, the value of all other statistics remains virtually unchanged, and the overall fit of the simulated cross-tabulations to the empirical data is only marginally improved – the range of the dissimilarity index largely overlaps with the range obtained under the previous model variant.

By contrast, a noticeable fit improvement appears when the last mechanism hypothesised is introduced, that is, the network-based interdependences among agents' educational choices (see Eq. (4)). As regards network parameterisation, the following choices were made: (1) each agent has, on average, four direct friends; (2) only 10% of all links present in the system relate agents belonging to different educational backgrounds; (3) these inter-group links are mainly of a short-distance type – that is, about 60% of inter-group links put in contact agents with educational backgrounds at distance 1 (meaning with agents from the group just above/below them). These choices aim to mimic characteristics of empirical social networks, namely, that the number of closest friends substantially affecting specific behaviours tends to be relatively small (for instance, McPherson, Smith-Lovin, & Brashears, 2006 found a size ranging between 2 and 3 for confident discussions networks; Christakis & Fowler, 2007, found a friendship average degree of around 1 with range from 0 to 8, see also Fowler & Christakis, 2008; Snjiders & Steglich, 2013, state that friendship networks usually exhibit average degrees between 3 and 4), and, on the other hand, that both 'strong' and 'weak' friendship ties are overwhelmingly homophilic (on education-based mate selection, see Blossfeld, 2009, and Skopek, Schulz, & Blossfeld, 2011, for on-line dating settings; on the social segregation of 'weak' ties, see DiPrete et al., 2011; on homophily more generally, see McPherson, Smith-Lovin, & Cook, 2001).

Under this parameterisation (alternative ones will be studied in the next section), the introduction of the network-based social influence mechanism leads to aggregate results that are very much in line with empirical observations (notably, 3 out of 6 statistics almost completely overlap with their empirical counterparts). In particular, the presence of local dyadic interactions between agents increases the percentage of educationally immobile agents, the overall intensity of inequality of educational opportunity, and, quite remarkably, the competitive educational advantage of the highest agent group (see Table 2f, columns 'ip', 'agor' and 'hggor', respectively). These indicators are especially important because they testify to the capacity of the network-based mechanism to segregate educational choices to a larger extent than the three previous 'atomistic' model variants were able to do, thus bringing the simulated educational stratification closer to the strong level of inequality exhibited by the actual French data.

In order to see the net effect of local dyadic interactions among agents more directly, let us re-run the simulation under discussion with exactly the same distributions of agents' ability and benefit perceptions (see Appendix A, Fig. A.1, dashed lines) but turning off the social influence term. Fig. 2 reports the result of this counterfactual by focusing on the

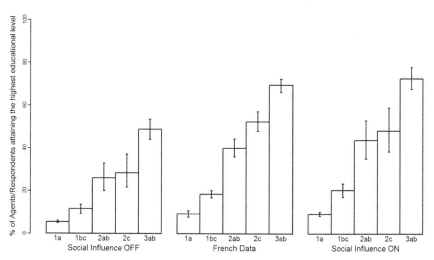

Fig. 2. Percentages of Agents Attaining the Highest Educational Level within the Five Agent Groups Averaged over 100 Replications of the Model (Bars Give the Values within Which Fall 95% of the Model Replications) When the Social Influence Term (SI) is Turned Off/On.

percentages of agents attaining the highest educational level within each of
the five groups of agents.

Three facts appear. First, the differentiation of educational choices across
agent groups is much more pronounced when the social influence term is
present. Given that the differentiation of ability and benefit across groups is
exactly the same under the two experimental conditions, this means that
network-based interdependences among agents' educational choices have
the capacity to progressively amplify the initial differentiation of ability and
benefit perceptions. Second, this segregating effect of local dyadic
interactions operates much more intensely, the higher the agent's group.
Finally, no matter what group is considered, the empirical percentages
observed in the French data fall within the range of the simulated
percentages only when the social influence term is turned on, thereby
suggesting that the actual deep stratification of educational choices cannot
be fully explained by postulating only a socially differentiated structure of
ability and perceived benefits.

Fig. 3 clarifies the source of this segregating effect sustained by local
dyadic interactions between agents. For each educational level that agents
must choose, the graphs report the proportion of agents' neighbours who

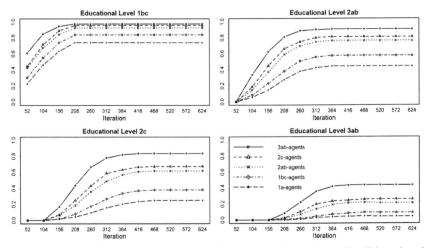

Fig. 3. Average Proportion of Agents' Neighbours Who Chose the Educational
Level that the Agent is Evaluating at Instant *t* (Proportions Are Averaged over 100
Replications; Variability Across Replications Is Omitted to Make Graphs More
Readable).

chose the educational level. To understand the model dynamic, this is the most appropriate piece of information because it is in this that the social influence term basically consists (see Eq. (4)).

The curves show that, as a consequence of the initial differentiation of ability and perceived benefits, the higher the agent's group, the richer his/her local neighbourhood in terms of contacts making a positive choice – which holds at each transition. When one considers that, under the present network parameterisation, agents tend to be linked mainly with agents having similar ability and benefit perceptions, it is clearly apparent that, at each transition, stronger support from the agent's neighbours will thus benefit precisely those agents who already have higher starting values on ability and perceptions of education benefits. As a result, the initial differentiation of ability and perceived benefits is dynamically deepened and widened by means of a cumulative process (see Merton, 1968, pp. 606, 610), in which the amplification mechanism (see Boudon, 1979, pp. 156–157) – the social multiplier if one prefers (see Durlauf, 2006; Durlauf & Cohen-Cole, 2004) – is based here on the socially segregated composition of agents' ego-centred dyadic networks.

While, as argued, the presence of this amplifying process fuelled by local dyadic interactions between agents is necessary to get closer to the actual cross-sectional educational stratification observed in France, to conclude it should be acknowledged that the simulated data generated under the full model do not fit perfectly with the empirical observations. Between about 11% and 13% of cases are still misclassified even when dynamic network-based interdependences among agents' educational choices are included in the simulation (see Table 2f, column 'di'). A careful comparison of the simulated and empirical cross-tabulations shows that this gap is mainly due to the fact that the current model parameterisation tends to allow too many agents belonging to the lowest educational group to go beyond the first educational transition while not leading enough agents belonging to the middle groups beyond the same point (see Appendix A, compare Tables A.2a and A.2f). Among the statistics computed on the simulated data, this under/overproduction is reflected by the value of the generalised odds ratio summarising the relative position of the lowest group of agents. Compared to the empirical value, the simulated one, although it is the best among the four model variants simulated, is still not high enough, which suggests that the full model is too 'generous' with respect to agents belonging to the lowest group.

To correct for this problem, it would suffice to introduce an additional differentiation in agents' abilities and/or perceived benefits with the aim of representing the existence of specific barriers/advantages at some educational transition for some group of agents. While one may find theoretical/empirical justifications for such modifications, I will not follow this strategy for two reasons. On the one hand, this strategy would imply that the mechanisms postulated are believed to be the only ones at work, which is a position that I would not endorse. Conceptualising additional substantive mechanisms may thus be a strategy to reduce the gap between simulated and empirical data that is more reasonable than introducing fine-tuning *post-hoc* modifications of the existing mechanisms (on this point, see Appendix B). On the other hand, the proximity reached between simulated and empirical data seems quite remarkable given the relatively limited number of parameters that have been manipulated. In particular, ability/perceived benefits were assumed to be differentiated only across groups of agents but not across educational levels. This means that the formal model proposed was able to approximate all the qualitative features of an empirical complex structure contained in a 5×5 cross-tabulation by manipulating only 10 parameters out of the 16 independent parameters that might have been manipulated (see Appendix A, Table A.1). In terms of model parsimony, this is a significant result.

SENSITIVITY ANALYSIS OF THE SOCIAL INFLUENCE MECHANISM

By means of computer simulations, the previous section aimed to prove that a network-based social influence mechanism must be postulated so as to match closely the stratification of educational choices across educational backgrounds observed in the French data. In particular, the amplifying process triggered by this mechanism is necessary to reproduce the large gap at the highest educational levels between the lowest and the highest social groups. This result was produced under a specific network parameterisation (see Appendix A, Table A.1), which, as said above, attempted to mimic some basic empirical regularities of real friendship networks. The present section assesses the robustness of this result against alternative network parameterisations.

In this respect, the first parameter manipulation to be performed concerns the average degree of the network in which agents are embedded. Fig. 4 focuses on the percentage of agents attaining the highest educational level within each group and plots it as a function of increasing average network degrees, 4 being the value adopted in the simulation previously performed to

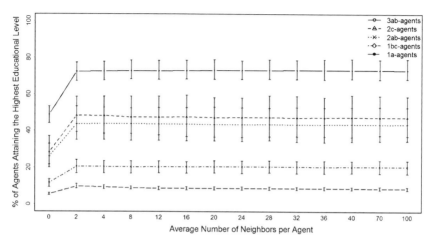

Fig. 4. Percentages of Agents Attaining the Highest Educational Level within Each of the Five Groups of Agents Averaged over 100 Replications of the Model under Different Values of the Parameter *K*, that is the Average Number of Neighbours with Whom Each Agent is in Contact (Bars Give the Values within Which Fall 95% of the Model Replications).

approximate the French educational stratification. As the low probability of inter-group link formation is unchanged, this parameter manipulation thus mainly amounts to progressively increasing the number of direct contacts that each agent establishes within his/her own group. In terms of Granovetter's (1973, 1983) distinction between 'strong' and 'weak' ties, it is mainly the amount of the agent's 'strong' in-group ties that it is made variable here.

The main result is that the model's aggregate behaviour is remarkably stable, and hence robust to the modification of the average number of contacts that each agent is allowed to establish (mainly) within the group to which s/he belongs. The curves show that, no matter what group of agents is considered, the only significant difference observed is between the situations in which no contact at all exists – this is simply the model without the social influence term – and those where a few neighbours are allowed to influence the agent's educational choices. Even extremely high (and unrealistic – it is becoming well known that relevant contacts are relatively limited even within web-based social networks and exchanges: see Easley & Kleinberg, 2010, pp. 54–58; Skopek et al., 2011, p. 185) network degrees leave the percentage of agents attaining the highest educational level virtually unchanged. Thus, in the present model, 'strong' in-group ties do not necessarily have undesirable effects. On the contrary, when there are few of them, they sustain agents' educational choices; when they are too numerous, at worst, they do not significantly change agents' behaviour.

The way in which the network-based social influence mechanism is formalised here explains this result (see Eq. (4)). In fact, the fractional form of this term implies that, for a given distribution of agents' ability and perceived benefits, increasing the size of the agent's neighbourhood will not affect his/her educational choices because numerical changes in the numerator, that is, the number of contacts choosing the educational level that the agent is evaluating, will be neutralised by similar size changes in the denominator, that is, the total number of the agent's neighbours. Under increasing neighbourhood sizes, when anything else is unchanged in the model parameter setting, both quantities tend to increase to a similar extent, thus producing virtually no effect at the aggregate level (the analysis that numerically proves this statement is available upon request).[10]

Substantially, this result suggests that if, in the reality, actors were influenced by the proportion of their contacts making a certain choice rather than by their absolute number, being exposed to a large fraction of contacts may have, at aggregate level, similar effects as being exposed to a few neighbours. In the case of educational choices, this seems realistic. If local dyadic interactions matter, as assumed earlier, because interacting with others enables actors to share cognitive and material resources as well as to establish contact with specific identity models, a given actor may share, say, car, housing, course notes and normative models with a few fellow students but, because of time and cognitive limitations, not with tens of them. If so, only a relatively small size of the actor's friendship network will be really effective.

All other things being equal, modifying the agents' probability, and hence the amount of the inter-group links, should generate more visible effects. In this case, in fact, for a given number of neighbours, more or fewer contacts with agents outside an agent's group should imply a modification of the educational composition of the agent's neighbourhood. The social influence exerted on the agent should thus be qualitatively different, and this should impact to some extent on the agent's educational choices.

Fig. 5 focuses on the percentage of agents attaining the highest educational level within each group and plots it as a function of values of the probability of establishing contacts outside an agent's group ranging from 0 to 1, which amounts to moving progressively from five disconnected regular networks where the probability of inter-group linkage is 0 – under

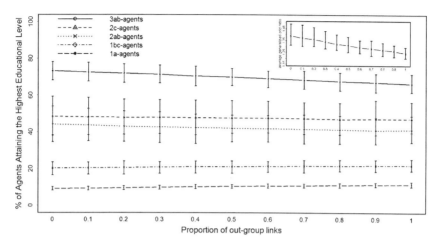

Fig. 5. Percentages of Agents Attaining the Highest Educational Level within the Five Groups of Agents Averaged over 100 Replications of the Model Under Different Values of the Parameter *p*, that is the Probability that an Agent's In-Group Link is Disconnected and Rewired to an Agent Belonging to a Different Group (Bars Give the Values within Which Fall 95% of the Model Replications). The Small Right-Corner Graph Plots the Average Generalised Odds Ratio Computed on the Simulated Cross-Tabulations – the Closer the Coefficient to 1, the Less Inequality of Educational Opportunity is Present in the Table (Central Points and Bars Have the Same Interpretation as Above). To Be Noted Is that the Average Network Degree Is Kept at 4, that is the Value Adopted to Approximate the French Educational Stratification.

this condition, agents only have in-group links – to a single random network where the probability of inter-group linkage is 1 – here agents only have out-group links (for the case of a one-group population, see Watts, 1999, pp. 503–509). In terms of Granovetter's (1973, 1983) distinction between 'strong' and 'weak' ties, this experimental setting thus amounts to manipulating the agent's proportion of 'weak' out-group ties.

Two main results ensue. On the one hand, for a large range of increasing heterophily level around the low value adopted to approximate the actual French educational stratification, that is, 0.1, the aggregate behaviour of the model is virtually insensitive to changes in the probability of creating inter-group links. Similarly to what was observed with respect to modifications of the average network, the results presented in the previous section are thus quite robust to alternative network parameterisations. On the other hand, if one considers the entire range of the probability of inter-group link formation – thus including in the analysis a quite unrealistic level of heterophily, values higher than 0.5 meaning that out-group links tend to become more frequent than in-group links – the curves plotted in Fig. 5 show that the gap between highest and lowest groups at the highest educational transition tends to be reduced.

The upper right-corner subplot in Fig. 5 testifies that this effect is not localised to the distribution of choices at the highest educational level. It shows, in fact, that if one computes the average generalised odds ratio on the simulated cross-tabulations generated under increasing levels of ego-centred network heterophily, then the value of this synthetic coefficient clearly exhibits a decreasing tendency, suggesting that the overall amount of inequality of educational opportunity is reduced by allowing agents to make contacts with an increasing number of agents with educational backgrounds different from their own. In the present model, in line with Granovetter's original argument, 'weak ties' thus generate desirable consequences at the aggregate level, namely, more educational fluidity. However, contrary to the idea that 'weak ties' tend to generate positive effects *in general*, closer inspection of the curves plotted in Fig. 5 shows that, while the lowest group agents tend more frequently to reach the highest educational level when the proportion of inter-group links increases, the contrary holds for the highest group agents, while the in-between agent groups do not exhibit any particular trend.[11]

This asymmetry arises from the way in which the network linking agents is created within the artificial society studied here. On the one hand, as shown by Eq. (4), dyadic links are not weighted, which implies that the educational choice of an upper-group agent matters for the educational choice of a lower-group agent exactly to the same extent as the choice of the latter matters for the choice of the former. On the other hand, since the network-building algorithm requires the network degree to be kept constant, each inter-group link that has been created replaces one in-group link (see footnote 7). Under these conditions, when the out-group links tend to put into contact agents (mainly) belonging to groups at a one-step distance (see Appendix A, Table A.1), agents at the very bottom of the group hierarchy will benefit from being more and more in contact with agents just above them, who tend to make slightly more positive choices than they do. Agents in the middle of the group hierarchy will be stretched by counterbalancing tendencies, agents above them making slightly more positive choices whose positive influences will be neutralised by agents below them making educational choices slightly less positive than theirs. The educational outcomes of highest group agents can instead only become worse, their neighbourhood becoming progressively filled with agents below them who make less positive educational choices than they do.

This result thus illustrates, in the context of a theoretical model of a specific relevant social behaviour, that is, educational choices, the counter-intuitive results obtained by Centola, Eguiluz, and Macy (2007) and Centola and Macy (2007) using strictly comparable network topology, who demonstrated that the 'strength of weak ties' does not hold in general. Under certain conditions, namely when, for some or other reason, a given behaviour is 'costly, risky or controversial', the support of those in the best position to make the choice – that is, in the present case, agents with the same educational background – is crucial for adopting the behaviour. When heterophily increases beyond a certain level, within the artificial society studied here, highest groups agents can no longer profit from relational proximity with agents with a similar capacity to make costly educational choices, thus losing part of their competitive advantage at the highest educational transition.

DISCUSSION

Section 'Computational modelling of educational preference formation' developed a generative formal model of the macro-level structure of educational inequality which frames educational choices as the result of both subjective ability/benefit evaluations and peer-group pressures, thus enriching rational-choice explanations of educational choices in sociology through theoretical insights deriving from heterodox theoretical perspectives in economics of inequality and of education.

By means of agent-based computational simulations, the macro-level consequences of this model have been tested against French empirical data. By introducing the hypothesised mechanisms sequentially and by quantify-ing the proximity between the simulated and the empirical educational stratifications for each combination of mechanisms, section 'Computational results, empirical data and model dynamic' has deductively proved that ability and subjective perceptions of education benefits, no matter how intensely differentiated across agent groups, are not sufficient *on their own* to generate the actual stratification of educational choices across educational backgrounds existing in France at the beginning of the twenty-first century. By computational counterfactual manipulations, it has been proved that network-based interdependences among educational choices contribute, *over and above* the differentiation of ability and of benefit perceptions, to the genesis of educational stratification by reinforcing, hence accentuating, the segregation of the educational choices that agents make on the basis of purely private ability/benefit calculations.

It should now be emphasised that the results presented in section 'Computational results, empirical data and model dynamic' (see Table 1) allow, although imperfectly, assessment of the relative generative power of each of the mechanisms postulated. In particular, close inspection of the variations of the dissimilarity index across the model variants that have been simulated suggests that (1) the differentiation of ability across agent groups leads to the largest reduction, that is, around 17 percentage points, in the dissimilarity index value compared to the baseline model in which none of the mechanism hypothesised was at work; (2) the differentiation of education benefit perceptions across agent groups is the second most powerful factor, leading to an around 9 additional percentage-points reduction of the dissimilarity index compared to the ability-based model variant; (3) the network-based social influence mechanism comes in the third position, yielding around 4 more additional percentage-points in the dissimilarity index reduction compared to the model variant in which ability, benefit and the multiplicative term between these two factors were at work – the multiplicative term between ability and benefit coming last with only about 1 percentage-point of dissimilarity index reduction.

Although the paper has demonstrated that the network-based social influence mechanism is necessary to match the empirical data closely, it does not lead to the conclusion that all social interactions matter. Quite the contrary, the 'explanatory' hierarchy established on the basis of the dissimilarity index reduction is very much in line with statistically based empirical studies on educational inequalities which suggest that, while ability/cognitive skills systematically exhibit very high predictive power (see, for instance, Gabay-Egozi et al., 2010; Stocké, 2007), peer effects, when statistically significant, tend to be relatively weak (for an overall assessment, see, for instance, Breen & Jonsson, 2005, p. 229). In this respect, the main contribution of the present simulation-based study is its demonstration that, although their quantitatively average net effect might be modest, dyadic social interactions should not be discarded on a theoretical level because, without them, the actual level of educational inequality could not be accounted for. While the network-based social influence mechanism cannot generate *on its own* educational choice differentials across social backgrounds, the analyses reported here prove that it is necessary to assume that the mechanism is at work to account for the actual deep social segregation of educational choices across social groups, especially when the gap between highest and lowest social groups at the highest educational levels is considered.

Section 'Sensitivity analysis of the social influence mechanism' has shown that this result is robust over a wide range of different, but still realistic, network parameterisations, with respect to both the local density of the network in which agents are embedded and the amount of heterophily allowed within the network. However, it is important to be aware of the specific way in which the network-based social influence mechanism has been conceptualised here.

In this regard, the following simplifications warrant especial attention. First of all, the network linking artificial agents is assumed to be static during the simulation – the educational states of agents' neighbours thus dynamically change but the set of neighbours does not. Second, each tie is assumed to be symmetric and is not weighted – dyadic influences are thus systematically bidirectional and of equal intensity. Third, agents' sensitivity to neighbours' educational choices is not modelled – agents are thus homogenous with respect to how they react to social influence. Finally, the agent's network does not contain any spatial/geographical dimension.

Without a doubt, enriching the model with more conceptually refined solutions on each of these aspects would lead to stimulating theoretical insights. Assuming, for instance, that friendship networks evolve during an agent's school career – that is, allowing lower-group agents who succeed to become progressively more frequently in contact with higher-group agents – would be an interesting theoretical development. Introducing asymmetric and weighted ties – that is, assuming that a higher-group agent is less affected by the choice of a lower-group neighbour than the latter is affected by the choice of the former – would make the model more realistic. Embedding friendship networks in spatial neighbourhoods – that is, limiting the probability that geographically distant agents interact with each other – would also increase the model's applicability. My expectation, however, is that unless the first modification is given an unrealistically high (numerical) power, these modifications can only strengthen the main result produced by the model studied here: that is, network-based interdependences among educational choices tend to reinforce and accentuate the differentiation across social groups in individuals' ability- and benefit-based calculations, thus helping to explain the actual high level of social segregation of educational choices.

Moreover, it should not be overlooked that additional hypotheses, no matter how theoretically realistic they may appear, imply more parameter values to be initialised, which, from the standpoint of an empirically oriented variant of the simulation methodology, means in turn more empirical data to be collected in the hope of eventually being able to parameterise the model by means of real-world data.

This, in my opinion, is the main limitation of the present study. While the macro-level consequences of each variant of the formal model have been systematically matched against aggregate individual-level survey data, the parameter values on which each micro-level mechanism relies only come from arbitrarily chosen numerical values. Although these choices can be justified, and although their aggregate consequences have been proved to be realistic, so proving the generative sufficiency of the mechanisms at hand (see Epstein, 2006, chs. 1–2), I believe that it would be highly appreciable to input agents' ability and education benefit perceptions on the basis of representative individual survey data. This, I maintain, is the further step most needed for the present work. Besides providing a full example of a truly empirically calibrated agent-based model (on this concept, see Hedström, 2005, ch. 6), introducing such micro-level empirical bases into model parameters would also enable more solid assessment of the relative explanatory power of the theoretical mechanisms that the model assumes to be at work. After all, this is probably what formal modelling – here in its agent-based computational variant – is fundamentally meant to do: point out relevant parameters for which richer and more detailed empirical information is needed (see Breen, 2009; White, 2000).

CONCLUSION

Overall, although imperfect, the formal model at the centre of the paper and the research strategy adopted to study it seem to open promising avenues for future research. On a theoretical level, the model has the interest of linking the macro-level structure of educational inequalities with the way in which group belonging biases the heterogeneity of actors in ability, preferences and social contacts: a factor that has been under-investigated within the socio-logical rational-choice approach to educational choices. The article thus suggests an explanatory factor that may also help to enhance understanding of the long-term evolution of educational inequalities. As pointed out by Breen et al. (2010, pp. 1515–1516), in fact, studies of educational inequalities now need to explain the mix of temporal reduction and stability of class differentials in educational attainment. Paying closer attention to friendship networks may help. As suggested by Blossfeld and Timm (2003a), educational homogamy induces network segregation. There are strong theoretical reasons to expect that the expansion of educational systems, and hence increasing duration in school, leads to a high level of educational homogamy across cohorts (for some confirmatory empirical evidence, see Blossfeld & Timm, 2003b). As a consequence, one may expect in turn that social segregation in friendship network at best does not change and, at worst, increases across generations (some signs of an increasing network homogeneity along several socio-demographic traits, including education, were discovered by McPherson et al., 2006, pp. 361–362, 371). Network homophily may thus contribute to explaining the observed mix of change and stability of educational inequality in that stable or even increasing levels of social homophily may counterbalance (or attenuate) the equalising effects of long-term potentially converging benefit and cost perceptions of education across social classes, as well as the effects of educational policies aimed at reducing performance gaps across social groups. On a methodological level, the paper's contribution seems to be twofold. On the one hand, it contributes to the literature on neighbourhood effects by suggesting that agent-based computational simulations can be fruitfully exploited to analyse formal models containing network-based mechanisms. On the other hand, it reinforces the presence of this technique within the sociology of stratification and social mobility and proves that agent-based models are powerful tools with which to design complex sets of hypotheses linking structures, actors and networks, and to test the macro-level consequences of these hypotheses. This test having been performed against empirical data, the paper also suggests the interest of reinforcing an interface among formal theoretical modelling, the quantitative analysis of empirical data and computational techniques – a research strategy which is still too rarely followed in the quantitative analysis of social stratification (for a notable exception, see Bruch & Mare, 2006). Thus, despite the limitations explicitly discussed in the previous section, I would be more inclined to keep on cooking rather than abandon this multi-faceted research strategy.

ACKNOWLEDGEMENTS

Preparatory work for this article was presented at the Sociology Seminar Series (Nuffield College, University of Oxford), at the GSADI Ph.D. Seminar Series (Universitat Autònoma de Barcelona), at the Analytical-Quantitative Sociology Seminar (University of Oslo) and at the Sociology Colloquium Series (MZES, University of Mannheim). I am very grateful to the participants at these seminars for their comments and suggestions. Carlo

Barone is the person who has influenced me most in writing the final version of the article: I would like to thank him for the time he devoted to questioning my conception of simulation and of educational choices. I have also greatly benefited from discussing the article with Clemens Kroneberg, as well as from responding to Andreas Wimmer, Flaminio Squazzoni, Pablo Jensen and Torkild Lyngstad, who carefully commented on a previous version of the manuscript. The comments of two anonymous referees have also been of invaluable help, as well as Gunn Birkelund's regular encouragements. I am greatly indebted to Louis-André Vallet for providing me with his SAS syntax to recode French educational and occupational information into the Casmin schema. I obtained the French dataset from the Reseau Quetelet, which I thank for its efficiency. Last but not least, I wish to express my gratitude to Adrian Belton for revising my English. The usual disclaimers apply.

NOTES

1. The present paper extends Manzo (2009) in several respects: (1) the formal model presented in section 'Computational modelling of educational preference formation' is designed to generate new, and more recent, empirical data; (2) the *explanandum* is different, in that these data concern the statistical association between individuals' educations and the educations of their parents, rather than the statistical association between individuals' educations and the social class of their parents; (3) the formal model is extended to represent five social groups instead of four; (4) the formal model is implemented in NetLogo instead of Java (whose original code was due to Frédéric Amblard). Compared to Manzo (2011), the paper takes some additional steps further: (1) the formal model is now a truly probabilistic model; (2) the formal model is now able to accommodate a representation of the effect of ability on educational choices; (3) the number of parameters adopted to represent actors' subjective benefits and costs is dramatically reduced from 100 to 10; (4) the simulated agents' scheduling has been greatly simplified, all agents being now sequentially updated at each iteration.

2. Cobalti (1989) proposed using generalized odds ratios as measures of association to describe the relative aspect of social mobility in easily interpretable terms. He later extended this proposal to analysis of the inequality of educational opportunities (see Cobalti, 1992, pp. 139–142). Formally, generalized odds ratios are simply the geometric means of all the 'basic sets' forming a given cross-tabulation (see Goodman, 1969). As demonstrated by Kaufman and Schervish (1987, p. 233), there is a direct link between log-linear models and generalized odds ratios: for a two-way cross-tabulation, the generalized odds ratios for a given cell can be computed by raising the corresponding multiplicative parameter of the saturated model at power $(l \times c)/(l-1 \times c-1)$, where l and c are the number of the table's rows

and columns. I built on this relation to compute the coefficients reported in Table 2. Log-linear model estimations were performed with the functions 'loglm' and 'gnm' (for the 'uniform difference' model, see footnote 2) contained in the 'MASS' and 'gnm' *R* packages, respectively.

3. By exclusively focusing on the aggregate cross-tabulation between individuals' educational background and their educational achievement (see Pfeffer, 2008), I am following the numerous empirical analyses of social and educational mobility that have proved that the basic structure of the cross-sectional association between the two variables is largely invariant across several otherwise important socio-demographic factors, mainly sex and geographical areas of residence. I myself tested this hypothesis for the French data that I focus on here by performing a log-linear analysis of the three-way cross-tabulations of respondents' highest educational levels by their parents' education and sex. The results of this analysis (available upon request) clearly suggested that almost all the variation of respondents' educational attainments was due to their educational backgrounds. The 'constant association' model, in fact, absorbs more than 99% of the residuals produced by the baseline model – here the 'conditional independence' model, which unrealistically postulates that respondents' education only co-varies with gender. By contrast, the 'uniform difference' model (Xie, 1992), which posits that the educational–origin–destination association differs between men and women by a multiplicative factor β, only adds about 0.01% to the variance explained by the 'constant association' model, and the dissimilarity index is virtually unchanged (for a recent review of these statistical models, see Breen, 2004, ch. 2). Thus, the extent of the variations of educational outflows and opportunities across genders does not seem large enough to justify the introduction of specific hypotheses linking families' educational strategies to offspring's sex into the explanatory formal model that I discuss in the next section (for a recent comparative analysis of gender differences in educational inequality which would justify this simplification, see Breen et al., 2009).

4. The choice of $c = 1.5$ is due to the fact that the model contains three terms (see Eq. 2), each of which will range between 0 and 1, so that the theoretical minimum value for P_{igL} will be 0, whereas the maximum will be 3. Centring the logistic on 1.5 rather than leaving it centred on 0 thus allows the three terms to fall within a large range of the x-axis, thereby avoiding high probabilities of making the choice even when no mechanisms are present (i.e. when, by construction, $P_{igL} = 0$).

5. Despite the frequent use of the normal distribution to approximate the distribution of ability, it is long-standing argument in economics that 'there is little reason to assume that ability is in fact normally distributed' (see Mayer, 1960; more recently, see Koerselman, 2011). From a descriptive point of view, assuming a log-normal distribution allows better account to be taken of the frequently observed skewed form of the distribution of ability. From a numerical point of view, this choice also avoids the problem of negative values of ability for which a clear substantive interpretation is not immediately apparent.

6. This interaction-based exposure effect has proven to be relevant for such diverse choices as whether or not to commit suicide (Hedström, Liu, & Nordvik, 2008), whether or not to get divorced (Åberg, 2009), whether or not to pay taxes (Hedström & Ibarra, 2010).

7. To create the artificial network, the specific algorithm that I adopted extends
the algorithm proposed by Watts and Strogatz (1998; see also Watts, 1999, pp. 503–
506, 524) to the situation where several groups of agents are present and the rewiring
process must consequently apply to the creation of links among groups. It can be
summarized as follows: (1) first, a regular network of symmetric and non-weighted
links is created within each of the five group of agents, each of the agent having K
links; (2) then, each link is considered and, with probability p, is rewired outside the
agent's group; (3) finally, the educational group of the potential out-group neighbour
is determined according to the following probabilistic criterion: the more distant the
focal agent's and potential neighbour's educational backgrounds, the lower the
probability that a link between the two agents will be created. Note that K, the
average number of links among agents set in step 1 is kept constant when rewiring
steps 2 and 3 are realized. The rationale behind this choice is that it enables
evaluation of the relative impact on the outcome of interest (educational choices,
here) of the local density of the network or of the fraction of long ties (the out-group
links, here) (see Centola & Macy, 2007, p. 711) – this experimental manipulation will
be performed in section "Sensitivity analysis of the social influence mechanism".
Note also that I adopt the simplest concept of distance among agents' educational
backgrounds, namely the absolute value of the difference between educational group
indexes (ranging from 1, the most advantaged educational background, to 5, the
most disadvantaged one).

8. The program is written in NetLogo 5.0 (see Tisue & Wilensky, 2004a, b).
Currently, Railsback and Grimm (2012) constitute the best introduction to Netlogo
as a programming language for agent-based model building. To appreciate the power
Netlogo has achieved, compare Lytinen and Railsback (2012) to Railsback, Lytinen,
& Jackson (2006).

9. From a logical point of view, this parameter tuning operation is equivalent to
what is done in statistical modelling when, given some identification constraints, one
looks for parameter values which minimize the distance between fitted and observed
values. As correctly pointed out by Snijders and Steglich (2013), however, unlike
statistical modelling, agent-based modelling is not meant for causal inference. As a
consequence, parameter search procedures in agent-based modelling do not need to
rely on assumptions about variable and error distributions because parameters are
not supposed to provide efficient and robust estimations of average effects
generalized to the population, but only to express theoretically meaningful and
realistic relations among (some of the) variables on which algorithms rely.

10. It should be noted that this numerical phenomenon implied by the fractional
form of the social influence term adopted here is part of a deeper phenomenon
related to the two ways in which threshold effects more generally can be formalized.
As pointed out by Centola and Macy (2007, p. 711), 'fractional' thresholds, that is
thresholds based on the proportion of an agent's neighbours doing something
instead of the absolute number of neighbours, implies that both 'adopters' and
'nonadopters' influence the agent's behaviour. Under the 'fractional' threshold, when
the agent's neighbourhood size increases, it is thus also possible that, if the fraction
of adopters is limited, the amount of influence undergone by the focal agent
decreases instead of increasing because the fraction of 'nonadopters' will weigh more.
Although tiny, a trace of this counterintuitive effect is present in Fig. 4, namely

among agents belonging to the lowest group for whom, given their average level of ability/perceived benefits, highest educational choices are not so frequent. For them, a slight decreasing trend is visible as the average number of agents with whom they are in contact increases. Given variability across replications, however, it would not be justified to exaggerate the importance of this effect in the present model.

11. All the trends described would be even more marked if one simulated the model under increasing values of the inter-group link probability but applying an alternative, although far less realistic, configuration of these links on the basis of which the more distant the focal agent's and potential neighbour's educational backgrounds, the higher the probability that the out-group link will be created (such a modification amounts to manipulating parameters PG_{GSD}, see Appendix A, Table A.1). This configuration is thus the exact contrary of the one I have adopted throughout the paper, in that the majority of out-group links would in this case be between maximally socially distant agents rather than between agents at a social distance equal to 1 (results are available upon request).

REFERENCES

Åberg, Y. (2009). The contagiousness of divorce. In P. Hedström & P. Bearman (Eds.), *The Oxford handbook of analytical sociology* (pp. 342–364). Oxford: Oxford University Press.

Agirdag, O., Van Houtte, M., & Avermaet, P. V. (2011). Why does the ethnic and socio-economic composition of schools influence math achievement? The role of sense of futility and futility culture. *European Sociological Review*. doi:10.1093/esr/jcq070.

Akerlof, G. (1997). Social distance and social decisions. *Econometrica*, 65(5), 1005–1027.

Akerlof, G. E., & Kranton, R. E. (2002). Identity and schooling: Some lessons for the economics of education. *Journal of Economic Literature*, 40(4), 1167–1201.

Albouy, V., & Wanecq, T. (2003). Les inégalités sociales d'accès aux grandes écoles. *Economie et Statistique*, 361, 27–52.

Andrew, M., & Hauser, R. M. (2011). Adoption? Adaptation? Evaluating the formation of educational expectations. *Social Forces*, 90(2), 497–520.

Ballarino, G., & Bernardi, F. (2001). Uso di dati time-budget per lo studio delle risorse familiari: Capitale sociale e culturale dei genitori dei bambini in età scolare in Italia. *Quaderni di Sociologia*, 2, 7–36.

Becker, R. (2003). Educational expansion and persistent inequality of education. Utilizing subjective expected utility theory to explain increasing participation rates in upper secondary school in the federal republic of Germany. *European Sociological Review*, 19(1), 1–24.

Blossfeld, H.-P. (2009). Educational assortative marriage in comparative perspective. *Annual Review of Sociology*, 35, 513–530.

Blossfeld, H.-P., & Timm, A. (2003a). Educational systems as marriage markets in modern societies: A conceptual framework. In H.-P. Blossfeld & A. Timm (Eds.), *Who marries whom? Educational systems as marriage markets in modern societies* (pp. 9–18). Dordrecht: Kluwer Academic Publishers.

Blossfeld, H.-P., & Timm, A. (2003b). Assortative mating in cross-national comparison: A summary of results and conclusions. In H.-P. Blossfeld & A. Timm (Eds.), *Who marries whom? Educational systems as marriage markets in modern societies* (pp. 331–342). Dordrecht: Kluwer Academic Publishers.

Borrill, P., & Tesfatsion, L. (2010). *Agent-based modeling: The right mathematics for the social sciences?* Working Paper No. 10023. Iowa State University, Department of Economics.

Boudon, R. (1974). *Education, opportunity, and social inequality.* New York: Wiley & Sons.

Boudon, R. (1979). *La logique du social.* Paris: Presses Universitaires de France.

Brännström, L. (2008). Making their mark: The effects of neighbourhood and upper secondary school on educational achievement. *European Sociological Review, 24*(4), 463–478.

Brauns, H., & Steinman, S. (1997). *Educational reforms in France, West-Germany, the United Kingdom and Hungary: Updating the Casmin educational classification.* Working Papers 21. Mannheim.

Breen, R. (1999). Beliefs, rational choice and Bayesian learning. *Rationality and Society, 11*(4), 463–480.

Breen, R. (Ed.). (2004). *Social mobility in Europe.* Oxford: Oxford University Press.

Breen, R. (2009). Formal theory in the social sciences. In P. Hedström & B. Wittrock (Eds.), *Frontiers of sociology* (pp. 209–230). Leiden: Brill.

Breen, R., & Goldthorpe, J. (1997). Explaining educational differentials: Towards a formal rational choice theory. *Rationality and Society, 9*(3), 275–305.

Breen, R., & Jonsson, J. O. (2005). Inequality of opportunity in comparative perspective: Recent research on educational attainment and social mobility. *Annual Review of Sociology, 31*, 223–243.

Breen, R., Luijkx, R., Müller, W., & Pollak, R. (2009). Nonpersistent inequality in educational attainment: Evidence from eight European countries. *American Journal of Sociology, 114*(5), 1475–1521.

Breen, R., Luijkx, R., Muller, W., & Pollak, R. (2010). Long-term trends in educational inequality in Europe: Class inequalities and gender differences. *European Sociological Review, 26*(1), 31–48.

Breen, R., & Yaish, M. (2006). Testing the Breen-Goldthorpe model of educational decision making. In L. Stephen, D. B. Morgan, D. Grusky & G. S. Fields (Eds.), *Frontiers in social and economic mobility.* Stanford, CA: Stanford University Press.

Bruch, E., & Mare, R. (2006). Neighborhood choice and neighborhood change. *American Journal of Sociology, 112*(3), 667–709.

Burke, M. A., & Heiland, F. (2006). The strength of social interactions and obesity among women. In F. C. Billari, T. Fent, A. Prskawetz & J. Scheffran (Eds.), *Agent-based computational modelling* (pp. 117–137). Heidelberg: Physica-Verlag HD.

Centola, D., Eguiluz, V. M., & Macy, M. W. (2007). Cascade dynamics of complex propagation. *Physica A, 374*, 449–456.

Centola, D., & Macy, M. W. (2007). Complex contagions and the weakness of long ties. *American Journal of Sociology, 113*(3), 702–734.

Cheadle, J. E. (2008). Educational investment, family context, and children's math and reading growth from kindergarten through third grade. *Sociology of Education, 81*(1), 1–31.

Christakis, N. A., & Fowler, J. H. (2007). The spread of obesity in a large social network over 32 years. *New England Journal of Medicine, 357*(4), 370–379.

Cobalti, A. (1989). A relative mobility table. A modest proposal. *Quality and Quantity, 23*(2), 205–220.

Cobalti, A. (1992). Origine sociale e livello di istruzione: Un modello. *Polis, 6*(1), 117–145.

Cohen-Cole, E., & Zanella, G. (2008). Unpacking social interactions. *Economic Inquiry*, *46*(1), 19–24.

Collins, R. (1979). *The credential society*. New York: Academic Press.

Davies, R., Heinesen, E., & Holm, A. (2002). The relative risk aversion hypothesis of educational choice. *Journal of Population Economics*, *15*(4), 683–713.

Davison, A., & Hinkley, D. (1997). *Bootstrap methods and their application*. Cambridge: Cambridge University Press.

DiPrete, T. A., Gelman, A., McCormick, T., Teitler, J., & Zheng, T. (2011). Segregation in social networks based on acquaintanceship and trust. *American Journal of Sociology*, *116*(4), 1234–1283.

Duncan, G. J., & Murnane, R. (2011). *Whither opportunity? Rising inequality, schools, and children's life chances*. New York: Russell Sage.

Durlauf, S. (1999a). The memberships theory of inequality: Ideas and implications. In E. Brezis & P. Temin (Eds.), *Elites, minorities, and economic growth*. Amsterdam: North Holland.

Durlauf, S. (1999b). How statistical mechanics contribute to study of science. *Proceedings of the National Academy of Sciences*, *96*(19), 10582–10584.

Durlauf, S. (2001). A framework for the study of individual behaviour and social interactions. *Sociological Methodology*, *31*(1), 47–87.

Durlauf, S. (2002). The memberships theory of poverty: The role of group affiliations in determining socioeconomic outcomes. In S. Danziger & R. Haveman (Eds.), *Understanding poverty in America*. Cambridge: Harvard University Press.

Durlauf, S. (2006). Groups, social influences, and inequality: A memberships theory perspective on poverty traps. In S. Bowles, S. Durlauf & K. Hoff (Eds.), *Poverty traps*. Princeton, NJ: Princeton University Press.

Durlauf, S., & Cohen-Cole, E. (2004). Social interactions models. In K. Lempf-Leonard (Ed.), *Encyclopedia of social measurement*. Academic Press.

Durlauf, S. N., & Ioannides, Y. M. M. (2010). Social interactions. *Annual Review of Economics*, *2*, 451–478.

Duru-Bellat, M., Kieffer, A., & Reimer, D. (2011). Les inégalités d'accès à l'enseignement supérieur: Le rôle des filières et des spécialités. *Une Comparaison entre l'Allemagne de l'Ouest et la France, Économie et Statistique* (433–434), 3–22.

Easley, D., & Kleinberg, J. (2010). *Networks, crowds, and markets: Reasoning about a highly connected world*. Cambridge: Cambridge University Press.

Epstein, J. (2006). *Generative social science: Studies in agent-based computational modeling*. Princeton, NJ: Princeton University Press.

Erikson, R., & Goldthorpe, J. (1992). *The constant flux: A study of class mobility in industrial society*. Oxford: Clarendon Press.

Falch, T., & Massih, S. S. (2011). The effect of education on cognitive ability. *Economic Inquiry*, *49*(3), 838–856.

Fekjær, S. N., & Birkelund, G. (2007). Does the ethnic composition of upper secondary schools influence educational achievement and attainment? A multilevel analysis of the Norwegian case. *European Sociological Review*, *23*(3), 309–323.

Fischer, C. S., Hout, M., Jankowski, M. S., Lucas, S. R., Swidler, A., & Vos, K. (1996). *Inequality by design: Cracking the bell curve myth*. Princeton, NJ: Princeton University Press.

Fowler, J. H., & Christakis, N. A. (2008). The dynamic spread of happiness in a large social network: Longitudinal analysis over 20 years in the Framingham heart study. *British Medical Journal*, *337*, a2338.

Gabay-Egozi, L., Shavit, Y., & Yaish, M. (2010). Curricular choice: A test of a rational choice model of education. *European Sociological Review*, *26*(4), 447–463.

Gambetta, D. (1987). *Where they pushed or did they jump? Individual decision mechanisms in education*. Cambridge: Cambridge University Press.

Gintis, H., & Bowles, S. (2002). Intergenerational inequality. *Journal of Economic Perspectives*, *16*(3), 3–30.

Gintis, H., Bowles, S., & Osborne, M. (2001). Incentive-enhancing preferences: Personality, behavior, and earnings. *American Economic Review*, *91*(2), 155–158.

Goldthorpe, J. (2001). Causation, statistics, and sociology. *European Sociological Review*, *17*(1), 1–20.

Goldthorpe, J. H. (1996). Class analysis and the reorientation of class theory: The case of persisting differentials in education attainment. *The British Journal of Sociology*, *47*(3), 481–505.

Goodman, L. A. (1969). How to ransack social mobility tables and other kinds of cross classification tables. *American Journal of Sociology*, *75*(1), 1–40.

Goux, D., & Maurin, E. (2007). Close neighbours matter: Neighbourhood effects on early performance at school. *The Economic Journal*, *117*(523), 1193–1215.

Granovetter, M. (1973). The strength of weak ties. *American Journal of Sociology*, *78*(6), 1360–1380.

Granovetter, M. (1978). Threshold models of collective behavior. *American Journal of Sociology*, *83*(6), 1420–1443.

Granovetter, M. (1983). The strength of weak ties: A network theory revisited. *Sociological Theory*, *1*, 201–233.

Granovetter, M. (1988). Threshold models of diversity: Chinese restaurants, residential segregation and the spiral of silence. *Sociological Methodology*, *18*, 69–104.

Granovetter, M., & Soong, R. (1983). Threshold models of diffusion and collective behavior. *Journal of Mathematical Sociology*, *9*, 165–179.

Haller, A. O., & Woelfel, J. (1972). Significant others and their expectations: Concepts and instruments to measure interpersonal influence on status aspirations. *Rural Sociology*, *37*(4), 591–622.

Harding, D., Gennetian, L., Winship, C., Sanbonmatsu, L., & Kling, J. (2011). Unpacking neighborhood influences on education outcomes: Setting the stage for future research. In G. J. Duncan & R. Murnane (Eds.), *Whither opportunity? Rising inequality, schools, and children's life chances* (pp. 277–299). New York: Russell Sage.

Hedstrom, P. (1998). Rational imitation. In P. Hedstrom & R. Swedberg (Eds.), *Social mechanisms. An analytical approach to social theory*. Cambridge: Cambridge University Press.

Hedstrom, P. (2005). *Dissecting the social: On the principles of analytical sociology*. Cambridge: Cambridge University Press.

Hedström, P., & Bearman, P. (2009). What is analytical sociology all about? An introductory essay. In P. Hedström & P. Bearman (Eds.), *The Oxford handbook of analytical sociology* (pp. 3–24). Oxford: Oxford University Press.

Hedström, P., & Ibarra, R. (2010). On the contagiousness of non-contagious behavior: The case of tax avoidance and tax evasion. In H. Joas & B. Klein (Eds.), *The benefit of broad horizons: Intellectual and institutional preconditions for a global social science* (pp. 315–336). Leiden: Brill.

Hedström, P., Liu, K.-Y., & Nordvik, M. (2008). Interaction domains and suicides: A population-based panel study of suicides in the Stockholm metropolitan area, 1991–1999. *Social Forces*, *87*(2), 713–740.

Herrnstein, R. J., & Murray, C. (1994). *The bell curve: Intelligence and class structure in America life*. New York: Free Press.

Hillmert, S., & Jacob, M. (2003). Social inequality in higher education. Is vocational training a pathway leading to or away from university? *European Sociological Review, 19*(3), 319–334.

Holm, A., & Jaeger, M. M. (2008). Does relative risk aversion explain educational inequality? A dynamic choice approach. *Research in Social Stratification and Mobility, 26*(3), 199–219.

Ichou, M., & Vallet, L.-A. (2011). Do all roads lead to inequality? Trends in French upper secondary school analysed with four longitudinal surveys. *Oxford Review of Education, 37*(2), 167–194.

Jackson, M. (Ed.). (2012). *Determined to succeed? Performance, choice and education*. Stanford, CA: Stanford University Press.

Jackson, M., Erikson, R., Goldthorpe, J. H., & Yaish, M. (2007). Primary and secondary effects in class differentials in educational attainment: The transition to A-Level courses in England and Wales. *Acta Sociologica, 50*(3), 211–229.

Jaeger, M. M. (2007). Economic and social returns to educational choices. Extending the utility function. *Rationality and Society, 19*(4), 451–483.

Jonsson, J. O., & Erikson, R. (2000). Understanding educational inequality: The Swedish experience. *L'Année Sociologique, 50*(2), 345–382.

Kaufman, R. L., & Schervish, P. G. (1987). Variations on a theme. More uses of odds ratios to interpret log-linear parameters. *Sociological Methods and Research, 16*(2), 218–255.

Keller, S., & Zavalloni, M. (1964). Ambition and social class: A respecification. *Social Forces, 43*(1), 58–70.

Koerselman, K. (2011). *Bias from the use of mean-based methods on test scores, Swedish Institute for Social Research (SOFI)*. Working Paper 1/2011. Stockholm University.

Kroneberg, C., & Kalter, F. (2012). Rational choice theory and empirical research. Methodological and theoretical contributions in Europe. *Annual Review of Sociology, 38*, 73–92.

Law, A. M. (2007). *Simulation modeling and analysis*. New York: McGraw-Hill.

Limpert, E., Stahel, W. A., & Abbt, M. (2001). Log-normal distributions across the sciences: Keys and clues. *Bio Science, 51*(5), 341–352.

Lucchini, M., Della Stella, S., & Pisati, M. (2010). *The weight of the genetic and environmental dimensions in the inter-generational transmission of educational success*. European Sociological Review. doi:10.1093/esr/jcr067.

Lytinen, S. L., & Railsback, S. F. (2012). The evolution of agent-based simulation platforms: A review of NetLogo 5.0 and ReLogo. Proceedings of the fourth international symposium on agent-based modeling and simulation (21st European Meeting on Cybernetics and Systems Research [EMCSR 2012]). Vienna, Austria, April 2012.

Manski, C. (1993a). Identification of endogenous social effects: The reflection problem. *Review of Economic Studies, 60*(3), 531–542.

Manski, C. (1993b). Identification problems in social sciences. *Sociological Methodology, 23*, 1–56.

Manski, C. (2000). Economic analysis of social interaction. *Journal of Economic Perspectives, 14*(3), 115–136.

Manzo, G. (2006). Generative mechanisms and multivariate statistical analysis. Modeling educational opportunity inequality by Multi-Matrix Log-Linear topological model: Contributions and limits. *Quality and Quantity, 40*(5), 721–758.

Manzo, G. (2007). Variables, mechanisms, and simulations: Can the three methods be synthesized? A critical analysis of the literature. *Revue Française de Sociologie – An Annual English Selection, 48*(Suppl.), 35–71.

Manzo, G. (2009). *La spirale des inégalités. Choix scolaires en France et en Italie au XX siècle.* Paris: Presses de l'Université Paris-Sorbonne.

Manzo, G. (2010). Analytical sociology and its critics. *European Journal of Sociology, 51*(1), 129–170.

Manzo, G. (2011). *Educational choices and educational traps. Towards an integration between computational and statistical modelling in the sociology of social stratification.* GEMASS Working Papers, GeWop 2011, no. 1.

Mastekaasa, A. (2006). Educational transitions at graduate level: Social origins and enrolment in PhD programmes in Norway. *Acta Sociologica, 49*(4), 437–453.

Mayer, T. (1960). The distribution of ability and earnings. *The Review of Economics and Statistics, 42*(2), 189–195.

McPherson, J., Smith-Lovin, L., & Cook, J. (2001). Birds of a feather: Homophily in social networks. *Annual Review of Sociology, 27*, 415–444.

McPherson, M., Smith-Lovin, L., & Brashears, M. E. (2006). Social isolation in America: Changes in core discussion networks over two decades. *American Sociological Review, 71*, 353–375.

Merton, R. K. (1968). The Matthew effect in science. The reward and communication systems of science are considered. *Science, 159*(810), 55–63.

Morgan, S. L. (2005). *On the edge of commitment: Educational attainment and race in the united states.* Stanford, CA: Stanford University Press.

Mouw, T. (2006). Estimating the causal effect of social capital: A review of recent research. *Annual Review of Sociology, 32*, 79–102.

Müller, W., & Karle, W. (1993). Social selection in educational systems in Europe. *European Sociological Review, 9*(1), 1–23.

Müller, W., Lüttinger, P., König, W., & Karle, W. (1989). Class and education in industrial nations. *International Journal of Sociology, 19*(3), 3–39.

Need, A., & de Jong, U. (2000). Educational differentials in the Netherlands: Testing rational choice theory. *Rationality and Society, 13*, 71–98.

Orléan, A. (1995). Bayesian interactions and collective dynamics of opinion: Herd behavior and mimetic contagion. *Journal of Economic Behavior and Organization, 28*(2), 257–274.

Pfeffer, F. T. (2008). Persistent inequality in educational attainment and its institutional context. *European Sociological Review, 24*(5), 543–565.

Raftery, A. E., & Hout, M. (1993). Maximally maintained inequality: Expansion, reform and opportunity in Irish education, 1921–1975. *Sociology of Education, 66*, 41–62.

Railsback, S. F., & Grimm, V. (2012). *Agent-based and individual-based modeling: A practical introduction.* Princeton, CA: Princeton University Press.

Railsback, S. F., Lytinen, S. L., & Jackson, S. K. (2006). Agent-based simulation platforms: Review and development recommendations. *Simulation, 82*, 609–623.

Reynolds, J. R., & Johnson, M. K. (2011). Change in the stratification of educational expectations and their realization. *Social Forces, 90*(1), 85–110.

Rolfe, M. (2009). Conditional choice. In P. Hedström & P. Bearman (Eds.), *The Oxford handbook of analytical sociology* (pp. 419–447). Oxford: Oxford University Press.

Sampson, R., Morenoff, J. D., & Gannon-Rowley, T. (2002). Assessing neighbourhood effects: Social processes and new directions in research. *Annual Review of Sociology, 28,* 443–478.

Schelling, T. C. (1971). Dynamic models of segregation. *Journal of Mathematical Sociology, 1,* 143–186.

Schelling, T. C. (1973). Hockey helmets, concealed weapons and daylight saving. A study of binary choices with externalities. *Journal of Conflict Resolution, 17*(3), 381–428.

Schizzerotto, A. (1997). Perché in Italia ci sono pochi diplomati e pochi laureati? Vincoli strutturali e decisioni razionali degli attori come cause della contenuta espansione della scolarità superiore. *Polis, 11*(3), 345–365.

Selz, M., & Vallet, L.-A. (2006). La démocratisation de l'enseignement et son paradoxe apparent (pp. *Données Sociales, La Société Française,* INSEE, Paris.

Sewell, W. H., Hauser, R. M., Springer, K. W., & Hauser, T. S. (2003). As we age: A review of the Wisconsin longitudinal study, 1957–2001. *Research in Social Stratification and Mobility, 20,* 3–111.

Shalizi, C. R., & Thomas, A. C. (2011). Homophily and contagion are generically confounded in observational social network studies. *Sociological Methods and Research, 40*(3), 211–239.

Shavit, Y., & Blossfeld, H.-P. (Eds.). (1993). *Boulder, CO.* Westview Press.

Shoam, Y., & Leyton-Brown, K. (2009). *Multiagent systems: Algorithmic, game-theoretic, and logical foundations.* Cambridge: Cambridge University Press.

Skopek, J., Schulz, F., & Blossfeld, H.-P. (2011). Who contacts whom? Educational homophily in online mate selection. *European Sociological Review, 27*(2), 180–195.

Snjiders, T. A. B., & Steglich, C. E. G. (2013, forthcoming). Representing micro-macro linkages by actor-based dynamic networks models, Sociological Methods and Research.

Sobel, M. E. (2006). Spatial concentration and social stratification: Does the clustering of disadvantage 'Beget' bad outcomes? In S. Bowles, S. N. Durlauf & K. Hoff (Eds.), *Poverty traps* (pp. 204–229). New York: Russell Sage Foundation.

Stocké, V. (2007). Explaining educational decision and effects of families social class position: An empirical test of the Breen–Goldthorpe model of educational attainment. *European Sociological Review, 23*(4), 505–519.

Stocké, V. (2008). *Educational decisions as rational choice? Testing the Erikson-Jonsson model.* Working Papers 504, Universität Mannheim.

Stonedahl, F., & Wilensky, U. (2010). *Evolutionary robustness checking in the artificial Anasazi model.* Proceedings of the AAAI fall symposium on complex adaptive systems: Resilience, robustness, and evolvability. November 11–13, 2010. Arlington, VA.

Thélot, C., & Vallet, L.-A. (2000). La réduction des inégalités sociales devant l'école depuis le début du siècle. *Économie et Statistique, 334,* 3–32.

Tisue, S., & Wilensky, U. (2004a). NetLogo: Design and implementation of a multi-agent modeling environment. Evanston, IL, Center for Connected Learning and Computer-Based Modeling, Northwestern University. http://ccl.northwestern.edu/papers/

Tisue, S., & Wilensky, U. (2004b). NetLogo: A simple environment for modeling complexity. Evanston, IL, Center for Connected Learning and Computer-Based Modeling, Northwestern University. http://ccl.northwestern.edu/papers/

Vallet, L. A., & Selz, M. (2007). Evolution historique de l'inégalité des chances devant l'école: Des méthodes et des résultats revisités. *Education & Formation, 74,* 65–74.

Van de Werfhorst, H. G. (2009). Credential inflation and educational strategies: A comparison of the United States and the Netherlands. *Research in Social Stratification and Mobility*, *27*, 269–284.

Van de Werfhorst, H. G., & Hofstede, S. (2007). Cultural capital or relative risk aversion? Two mechanisms for educational inequality compared. *The British Journal of Sociology*, *58*, 391–415.

VanderWeele, T. J. (2011). Sensitivity analysis for contagion effects in social networks. *Sociological Methods & Research*, *40*(2), 240–255.

Watts, D. J. (1999). Networks, dynamics, and the Small-World phenomenon. *American Journal of Sociology*, *105*(2), 493–527.

Watts, D. J. (2004). The new science of networks. *Annual Review of Sociology*, *30*, 243–270.

Watts, D. J., & Strogatz, S. H. (1998). Collective dynamics of 'Small-world' networks. *Nature*, *393*, 440–442.

White, H. (2000). Parameterize: Notes on mathematical modeling for sociology. *Sociological Theory*, *18*(3), 505–509.

Winship, C., & Korenman, S. (1997). Does staying in school make you smarter? The effect of education on IQ in the bell curve. In B. Devlin, S. E. Fienberg, D. P. Resnick & K. Roeder (Eds.). *Intelligence, genes and success: Scientists respond to the Bell curve* (pp. 215–234, ch. 10). Springer-Verlag.

Wooldridge, M. (2009). *An introduction to multi agent systems*. John Wiley and Sons, Ltd.

Xie, Y. (1992). The log-multiplicative layer effect model for comparing mobility tables. *American Sociological Review*, *57*(3), 380–395.

APPENDIX A

Table A.1. Number, State and Initialisation Values of the Model
Parameters Concerned by the Simulation.

Parameter	Number of Independent Parameters	State and Initialisation Values
Mean of the log-normal distribution of agents' ability (A_g)	5	Manipulated
Variance of the log-normal distribution of agents' ability (σ_A^2)	1	Set to 0.25
Mean of the log-normal distribution of agents' perceived benefits (B_g)	5	Manipulated
Variance of the log-normal distribution of agents' perceived benefits (σ_B^2)	1	Set to 0.25
Network average degree (K)	1	Set to 4
Probability of out-group links (p)	1	Set to 0.1
Probability of out-group links as function of the 'Social' distance among groups ($P_{GSD \in [1,2,3,4]}$)	3	Set to 0.6, 0.25, 0.10, 0.05
Maximum number of times the educational level L can be evaluated F	1	Set to 3

Table A.2. Percentage of Actors/Agents Reaching a Given Educational Level (Columns) within a Given Educational Background/Agent Group (Rows) – French Real-Data Cross-Tabulation (Average of 100 Bootstrapped Cross-Tabulations) and Simulated Cross-Tabulations Generated by Each Model Variant Discussed in Section 'Computational Results, Empirical Data and Model Dynamic' (Average Over 100 Replications).

	1a	1bc	2ab	2c	3ab	N
(a) French Empirical Data						
1a	48.90	20.38	14.33	7.21	9.17	1,418
1bc	15.34	24.39	25.53	16.22	18.51	1,769
2ab	7.66	8.96	23.80	19.60	39.98	524
2c	5.63	5.73	16.80	19.53	52.31	380
3ab	4.76	2.79	8.13	14.81	69.51	909
(b) 'Straw Man' Model: All Mechanisms Are Absent						
1a-agents	54.69	24.69	11.31	5.11	4.20	1,418
1bc-agents	54.67	24.88	11.19	5.14	4.12	1,769
2ab-agents	54.80	24.54	11.30	5.05	4.31	524
2c-agents	54.79	24.46	11.27	5.20	4.27	380
3ab-agents	54.38	25.03	11.22	5.11	4.26	909
(c) Model Variant 1: Ability						
1a-agents	44.73	24.43	13.26	8.42	9.15	1,418
1bc-agents	33.95	22.71	14.22	9.34	19.78	1,769
2ab-agents	29.47	21.57	13.16	11.32	24.47	524
2c-agents	31.10	21.56	14.17	12.56	20.61	380
3ab-agents	34.31	19.29	13.89	10.26	22.23	909
(d) Model Variant 2: 'Model Variant 1' + Perceived Benefits						
1a-agents	45.01	24.37	13.23	8.33	9.06	1,418
1bc-agents	34.51	22.82	14.14	9.25	19.28	1,769
2ab-agents	17.23	14.43	12.79	10.17	45.38	524
2c-agents	15.52	14.20	11.28	10.95	48.04	380
3ab-agents	14.36	10.31	11.34	7.62	56.36	909
(e) Model Variant 3: 'Model Variant 2' + Ability/Benefits Interaction						
1a-agents	45.52	24.43	13.07	8.21	8.77	1,418
1bc-agents	36.01	23.15	13.96	9.03	17.85	1,769
2ab-agents	17.06	14.35	12.25	9.92	46.42	524
2c-agents	14.24	12.64	10.59	9.93	52.60	380
3ab-agents	11.45	8.59	9.60	6.79	63.56	909
(f) Model Variant 4: 'Model Variant 3' + Social Influence						
1a-agents	37.67	26.26	16.41	10.45	9.21	1,418
1bc-agents	25.79	24.58	17.20	12.02	20.40	1,769
2ab-agents	12.73	14.98	14.19	14.37	43.73	524
2c-agents	11.29	13.09	12.84	14.63	48.14	380
3ab-agents	5.64	5.89	7.11	8.79	72.57	909
(g) Model Variant 5: 'Model Variant 4' + Inflation Spiral Mechanisms (see Appendix B)						
1a-agents	31.88	24.91	17.61	11.89	13.71	1,418
1bc-agents	18.11	20.95	16.52	13.13	31.29	1,769
2ab-agents	8.34	11.46	12.10	12.24	55.86	524
2c-agents	7.88	9.75	10.68	11.86	59.83	380
3ab-agents	4.10	4.60	5.25	6.17	79.88	909

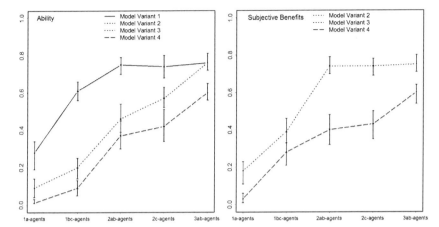

Fig. A.1. Effective Mean Values (Averaged over 100 Replications) of Agents' Ability (Left) and Perceived Benefits (Right) as a Function of Agents' Group for Each Model Variant (Bars Give Values within Which Fall 95% of Model Replication). Example: Under Model Variant 1, the Mean of Ability Distribution for Agents Belonging to the Lowest Group (1a-Agents) Ranges across Replications between ≈ 0.20 and ≈ 0.37.

APPENDIX B

As I have stressed in the discussion section, the formal model presented here contains several simplifying assumptions. In particular, with regard to the way in which actors evaluate the net benefits of a given educational level, both its pay-offs on the job market and the actor's subjective evaluation of these pay-offs from the point of view of the social group to which s/he belongs are conflated into a single parameter, B_{ig} (see section 'Computational modelling of educational preference formation'; Eq. (2)).

On a conceptual level, however, separating these two components would be appreciable. Such analytical decomposition would allow more direct representation of the inflation spiral in which educational choices tend to be trapped in the long run. While an explicit representation of this process is absent from Breen and Goldthorpe's (1997) formal model, Goldthorpe's (1996) first discursive outline of the model explicitly acknowledged that when education is considered a positional good, its value decreases as more people obtain a given educational qualification, thus progressively modifying actors' subjective incentives to do their best to go beyond that qualification if they want to maintain their relative position in the social hierarchy (see already Boudon, 1974, ch. 8; for a historical outline of education inflation dynamics, see Collins, 1979). Recent empirical analyses have shown that individuals' expectations/ambitions about going beyond the upper secondary level increase in the long run (see Reynolds & Johnson, 2011) and that the inflation trend of higher educational certificates induces increasing proportions of all social classes to try and obtain them (see Van de Werfhorst, 2009).

Eq. (B.1) slightly modifies Eq. (2) (see section 'Computational modelling of educational preference formation') in order to accommodate in a simple way an explicit representation of this process of educational inflation and its effect on actors' beliefs. To this end, the two following terms are introduced into the original Eq. (2): (a) the term OR_{Lt} – that is, the pay-off from educational level L on the job market at the instant t (OR stands for objective returns) and (2) the term NC_{Lt} – that is, the overall number of choices that a given educational level L has received at the instant t from all agents living in the artificial society (N being the total number of artificial agents). These two terms are then made to interact in a specific way.

On the one hand, the diffusion of educational choices at the aggregate level is assumed to affect the agent's educational choice by progressively reducing the objective return OR_{Lt} of educational level L, thereby indirectly depressing the agent's evaluation of educational level L. However, on the other hand, it is also assumed that artificial agents actively react to this inflation dynamic of educational levels by iteratively readjusting their initial subjective perception B of the benefits of the educational level L: that is, the larger the proportion of favourable choices for L, the more perceived benefits are upwardly reevaluated.

$$P_{igL} = A_{ig} + \frac{1}{\ln(NC_{Lt-n})}\mathrm{OR}_{Lt} + (\phi(A) \times B_{ig})^{1-\frac{NC_{Lt-n}}{N}} + SI_{igL} \qquad \text{(B.1)}$$

Thus, the main difference between the model studied in the article and the generalisation presented here is the introduction of a second source of externalities among agents' educational choices, which instead of being based on the educational choices performed by agents' closest contacts, derive from the educational behaviour of the population of agents considered as a whole (*NC*). As the detailed simulation algorithm clarifies (see Fig. 1, step 2.2), however, since the total number of choices NC_{Lt} in favour of each educational level is computed, and put back into the agent's education behavioural function [B.1], every 52 iterations, the two forms of social externalities do not operate on the same temporal scales. While the network-based social influence is continuously at work, the population-based feedbacks triggered by the diffusion of education levels are activated only discretely.

According to Goldthorpe's (1996) verbal analysis, if dynamic belief updates of this kind were at work under the pressure of a process of education devaluation, one should expect to find that, *ceteris paribus*, class differentials in educational choices persist because the educational race becomes increasingly intense for every social group.

In order to test this hypothesis, exactly the same set of simulations that enabled best approximation of the educational stratification empirically observed in France – that is, the model containing all the mechanisms postulated (see section 'Computational results, empirical data and model dynamic'; Table 2f) – were re-run by introducing the two additional mechanisms formalised by Eq. (B.1). To initialise the four parameters of which the term OR consists, I took the proportion of French respondents reaching the service class at the end of their occupational careers (for the CASMIN occupational schema adopted here, see Breen, 2004, p. 12) among those reaching one of the five educational levels – thus representing the objective return associated with a given educational level as the capacity of this level to ensure a place among the most advantageous social positions.

The results reported in Table 2g (see section 'Computational results, empirical data and model dynamic') confirm this expectation. The statistics computed on the simulated data show that, when artificial agents are assumed to constantly upwardly revaluate their initial appreciation of education benefits as a function of the devaluation of educational level, while the overall proportion of agents reaching the highest educational level increases (the proportion of upwardly agents is higher than in the model without the 'inflation' spiral; see also Appendix A, Table A.2g), the overall level of inequality of educational opportunity, as measured by the average generalised odds ratios, is virtually unchanged and so are the coefficients expressing the relative positions of the highest and the lowest group of agents (see columns 'agor', 'hggor', 'lggor', respectively).

That said, I would stress the exploratory value of the test performed. Rigorous study of the generative power of the two mechanisms representing the inflation spiral and its effect on individuals' belief updating would require testing the computational model against a distribution of empirical cross-tabulations covering a series of cohorts instead of using a cross-sectional cross-tabulation. This would certainly be a step forward in developing the present study.

OCCUPATIONAL STANDING AND OCCUPATIONAL STRATIFICATION BY COGNITIVE ABILITY

Min-Hsiung Huang

ABSTRACT

There is a popular psychometric thesis suggesting that people with different levels of cognitive ability end up in different occupations because some occupations require greater intelligence than others for successful performance. To examine several central claims of the psychometric thesis, this study uses two kinds of data for analysis: one is cross-sectional and occupation-level data from various sources dated as early as World War I and the other is longitudinal and individual-level data from the National Longitudinal Survey of Youth 1979 Cohort (NLSY79) and the Wisconsin Longitudinal Study (WLS) in the United States. Findings of this study suggest that occupational segregation by cognitive ability is much less intensive than that suggested by the psychometric theory, and there is no evidence of a trend of increasing cognitive partitioning by occupation over time.

Keywords: Cognitive ability; IQ; occupation; occupational prestige; WLS; NLSY79

Class and Stratification Analysis
Comparative Social Research, Volume 30, 101–127
Copyright © 2013 by Emerald Group Publishing Limited
All rights of reproduction in any form reserved
ISSN: 0195-6310/doi:10.1108/S0195-6310(2013)0000030008

INTRODUCTION

There is a psychometric theory of occupational inequalities, which suggests that some occupations require greater intelligence than others for success-ful performance; therefore, people who differ in cognitive ability end up in different occupations (Dawis, 1994; Gottfredson, 1997, 2000, 2003; Herrnstein & Murray, 1994; Jensen, 1980, 1998; Matarazzo, 1972; Tyler, 1965; Wechsler, 1958). The essence of this psychometric thinking involves the following five propositions:

First, average IQ scores of members of different occupations vary greatly because occupations differ in the complexity of their demands. The range of occupational mean IQ scores embraces 4.5 standard deviations, compared to a normal distribution of individual IQ scores that usually covers 6–8 standard deviations (Jensen, 1980, pp. 341–342).

Second, there is a high degree of correlation between average IQ by occupation and the prestige of occupations because a hierarchy of occupational prestige largely reflects the intelligence demanded by the various occupations (Jensen, 1998, pp. 292–293). Jensen (1980, p. 340) suggested a correlation of 0.90–0.95 between occupational prestige ratings and occupational average IQ scores.

Third, the range of IQ scores within occupations is much smaller than that within the general population. For example, Gottfredson (1997, p. 90) suggests that average standard deviation of IQ among individuals in an occupation is only about 50–58% as great as that in the general population.

Fourth, the higher the average IQ score of an occupation, the smaller the dispersion of IQ scores within the occupation (Gottfredson, 1997, p. 90; Jensen, 1998, p. 293). This occurs because only those who come from the upper end of the cognitive ability distribution are competent enough to succeed in high-status occupations. Unlike high-status occupations, low-status occupations do not require high intelligence. Thus, low-status occupa-tions could include people who range widely in cognitive ability distribution. This also leads to a hypothesis that "occupations differ more in the minimum than in the average IQ levels of their members" (Gottfredson, 1984, p. 27).

Fifth, the efficiency in sorting people to jobs by cognitive ability is expected to increase as a society becomes more industrialized and technolo-gically advanced. Advances in technology not only create a greater variety of jobs to be more freely pursued by individuals but also lead to better worker-job cognitive matches as individuals seeking better jobs, and employers searching for more able workers to maximize economic efficiency (Gottfredson, 2003; Herrnstein & Murray, 1994).

This study aims to address the foregoing five propositions that are key to the "modified functional" theory of occupational inequalities (Gottfredson, 1984, 1985, 1986). These five propositions imply that the importance of cognitive ability for occupational success is functional, critical, and fundamental. It is functionally important because cognitive ability has an actual impact on employment productivity. It is critically important because of the threshold property of IQ in relation to occupational status, and the critical thresholds of IQ scores are higher for occupations of higher status. Also, it is fundamentally important because the occupational prestige hierarchy is based primarily on occupational differences in the degree of intellectual difficulty.

The remainder of this paper is organized as follows. In the next section, I review the empirical studies used to support the foregoing five propositions. Then I introduce the data sets used for the present analysis. Subsequently, I report the findings of this study. The last section concludes.

SURVEY OF RESEARCH

The Range of Occupational Mean IQ

To report the range of occupational mean IQ scores, Jensen (1980) stated the following:

> To gain an accurate impression of the full range of mean intelligence differences between occupational levels, we must look at a representative sample of the working population that has not been previously selected on intelligence or education. The U.S. Department of Labor has obtained such information (See Manpower Administration, 1970). A representative sample of 39,600 of the employed U.S. labor force in the age range from 18 to 54 years was given the U.S. Employment Services General Aptitude Test Battery. The sample contains 444 of the specific occupations listed in the U.S. Department of Labor's Dictionary of Occupational Titles (1965). (pp. 341–342)

With this sample, Jensen (1980) reported that the IQ means of the 444 specific occupations range from 55 for tomato peelers to 143 for mathematicians. Because the overall mean General Aptitude Test Battery (GATB) General Intelligence score is 100 with a standard deviation of 20, Jensen suggested a range of occupational mean IQ as wide as 4.45 standard deviations, compared to a normal distribution of individual IQ scores that usually covers 6–8 standard deviations.

However, according to the *Manual for the USES General Aptitude Test Battery*, the GATB sample is not nationally representative, nor is it a sample of a given time point. Moreover, both test and occupational data were collected at the same time. Hauser (2002) further suggested that "the GATB data were collected somewhat haphazardly, over a period of years, from the late 1940s to the late 1960s, and in samples of highly variable size, definition, and quality" (p. 27). For these reasons, the findings of Jensen (1980) should be interpreted with caution.

Correlation between Occupational Mean IQ and Occupational Prestige

With respect to the correlation between occupational mean IQ and occupational prestige, Jensen (1980) posited that "correlations between average prestige ratings and average IQs in occupations are very high – .90 to .95 – when the averages are based on a large number of raters and a wide range of rated occupations" (p. 340). This statement, however, was made without the support of data including occupational average IQs of a wide range of rated occupations.

Jensen reported a correlation of 0.91 between the 1964 National Opinion Research Center (NORC) ratings of occupational prestige and the Barr scale of occupations. The Barr scale (Terman, 1925, p. 66) is a subjective measure of the level of cognitive demand in an occupation based on 20 judges and a total of 121 specific occupations. The Barr scale, therefore, is not equivalent to occupational mean IQs that are measured objectively.

The high degree of correlation of 0.91 between the Barr scale and the occupational prestige ratings may be due to the fact that the Barr scale, a subjective measure of intellectual demand in occupations, is more a measure of occupational prestige than a measure of occupational differentials in intellectual demand. For example, Hakel, Hollmann, and Ohnesorge (1971) found that when subjects are asked to rank occupations on the basis of incumbents' average intelligence, they often make incorrect decisions by choosing the more prestigious occupations as occupations of higher average intelligence. They concluded, "Prestige is so potent a factor that it obscures differences between occupations in intelligence unless those differences actually run parallel to differences in prestige" (Hakel et al., 1971, p. 71).

Dispersion of IQ Scores within Occupations

The extent of individual variation in IQ within occupations is indicative of the degree to which occupations are segregated by cognitive ability. Based on

80 job categories listed in Table 3 of the Wonderlic Personnel Test Manual (Wonderlic & Associates, 1983), Sackett and Ostgaard (1994) estimated that the standard deviation in IQ among the job applicant pools for all jobs is about 10% less than the standard deviation of IQ in the general population. Hunter, Schmidt, and Judiesch (1990, p. 38) analyzed data from 515 U.S. Employment Service studies and estimated that the standard deviation of IQ scores of incumbents is 71% as large as the standard deviation of the IQ scores of applicants. These two estimates together suggest that the average standard deviation in IQ among incumbents in an occupation is about 63% as large as the standard deviation of IQ in the general population. Gottfredson (1997, p. 90) came up with a different estimate, suggesting that the average standard deviation of IQ among incumbents in an occupation is only about 50–58% as large as in the general population.

Using data from the GATB – produced by the U.S. Department of Labor (1970) – a sample Jensen (1980) incorrectly claimed to be nationally representative, Jensen (1980) found that "analysis of variance shows that of the total population variance in test scores, 47 percent of it is variation between the means of occupations and 53 percent is individual variation within occupations" (p. 343). Jensen (1998) revised this statement in a later publication, suggesting that "since about 10 percent of the within-occupations variance is attributable to measurement error, the true within-occupations variance constitutes only 43 percent of the total G-score variance" (p. 293).

Correlation between Occupational Mean IQs and Intra-Occupational Variations of IQ

The study of Harrell and Harrell (1945) is among the first in reporting a decreasing pattern in within-occupation IQ variance as the standing of an occupation increases. They used the Army General Classification Test (AGCT) data from 18,782 white enlisted men of the U.S. Army Air Forces Air Service Command.[1] These enlisted men reported their previous civilian occupations, and this made possible for estimating AGCT means, medians, and standard deviations for a total of 74 occupations; within each occupation, there were at least 21 cases. Harrell and Harrell offered the following speculation: "Evidently a certain minimum of intelligence is required for any one of many occupations and a man must have that much intelligence in order to function in that occupation, but a man may have high intelligence and be found in a lowly occupation because he lacks other qualifications than intelligence" (p. 239). The negative correlation between

occupational mean AGCT scores and intra-occupational standard deviations of AGCT is as high as −0.89 in the study of Harrell and Harrell. Using
the U.S. Army records of 1944 for 81,553 white enlisted men, drawn from
227 civilian occupations, Stewart (1947) reported a negative correlation
between occupational hierarchy and AGCT variability within occupations
($r = -0.81$). That is, the lower the AGCT level of an occupation, the greater
the intra-occupational variability in AGCT.

These two early studies are often cited by researchers to support the
argument that persons with high intelligence can be found in nearly all
occupations, but persons with low intelligence can only be found in lowly
occupations (e.g., Herrnstein, 1971; Jensen, 1980). For example, Jensen
(1980) suggested that a certain threshold level of intelligence is necessary but
not sufficient for success in most occupations. Therefore, it is easier to predict
a person's occupational status if this person has a low IQ rather than a high
IQ. The nature of the correlation between IQ and occupational status,
according to Jensen (1980, p. 364), is that of the "twisted-pear" correlation
(Fisher, 1959; Storms, 1960). Because of the existence of the twisted-pear
correlation between IQ and occupation, Jensen suggested that the low partial
correlation between IQ and occupation (after holding educational attainment constant) does not contradict or invalidate the importance of the
threshold property of the relationship between IQ and occupation.

Jensen's (1980) interpretation of the negative correlation, while intriguing,
should be taken with caution. The negative correlation between the means
and the standard deviations of the AGCT scores across occupational levels
appeared in the military data may be a consequence of the low ceilings on
tests, along with the censoring of high scorers (military officers were not
tested). For example, Stewart (1947) suggested that:

> Because of the selective effect of deferments, rejections, and discharges, the Army
> population representing any given occupation was not the same as the total civilian
> population for that occupation. In addition, the fact that AGCT scores were not
> available for officers also tended to make the AGCT distributions for some occupations
> less completely representative of their counterparts in the total civilian population.
> Professional and higher-level non-professional occupations may be expected to have
> been particularly distorted. (p. 28)

Increasing Efficiency in Sorting People to Jobs by Cognitive Ability over Time

One key argument of *the Bell Curve* by Herrnstein and Murray (1994) is that
those with high intelligence are becoming separated from those of average

and below-average intelligence in the occupational sphere since 1940. Those with high IQs, according to Herrnstein and Murray, have become more concentrated in the "high-IQ professions," which include accountants, architects, chemists, college teachers, computer scientists, dentists, engineers, lawyers, mathematicians, natural scientists, physicians, and social scientists.

Based on the assumption that half of the incumbents of the high-IQ professions had IQs of 120 or higher throughout the period between 1900 and 1990, they showed that people with an IQ of 120 or higher have become more concentrated in these occupations. Herrnstein and Murray reported that "in 1900, the number of jobs in the high-IQ professions soaked up only about one out of twenty of these talented people. By 1990, they soaked up almost five times as many, or one out of four" (p. 55).

Huang (2001), however, found the conclusions of Herrnstein and Murray (1994) unconvincing. The assumption that half of the incumbents of the high-IQ professions *must* had IQs of 120 or higher throughout the period between 1900 and 1990, according to Huang, predetermines the finding of an increasing concentration of high-IQ persons in high-IQ professions over time. Using data from the General Social Survey, 1974–1998, Huang found a decrease in the average level of verbal ability among incumbents of high-IQ professions, as more and more people became engaged in these professions.

DATA

An ideal data set for this analysis would consist of several nationally representative longitudinal samples covering a time span of several decades and including the same IQ measures over time. In each nationally representative longitudinal sample, respondents are first interviewed during childhood and given a complete IQ test, after which respondents are regularly followed and interviewed until old age with their occupational information collected in every follow-up. In addition, each longitudinal sample should include a sufficient number of cases within each occupation, so the mean and the distribution of individual IQ scores within each occupation can be estimated correctly. Such ideal data, however, do not exist. In reality, data containing both measures of cognitive ability and occupational information are rare and less than ideal in many respects. Given these data limitations, the present study uses two kinds of data: one is cross-sectional and occupation-level data from various sources dated as early as World War I and the other is longitudinal and individual-level data from the National Longitudinal Survey of Youth 1979 Cohort (NLSY79) and the Wisconsin Longitudinal Study (WLS) in the United States.

Cross-Sectional Occupation-Level Data

Fryer (1922).
Empirical studies on the relationship between cognitive ability and occupation started as early as World War I, when a group test of intelligence, the Army Alpha, was used to screen World War I draftees and assign jobs. To present a list of "occupational-intelligence standards," Fryer (1922) collected data mainly from the U.S. Army, reaching a total of nearly 60,000 male respondents. In the Army data, respondent IQ score was based on (a) the Alpha test which was a paper-and-pencil group test with eight subtests used in the U.S. Army (Yerkes, 1921, pp. 219–234) and (b) the "Business Alpha" which is a 20-minute intelligence test designed and standardized for vocational and business purposes (Fryer, 1922, p. 276). Data on occupations are based on individuals' civilian occupations prior to entering the Army, and the Alpha test was administered after entering the Army. Based on these data, Fryer presented a list of 96 occupations with their average IQ scores and the score range between the first and the third quartile.

Pond (1933).
At the Scovill Manufacturing Company of Waterbury in Connecticut, all newly hired employees, and all those who were to be transferred to new projects, were given an intelligence test: either the Army Alpha or the Army Beta test. The Beta test was designed as an alternative to the Alpha test for those who were illiterate or had poor language skills. Pond (1933) collected data from the male employees who were hired or transferred into new work during the period from December 1, 1923, to December 31, 1928. The age of employees ranged from 16 to over 70, although most employees were aged between 20 and 40. The total number of employees is 9,075, and each occupation has at least 40 cases. Using the company data, Pond (1933) reported the number of incumbents in their position, mean IQ score, total range in IQ scores, and IQ scores at the 25th and the 75th percentiles for each occupation in a list of 44 occupations.

Stewart (1947).
One of the most extensive research projects addressing the segregation of occupations by cognitive ability was conducted by Stewart (1947). For each

occupation, Stewart reported the median score, the standard deviation, and the scores at the 10th, 25th, 50th, 75th, and 90th percentiles on the AGCT, based on 81,553 white enlisted men in 227 civilian occupations. Intra-occupational standard deviations in test scores and the individual test scores within an occupation at different percentiles were made available for 167 occupations only. For the standardization population, the AGCT has a mean of 100 and a standard deviation of 20.

Stewart's study was confined to white enlisted men who were not officers, which implies that the high-scoring members of the high-scoring occupations are less likely to have been included in the data. On the other hand, those with extremely low scores were not permitted to enlist in the military. Therefore, the Stewart data are truncated at both ends. The Stewart data on occupations were based on individuals' civilian occupations prior to entering the Army, and the AGCT test was administered after entering the Army.

U.S. Department of Labor (1970).
Another large set of data comes from the U.S. Employment Service (Table 9-2, U.S. Department of Labor, 1970). In this data set, cognitive ability is measured by the GATB, which has a mean of 100 and a standard deviation of 20 in the general population. This sample contains 444 occupations and includes 39,600 men and women, aged 18–54. The GATB sample is not nationally representative, nor is it a sample of a given time point. The GATB data were collected from the late 1940s to the late 1960s, and the samples collected vary in size and quality. Individual test results and occupational information were collected at the same time. The authors of the study stated: "The type of sample is designated as applicant, apprentice, employee, student, or trainee, representing the status of the individuals comprising the sample at the time when the tests were administered" (U.S. Department of Labor, 1970, p. 63). Therefore, not all respondents in the GATB sample were incumbents in a particular occupation.

Wonderlic, Inc. (2002).
Coming from a commercial source, the Wonderlic sample contains job applicant pools for 72 occupational categories listed in Table 3 of the *Wonderlic Personnel Test and Scholastic Level Exam User's Manual* (Wonderlic, Inc., 2002). The Wonderlic sample was gathered over several decades and it had a sample size of 80,417 male and female appli-cants who took the Wonderlic Personnel Test (WPT). The WPT is a

self-administered test containing 50 questions administered over exactly 12 minutes. The WPT was standardized based on the adult working population with a mean of 21.06 and a standard deviation of 7.12. The WPT scores were made comparable with test scores in the Wechsler Adult Intelligence Scale and the GATB (Wonderlic, Inc. 2002, p. 20). For each occupation, the study of Wonderlic Inc. (2002) listed the number of incumbents; the mean, the mode, and the standard deviation of individual WPT scores; and WPT scores at the 25th and the 75th percentiles. It should be noted that the Wonderlic sample consists of job applicants, not occupational incumbents.

For all the occupation-level data sets listed above, I assign each occupation a code based on the 1970 U.S. census occupational codes. Based on the occupational code, I also assign each occupation a two-digit Hodge–Siegel–Rossi occupational prestige score (Hodge, Siegel, & Rossi, 1964). This is for estimating the correlation between occupational prestige ratings and occupational mean IQ levels. Among all the five data sets listed above, only the Wonderlic sample (Wonderlic, Inc., 2002) and the GATB sample (U.S. Department of Labor, 1970) include female respondents. Because cognitive ability and occupational information of respondents were measured and collected at the same time point, all occupation-level data sources listed above share one common disadvantage: the ordering of occupations by mean IQ reflects not only the screening of occupations by innate ability but also the influence of educational and occupational experience on cognitive development. It is possible that intelligence is a result rather than a cause of occupational differences. For example, some sociological studies found that job complexity has a positive impact on intellectual skills; furthermore, the influence of job on intellectual skills is greater than the reverse (Kohn & Schooler, 1973, 1978, 1982; Kohn, Naoi, Schoenbach, Schooler, & Slomczynski, 1990).

Individual-Level Data

The occupation-level data sets listed above were not based on a nationally representative sample and a research design in which respondent cognitive abilities were measured before they entered the labor market. Therefore, in this analysis, I use panel data from the NLSY79. Because data from the NLSY79 used in this analysis are limited to those aged 25-42 years, I also use panel data from the WLS, which is a state-representative sample. The NLSY79 includes male and female respondents, as does the WLS.

The National Longitudinal Survey of Youth 1979 Cohort

The NLSY79 was designed to represent the noninstitutionalized civilian part of young people living in the United States in 1979 and born between 1957 and 1964. The NLSY79 respondents were first interviewed in 1979 and were followed and interviewed annually until 1994 and biennially since. However, data collected in and after the 2002 follow-up survey are not used for analysis because respondent occupations are based on the 2000 U.S. census occupational codes, which differ from the 1980 U.S. census occupational codes used in the NLSY79 before 2002.

The NLSY79 data for a single year does not have a sufficiently large sample size to address the proposed research questions. To obtain a better approximation, I treat each person-year as a separate observation, from the 1983 NLSY79 to the 2000 NLSY79, including only those persons aged 25–42. All occupations with a sample size of less than 15 different members are excluded from the analysis. Therefore, the total sample provides 118,179 observations, based on 11,279 respondents who worked in 369 occupations. These 118,179 observations include repeated measures of the same individual within occupations, as well as repeated measures of the same individual differently employed. The fact that there are some repeated measures of the same individual within occupations indicates that some respondents did not change their occupations for some years, while the fact that there are a number of repeated measures of the same individual between occupations indicates that some respondents changed occupations as they aged. When repeated measures of the same individual within occupations are excluded, the sample size is reduced to 63,809 observations. Therefore, two sets of data are analyzed with respect to the NLSY79: one has a sample of 118,179, including 60,652 male and 57,527 female observations, while the other has a sample size of 63,809, including 32,966 male and 30,843 female observations. When there is a concern that respondent gender may make a difference in results, I analyze the male sample only. In the male sample, the total number of occupations for analysis is reduced to 304, and within each of these 304 occupations, there are more than 15 different individual respondents.

In each survey year of NLSY79, a set of sampling weights is constructed to provide an estimate of how many individuals in the United States each respondent represents. Thus, sampling weights are applied when analyzing data from the NLSY79.

The Armed Services Vocational Aptitude Battery (ASVAB) was administered in 1980 to NLSY79 respondents aged 15–22 years. The ASVAB consists of a battery of 10 tests. To obtain an Armed Forces

Qualifications Test (AFQT) score for each respondent, I follow a calculation procedure to produce the 1989 revised AFQT scores, which are derived from the verbal and mathematical components of the ASVAB (Zagorsky & White, 1999). The AFQT is a general measure of training potentiality and used to screen applications for the Armed Forces in the United States. According to Herrnstein and Murray (1994), the AFQT is a good measure of general cognitive ability. Like Herrnstein and Murray, I create age-equated AFQT scores based on separate distributions by birth year (Herrnstein & Murray, 1994, p. 570). I correct age-equated AFQT scores for skew and transform them to have a mean of 100 and a standard deviation of 15. Similarly, I set all scores greater or smaller than three standard deviations from the mean at three standard deviations.

The Wisconsin Longitudinal Study
The WLS has a history of more than 50 years and is still ongoing.[2] The fifth WLS follow-up study was scheduled for 2010, when the primary respondents (a random sample of a third of all high school graduates of 1957 in Wisconsin) were around 71 years old. Survey data were collected from these graduates or their parents in 1957, 1964, 1975, 1992, 2004, and 2010. In 1977, survey data from a subsample of 2,000 siblings of the primary respondents were collected. In the 1992-1993 round of the WLS, the sample was expanded to include a randomly selected sibling of every primary respondent who has at least one brother or sister.

Respondents' test scores were obtained from records of the Wisconsin State Testing Service, which routinely and almost universally assessed the performance of Wisconsin secondary school students on the Henson-Nelson Test of Mental Ability from 1933 to the late 1950s or early 1960s. Almost all of the 1957 graduates took the Henmon-Nelson test in the junior year of high school, but for their siblings, the test was sometimes taken in the senior or sophomore year. The main disadvantage in using test score data from the WLS is the truncation of the educational distribution at the lower end, because high school graduation rates were 75–80% among men, and higher among women, in Wisconsin in 1957. In addition to the disadvantage of truncation, not all respondents, especially siblings, took the Henmon-Nelson test in the same year. Because some respondents took the Henmon-Nelson test in both the freshman and junior years, junior year raw scores on the Henmon-Nelson test for all of the graduates and siblings were estimated. These raw scores were then again normalized to a set of IQ equivalents, based on the percentile distribution of Henmon-Nelson scores of all Wisconsin high school juniors in 1951 (Hauser, 2002). Because of the truncation and the normalization of scores, the Henmon-Nelson test scores in the WLS are not equivalent to the AFQT scores in the NLSY79.

To rank occupations by incumbents' Henmon-Nelson IQ, I use data from the graduates as well as a random subsample of their brothers and sisters. I treat each person-year or person-job as a separate observation, from respondent's first job in young adulthood to respondent's current job in ages 53–54 in the early 1990s, based on the 1970 census occupational classification. Occupational information collected in and after the follow-up of 2004 is not used for analysis because many respondents have already retired from their jobs. All occupations with a sample size of less than 15 different members are excluded from the analysis. This treatment of data results in 99,659 observations, based on 15,429 respondents (including 9,577 graduates and 5,852 sibling respondents), employed in 261 occupations. These 99,659 observations include repeated measures of the same respondent within occupations, as well as repeated measures of the same respondent between occupations. When the repeated measures of the same individual within occupations are excluded, the sample size is reduced to 40,528 observations. Thus, two sets of data are analyzed with respect to the WLS: one based on a total number of 99,659 observations and the other based on a total number of 40,528 observations.

RESULTS

Occupational Differences in Mean and Minimum IQ

Every occupation-level data set used in this study provides the 25th percentile score within each occupation; therefore, a cognitive test score at the 25th percentile is taken as the minimum IQ of an occupation. For each data set used, occupations are ranked by mean and by minimum IQ (score at the 25th percentile) of their members, and some selective results are presented in Figs. 1–5 for data sets with more than 95 occupations. Each of these figures is based on a specific data set, which includes a large number of occupations and covers a wide range of occupational prestige ratings. In each figure, from Figs. 1 to 5, I add a note on the range of occupational prestige scores, indicating that a wide range of occupational prestige is covered.

When occupations are ranked by mean IQ scores of their members, a nonlinear slope appears, as demonstrated in Figs. 1–4. The slope gradually becomes upwardly steeper as it reaches the top; it also gradually becomes

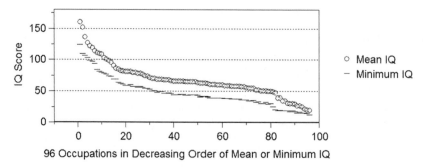

Fig. 1. Occupational Differences in Mean and Minimum IQ 96 Occupations Listed by Fryer (1922). *Note 1*: Occupational Minimum IQ is the IQ Score of the Incumbent Performing at the 25th Percentile within an Occupation. *Note 2*. The Occupational Prestige Scores Range from 14 (Farrier) to 82 (Physician).

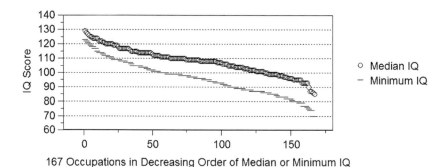

Fig. 2. Occupational Differences in Median and Minimum IQ 167 Occupations Listed by Stewart (1947). *Note 1*: Occupational Minimum IQ is the IQ Score of the Incumbent Performing at the 25th Percentile within an Occupation. *Note 2*: The Occupational Prestige Scores Range from 12 (Teamster) to 82 (Physician).

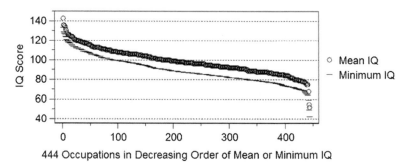

Fig. 3. Occupational Differences in Mean and Minimum IQ 444 Occupations Listed by U.S. Department of Labor (1970). *Note 1*: Occupational Minimum IQ is the IQ Score of the Incumbent Performing at the 25th Percentile within an Occupation. *Note 2*: The Occupational Prestige Scores Range from 12 (Charwoman) to 82 (Physician).

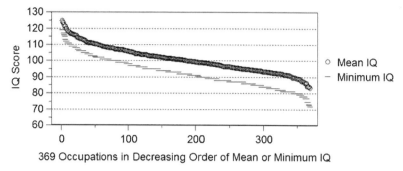

Fig. 4. Occupational Differences in Mean and Minimum IQ 369 Occupations in NLSY79, Age 25–42, $N = 118,179$. *Note 1*: Occupational Minimum IQ is the IQ Score of the Incumbent Performing at the 25th Percentile within an Occupation. *Note 2*: Occupational Prestige Scores Range from 17 (Food Preparation) to 86 (Physician).

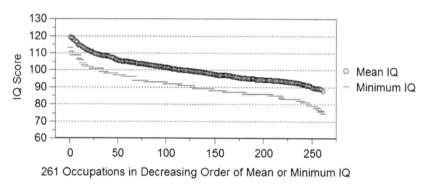

Fig. 5. Occupational Differences in Mean and Minimum IQ 261 Occupations in WLS, Age 54 or Less, $N = 99,659$. *Note 1*: Occupational Minimum IQ is the IQ Score of the Incumbent Performing at the 25th Percentile within an Occupation. *Note 2*: Occupational Prestige Scores Range from 17 (Charwoman) to 82 (Physician).

downwardly steeper as it reaches the bottom. Occupational differences in mean IQ are expanded by a few occupations that have very high mean scores and a number of occupations that have very low mean scores. Occupations are not equally spaced along the slope; differences in mean IQ between adjacent occupations are larger at the extremes of the range than they are in the middle.

Using data from the WLS, Fig. 5 shows a somewhat different nonlinear slope when 261 occupations are ranked by the mean IQ of their members. The slope gradually acquires a steeper upward slope as it reaches the top, but it does not gradually acquire a steeper downward slope as it reaches the bottom. This may be due to the fact that all WLS respondents are high school graduates and low-scoring occupations are not well represented in the WLS.

Occupations listed in the studies of Pond (1933) and Wonderlic, Inc. (2002) do not generate a similar nonlinear slope as presented in Figs. 1–4; an inconsistency that may be due to a very small number of occupations available for ranking in these two studies. The results based on the NLSY79 and the WLS, as presented in Figs. 4 and 5, are not significantly affected by excluding repeated measures of the same individual within occupations.

The majority of mid-range occupations do not differ substantially in mean IQ. For example, 54% of all 444 occupations listed in the study of U.S. Department of Labor (1970) have mean GATB scores that lie in a relatively small range, between 89 and 109, within 1 standard deviation of the GATB scores in the general population. For another example, in the NLSY79, about 65% of all occupations have mean AFQT scores of between 92.5 and 107.5: a score range equivalent to one standard deviation of the AFQT scores in the general population.

A comparison between a perfect normal distribution and several distributions of occupational mean IQ scores is demonstrated in Fig. 6, using data from the AGCT (Stewart, 1947), the GATB (U.S. Department of Labor, 1970), the NLSY79, and the WLS. As Fig. 6 shows, relative to a perfect normal distribution, the distribution of occupational mean IQ scores

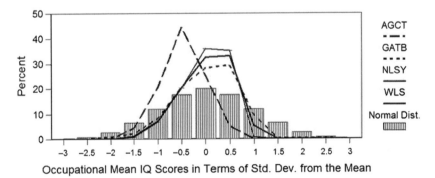

Occupational Mean IQ Scores in Terms of Std. Dev. from the Mean

Fig. 6. Comparing a Perfect Normal Distribution with Percentage Distribution of Occupation Mean IQ Scores: AGCT, GATB, NLSY79, and WLS. *Notes*: The Normal Distribution is in Bars. The AGCT Sample Has 222 Occupations (Stewart, 1947). The GATB Sample Has 444 Occupations (U.S. Department of Labor, 1970). The NLSY and the WLS Samples Have 369 and 261 Occupations, Respectively.

is much narrower and has a higher center peak; that is, there is a higher frequency of values near the mean. In the NLSY79 and the WLS, the range of occupational mean IQ scores embraces only 2.5 standard deviations, compared to a range of 6–8 standard deviations in individual IQ score distribution of the general population. In the AGCT sample, it covers only 2 standard deviations.

Another way to demonstrate occupational differences in their members' IQ scores is to display individual IQ score distributions for members of high scoring, low scoring, and other occupations. Using data from the NLSY79, the most recent data and thus should reveal the most intensive cognitive partitioning by occupation, Fig. 7 shows the AFQT percentage distributions of members in the top 12 high-scoring occupations, bottom 12 low-scoring occupations, and the rest of the occupations. These three distributions largely overlap. Some members of the low-scoring occupations have the same, or higher, IQ scores as those in the top-scoring occupations.

The hypothesis that occupations differ more in the minimum than in the mean IQ levels of their members is generally not supported, as indicated in Table 1. Only the study of Stewart (1947) demonstrates a somewhat larger standard deviation in minimum IQ scores than in mean IQ scores.

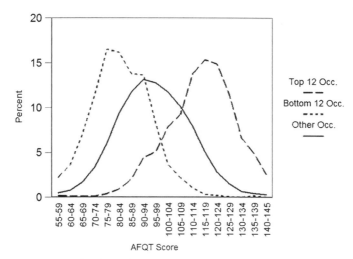

Fig. 7.   AFQT Distributions of Persons in High-Scoring, Low-Scoring, and Other Occupations in NLSY 1983–2000, Age 25–42. *Note*: I Treat Each Person-Year as a Separate Observation, from the 1983 NLSY to the 2000 NLSY, Including Only Those Who Are of Age 25 or Older.

Table 1. Mean and Standard Deviation of Occupational Mean and
Minimum IQ Scores.

Data Source	Occupational Mean IQs		Occupational Minimum IQs	
	Mean	Std. Dev.	Mean	Std. Dev.
Fryer (1922)	67.8	27.1	47.4	23.0
Pond (1933)	133.4	13.4	120.6	14.6
Stewart (1947)	108.0	9.2	95.8	11.7
U.S. Department of Labor (1970)	98.9	12.8	89.4	13.3
Wonderlic, Inc. (2002)	21.9	3.8	17.3	4.0
NLSY79 ($N=118,179$)	100.1	8.2	92.5	8.9
NLSY79 ($N=63,809$)	97.5	7.6	88.2	7.8
WLS ($N=99,659$)	100.1	7.0	90.8	7.4
WLS ($N=40,528$)	100.3	6.6	90.9	7.0

Notes: Different IQ measures are used in different studies. Occupational minimum IQ score refers to the 25th percentile score within an occupation. As indicated in the text, the Wonderlic Personnel Test (WPT) was standardized based on the adult working population with a mean of 21.06 and a standard deviation of 7.12.

Occupational Prestige and Occupational Mean IQ

Table 2 shows that the correlation between occupational prestige ratings and occupational average IQ scores is around 0.7 or lower for the data sets used in this study. This is much lower than a correlation of 0.95 suggested by Jensen (1980, p. 340).

It should be noted that a correlation of 0.7 reported in this study does not necessarily reflect the degree of consistency between the hierarchy of occupational prestige and the ordering of occupational differences in terms of the demand for cognitive ability. A correlation between two aggregated variables, as displayed in Table 2, tends to conceal intra-group variation and is often much stronger than a correlation between two nonaggregate variables (Raudenbush & Bryk, 2002). This is known as an ecological fallacy. A nonaggregate level analysis would yield a much lower correlation than those presented in Table 2. Hauser (2002), for example, analyzed individual-level data from the WLS and reported a correlation of 0.45 between occupational status and the Henmon-Nelson IQ test scores after corrected for unreliability in the IQ test.

The correlation between occupational prestige and occupational mean IQ may not take place naturally through occupational demands for cognitive ability. The correlation may exist because initial admission to many

Table 2. Correlations between Occupational Prestige, Occupational Mean/Median IQ, and the Intra-Occupational Standard Deviation of IQ.

	Prestige	Mean IQ
Fryer (1922), 96 occupations		
Prestige		
Mean IQ	0.68***	
Std. Dev.	0.42***	0.60***
Pond (1933), 44 occupations		
Prestige		
Mean IQ	0.33*	
Std. Dev.	−0.12	−0.39**
Stewart (1947), 167 occupations		
Prestige		
Mean IQ	0.60***	
Std. Dev.	−0.47***	−0.81***
U.S. Department of Labor (1970), 444 occupations		
Prestige		
Mean IQ	0.65***	
Std. Dev.	−0.24***	−0.26***
Wonderlic, Inc. (2002), 72 occupations		
Prestige		
Mean IQ	0.63***	
Std. Dev.	−0.15	−0.32**
NLSY79, N = 118,179, 369 occupations		
Prestige		
Mean IQ	0.74***	
Std. Dev.	−0.09	0.00
NLSY79, N = 63,809, 369 occupations		
Prestige		
Mean IQ	0.72***	
Std. Dev.	0.16**	0.18***
NLSY79, N = 60,652, men only, 304 occupations		
Prestige		
Mean IQ	0.71***	
Std. Dev.	−0.30***	−0.10
NLSY79, N = 32,966, men only, 304 occupations		
Prestige		
Mean IQ	0.72***	
Std. Dev.	−0.06	0.05
WLS, N = 99,659, 261 occupations		
Prestige		
Mean IQ	0.73***	
Std. Dev.	−0.14	−0.02
WLS, N = 40,528, 261 occupations		
Prestige		
Mean IQ	0.74***	
Std. Dev.	−0.18**	−0.06

*Significance levels: 5%.
**Significance levels: 1%.
***Significance levels: 0.1%.

prestigious occupations depends on test scores (Neisser et al., 1996, p. 87). Occupational differences in mean IQ can be structured by the fact that test scores are used for admission to higher education and job entry, whether or not the use of test scores for admission is truly necessary and rational.

Individual Variation in IQ within Occupations

Based on an analysis of variance, Table 3 reports the percentage of total variance in test scores that occurs within occupations for most data sets used this study.[3] Because the standard deviation of individual test scores within an occupation was not reported in the studies of Fryer (1922) and Pond (1933), these two data sets cannot be used for an analysis of variance. Using data from the GATB collected by the U.S. Department of Labor (1970), I estimate that 46% of the total variation in GATB scores is individual variation within occupations, and it is 49% when Stewart's (1947) AGCT data are analyzed. For the rest of the three data sets, as

Table 3.   Percent of Total Variance in Individual IQ Scores that Occurs within and between Occupations with Correction for Unreliability in the IQ Tests.

	% within Occupations	% between Occupations
Stewart (1947), 167 occupations		
AGCT	49	51
U.S. Department of Labor (1970), 444 occupations		
GATB	46	54
Wonderlic, Inc. (2002), 72 occupations		
WPT	76	24
NLSY79, 369 occupations, N = 118,179		
AFQT	74	26
NLSY79, 369 occupations, N = 63,809		
AFQT	80	20
NLSY79, 304 occupations, men only, N = 60,652		
AFQT	68	32
NLSY79, 304 occupations, men only, N = 32,966		
AFQT	76	24
WLS, 261 occupations, N = 99,659		
Henmon-Nelson IQ	79	21
WLS, 261 occupations, N = 40,528		
Henmon-Nelson IQ	82	18

Table 3 shows, the percentage of total variance in test scores that occurs within occupations is much higher, 76% in the WPT data from the study of Wonderlic, Inc. (2002), 68–80% in the NLSY79, and 79–82% in the WLS. A higher percentage found in these three data sources may be, in part, due to the inclusion of female respondents. There is as much variation in IQ scores for women as there is for men; however, women traditionally find themselves employ in a small number of occupations. The inclusion of female respondents, therefore, is likely to result in a higher percentage of total variance in test scores that occurs within occupations. This gendered explanation, however, is not supported by the GATB sample. The GATB sample includes both men and women, but it does not bring about a higher percentage of total variance in test scores that occurs within occupations.

To examine whether respondent gender makes a difference in results, I use data from the NLSY79 and exclude all female respondents, and the results are presented in Table 3. Before excluding all female observations, the percentage of total variance in test scores that occurs within occupations is 74% in the sample, which includes repeated measures of the same individual within occupations ($N = 118,179$), and it is 80% in the sample that does not include repeated measures of the same individual within occupations ($N = 63,809$). After excluding all female observations, these two percentages are reduced to 68% and 76%, respectively. Therefore, when female respondents are excluded, the percentage of total variance in test scores that occurs within occupations decreases modestly.

Intra-Occupational Dispersion of IQ and Level of Occupational Prestige

This section presents results regarding whether or not the intra-occupational standard deviation of IQ tends to be smaller for occupations that have higher social standing and higher mean IQ levels. Only in the study of Stewart (1947), as indicated in Table 2, was there a highly negative correlation between occupational mean IQs and intra-occupational standard deviation of IQs. Because women encompass the full range of IQ and are more likely to concentrate on a few white-collar occupations (such as teachers, nurses, secretaries, and librarians) that are primarily found in the upper-middle range of the occupational hierarchy, the inclusion of female respondents could diminish the negative correlation. The WLS, the NLSY79, the Wonderlic, and the GATB samples include men and women, and none of these data sets shows a very strong negative correlation between occupational mean IQ and intra-occupational standard deviations of IQ, as indicated in Table 2.

The NLSY79 sample includes male and female respondents and a large number of occupations that encompass the full range of occupational prestige ratings. Therefore, it is possible to test whether the exclusion of female respondents would result in a negative correlation between occupational mean IQ scores (or occupational prestige) and intra-occupational standard deviation of IQ scores. The results are presented in Table 2. Before excluding all female observations, the correlation between occupational prestige and intra-occupational standard deviation in IQ scores is -0.09 in the NLSY79 sample, which includes repeated measures of the same individual within occupations ($N = 118,179$). When all female observations are excluded, however, the negative correlation turns higher ($r = -0.3$) and reaches statistical significance. Therefore, the negative correlation between occupational standing (either occupational prestige or occupational mean IQ) and the intra-occupational standard deviation of IQ, if such a correlation exists, is modest and confined to men in the labor force. When female respondents are included, the modest negative correlation falls to zero.

Changes in Cognitive Partitioning by Occupation over Time

This study uses data sets collected at different points in time. Early data sources include the studies of Fryer (1922), Pond (1933), Stewart (1947), and the U.S. Department of Labor (1970), followed by the study of Wonderlic, Inc. (2002) and data from the WLS, whereas the NLSY79 is the most recent data set used in this analysis. If cognitive partitioning by occupation has become more intensive over time, the correlation between occupational prestige and occupational mean IQ should have increased, the percentage of total variance in IQ test scores that occurs within occupations should have decreased, and occupational differences in the mean IQ scores of their members should have been magnified. This study, however, does not find these changes over time. This finding is consistent with that of Strenze (2007) who conducted a meta-analysis of the longitudinal studies that have examined the predictive power of cognitive ability on socioeconomic success. Neither did Strenze find an increasing predictive power of cognitive ability on occupational success over time.

CONCLUSION

The extent to which occupations sort people by IQ has been studied for decades. This line of research contains five key questions. First, to what extent do occupations differ in average measured cognitive ability of their members? Second, to what extent are high-scoring occupations those of higher prestige? Third, to what extent do people in the same occupation have similar IQs? Fourth, do cognitive requirements create a "floor" for the IQ scores of the people who eventually become incumbents of the occupation? Finally, has cognitive partitioning by occupation increased over time?

In response to these questions, the conventional psychometric wisdom suggests that occupations are highly segregated by cognitive ability. Occupational differentials in cognitive ability are a direct result of occupational differentials in minimum IQ threshold for successful task performance. Because occupations differ in intellectual demands and society rewards talent and merit, the occupational prestige hierarchy mainly reflects occupational differences in the degree of intellectual difficulty.

Findings of this study, however, challenge the conventional psychometric wisdom. This study finds that the distribution of individual IQ test scores within an occupation largely overlaps with the same distribution of another occupation. The magnitude of occupational differences in mean IQ is mainly driven by a handful of high-scoring occupations on the top and a few low-scoring occupations on the bottom. For the great majority of occupations in the middle range, they differ modestly in mean IQ. The correlation between the two aggregate variables, occupational prestige ratings and occupational mean IQ scores, is much lower than what was suggested by Jensen (1980). The variation in IQ within occupations is very large; about three-fourths of the variation in IQ is individual variation within occupations. Top-scoring occupations have intra-occupational standard deviations of IQ as large as those in other occupations. This study also finds no support for a trend of increasing cognitive partitioning by occupation over time.

This study finds a modest degree of occupational segregation by cognitive ability. This modest degree of segregation, however, does not necessarily represent the degree of an actual impact of cognitive ability on occupational success – an impact, according to the psychometric theory, takes place naturally and functionally due to occupational demands on intellectual ability. In a test-centered society in which people believe that the use of tests is both fair and efficient, ability testing has been institutionalized for admission to higher education and job entry. In such a society, market competition for entering prestigious occupations favors individuals whose high-IQ scores permit them to succeed an entrance exam and attend prestigious colleges, even though a high IQ may not actually be necessary for satisfactory performance in a prestigious occupation. Therefore, a high concentration of high-IQ persons in one particular occupation does not necessarily suggest that this occupation must involve a high degree of work complexity and that only persons with very high IQs can meet the cognitive demands.

The importance of personality traits (or noncognitive skills) on occupational success has increasingly been recognized (Bowles, Gintis, & Osborne, 2001; Cobb-Clark & Tan, 2011; Heckman, Stixrud, & Urzua, 2006). Bowles et al. (2001), for example, find that the noncognitive component of the returns to schooling is much larger than that of the cognitive component. People with different levels of cognitive ability from diverse social background compete for high-paying and prestigious positions. In such competitive conditions, cognitive ability matters, but many other factors such as helpful social and economic networks and resources, occupational aspiration, persistence, special talents, and educational credentials also play an important role in shaping occupational stratification.

ACKNOWLEDGMENT

I thank two anonymous reviewers for their helpful comments on an earlier version of this paper.

NOTES

1. The AGCT of the World War II is an improved version of the Army Alpha test used in the World War I. The AGCT aims to measure general learning ability that could be used to assign new recruits to jobs. The AGCT contains four subtests: verbal, arithmetic computation, arithmetic reasoning, and pattern analysis (Zeidner & Drucker, 1983).

2. See Hauser (2009) and Huang and Hauser (2010) for an introduction of the WLS.

3. Estimates presented in Table 3 are corrected for unreliability in the IQ tests, using a reliability measure of 0.84 for the Henmon-Nelson IQ score, 0.94 for the AFQT, 0.91 for the WPT, 0.83 for the GATB, and 0.90 for the AGCT. These reliability measures are from several sources. Hauser and Palloni (2011) report a reliability of 0.84 in the Henmon-Nelson IQ test. The reliability estimates of the AFQT, ranging from 0.93 to 0.94, are reported on the official site of the ASVAB (http://www.official-asvab.com/reliability_res.htm#table2). As to the WPT, reliabilities range between 0.88 and 0.94 (McKelvie, 1989; Wheeless & Serpento, 1982).

Reliability measures of the GATB range from 0.79 to 0.93 (Jaeger, Linn, & Tesh, 1989, p. 316). Capshew (1999, p. 103) suggests a reliability estimate of 0.90 for the AGCT.

REFERENCES

Bowles, S., Gintis, H., & Osborne, M. (2001). The determinants of earnings: A behavioral approach. *Journal of Economic Literature, 22*(4), 1137–1176. doi:10.1257/jel.39.4.1137.

Capshew, J. H. (1999). *Psychologist on the march: Science, practice, and professional identity in America, 1929–1969*. Cambridge: Cambridge University Press.

Cobb-Clark, D. A., & Tan, M. (2011). Noncognitive skills, occupational attainment, and relative wages. *Labour Economics, 18*(1), 1–13. doi:10.1016/j.labeco.2010.07.003.

Dawis, R. V. (1994). Occupations. In R. J. Sternberg (Ed.), *Encyclopedia of human intelligence* (Vol. 2, pp. 781–785). New York: Macmillan.

Fisher, J. (1959). The twisted pear and the prediction of behavior. *Journal of Consulting Psychology, 23*(5), 400–405. doi:10.1037/h0044080.

Fryer, D. (1922). Occupational-intelligence standards. *School and Society, 16*, 273–277.

Gottfredson, L. S. (1984). *The role of intelligence and education in the division of labor.* Report No. 355, Johns Hopkins University, Center for Social Organization of Schools, Baltimore, MD.

Gottfredson, L. S. (1985). Education as a valid but fallible signal of worker quality: Reorienting an old debate about the functional basis of the occupational hierarchy. In A. C. Kerckhoff (Ed.), *Research in sociology of education and socialization* (Vol. 5, pp. 123–169). Greenwich, CT: JAI Press.

Gottfredson, L. S. (1986). Societal consequences of the g factor in employment. *Journal of Vocational Behavior, 29*, 379–410. doi:10.1016/j.bbr.2011.03.031.

Gottfredson, L. S. (1997). Why g matters: The complexity of everyday life. *Intelligence, 24*(1), 79–132. doi:10.1016/S0160-2896(97)90014-3.

Gottfredson, L. S. (2000). Intelligence. In E. F. Borgatta & R. J. V. Montgomery (Eds.), *Encyclopedia of sociology* (2nd ed., pp. 1359–1386). New York: Macmillan.

Gottfredson, L. S. (2003). G, jobs, and life. In H. Nyborg (Ed.), *The scientific study of general intelligence: Tribute to Arthur R. Jensen* (pp. 293–342). New York, NY: Pergamon.

Hakel, M. D., Hollmann, T. D., & Ohnesorge, J. P. (1971). Relative influence of prestige as a determiner of intelligence judgments for occupations. *Journal of Vocational Behavior, 1*(1), 69–74. doi:10.1016/0001-8791(71)90007-8.

Harrell, T. W., & Harrell, M. S. (1945). Army general classification test scores for civilian occupations. *Educational and Psychological Measurement, 5*(3), 229–239. doi:10.1177/001316444500500303.

Hauser, R. M. (2002). *Meritocracy, cognitive ability, and the sources of occupational success.* CDE Working Paper 98-07, University of Wisconsin-Madison, Center for Demography and Ecology, Madison, WI.

Hauser, R. M. (2009). The Wisconsin longitudinal study: Designing a study of the life course. In H. G. Elder Jr. & J. Z. Giele (Eds.), *The craft of life course research* (pp. 29–50). New York: Guilford Press.

Hauser, R. M., & Palloni, A. (2011). Adolescent IQ and survival in the Wisconsin longitudinal study. *The Journals of Gerontology, Series B: Psychological sciences and social sciences, 66B*(S1), 91–101. doi:10.1093/geronb/gbr037.

Heckman, J. J., Stixrud, J., & Urzua, S. (2006). The effects of cognitive and noncognitive abilities on labor market outcomes and social behavior. *Journal of Labor Economics*, *24*(3), 411–482. doi:10.1086/504455.

Herrnstein, R. J. (1971). *I.Q. The Atlantic Monthly*, *228*(3), 43–64.

Herrnstein, R. J., & Murray, C. (1994). *The bell curve: Intelligence and class structure in American life*. New York: Free Press.

Hodge, R. W., Siegel, P. M., & Rossi, P. H. (1964). Occupational prestige in the United States, 1925–63. *American Journal of Sociology*, *70*(3), 286–302. doi:10.1086/223840.

Huang, M.- H. (2001). Cognitive abilities and the growth of high-IQ occupations. *Social Science Research*, *30*(4), 529–551. doi:10.1016/j.bbr.2011.03.031.

Huang, M.-H., & Hauser, T. S. (2010). Tracking persons from high school through adult life: Lessons from the Wisconsin longitudinal study. *EurAmerica*, *40*(2), 311–358.

Hunter, J. E., Schmidt, F. L., & Judiesch, M. K. (1990). Individual differences in output variability as a function of job complexity. *Journal of Applied Psychology*, *70*(1), 28–42. doi:10.1037/0021-9010.75.1.28.

Jaeger, R. M., Linn, R. L., & Tesh, A. S. (1989). A synthesis of research on some psychometric properties of the GATB. In J. A. Hartigan & A. K. Wigdor (Eds.), *Fairness in employment testing: Validity generalization, minority issues, and the general aptitude test battery* (pp. 303–324). Washington, DC: National Academy Press.

Jensen, A. R. (1980). *Bias in mental testing*. New York: Free Press.

Jensen, A. R. (1998). *The g factor: The science of mental ability*. Westport: Praeger.

Kohn, M. L., Naoi, A., Schoenbach, C., Schooler, C., & Slomczynski, K. M. (1990). Position in the class structure and psychological functioning in the United States, Japan, and Poland. *The American Journal of Sociology*, *95*(4), 964–1008. doi:10.1086/229382.

Kohn, M. L., & Schooler, C. (1973). Occupational experience and psychological functioning: An assessment of reciprocal effects. *American Sociological Review*, *38*(1), 97–118. doi:10.2307/2094334.

Kohn, M. L., & Schooler, C. (1978). The reciprocal effects of the substantive complexity of work and intellectual flexibility: A longitudinal assessment. *The American Journal of Sociology*, *84*(1), 24–52. doi:10.1086/226739.

Kohn, M. L., & Schooler, C. (1982). Job conditions and personality: A longitudinal assessment of their reciprocal effects. *The American Journal of Sociology*, *87*(6), 1257–1286. doi:10.1086/227593.

McKelvie, S. J. (1989). The Wonderlic personnel test: Reliability and validity in an academic setting. *Psychological Reports*, *65*, 161–162. doi:10.2466/pr0.1989.65.1.161.

Matarazzo, J. D. (1972). *Wechsler's measurement and appraisal of adult intelligence* (5th ed.). Oxford, England: Oxford University Press.

Neisser, U., Boodoo, G., Bouchard, T. J. J., Boykin, A. W., Brody, N., Ceci, S. J., & Urbina, S. (1996). Intelligence: Knowns and unknowns. *American Psychologist*, *51*(2), 77–101. doi:10.1037/0003-066X.51.2.77.

Pond, M. (1933). Occupations, intelligence, age and schooling: Their relationship and distribution in a factory population. *The Personnel Journal*, *11*(6), 373–382.

Raudenbush, S. W., & Bryk, A. S. (2002). *Hierarchical linear models: Applications and data analysis methods* (2nd ed.). Thousand Oaks, CA: Sage Publications.

Sackett, P. R., & Ostgaard, D. J. (1994). Job-specific applicant pools and national norms for cognitive ability tests: Implications for range restriction corrections in validation research. *Journal of Applied Psychology*, *79*(5), 680–684. doi:10.1037/0021-9010.79.5.680.

Stewart, N. (1947). A.G.C.T. scores of army personnel grouped by occupation. *Occupations, 26*, 5–41. doi:10.1002/j.2164-5892.1947.tb00820.x.

Storms, L. H. (1960). Rationales for the twisted pear. *Journal of Consulting Psychology, 24*(6), 552–553. doi:10.1037/h0043285.

Strenze, T. (2007). Intelligence and socioeconomic success: A meta-analytic review of longitudinal research. *Intelligence, 35*(5), 401–426. doi:10.1016/j.intell.2006.09.004.

Terman, L. M. (1925). *Mental and physical traits of a thousand gifted children*. Stanford, CA: Stanford University Press.

Tyler, L. E. (1965). *The psychology of human differences* (3rd ed.). New York: Appleton-Century-Crofts.

U.S. Department of Labor. (1970). *Manual for the USES general aptitude test battery. Section III: Development*. Washington, DC: U.S. Government Printing Office.

Wechsler, D. (1958). *The measurement and appraisal of adult intelligence* (4th ed.). Baltimore, MD: Williams & Wilkins.

Wheeless, V. E., & Serpento, S. T. (1982). *An analysis of the Wonderlic personnel test (form A) as a factor in hiring clerical personnel in institutions of higher education*. West Virginia University, Morgantown, West Virginia, Office of Institutional Research. Unpublished.

Wonderlic, E. F., & Associates, Inc. (1983). *Wonderlic personnel test manual*. Northfield, IL: Author.

Wonderlic, Inc. (2002). *Wonderlic personnel test and scholastic level exam: User's manual*. Libertyville, IL: Wonderlic, Inc.

Yerkes, R. M. (Ed.). (1921). *Psychological examining in the United States army* (Vol. 15). Washington, DC: Washington Government Printing Office.

Zagorsky, J. L., & White, L. (1999). *NLSY79 user's guide: A guide to the 1979–1998 national longitudinal survey of youth data*. Washington, DC: U.S. Department of Labor.

Zeidner, J., & Drucker, A. J. (1983). *Behavioral science in the army: A corporate history of the army research institute*. Alexandria, VA, U.S. Army Research Institute for the Behavioral and Social Science.

PART II
RESEARCH DESIGNS

ANALYSING INTERGENERATIONAL TRANSMISSIONS: FROM SOCIAL MOBILITY TO SOCIAL REPRODUCTION

Steffen Hillmert

ABSTRACT

Social mobility research starts conventionally from the children's generation and looks at group-specific individual life chances. However, an immediate interpretation of these results as measures of social reproduction is often misleading. This paper demonstrates the usefulness of a related but alternative approach which looks at intergenerational links from the perspective of the parents' generation. It asks about the consequences of social inequality in this generation for the following generation(s). This includes questions of how the parental origin context is formed, whether there are any children at all and when they were born as well as the aspect of these children's relative chances of attaining particular social positions. As an empirical example, the paper describes patterns of educational reproduction in (West) Germany during the mid- and late 20th century. Simulations allow assessing the relative importance

Class and Stratification Analysis

Comparative Social Research, Volume 30, 131–157
ISSN: 0195-6310/doi:10.1108/S0195-6310(2013)0000030009

*of various partial processes of social reproduction. A large proportion
of the observed levels of educational reproduction can be attributed to
family-related processes such as union formation. Drawing together
analyses from various areas, the paper combines questions of social
mobility research with a demographic perspective and broadens the
analytical basis of inequality research for systematic comparative
research.*

Keywords: Social reproduction; social inequality; social mobility;
education; intergenerational transmission; simulation

Sociological analyses of intergenerational social mobility and reproduction
have always stressed the importance of the family of origin for the creation
and transmission of social inequality. For example, educational and
occupational opportunities of children decisively depend on family background and the social situation of the parents. In this context, one often
speaks of a social 'inheritance' of status. Characteristics relevant for social
inequality are transmitted from parents to children. This happens through
biological (genetic) as well as social processes, in particular, learning within
the family environment. In addition, the social situation of the family and its
economic, cultural and social 'capital' (Bourdieu, 1986a) define specific
chances for the children – regarding in particular institutionalised forms of
education, learning and development. Moreover, there is the direct transfer
of resources by donations or inheritance, particularly in the case of
economic capital. Conceptually, it is important that both parents are
involved in the transfer of characteristics relevant for social inequality.
Hence, the *composition* of the parental context becomes crucially important
for the situation of the children. While the biological definition of the two
parents is unequivocal, there is much greater variation in social terms –
especially along the life course.

While intergenerational social transmission takes considerable time and
may stretch across a number of generations, conventional studies of social
reproduction are often rather historical snapshots and characterised by
typical restrictions. They mostly focus on estimating the *effects* of social
origin characteristics on the attainment of the children. Such investigations
yield important insights into the process of intergenerational status
transmission; however, other, chronologically preceding aspects which are
conditions for this transmission often remain out of sight. This applies to the
actual distribution of the social origin indicators at the level of families and

to the *causes* of this distribution. If one is interested from a social-structural perspective in the active *reproduction* of education or social status across generations, additional questions arise: Who of a generation of (potential) parents does actually have children at all, how many children do parents have and when do they have them? This also depends on social conditions. One may ask whether and how these additional processes are associated with well-known inequalities like social inequality in education or, in other words, how these inequalities are related to family structures and the population development.

This paper looks at the role of the family in the process of the inter-generational transmission of social inequality. It follows previous studies when describing origin-related social inequalities, but also accounts for the mentioned restrictions by investigating central family-related aspects in intergenerational social reproduction. Apart from presenting selected empirical results, the aim is to demonstrate the broader conceptual possibilities of an inequality-related research that incorporates family dynamics. Such an approach may provide the basis for comparative research which builds upon, but also reaches beyond conventional social mobility research. After outlining the fundamental conceptual issues, the theoretical foundations of the basic mechanisms of intergenerational social reproduction are concisely reviewed. The following section discusses analytical options of the social reproduction approach. These steps are empirically illustrated using intergenerational *educational* reproduction in (West) Germany as an example. The paper concludes with a brief discussion of implications for comparative research.

CONCEPTUAL PERSPECTIVES

Questions of social mobility and social reproduction have always been at the centre of sociological analyses. According to Sorokin (1959), *social mobility* can be defined as the movement of individuals or social units among the social positions in a society which form structures of social inequality. Social mobility is seen as a consequence of both individual efforts and structural change; it is also regarded as an indicator of the individual or group-related stability of social advantage and disadvantage. An underlying assumption of mobility research is that the permanence or transience in holding social positions also influences the social definition of identities and interests. In this sense, social mobility can be understood as a process mediating between social structure, individual action and motivation. Social mobility has also important effects on social integration in a society. From a liberal perspective, social mobility helps to stabilise the political order. It can legitimise social class and status inequalities, in particular, if it is associated with meritocratic principles. On the other hand, however, it can also reduce social class identification and the potential of collective class action. In view of the possibility of (upward) mobility, collective action tends to be given up in favour of individual solutions (Blau & Duncan, 1967; Erikson & Goldthorpe, 1992).

Along with theoretical considerations, there is a long tradition of mainly descriptive research looking at the actual levels and patterns of mobility. Research of this kind looks at both *intragenerational* mobility, that is social mobility within individual life courses, and *intergenerational* mobility, that is social mobility between the different generations of a family. In most cases, this means that socio-economic positions are compared between parents and their children. According to the systematisation by Ganzeboom, Treiman, and Ultee (1991), thematically broadly defined socio-structural studies were succeeded by more specific analyses estimating the role of social background in the process of status attainment, before models of intergenerational mobility tables dominated the scene (see also Treiman & Ganzeboom, 2000). Given the temporal distance between the generations, the analysis of intergenerational mobility is necessarily associated with a long-term perspective. Social mobility has been analysed with regard to both historical trends and international comparisons (e.g. Breen, 2004; Erikson & Goldthorpe, 1992; Featherman & Hauser, 1978).

In probably most studies on the intergenerational transmission of social inequality, the term *social reproduction* is used to denote a strong association between the social positions of different generations – in a way as a counter-concept to social mobility. Alternatively, however, two paradigms of intergenerational inequality research can be distinguished; in one of these, the term gets a specific meaning. They could be labelled as (1) 'origin-specific chances' and (2) 'total social reproduction'.

(1) Analyses of origin-specific chances take the *children's generation* as a starting point. For example, occupational attainment is compared among persons with regard to their *social background,* that is to the status of their parents. Regarding the individuals in the analysis, the question asked is essentially: 'Where do they come from?' This is by far the more frequent analytical approach. It also corresponds to the modern idea of individual life courses. It puts life chances of the children into the centre of attention and it can be related to individual rights; if

necessary, it can also be used to discuss possible policy interventions. However, this analytical approach is essentially concerned with *conditional* origin-specific chances. They are conditional on the formation of the origin context as well as on the very existence of the children whose life situation is analysed. If one is interested in the analytical questions of intergenerational *social reproduction* in societies, it appears that an immediate interpretation of the conventional results as the overall extent of such reproduction is often misleading (Duncan, 1966; Sakamoto & Powers, 2005).

(2) An alternative approach – rooted in traditional concepts of demography (Mackenroth, 1953; Matras, 1967) and in recent years mainly inspired by the work of Mare (1997) and colleagues – looks at intergenerational associations from the *perspective of the parental generation* and asks about the consequences for the following generation(s): 'Where do they go?' This includes questions of how the origin context *originates*, whether there are *at all* children descending from a particular relationship, *how many* children and *when* they are born. Finally, there is the important aspect of the relative social chances of these children. While the parents of a certain cohort of children will represent a wide spectrum of birth cohorts, an analysis from the parental perspective will normally start with a particular cohort of individuals and then look at the social positions of their descendants in the following generations. When the natural population process is included, conceptual limitations of social mobility analyses, which result from the conventional conditioning on the children, can be overcome. In order to adequately describe the path of social status transmission from one generation to the next, it should be distinguished between at least three *partial processes* in the process of intergenerational social reproduction (cf. Maralani & Mare, 2005): socially selective partner choice, socially selective fertility, and socially selective status attainment. In both conceptual and empirical regards, it is suitable to start from individuals and to model their partner choices and fertility behaviour.

An analytical view on intergenerational social reproduction follows a number of steps:

- Individuals in the (potential) parents' generation need to be located within a *space of social inequality*, defined by, for example, occupational status or education (the *social origin* from the perspective of the next generation).
- On the basis of this classification, socially *selective partner choice* and the formation of households and parental contexts can be studied. This

includes essentially two questions: Who has a partner at all? And who marries whom?

- Conditional on – among other factors – the results of this union formation, socially *selective fertility* can be observed.
- Conditional on these mechanisms is finally socially *selective status attainment* of the members of the children's generation. From the point of view of the parents' generation, this result can be called *social destination*. Again, individuals are positioned within a common space of social inequality.

In reality, the process of intergenerational social reproduction is more complicated. In particular, the part of the individual status acquisition can be further differentiated. First, there is the acquisition of qualifications, and second, there are returns in the labour market from these qualifications. Again, educational attainment plays the dominant role. Nevertheless, the three steps form the simplest model connecting individuals of two successive generations, thus describing an entire cycle of intergenerational reproduction. This cycle can be seamlessly extended across more than two generations, accounting for the fact that the social reproduction between two generations is embedded in a long-term 'stream of reproduction' which has no definite beginning or end. In our simplified version, effects of mortality are neglected. The model serves first of all as a specification of phenomena that are appropriate for explanatory models, not as a causal model of explanation itself.

Such an analytical approach is based conceptually on ideas of life-course research. Areas of life are interdependent and life courses are embedded in longer-term generational relations and a number of relevant institutional contexts (Elder, 1985; Mayer, 2009). A comprehensive approach therefore needs to draw upon research from a number of research fields; given the restricted scope of this paper, such a summary has to be selective. Moreover, the following empirical analyses simplify the life-course dimension considerably by neglecting information on the timing of life events (marriages, births, attainment of qualifications, etc.) and sequential information (e.g. the sequence of successive partners).[1] Even in such a simplified form, however, the social reproduction approach is able to cover much broader range of selective social mechanisms than conventional studies that analyse origin-specific chances. Fig. 1 illustrates this fact.

While conventional approaches start from individual children and look for their social origin, that is their parents' (or parent's) social status, as a determinant of individual life chances, the social reproduction approach

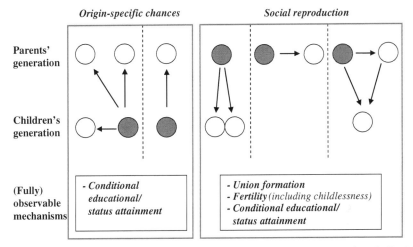

Fig. 1. Comparing Two Analytical Perspectives on Intergenerational Social Transmission. *Note*: Displayed Are Examples of Possible, Typical Family Constellations. Individuals Are Represented by Circles. Filled Circles Denote the Primarily Sampled Individuals; Arrows Denote the Direction of Collecting Information About Family Members.

starts from individual (potential) parents and looks at both their union formation and fertility before turning to the life chances of their children. This means that there is relevant variation among origin contexts as well as among offspring; in particular, persons who remain childless are represented in the sample. This is obviously not the case if information about the parental generation is collected indirectly from the children's generation. The intention of the social reproduction approach is to study how children with certain levels of attainment are 'generated' from one generation to another. Rates of intergenerational reproduction in this sense are relevant for a better historical understanding of social dynamics in general and the stability of social collectivities in society in particular.

THEORETICAL BACKGROUND

While a large part of the more recent research on social mobility is descriptive, there has also been a long-term tradition of explanatory approaches focusing on individual mobility and collective mobility patterns. Social mobility research has concentrated on two central subjects, occupational and marriage mobility, whereby marriage mobility has been traditionally seen as a possible strategy for women to compensate for missing opportunities for occupational upward moves (Geißler, 2002). An important conceptual differentiation is between *absolute* and *relative* mobility. Absolute mobility rates, looking at instances of mobility in general, can be strongly influenced by structural change as expressed by the 'marginal distributions' of social positions at any point in time. As a result of this development, often a majority of individuals are socially mobile. This kind of mobility is often regarded as involuntary, or an action-based theoretical explanation of it is skipped altogether. Relative mobility rates – also called *social fluidity* – describe the relative chances to which people with particular origin positions reach particular destinations. Comparing different groups in this regard, they represent the degree of 'social openness' within a society. In action-based theoretical explanations for intergenerational mobility or its absence, the dominant assumption is the motive of intergenerational status preservation – in particular with regard to *counter mobility* found in transient situations of intergenerational status inconsistency (Goldthorpe, Llewellyn, & Payne, 1987). However, there are also typical intentions of upward social mobility. In regard to the relevant mechanisms, social mobility must be understood as being accomplished by intervening processes. Again, this applies in particular to educational attainment.

The theoretical basis of *social reproduction* is even more diverse. This is not least due to its mediating position between sociological and demographic perspectives; so far, they have not led to specific hypotheses about the internal structure of social reproductive processes. In a broad sense, a similar emphasis on absolute quantities in selective reproduction can be found in biological theories of evolutionary optimisation which relate parental investments and reproductive success not only to the immediate descendants, but also to relatives ('inclusive fitness'; cf. Hamilton, 1964). In social science, materialist approaches construct a close connection between the relations of social inequality in a society and the degree of intergenerational transmission of resources within families (Bowles & Gintis, 2002). In an ethnological perspective (Bourdieu, 1976) it becomes clear that marriage strategies can be explicitly aimed at the reproduction of social structures, and also for modern societies, adequate marriage and occupational investments can be regarded as compensatory strategies of status preservation that actors are more or less conscious about (cf. Bourdieu, 1986b). As a contrast, one could follow Lipset and Zetterberg's (1959) thesis of the similar and generally increasing social openness of modern societies which expresses itself in both social heterogamy, that is diverse marriage patterns, and increasing levels of intergenerational social mobility. Apart from that, inherent statistical connections between mobility patterns and opportunity structures of partner choice have repeatedly been pointed out (Collins, 1986).

Following theories of action, two essential questions which go beyond the single partial processes are as follows: First, are the relevant decisions primarily a result of personal criteria or do they represent more or less specifically defined collectivities ('classes for itself')? Second, do the relevant partial processes interact 'behind the backs' of individuals and families[2] or is there a general logic of action for social *reproduction* in the sense of a conscious combination of several partial processes? These questions have hardly been solved yet. In theoretical regards, it is far from clear whether the relevant decisions are made separately for the different domains of life and with specific rationalities or whether there is a general logic of action in social and educational reproduction, which could also provide the basis for actor-related explanations. At the moment, it is often even difficult to find clear explananda of social reproduction. Each of the specified partial processes – partner choice, fertility, and educational or status attainment – has been documented in detail, but the interaction of these processes has so far only insufficiently been analysed.

Status Attainment, Educational Inequality and Family Structures

The analysis of occupational status acquisition as a function of parental status and educational attainment (cf. Blau & Duncan, 1967) has developed into a prominent field of inequality research. In modern societies, formal education has become the most important mechanism of the (conditional) status transmission between the generations. There is a close connection between, on the one hand, unequal access to education and educational attainment and, on the other hand, educational consequences in the labour market and in other areas of life. The German labour market in particular is structured by formal educational qualifications, and this includes high risks of exclusion for the unqualified. Returns to education and training regarding positions in the labour market have been remarkably stable during the last decades. In spite of educational expansion this applies in particular to academic training (Becker & Hadjar, 2009; Hillmert, 2002; Müller, 1998). The degree of the structuration of life courses by social origin and education has rather increased in the post-war period (Mayer &

Blossfeld, 1990). Intergenerational educational mobility has therefore itself become a relevant topic for social mobility research, and in the following, we concentrate on educational reproduction. Research on selective educational opportunities in connection with social background – education, income, occupational status of the parents – forms the core of educational sociology. Educational opportunities are measured by competence acquisition as well as educational participation, and, above all, as attainment of certain educational qualifications. For (West) Germany as well as for many other industrial countries empirical studies have found reduced inequalities in the long run, but they have remained on a high level (Breen & Jonsson, 2005; Breen, Luijkx, Müller, & Pollak, 2010; Pfeffer, 2008). Such origin-related inequalities can be attributed to a number of factors. An important conceptual distinction for a life-course oriented analysis is between primary and secondary effects with regard to transitions in educational careers (Boudon, 1974). While primary effects refer to the conditions acquired up to certain transitions – in particular cognitive abilities and competencies – secondary effects refer to selective decisions associated with these transitions. In theoretical terms, this reflects the socialisation function of the family including its cultural resources (De Graaf, De Graaf, & Kraaykamp, 2000) as well as family decisions concerning important educational transitions. Action-theoretical models of decisions have once again stressed the motive of labour-market returns to education and intergenerational status preservation (cf. Breen & Goldthorpe, 1997; Hillmert & Jacob, 2003; Stocké, 2007). Educational decisions must be related to specific institutional contexts which define the respective times and alternatives of decision (Hillmert, 2007). 'Discriminating' institutional selection processes may also play a role (Bourdieu & Passeron, 1977). Gender differences in educational behaviour form another important dimension of inequality. Traditional educational disadvantages of girls have turned into relative advantages since the 1980s – at least with regard to school education. This development is valid for most modern societies; the causes for this development, however, are not entirely clear (Buchmann, DiPrete, & McDaniel, 2008). In the 20th century, effects of social background have developed for both genders in a similar manner (Breen et al., 2010). Incomplete families – in the sense of an at least temporary absence of one or both parents – are another aspect of the role of social origin and family structures for educational attainment. Studies have repeatedly shown better educational opportunities for children who grow up with both (natural) parents. This is also true in comparison with step families. A large part of the effects can obviously be attributed to a lack of resources; however, the problems of causal conclusions are increasingly stressed (Francesconi, Jenkins, & Siedler, 2010). The role of *siblings* in educational attainment has also been thoroughly analysed. Sibling effects on education show up with regard to the number, the age and the gender of siblings and a child's own position in the order of birth. Typical explanations for (negative) sibling effects point either to cognitive influences or to family resources and their sharing among more or less children. Again, however, there is increasing doubt about the causality of the described effects (Jæger, 2009; Steelman, Powell, Werum, & Carter, 2002).

Formation of the Parental Context

The formation of parental contexts can also be described with reference to socio-structural characteristics like education. An important type of structural effects concerns the 'marriage market' and the group-specific formation of marriages and partnerships. This includes questions of whether persons marry at all, and, if so, who marries whom. The cultural capital of the family of origin influences not only educational attainment but also marital success. Just like educational decisions, marriage behaviour can be interpreted as an expression of strategies of status preservation (DiMaggio & Mohr, 1985). Relevant is in particular the phenomenon of *social homogamy*, that is the fact that individuals with similar educational or status background tend to join as (marriage) partners. For social inequality, this means that the individual-level distribution of resources is reproduced on the level of families and households. Relative social advantage and disadvantage concentrate there even stronger. In statistical terms, education has gained importance as a means of homogamy during the 20th century, and this is also probably true for education as a criterion of individual partner choices. Patterns of homogamy can be explained by typical preferences, opportunity structures created by the educational system and the growing labour-market integration of women, which has been accompanied by parallel changes in education and social roles (Blossfeld, 2009). However, the exact historical trends during the last decades are not exactly clear and also depend on the actual operationalisation (Blossfeld & Timm, 2003).

Selective Fertility

Particularly relevant for the aspect of social *reproduction* is the fact of socially selective fertility. A negative association between education and fertility can be seen in West Germany (Kreyenfeld & Konietzka, 2008) and many other countries (Martin, 1995). In contrast to classical assumptions of Human Capital Theory (Becker, 1973), however, this is to a large extent the effect of a procrastination of family formation during times of vocational training or higher education (cf. Blossfeld & Huinink, 1991). It can also be expected that the relative instrumental 'value of children' for achieving valued goals – in emotional, economic and normative respect – is different for various socio-economic groups (Hoffman & Hoffman, 1973). The analysis of education-specific fertility requires again that both partners are considered. Bargaining approaches highlight the fact that family decisions are not necessarily approached consensually (Corijn, Liefbroer, & De Jong Gierveld, 1996). While parental status is an important determinant of fertility behaviour, this is also increasingly influenced by the specific family tradition net of their socio-economic position (Murphy & Wang, 2001).

ANALYSING SOCIAL REPRODUCTION

If the process of social reproduction is conceptualised as the sum of partner choice, fertility and individual attainment, three analytical perspectives are of particular interest:

First, one can look for similarities or analogies in the determinants and the consequences of the different partial processes. Here, previous research has shown that educational attainment – parental education and own education – has a determining influence on these partial processes. The social reproduction approach allows estimating combined or *total effects* of social origin that are mediated by the three partial processes. Adequate *dependent variables* for such effects are *relative chances* of attainment or *absolute levels* of group-specific reproduction.[3] Most studies restrict themselves to studying associations between two family generations, but empirical evidence on the long-term effects of (grand-)parental status suggests that it would be more adequate to include at least three generations (cf. Mare, 2011).[4] It also reminds of the fact that these social processes happen within a continuous stream of reproduction where children at some point tend to become parents.

Second, in the sense of a *decomposition,* one can ask how important the different partial processes are for the overall result of social reproduction across generations and how this relative importance differs among various social contexts.

Third, there are possible connections or exchange relations ('trade-offs') between the partial relations (cf. Mare, 1997), which may also be used for an evaluation of the (net) effects of political interventions. Trade-offs between partial processes – for example, 'the lower fertility of a particular social category, the higher their educational investments in their (smaller number of) children' as predicted by economic theories of the family – can be expected to exist not only on the level of whole societies but on various analytical levels. On the level of social groups, we compare the behaviour of educational and status groups in a number of dimensions. Such exchange relationships can also be expected on the micro level of individuals and families, as even within particular groups, specific trade-offs may be a result of individual choice. An action-based explanation of such trade-offs between partial processes implies an assumption of common goals or strategies like status preservation.

Comparative analyses do not really add another perspective, but they can rather use these three perspectives for a further extension. For example, the relative importance of the various partial processes may differ between countries even if overall results of social reproduction are similar, and it would be highly interesting to relate such differences to specific institutional configurations or welfare regimes. The analysis of trade-offs between various forms of social selectivity is by definition comparative. On the macro level of societies, we may observe such trade-offs in international and historical comparisons.

Previous empirical findings that follow a similar approach are mixed with regard to mutual relationships between the processes. Analyses on the United States have shown, for example, that the effects of differential fertility on educational mobility are relatively small (cf. Mare, 1997), while they have had a larger impact in rapidly changing developing countries (Mare & Maralani, 2006). In general, the role which the partial processes play for the whole process of status reproduction in a certain society depends on how significantly they vary among social groups, on how fast they change and how closely they are connected with each other. Given the likely international variations in these features, the model provides a reasonable analytical basis for comparative research.

SOME EMPIRICAL ILLUSTRATIONS

In the following, selected aspects of the social reproduction approach are illustrated by empirical evidence from (West) Germany. Questions of intergenerational *educational* reproduction during times of educational expansion are used as an example. Educational expansion in Germany during the 20th century was by no means a linear process (Mayer, Schnettler, & Aisenbrey, 2009), but historical conditions that were full of change have been accompanied by a relatively high level of institutional stability. Since the Weimar Republic, the German education system or rather the education systems of the federal states have been characterised by structural characteristics like a universal elementary school, an essentially three-tier secondary school system, a broadly developed vocational training system and a system of higher education which has been differentiated only in the last decades (cf. also Cortina, Baumert, Leschinsky, Mayer, & Trommer, 2008).

There is no comprehensive data source that contains all the information needed to analyse our specific research questions in quantitative terms. The empirical basis for the following analyses is therefore provided by a combined dataset created out of 14 different surveys conducted in West Germany between 1970 and 2008 (e.g. Buis, Mönkediek, & Hillmert, 2012).[5] They include census and micro-census data and together cover most of the 20th century, represented by the cohorts born between 1895 and 1978. For the parental birth cohorts that were included in the following analyses (i.e. 1925–1950), the sample size is between 55,000 and 200,000 per annual cohort. The collected information was harmonised among all of the original data sources and combined into a unique dataset. The typical design of most surveys in Germany (as elsewhere) has been to take a cohort of children and collect information on the education of their parents, while a social reproduction approach would rather require data on parental cohorts and the education of their offspring. Therefore, our analysis follows a multi-stage procedure: In a first step, the partial processes are estimated separately. In a second step, these results are combined using a simulation technique in order to get an estimate of the overall process. In a third step, this combination is modified using 'counterfactual' assumptions to assess the relative importance of the partial processes.

As socially selective partial processes, we estimate from the empirical data: the distribution of education in a particular cohort of women; marriage and cohabitation rates; assortative mating of women with regard to education; fertility patterns of women conditional on partner choice and educational attainment of the offspring conditional on the parental education and family size. Table A.1 in the appendix gives an overview over the different statistical procedures that are used for estimating these conditional probabilities. The statistical combination of the estimated partial processes is achieved by a simulation. This means that the individual life events and (yearly) values for particular variables are assigned at random to a given population on the basis of the group-specific probabilities defined by the empirically estimated parameters. The basic algorithm starts with initial populations of women – with various levels of educational attainment – of the 1925+ birth cohorts; it assigns to the individuals their most likely marital status, educational level of their partners, number, years of birth, gender and educational attainment of their children (if they have any children). The process of natural reproduction works in this model only through the population of women. The reason for this conceptual choice is that reliable data on fertility is normally only available for women. Men do, however, show up as spouses of the women and (married) fathers.

Our analyses abstract from the complexity of empirical life courses in a number of ways: We only consider (a maximum of) one partner per women, not a possible sequence of partners.[6] Deliberately only few grouping variables are used for all generations, in particular educational attainment. For the purposes of a 'sophisticated description' (Goldthorpe, 2007), the goal is the systematic description of social inheritance across generations and the identification of multiple effects and possible explananda, not the causal explanation of individual educational behaviour or the explanation of a maximum of variance. The central indicator of educational attainment refers to attained educational qualifications. Compared to occupational careers, these characteristics can be determined relatively early in the life course. This makes it easier to find longitudinal data with a sufficiently large observation window.

Fig. 2 presents the distribution of educational attainment across birth cohorts since 1925. In this figure, five levels of educational attainment are distinguished. *Basic*: This category contains persons with lower or intermediate general secondary education (i.e. 'Volks-/Hauptschule' or 'Realschule' school leaving certificates) and no formal vocational training; *Lower vocational* consists of persons with lower-level general secondary education and non-academic vocational training; *Medium vocational* denotes a combination of intermediate general secondary qualifications and non-academic vocational training; *Upper secondary* includes both persons with only upper general secondary school qualifications ('Abitur') and persons with a combination of upper general secondary schooling and non-academic vocational training; *Higher* contains all persons who have attained a tertiary degree.

Consistent with previous research (cf. Cortina et al., 2008), a first historical phase was characterised by the expansion of vocational training –

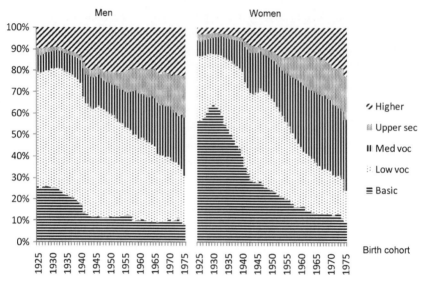

Fig. 2. Educational Attainment by Sex and Birth Cohort (Percentages), 1925–1975.
Data: Combined Census and Survey Data, West Germany.

especially among females – while the proportions of the higher qualified
('upper secondary' and 'higher') grew significantly in the later cohorts.
Educational expansion has in general been more distinctive for young
women than young men. Females had much lower average levels of
educational attainment than males in the older cohorts but improved their
attainment within a short time. In the youngest birth cohorts, educational
attainment of males and female has been nearly equal.

Also in these data, educational attainment depends strongly on social
(educational) background. We use odds ratios to describe the relative
differences in children's educational attainment, depending on the mothers'
level of education. For the sake of simplicity, only two educational
categories – individuals with and without higher (i.e. tertiary) education –
are distinguished. To evaluate the effects of differential fertility as well as
educational inequality, we compare simulated distributions of education in
different scenarios. The simulation based on the observed associations in the
different model parts is used as the reference. In Fig. 3, social inequality in
the empirical educational distributions of children is compared with suitable
counterfactual distributions. These are calculated as the distributions that
would, for example, result if the partners met not according to the empirical

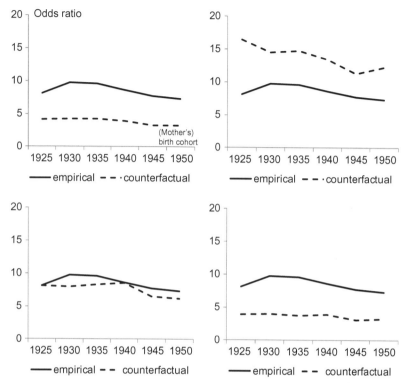

Fig. 3. Trends in Educational Inequality (Relative Chances of Attaining Higher Education) Under Different Scenarios, by Mother's Birth Cohort. *Note*: The Lines Represent Relative Chances (Odds Ratios) of Attaining Higher Education vs. Not Attaining Higher Education. Compared Are Children of Mothers with and without Higher Education. Displayed Are the Empirical Trend Across Birth Cohorts and Various Counterfactual Trends – Clockwise Starting with Upper Left Diagram: Marriage at Random; Marriages by Educational Rank Order; Equal Fertility; Both Marriage at Random and Equal Fertility. *Data*: Combined Census and Survey Data, West Germany.

patterns, but – at least with regard to education – by chance. Assuming statistical independence, these distributions are generated by multiplying the marginal distributions of the cohort-specific marriage contingency tables. Holding everything else constant, which educational attainment would then result for the children of a mother with a particular level of schooling, and how would inequality between groups change?

The empirical development regarding origin-related inequality in the attainment of higher education – indicated by the solid line – follows a slightly downward trend when we compare among the offspring of mothers who were born between 1925 and 1950. However, inequality has remained on a high level. Comparisons with the counterfactual trends indicate that the level of inequality would have been much lower, if marital unions had been formed randomly with regard to education and not along educational boundaries. The values for the counterfactual educational distributions are clearly lower; they fluctuate, but on average they are about half as large as the corresponding empirical values. To express it differently, in these cases, approximately half of the empirically observed inequality between children of parents from two different educational groups can be attributed to the fact that these parents have chosen their partners not randomly, but that they chose *specific* (types of) partners who – according to their social position – have themselves typical influences on the education of the children. On the other hand, the level of inequality would have been much higher, if marriage patterns had been strictly oriented at the order of the partners' educational level. Hence, the empirical level of assortative mating has been between these two extremes. For the *relative chances* of education, fertility (timing) differences between educational groups have obviously had no large effect.

This leads to the final analyses of absolute intergenerational educational reproduction. The empirical level of this reproduction depends strongly on the specific measures that are used. An important alternative is, for example, whether reproduction is brought about by all children of a parent or whether it is secured only by children of the same sex as the parent. The latter rates are necessarily much lower, but they can be informative about intergenerational continuities particularly in times with a high level of inequality between genders.

Additional analyses show that in all cohorts, the low educated and particularly the higher educated had relatively high social reproduction rates, while the intermediate groups had much lower rates (numerical results not presented). Note that such differences between educational levels are not necessarily an indicator of social inequality between these groups. Given their different sizes, it is statistically more likely for some groups to have higher reproduction rates than for others, even if there is no relationship between origins and destinations. In fact, a number of statistical measures use this assumption of independence to derive a standard against which the empirical values can be assessed. When comparing these reference values with the empirical results, it becomes clear that all educational groups have a higher than random reproduction rate; but again, this applies in particular to the higher educated.

In Fig. 4, we select a specific rate of reproduction for a more detailed analysis. The example is the reproduction among the high qualified, that is we look at (all of) the children of mothers who have attained a higher level of education. The lines represent the degree to which the number of women

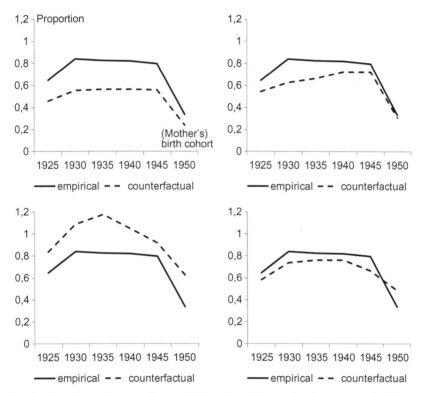

Fig. 4. Trends in Absolute Rates of Educational Reproduction among the Higher Educated Under Different Scenarios, by Mother's Birth Cohort. *Note*: The Lines Represent the Degree to Which the Number of Women with Higher Education is Replaced in the Next Generation by Their Own Children Who Attain Themselves Higher Education. Displayed Are the Empirical Trend Across Birth Cohorts and Various Counterfactual Trends – Clockwise Starting with Upper Left Diagram: Marriage at Random; Marriages by Educational Rank Order; Equal Fertility; Both Marriage at Random and Equal Fertility. *Data*: Combined Census and Survey Data, West Germany.

with higher education is replaced in the next generation by their own children who attain themselves higher education. For the youngest parental cohorts, this information is probably 'right censored', as these cohorts had not completely finished their fertility period when the data were collected. This might explain the significant drop in the educational reproduction rates. More important than a thorough interpretation of this trend, however, is that we can use this example to look once again at the effect of counterfactual changes in family formation processes. It turns out that while random partnership formation tends to reduce educational reproduction rates, equal fertility has a counter-acting effect. This means that in real life – which is characterised by both social homogamy and selective fertility – the high reproduction rates of the high qualified are partly due to their specific marriage patterns, but are also limited by the relatively low fertility of this group. 'Net educational reproduction rates' – that is the proportions to which a cohort of mothers is replaced by *daughters* with the same level of education – are approximately 50 percent of the respective proportions that include *all* children,[7] and all trends across cohorts are very similar.

Substantive interpretations of such counterfactual scenarios imply another type of assumptions. These additional assumptions concern the 'demand side' of educational opportunities and the allocation process that determines which children attain which level of education. This is especially obvious if the counterfactual scenarios predict a change in the overall number of children, but it is already relevant if empirical and counterfactual situations differ with regard to the number of children from any specific background. In this case, it is unlikely that the final counterfactual distribution will remain exactly the same as the empirical educational distribution, given the fact that quantities in various school tracks are normally not fixed and that allocation is (legally) supposed to be based on the ability and achievement of the actual population of students. But – given other well-known facts, competition and non-meritocratic inequality – how exactly does the allocation process work? In our example, we have used the simple assumption that also under counterfactual conditions the proportions of attainment in any of the groups remain constant. Alternative scenarios might assume, for example, that the school system expands or contracts completely exogenously and disproportionately on different levels. A thorough discussion of these scenarios, their theoretical foundations and their interactions with the scenarios of family formation mentioned above would be beyond the scope of this paper. It may be sufficient to state that both 'demand side' and allocation can be modelled on the basis of plausible assumptions. Moreover, systematic considerations about these issues are important also for the interpretation of results from conventional mobility research, which all too often takes 'structural change' as completely exogenous. At least in the context of education, this is a very strong assumption.

SUMMARY AND OUTLOOK

This paper has focused on historical trends in a single country, but it also proposes a research perspective that can serve as a promising basis for systematic (international) comparative research. The specific results serve as examples for the broad applications of such an approach. They are valid in their specific historical context and are subject to a number of restrictions. Especially if causal questions are of interest, having even more detailed data on educational success, family structure and possible transmission mechanisms would be desirable. This includes measures of individual achievement as well as attempts to control unmeasured factors (on the role of inherited endowments, cf. Behrman, Rosenzweig, & Taubman, 1994). However, the available analyses already prove that family-related analyses of social and educational inequality offer still considerably broader possibilities than 'only' a description of origin-related educational opportunities for children from certain cohorts. In particular, long-term processes of social reproduction in society can be studied by taking the partial processes of partnership formation and fertility into account. Obviously, a large proportion of the observed educational reproduction can be attributed to these partial processes which are essentially located outside the educational system – and which are therefore sensitive to interventions of educational policy only to a rather small degree. Therefore, international comparisons which refer not only to (conditional) educational opportunities but also to *all* selective processes of social reproduction are a consistent application of such an approach. Empirical comparisons could refer in particular to the relative contribution of the specified partial processes for the progression and the results of intergenerational, educational and social reproduction; international differences in these relative contributions would be significant explananda. Given a sufficiently long series of cohorts, trends in these contributions and associations between them can themselves be modelled.

While this paper has been mainly concerned with the demographic aspects of social reproduction, there is still a more general point regarding data collection. Most empirical studies of intergenerational mobility are based on surveys in which individuals provide detailed information about themselves and basic information on their parents. Hence, much more is normally known about the destination generation than the origin generation, while obviously the parents rather than the children drive the reproduction process from one generation to another. It is therefore essential in surveys to ask respondents about relevant characteristics (education, occupation, etc.) not only of their parents but also of their children.[8]

Focussing on the parents' generation might prove to be difficult because potential children of recent cohorts, for example of parents born around 1965, are often too young to have attained relevant social characteristics. In general, the process of intergenerational reproduction extends considerably through time, in that sense linking various historical periods. This applies already for the reproduction process of a single parental cohort, so that the observation window for historical comparisons between various parental cohorts may become rather small even when long-term historical data are available.

Despite such practical limitations, conceptualising social transmission from the parents' generation can always be used as a heuristic tool for conventional social mobility analyses: It makes research sensitive to underlying assumptions like the causes of 'structural' changes. In general, however, a number of important theoretical questions are still open. It is worth noting that the partial processes relevant for social reproduction are analysed in great detail in different fields of sociology. It is therefore important to interpret the available results in close connection with one another, and this does not necessarily require a common statistical model.

ACKNOWLEDGEMENTS

Research for this paper was supported by the German Research Foundation (DFG), grant no. HI 767/6-1. I would also like to thank the anonymous reviewer for helpful comments.

NOTES

1. In principle, it is not difficult to add this information to an analytical model of social reproduction, as it is based on individual information.

2. In other words, this would mean that the social reproduction perspective is concerned (only) with a specific of *aggregation* of behaviour which is relevant for social reproduction but not necessarily intended to do so.

3. When using information on the timing of the relevant life events, the *speed* of social reproduction may be an additional dependent variable.

4. Including more than two generations opens up an additional perspective on the mechanisms of social reproduction with the question of how the intergenerational *transmission of* (demographic) *behaviour* – marriage patterns, fertility behaviour – contributes to social reproduction in the following generation.

5. For an extended project description, see http://www.socialreproduction.de

6. Instability of marital unions is not necessarily a problem for this approach, if remarriages tend to happen along the same educational lines.

7. This does not necessarily occur: The simulation model assumes equal probabilities for the birth of sons and daughters, but educational opportunities may develop differently for young men and women.

8. For a detailed consideration of parental characteristics in intergenerational transmission, see the paper by Spenner (1981) who analyses the covariation between the requirements, routines and rewards of the occupations of both parents and children.

REFERENCES

Becker, G. S. (1973). A theory of marriage: Part I. *Journal of Political Economy*, *81*, 813–846.

Becker, R., & Hadjar, A. (Eds.). (2009). *Expected and unexpected consequences of the educational expansion in Europe and the US*. Bern: Haupt.

Behrman, J. R., Rosenzweig, M. R., & Taubman, P. (1994). Endowments and the allocation of schooling in the family and in the marriage market: The twins experiment. *Journal of the Political Economy*, *102*, 1131–1174.

Blau, P. M., & Duncan, O. D. (1967). *The American occupational structure*. New York: Wiley.

Blossfeld, H.-P. (2009). Educational assortative marriage in comparative perspective. *Annual Review of Sociology*, *35*, 513–530.

Blossfeld, H.-P., & Huinink, J. (1991). Human capital investments or norms of role transition? How women's schooling and career affect the process of family-formation. *American Journal of Sociology*, *97*, 143–168.

Blossfeld, H.-P., & Timm, A. (Eds.). (2003). *Who marries whom? Educational systems as marriage markets in modern societies*. Dordrecht: Kluwer Academic.

Boudon, R. (1974). *Education, opportunity and social inequality. Changing prospects in Western Society*. New York: Wiley.

Bourdieu, P. (1976). *Entwurf einer Theorie der Praxis*. Frankfurt a. M.: Suhrkamp.

Bourdieu, P. (1986a). The forms of capital. In J. G. Richardson (Ed.), *Handbook of theory and research for the sociology of education* (pp. 241–258). New York: Greenwood Press.

Bourdieu, P. (1986b). *Distinction: A social critique of the judgement of taste*. London: Routledge.

Bourdieu, P., & Passeron, J.-C. (1977). *Reproduction in education, society and culture*. London: Sage.

Bowles, S., & Gintis, H. (2002). The inheritance of inequality. *Journal of Economic Perspectives*, *16*, 3–30.

Breen, R. (Ed.). (2004). *Social mobility in Europe*. Oxford: Oxford University Press.

Breen, R., & Goldthorpe, J. H. (1997). Explaining educational differentials. Towards a formal rational action theory. *Rationality and Society*, *9*, 275–305.

Breen, R., & Jonsson, J. O. (2005). Inequality of opportunity in comparative perspective: Recent research on educational attainment and social mobility. *Annual Review of Sociology*, *31*, 223–243.

Breen, R., Luijkx, R., Müller, W., & Pollak, R. (2010). Long-term trends in educational inequality in Europe: Class inequalities and gender differences. *European Sociological Review*, *26*, 31–48.

Buchmann, C., DiPrete, T. A., & McDaniel, A. (2008). Gender inequalities in education. *Annual Review of Sociology*, *34*, 319–337.

Buis, M. L., Mönkediek, B., & Hillmert, S. (2012). *Educational expansion and the role of demographic factors: The case of West Germany Population Review*, *51*, 1–15.

Collins, R. (1986). *Sociology of marriage and the family: Gender, love and property*. Chicago, IL: Nelson-Hall.

Corijn, M., Liefbroer, A. C., & De Jong Gierveld, J. (1996). It takes two to tango, doesn't it? The influence of couple characteristics on the timing of the birth of the first child. *Journal of Marriage and the Family*, *58*, 117–126.

Cortina, K. S., Baumert, J., Leschinsky, A., Mayer, K. U., & Trommer, L. (Eds.). (2008). *Das Bildungswesen in der Bundesrepublik Deutschland: Strukturen und Entwicklungen im Überblick*. Reinbek: Rowohlt.

De Graaf, N. D., De Graaf, P. M., & Kraaykamp, G. (2000). Parental cultural capital and educational attainment in the Netherlands: A refinement of the cultural capital perspective. *Sociology of Education*, *73*, 92–111.

DiMaggio, P., & Mohr, J. (1985). Cultural capital, educational attainment, and marital selection. *American Journal of Sociology*, *90*, 1231–1261.

Duncan, O. D. (1966). Methodological issues in the analysis of social mobility. In N. J. Smelser & S. M. Lipset (Eds.), *Social structure and mobility in economic development* (pp. 51–97). Chicago, IL: Aldina.

Elder, G. H. (Ed.). (1985). *Life course dynamics: Trajectories and transitions 1968–1980*. Ithaca, NY: Cornell University Press.

Erikson, R., & Goldthorpe, J. H. (1992). *The constant flux: A study of class mobility in industrial societies*. Oxford: Clarendon Press.

Featherman, D. L., & Hauser, R. M. (1978). *Opportunity and change*. New York: Academic Press.

Francesconi, M., Jenkins, S. P., & Siedler, T. (2010). Childhood family structure and schooling outcomes: Evidence for Germany. *Journal of Population Economics*, *23*, 1201–1231.

Ganzeboom, H. B. G., Treiman, D. J., & Ultee, W. C. (1991). Comparative intergenerational stratification research: Three generations and beyond. *Annual Review of Sociology*, *17*, 277–302.

Geißler, R. (2002). *Die Sozialstruktur Deutschlands: Die gesellschaftliche Entwicklung vor und nach der Vereinigung*. Opladen: Westdeutscher Verlag.

Goldthorpe, J. H. (2007). *On sociology* (Vol. I). Stanford: Stanford University Press.

Goldthorpe, J. H., Llewellyn, C., & Payne, C. (1987). *Social mobility and class structure in modern Britain*. Oxford: Oxford University Press.

Hamilton, W. D. (1964). The genetical evolution of social behavior I and II. *Journal of Theoretical Biology*, *7*, 1–52.

Hillmert, S. (2002). Labour market integration and institutions: An Anglo-German comparison. *Work, Employment & Society*, *19*, 675–701.

Hillmert, S. (2007). Soziale Ungleichheit im Bildungsverlauf: Zum Verhältnis von Institutionen und Entscheidungen. In R. Becker & W. Lauterbach (Eds.), *Bildung als Privileg. Ursachen von Bildungsungleichheit aus soziologischer Sicht* (pp. 71–98). Wiesbaden: VS Verlag für Sozialwissenschaften.

Hillmert, S., & Jacob, M. (2003). Social inequality in higher education: Is vocational training a pathway leading to or away from University? *European Sociological Review, 19,* 319–334.

Hoffman, L. W., & Hoffman, M. L. (1973). The value of children to parents. In J. T. Fawcett (Ed.), *Psychological perspectives on population* (pp. 19–76). New York: Basis Books.

Jæger, M. M. (2009). Sibship size and educational attainment: A joint test of the confluence model and the resource dilution hypothesis. *Research in Social Stratification and Mobility, 27,* 1–12.

Kreyenfeld, M., & Konietzka, D. (2008). Education and fertility in Germany. In I. Hamm, H. Seitz & M. Werding (Eds.), *Demographic change in Germany: The economic and fiscal consequences* (pp. 165–187). New York: Springer.

Lipset, S. M., & Zetterberg, H. L. (1959). Social mobility in industrial societies. In S. M. Lipset & R. Bendix (Eds.), *Social mobility in industrial society* (pp. 11–75). Berkeley, CA: University of California Press.

Mackenroth, G. (1953). *Bevölkerungslehre: Theorie, soziologie und statistik der bevölkerung.* Berlin: Springer.

Maralani, V., & Mare, R. D. (2005). *Demographic pathways of intergenerational effects: Fertility, mortality, marriage and women's schooling in Indonesia.* CCPR Working Paper 019-05. Los Angeles: UCLA.

Mare, R. D. (1997). Differential fertility, intergenerational educational mobility, and racial inequality. *Social Science Research, 26,* 263–291.

Mare, R. D. (2011). A multigenerational view of inequality. *Demography, 48,* 1–23.

Mare, R. D., & Maralani, V. (2006). The intergenerational effects of changes in women's educational attainments. *American Sociological Review, 71,* 542–564.

Martin, T. C. (1995). Women's education and fertility: Results from 26 demographic and health surveys. *Studies in Family Planning, 26,* 187–202.

Matras, J. (1967). Social mobility and social structure: Some insights from the linear model. *American Sociological Review, 32,* 608–614.

Mayer, K. U. (2009). New directions in life course research. *Annual Review of Sociology, 35,* 413–433.

Mayer, K. U., & Blossfeld, H.-P. (1990). Die gesellschaftliche Konstruktion sozialer Ungleichheit im Lebensverlauf. In P. A. Berger & S. Hradil (Eds.), *Lebenslagen, Lebensläufe, Lebensstile* (pp. 297–318). Göttingen: Schwartz.

Mayer, K. U., Schnettler, S., & Aisenbrey, S. (2009). The process and impacts of educational expansion: Findings from the German life history study. In R. Becker & A. Hadjar (Eds.), *Expected and unexpected consequences of the educational expansion in Europe and the US* (pp. 27–47). Bern: Haupt.

Müller, W. (1998). Erwartete und unerwartete folgen der bildungsexpansion. In J. Friedrichs, M. R. Lepsius & K. U. Mayer (Eds.), *Die Diagnosefähigkeit der Soziologie* (pp. 81–112). Opladen: Westdeutscher Verlag.

Murphy, M., & Wang, D. (2001). Family-level continuities in childbearing in low-fertility societies. *European Journal of Population, 17,* 75–96.

Pfeffer, F. T. (2008). Persistent inequality in educational attainment and its institutional context. *European Sociological Review, 24*, 543–565.

Sakamoto, A., & Powers, D. A. (2005). Demography of social stratification. In D. L. Poston & M. Micklin (Eds.), *Handbook of population* (pp. 383–416). New York: Kluwer Academic.

Sorokin, P. A. (1959, Origin 1927). *Social and cultural mobility*. Glencoe: Free Press.

Spenner, K. I. (1981). Occupations, role characteristics, and intergenerational transmission. *Sociology of Work and Occupations, 8*, 89–112.

Steelman, L. C., Powell, B., Werum, R., & Carter, S. (2002). Reconsidering the effects of sibling configuration: recent advances and challenges. *Annual Review of Sociology, 28*, 243–269.

Stocké, V. (2007). Explaining educational decision and effects of families' social class position: an empirical test of the Breen-Goldthorpe model of educational attainment. *European Sociological Review, 23*, 505–519.

Treiman, D. J., & Ganzeboom, H. B. G. (2000). The fourth generation of comparative stratification research. In S. A. Quah & A. Sales (Eds.), *International handbook of sociology* (pp. 123–150). London: Sage.

APPENDIX

Table A.1. Summary of the Statistical Procedures Applied in the Example (Estimation of the Partial Processes).

(Dependent) Variable	Estimation Method	Covariates
Respondent's (i.e. mother's) education	(Annual) row percentages of the conditional tables	Year of birth
Indicator of having a partner	(Annual) row percentages of the conditional tables	Year of birth, respondent's education
Partner's education	Multinomial logit model	Year of birth, respondent's education
Indicator of giving birth	Binary logit models	Respondent's age (15–49) and education, separately for each annual/biannual cohort
Children's education	Multinomial and binary logit models (sequential models)	Year of birth, respondent's education and (her) partner's education

INCHING UP: THE LABOUR MARKET POSITION OF THE SECOND-GENERATION IMMIGRANTS IN BRITAIN AND THE UNITED STATES (1990–2000)

Yaojun Li

ABSTRACT

We analyse the labour market position of the second-generation minority ethnic groups in Britain and the United States in 1990 and 2000 on the basis of micro-data from the two most recent censuses of the population. We find that they were making progress, although some groups were still facing considerable disadvantages. The second-generation men were doing better in the United States than in Britain at both time points but the gaps were being narrowed. The second-generation women in Britain lagged behind their American counterparts in the first period, but they were doing equally well in the two countries in 2001. The overall pattern is one of small but notable progress and shows somewhat greater support for the revised straight-line theory than for the segmented assimilation theory.

Keywords: Labour market position; second-generation; ethnic penalty; Britain; the United States

Class and Stratification Analysis
Comparative Social Research, Volume 30, 159–187
ISSN: 0195-6310/doi:10.1108/S0195-6310(2013)0000030010

INTRODUCTION

Both Britain and the United States have seen a large influx of non-white immigrants in the last 50 years and an increasing proportion of the populations in both countries are the second-generation immigrants. Over 30% of the US population and over 11% of the British population are composed of minority ethnic members, with the second-generation being 18% and 5%, respectively. With globalisation and the ageing population of whites, the proportion of minority ethnics in the two countries, just as in some other developed nations, is most likely to grow in the years to come. How well are the second generation doing in the labour market? Are they making progress or experiencing deterioration in the socio-economic fortunes? Which groups are making the greatest progress and which are experiencing persistent disadvantage and to what extent? Are the two countries converging or diverging in terms of second-generation integration?

This study seeks to address these questions by examining the labour market position of the second-generation minority ethnic groups in Britain and the United States. Using micro-data from the two most recent censuses of the population (1990/1–2000/1), the analysis compares the findings against the expectations from the revised straight-line and the segmented assimilation theories on second-generation integration. We also wish to find evidence for the longer-standing debate on American exceptionalism. The paper is structured as follows. In the next section, we give a brief review of the recent debate on the second-generation assimilation and the longer-term concerns with social fluidity. After that, we introduce data and methods, followed by the presentation of findings. In the final section, we sum up and give a brief discussion.

THEORETICAL CONTEXT

In the last few decades, waves of immigrants, largely from developing countries, have come to Britain and the United States in the wake of the post-war reconstruction in the former, and the 1965 Immigration and Nationality Amendments (Hart-Cellar Act) in the latter. The children of the immigrants now constitute an increasingly important force in the labour market in each country.[1] Academic interest in the immigrant integration has, in the last two decades, shifted from the first to the second generation, especially in the United States. While earlier studies tend to focus on ethnic disadvantage and racial discrimination faced by the first generation

(Daniel, 1968; Gordon, 1964; Jowell & Prescott-Clarke, 1970; Quillian, 1995; Stewart, 1983; Telles & Murguia, 1990), recent studies attaches great importance to understanding the processes of the second-generation attainment (Alba, Kasinitz, & Waters, 2011; Haller, Portes, & Lynch, 2011; Kasinitz, Mollenkopf, Waters, & Holdaway, 2008; Portes, Fernandez-Kelly, & Haller, 2005, 2009; Portes & Rumbaut, 2001; Vermulen, 2012; Waters, Tran, Kasinitz, & Mollenkopf, 2012).

There are two main theories in debate on the socio-economic fortunes of the second-generation: the revised straight-line and the segmented assimilation theories. The first, as espoused by Alba and his colleagues (Alba, 2005; Alba, Lutz, & Vesselinov, 2001; Alba & Nee, 2003; Alba et al., 2011; Farley & Alba, 2002; Waters et al., 2012), is a reformulated version of the classical assimilation theory developed by the founders of the Chicago School of Sociology, who tracked the integration profile of European immigrants in American society. The classical theory predicts a 'process of interpenetration and fusion' of immigrants (Park & Burgess, 1921, p. 735) as characterised by successive generational upward mobility, greater integration into the mainstream and reduced ethnic distinctiveness in terms of language use, residential concentration and marriage pattern (Warner & Srole, 1945). Later, Gordon developed a more systematic paradigm of assimilation including seven dimensions: cultural, structural, marital, identificational, attitude-receptional, behaviour-receptional and civic. Among these, structural assimilation, defined as large-scale entry into the institutions of the host society, that is, the labour market, is held as the 'keystone of the arch of assimilation' (Gordon, 1964, p. 80).

Following the classical assimilation model, Alba and his colleagues provide a reformulated straight-line assimilation theory, predicting a basically similar trajectory of upward mobility and gradual integration for contemporary immigrants, the second generation in particular, to that followed by European immigrants. The revised theory is grounded in structural changes in American society. During the last few decades, occupational structure in the United States continues to upgrade, with proportionally more professional and managerial positions than were available in the previous decades. At the same time, the baby-boom generation are coming to their retirement age, leaving many top positions open to competition (Hout, 2006), including competition among the new second generation. The civil rights movement also helped to change the attitude of the mainstream towards minority ethnic groups so that they can now compete in the labour market on a more equal footing than in the past (Model, 2005). These and other factors have created a fairly favourable environment for the incorporation of the new immigrants, second-generation in particular, into the socio-economic fabric of the United States (Perlmann & Waldinger, 1997). With the passage of time, ethnic boundaries are expected to become increasingly blurred (Alba, 2005).

Apart from the structural changes facilitating assimilation, the revised assimilation theory holds that being second-generation has advantages. The parental generation who are generally self-selected with extraordinary drive and determination and are willing to work very hard for a better life for themselves and their children are, however, disadvantaged for a variety of structural reasons such as lack of appropriate socio-cultural capital in the host society, unfamiliarity with the local labour market, poor English and societal and employer discrimination, which leave many of them unable to realise their own dreams and they have to place hope on their children for the fulfilment of their suppressed aspirations (Waters et al., 2012). Thus, one finds that most second-generation minority ethnic groups have higher levels of educational attainment than their white counterparts do (Li, 2009). Even though the 'drag effects' in one form or another (Darity & Mason, 1998) may still prevent the second generation from reaching their full potential, reinvigorated aspirations assisted by educational attainment would mean that they will have fewer disadvantages than their parents.

The revised straight-line assimilation theory does not deny that there are still prejudices in society and discriminatory practices by employers which can lead to disadvantages in the second-generation's labour market attainment, nor does it deny that there may be considerable differences in the disadvantages faced by different groups. What it posits is that, overall, the second generation will make greater advances as time progresses, leading to increasing integration into American socio-economic life. In this sense, it is a prospective theory.

Challenging this is the segmented assimilation theory proposed by Portes and his colleagues (Haller et al., 2011; Portes, 1997; Portes et al., 2005, 2009; Portes & Rumbaut, 2001; Portes & Zhou, 1993). This theory is also based on structural changes in the economy and on family socio-economic resources. Unlike the situation in the earlier decades of the 20th century, the new, knowledge-based, economy is, the authors argue, taking an hour-glass shape. The bifurcated class structure has well-paid professional and managerial jobs at the top (requiring high levels of human capital) and poorly paid jobs at the bottom (requiring little more than physical strength). The middle layer, namely, skilled manual and clerical jobs that earlier immigrants could obtain for work-life upward mobility, is increasingly squeezed out as globalisation and outsourcing has channelled such jobs, especially in the manufacturing and service sectors, into developing countries. As professional knowledge acquired through higher education is playing an ever more important role than before for access to the top jobs, whether one has the prerequisite human capital will determine success or failure in work-life mobility. Given this, the acculturation processes will play a vital role in determining whether the second-generation will have adequate qualifications for a successful career in the labour market.

According to the segmented assimilation theory, differences in family socio-economic condition, family structure and intra-ethnic community cohesion will generate three acculturation processes for the second generation: consonant, selective and dissonant assimilation. Children from professional families with high levels of human capital will undergo a process of consonant acculturation where parents and children jointly learn and accommodate to the language and culture of the host society, which fosters upward mobility into the upper middle class of the mainstream white population. Others from similar backgrounds or with lower levels of human capital but strong parental and co-ethnic control will experience selective acculturation, where the learning of English and the culture of the host society will proceed smoothly to promote upward mobility and to avoid downward mobility while at the same time parental socio-cultural tradition and intra-ethnic solidarity are firmly maintained. Still others from working-class families with poor socio-economic resources, little parental control and weak community support will have dissonant acculturation, ending up in intergenerational stagnation or downward mobility into low-paid and dead-end jobs; worse still, some of them, being vulnerably exposed to the pervasive and harmful influences of inner-city subcultures of gangs, drugs and teen pregnancy, will lead a life of arrest, incarceration or early death, and descend into the underclass of permanent poverty and social exclusion typical of African Americans (Portes & Zhou, 1993).

A comparison of the two theories shows that while the former focuses on trends, the latter concentrates more on inter-group differences. Yet, in spite of the apparent heatedness of the debate, the two sides do not seem to engage in direct dialogue. A look at the analyses used for supporting the respective hypotheses shows that the two groups of researchers do not use a common benchmark. Portes et al. (2009) used the well-performing Asian group as the reference category, whereas Waters et al. (2012) used poor-performing Puerto Ricans as the reference category. This naturally leads to different conclusions based on apparent differences.

Before we proceed to empirical analysis, it is necessary to have a brief review of the other research bearing on the debate. Quite a few studies have been conducted, mostly in the United States, with mixed results. Some researchers, such as Waldinger and Perlmann (1998) and Perlmann and Waldinger (1997), criticised the segmented assimilation theory for its characterisation of mobility experience by second-generation Europeans in the early 20th-century America. Using data from the 1970 Census of the Population, Waldinger (2007) further showed that manufacturing jobs did not play any important role for the upward mobility of Italians, as they 'made a living in other ways, showing no propensity for industrial work whatsoever' (p. 32). Others find evidence of second-generation progress as compared with first-generation immigrants (Waters & Jiménez, 2005; Waters, Ueda, & Marrow, 2007). Still others, doing case studies on specific groups or using large-scale survey analyses such as the Children of Immigrants Longitudinal Study (CILS), provide strong support to the segmented assimilation theory, such as Zhou and Bankston (2001) on Vietnamese, Vickerman (1999) on West Indians, Menjívar (2000) on Salvadorans, and Portes et al. (2009) on Haitians, Jamaicans and some other groups. As US society is so big, the diversity found in some specific, localised segments of ethnic experience would come as no surprise. Overall, the existing research provides no convincing evidence on the two theories.

At this conjuncture, one may ask whether the revised straight-line and the segmented assimilation theories, designed for second-generation integration in the United States, would apply to other countries such as Britain. Britain and the United States share many similarities. The most notable similarity is that they are commonly regarded as archetypical liberal capitalism. The free market, coupled with the meritocratic ideology in both countries, would, according to the liberal theory (Bell, 1972), promote open competition, resulting in greater social mobility and ethnic integration within, as well as greater convergence between, countries. The two countries also have many differences, such as those rooted in the immigration histories (Heath, 2007), the diversity and composition of immigrants (Hirschman, 2005), the educational systems, the social-political milieu including the civil-rights movements in the United States and the successive Race Relations Acts in Britain, the generosity of welfare regimes and the various equal opportunities regulations in Britain, and the stricter law enforcement in the United States (Model, 2005; Waters, 2008). Such differences will no doubt affect immigrant integration in the two societies. Apart from these, cultural-structural differences between the two countries may affect immigrant integration. From popular myths to sociological representation, the United States is seen as a land of opportunity with little socio-economic constraint, whereas Britain is often viewed as being hopelessly hampered by entrenched class disparity and social sclerosis (Olsen, 1982). The thesis of American exceptionalism is found in social science discourses dating from Tocqueville (1835) to Lipset (1991). Even scholars who lament on racial discrimination against the Blacks as a scar on American conscience[2] were amazed at long-range mobility by the sons of manual workers into the professional elite and held it as evidence of 'a grain of truth in the Horatio Alger myth' in American society (Blau & Duncan, 1967, p. 435). There has, however, been little research on whether the socio-economic situation of the second generation would present a similar or greater myth, or equally, a persisting scar on British as well as on American conscience (though see Li, 2010, 2012; Model, 2005).

Cross-national research on British and US social structures is not a common theme in sociological analysis, with only a few studies available. Erikson and Goldthorpe's (1985) and Kerckhoff, Campbell, and Wingfield-Laird's (1985) studies focused on class mobility and found a common underlying pattern, but showed little insight into ethnic fortunes. Owing to data limitation, comparative ethnic studies tend to look at a single group or similar groups at one time, without focusing on the second generation. For instance, Cheng (1994) examined the socio-economic situation of Chinese in the two countries, but the other ethnic groups were not directly compared. Model (2005) explored the labour market situation of several groups in the two countries in the earlier 1990s, but gave no evidence on the trends. Thus, a comparative research of ethnic relations, particularly with regard to the second generation, is, as Heath, Rothon, and Kilpi (2008, p. 224) put it, 'in its infancy'.

DATA AND METHODS

To try to address the questions outlined above, we use the most authoritative data available, namely, the Samples of Anonymised Records (SARs) from the 1991 and the 2001 censuses of the population in Great Britain and the Integrated Public Use Microdata Series (IPUMS) (Ruggles et al., 2008) from the 1990 and 2000 censuses of the population in the United States. We pooled the 1% Household and the 2% Individual SARs for 1991 and the 3% Individual SARs for 2001 (http://www.ccsr.ac.uk/sars/), and the 1% and the 5% IPUMS for 1990 and 2000 (http://usa.ipums.org/usa/sampdesc.shtml). The use of such large datasets is necessitated by the need to ensure large sample sizes for subgroups in ethnicity by gender combinations in each country and at each time point. All the respondents selected for use in the present analysis were born in the two countries, hence at least the second generation. As the British data contain no information on the year of arrival for those born abroad, we cannot include 1.5th generation in the study as Waters et al. (2012) did. The analysis is confined to men aged 16–64 years and women aged 16–59 years as they are generally the 'working-age' population. Full-time students are omitted from the analysis, as the decision to stay in school or enter the labour market might involve different processes between the majority and minority ethnic groups. For instance, the longer stay in education by the second generation could well be a 'pre-emptive strategy' against employer discrimination.

As our research is on the labour market position of the second generation, the most important first task is to code the variables on ethnicity and labour market position (employment status and social class) in a standardised way. With regard to ethnicity, we code the same categories for the two countries while taking into account some country-specific groups. For ethnicity in Britain, we follow standard practice in using the 1991 SARs and code six main categories: White, Black Caribbean, Black African, Indian, Pakistani/ Bangladeshi and Chinese. The White group includes White Irish (people from the Republic of Ireland rather than Northern Ireland) and White Other (from the Commonwealth countries and from Europe). An analysis by Li & Heath (2008, 2010) showed that White Other and White Irish fared equally well as did White British at the two time points in question in terms of employment and access to professional and managerial positions. It is thus reasonable to group all Whites into the same category for the present study. People of Pakistani/Bangladeshi origin are grouped together due to the need for consistency with the US data, where the sample sizes for them, especially in 1990, are too small to yield reliable results for separate analysis. In the 2001 SARs, ethnic categories, which were separately coded for England and Wales on the one hand, and for Scotland on the other, have been re-coded to ensure consistency across the three countries within Britain (Northern Ireland data are not used in this analysis as the minority ethnic groups were not differentiated) and with those used for the 1991 SARs. A fairly large number of people of mixed origins in the 2001 SARs identify themselves as 'White and Black Caribbean' and 'White and Black African' (0.45% and 0.15%, respectively, in England and Wales). Prior analysis shows them to bear closer resemblance to their Black than to their White peers in the labour market position. In the light of this, they are coded to their respective minority groups rather than to White groups.

In the US data, we code ethnicity with eight main categories, that is, six categories as in the SARs (with African Americans in the United States 'notionally' corresponding to Black Africans in Britain[3]), and two US-specific groups that have received much attention in academic research (Massey, 1995). A range of source variables in the IPUMS were used in coding the ethnic variable: single race identifier (*racesingd*), Hispanic origin (*hispand*), birth place (*bpld*) and first and second ancestry identifiers (*ancest1d* and *ancest2d*). The resulting categories are: (i) White; (ii) African American (who are third or higher generation); (iii) Black Caribbean who self-identify as being Black and have first or second ancestry with Jamaica, Anguilla, Antigua, Bahamas, Barbados, British Virgin Islands, Dominica, Grenada, Montserrat, St Kitts, St Vincent, Trinidad, British West Indies, West Indian (non-specified) and Guyana; (iv) Indian (who self-identify as being of Indian heritage); (v) Pakistani/Bangladeshi (who are similarly coded as Indians but combined due to their small size);[4] (vi) Chinese; (vii) non-Mexican Hispanic (hereafter called 'Hispanic'); and (viii) Mexican.[5]

With regard to labour market position, we combined employment status with class position following Goldthorpe (1987, p. 268). Thus, we first differentiated employed, unemployed, and inactive and then, among the employed, we further differentiated three classes: (i) a professional and managerial 'salariat' class; (ii) an intermediate class of routine non-manual, own account, manual supervisors and lower technicians; and (iii) a manual working class of skilled, semi- and unskilled workers including agricultural labourers. It is noted here that the official class schema changed between the 1991 and the 2001 censuses in Britain, with the Social-Economic Groups (SEGs) used in 1991 and the National Statistics Social-economic Classification (NS-SeC) in 2001. We follow the standard practice of converting the SEGs (Heath & McDonald, 1987) and the NS-SeC (Rose & O'Reilly, 1998) into the Goldthorpe class. For the US data, we coded the same three classes as in Britain using the standard occupational classification variable (*occ1990*). As lower managers and higher supervisors were coded as part of the salariat in the SARs, the same was done for the IPUMS. Combining employment status and class yields five categories: salariat, intermediate, working class, unemployed and inactive.[6] This classification is apt for ethnic analysis as their unemployment rates are usually found as disproportionally high (Berthoud, 2000; Heath & Li, 2008, 2010; Li & Heath, 2008).

We use descriptive data and conditional mixed-process (CMP) models (Roodman, 2009) in the analysis. The CMP first differentiates labour market participation and non-participation (active = 1 and inactive = 0) in the selection part and, for the regression, models a series of ordered categories from unemployment to access to the salariat. We control for education, marital status and presence of dependent children in the household, as these are usually found to have a considerable impact on people's labour market position. As age in the 2001 SARs is band-coded, we adopted the same bands for all data sources used.[7]

The analysis is conducted for men and women, and for each country, separately. We first present descriptive analysis, followed by multivariate modelling.[8] Various Wald tests[9] are conducted for within-country (over-time) changes and between-country differences. As the sample size (around 20 million records in total excluding first-generation immigrants) makes the analysis very time-consuming, we sub-sampled some big groups but kept smaller groups intact. This resulted in a reduced sample (N = 410,093) within the confines of our data selection which still contains large sizes for all subgroups by ethnicity, generation, sex, year and country.[10]

ANALYSIS

We first show the ethnic distribution of men and women in the labour market in Tables 1 and 2, respectively. Analysing the data of Table 1, we find that nearly one in four men in both countries were in the professional and managerial salariat class in the earlier period but, whereas the proportion stayed at a roughly similar level for US men in 2000, it increased by 9.5 percentage points (from 23.3% to 32.8%) for British men. This might raise doubts over the comparability of data. Yet, looking at women's data, it is reassuring to find that there is little difference in the proportions found in salariat positions in the two countries: 28.6% of British compared with 28.0% of US women were found in such positions in 2001. Given this, we have reasons to believe, as other researchers have also found (Devine, 1997), that American women are more likely to be in salariat positions than their male counterparts (with the latter being more likely to be in self-employment which is included in the intermediate class in this analysis).

Looking at ethnic differences among men, we find both differences between groups and pronounced disadvantages for some groups. In the British case, with the exception of Chinese, all minority groups were less, and Pakistanis/Bangladeshis less than half as, likely to be in the salariat and all, including Chinese, were two to three times as likely to be unemployed as Whites in 1991. In 2001, Black African, Indian and Chinese men surpassed White men in access to the salariat, but the unemployment rates for all minority groups were still two to three times as high (over four times in the

Table 1. Labour Market Position of White and Second Minority Men in Britain and the United States in 1990/1–2000/1 (percentage by row).

	Britain						United States					
	SC	INT	WC	UN	IN	(N)	SC	INT	WC	UN	IN	(N)
1990/1												
White	26.7	22.5	30.6	11.4	8.8	8,922	31.4	22.3	31.9	4.4	9.9	34,086
Black Caribbean	14.5	18.3	28.9	33.7	4.6	1,890	24.8	23.2	34.4	7.1	10.5	1,744
Black A/A American	17.1	22.6	17.8	37.5	5.1	320	12.8	23.4	30.8	10.8	22.2	17,912
Indian	18.6	27.4	24.7	27.0	2.3	1,072	39.1	29.4	14.1	5.8	11.5	550
Pakistani/Bangladeshi	12.7	25.2	18.5	38.1	5.5	600	31.8	29.3	18.5	12.4	8.0	70
Chinese	35.0	25.9	8.8	23.4	6.9	95	54.0	22.6	13.5	3.7	6.2	4,976
Hispanic	—	—	—	—	—	—	18.3	26.5	28.5	8.8	17.8	6,390
Mexican	—	—	—	—	—	—	16.2	26.0	36.8	8.5	12.4	11,368
(%)	23.3	22.4	28.8	18.2	7.3		24.6	23.6	30.7	7.1	14.0	
2000/1												
White	33.5	27.4	19.0	5.2	14.9	9,599	32.4	22.0	29.0	3.6	13.0	36,066
Black Caribbean	27.9	22.3	19.8	16.8	13.2	3,681	28.7	25.2	28.1	3.8	14.1	1,513
Black A/A American	36.7	18.8	13.4	18.3	12.8	1,006	13.7	22.7	25.0	9.1	29.4	22,873
Indian	41.7	24.1	15.1	11.6	7.5	2,630	45.5	17.8	9.3	14.7	12.8	2,296
Pakistani/Bangladeshi	22.7	21.2	18.4	22.7	15.0	1,988	40.8	32.4	8.7	10.9	7.2	321
Chinese	44.1	24.3	14.0	9.1	8.5	329	54.8	22.6	9.4	4.7	8.6	6,458
Hispanic	—	—	—	—	—	—	18.4	25.2	25.0	7.4	23.9	11,318
Mexican	—	—	—	—	—	—	16.4	26.8	29.8	7.2	19.7	14,336
(%)	32.8	24.8	18.2	10.9	13.4		25.4	23.3	25.6	6.4	19.3	

Notes:

1. SC: the professional and managerial salariat class; INT: the intermediate class of routine non-manual, own-account, lower supervisorial and lower technical workers; WC: the working class of skilled, semi-skilled and unskilled manual workers, including agricultural labourers; UN: the unemployed; and IN: the inactive.

2. Black A/A American: Black African in Britain and African American in the United States.

Table 2. Labour Market Position of White and Second-Generation Minority Women in Britain and the United States in 1990/1–2000/1 (Percentage by Row).

	Britain						United States					
	SC	INT	WC	UN	IN	(N)	SC	INT	WC	UN	IN	(N)
1990/1												
White	19.3	34.8	12.4	5.6	27.9	8,406	27.7	27.6	17.4	3.6	23.7	32,578
Black Caribbean	16.2	37.5	7.3	17.4	21.5	2,053	24.7	27.5	17.7	5.7	24.5	1,854
Black A/A American	15.5	26.6	6.1	26.5	25.4	339	17.7	22.6	24.9	9.3	25.5	20,660
Indian	13.5	36.4	11.0	18.0	21.0	1,021	32.4	29.4	11.8	5.5	20.9	489
Pakistani/Bangladeshi	7.5	19.0	7.6	22.6	43.4	669	19.2	26.9	20.1	5.3	28.5	72
Chinese	23.9	34.2	4.0	15.3	22.6	101	47.1	28.4	9.8	2.4	12.2	4,660
Hispanic	–	–	–	–	–	–	17.8	24.6	16.8	7.7	33.1	6,717
Mexican	–	–	–	–	–	–	16.9	27.7	19.2	6.9	29.4	11,300
(%)	17.6	34.3	11.0	10.2	27.0		23.5	26.0	19.3	6.1	25.2	
2000/1												
White	28.2	22.9	21.2	3.3	24.4	8,890	33.1	23.8	17.2	3.5	22.5	34,168
Black Caribbean	30.1	23.6	14.4	9.1	22.9	4,425	30.4	24.3	17.8	5.1	22.5	1,561
Black A/A American	34.6	20.6	13.5	10.7	20.5	999	21.6	21.3	22.6	8.7	25.8	25,365
Indian	35.5	24.7	12.0	8.8	19.1	2,612	40.0	23.2	9.8	10.4	16.6	2,086
Pakistani/Bangladeshi	15.2	15.4	12.2	12.7	44.5	2,229	35.8	29.0	8.9	7.6	18.8	286
Chinese	37.2	28.7	13.9	8.8	11.5	296	48.7	23.0	8.8	5.3	14.2	6,286
Hispanic	–	–	–	–	–	–	21.9	23.9	16.7	7.5	29.9	11,627
Mexican	–	–	–	–	–	–	21.9	26.8	19.0	6.3	26.0	13,935
(%)	28.6	22.4	16.9	6.9	25.3		28.0	23.5	18.1	6.2	24.2	

Notes:
1. SC: the professional and managerial salariat class; INT: the intermediate class of routine non-manual, own-account, lower supervisorial and lower technical workers; WC: the working class of skilled, semi-skilled and unskilled manual workers, including agricultural labourers; UN: the unemployed; and IN: the inactive.
2. Black A/A American: Black African in Britain and African American in the United States.

case of Pakistani/Bangladeshi men). Getting a job was much more difficult for the second-generation minority men than for Whites.

The British situation was largely mirrored in the US case. Thus, apart from Chinese, Indians and Pakistanis/Bangladeshis, all other groups were less likely to be in salariat positions, and all groups (except Chinese in 1990) were two to four times as likely to be unemployed as Whites. African American, Hispanic and Mexican men were less than half as likely to be in salariat positions as White men. It is also noticeable that the three groups were not only much more likely to be unemployed, but were around twice as likely to be inactive. Given that our samples pertain to working-age men who are not students, the high rates of inactivity are a good indication of hidden unemployment ('discouraged workers') among the groups rather than a genuine lack of desire for labour market participation.

Comparing the male profile of labour market positions in the two countries, one notable feature emerges with regard to Pakistani/Bangladeshi men. In Britain, they were very much disadvantaged both in access to the salariat and in avoidance of unemployment in the two years but in the United States, even though their access to the salariat was little different from that of the Whites, their unemployment rates were still three times as high as those for the Whites (12.4% versus 4.4% in 1990, and 10.9% versus 3.6% in 2000). This suggests that the superior education of Pakistani/Bangladeshi men in the United States failed to protect them from unemployment.

Women's profile has some resemblance to that of men (Table 2). With regard to British women, we find that they made much progress in the period covered. Whereas in 1991, all minority groups except Chinese were less likely than Whites to be in the salariat, the reverse was found in 2001, with the exception of Pakistani/Bangladeshi women. By contrast, while greater access to the salariat might be seen as positive social change, the relatively high rates of unemployment among all minority ethnic women, particularly in 1991, indicate a serious disadvantage. It is remarkable that even though the overall level of unemployment was much reduced in 2001, the relative rates stayed at much the same level, with those for minority ethnics being two to four times as high as for White women. Another striking feature that emerges from the data is that nearly half of the Pakistani/Bangladeshi women were economically inactive in both years (43.4% and 44.5%, respectively).

American women's profile mirrors that of American men closely. Chinese and Indian women were most likely to find themselves in the salariat, in chief contrast with African American, Hispanic and Mexican women.

Although the unemployment rates in the United States were lower than in Britain, African American, Hispanic and Mexican women were still more than twice to be unemployed as compared with White women.[11]

The discussion above is focused on access to the salariat and the avoidance of unemployment. There are other facets left unexplored such as relative position in the intermediate and working classes. Equally important is the extent of 'ethnic penalty', namely, the net disadvantages faced by minority ethnics when human capital (educational qualifications and labour market experience as indicated by age and age squared) and personal attributes (health, marital status and dependent children) are controlled for. In the following, we present findings from the CMP models as earlier discussed. As at least one 'identifying variable' must be used in the selection but not the regression part of the models, we use long-term limiting illness for this on the grounds that it would have a primary effect on labour market participation. The results, shown in Tables 3 and 4 for men and women, respectively, can be interpreted in a fairly straightforward manner. The lower part (selection model) estimates the likelihood of being economically active ('participation rates') and the upper part (regression model) estimates, for the economically active, the chances of gaining desirable and avoiding undesirable labour market positions. We ordered the data from unemployment to access to the salariat as indicating increasing social desirability of the positions. The coefficients in the selection model are logit, and those in the regression part ordinal logit, parameters. For men and women in each country and in each year, we construct two models: firstly without, and then with, socio-demographic controls.

Table 3 shows men's likelihood of labour market participation (selection model) and, among the economically active, their relative labour market position (regression model). Looking firstly at the selection model, we find that health, education, age and dependent children all had the effects in the expected direction. Thus, men with long-term limiting illness, no higher education and no partners were, in most cases, less likely to be in the labour market, whereas those in the middle ages and having dependent children were, other things being equal, more likely to be economically active. These variables also have basically the same direction in their effects on labour market position in the regression model, with the exception that having dependent children has a negative effect on labour market position. Combining the two aspects, the data suggest that having dependent children makes men more likely to be economically active, but less likely to have (better) jobs. The effect of marital status echoes findings by Chun and Lee (2001), although their focus was on earnings.[12]

Table 3. Conditional Mixture-Process Models on Male Labour Market Position in Britain and the United States (1990/1).

	1990/1 Britain		1990/1 United States		2000/1 Britain		2000/1 United States	
	Model 1	Model 2	Model 1	Model 2	Model 1	Model 2	Model 1	Model 2
Regression (LM position)								
White (ref)	0	0	0	0	0	0	0	0
Black Caribbean	-0.608***	-0.335***	-0.186***	-0.054	-0.342***	-0.214***	-0.030	0.045
Black A/A American	-0.555***	-0.528***	-0.408***	-0.250***	-0.195***	-0.401***	-0.141***	-0.044**
Indian	-0.373***	-0.158***	0.292***	0.310***	-0.027	-0.091**	0.120*	0.124*
Pakistani/Bangladeshi	-0.639***	-0.360***	-0.054	-0.140	-0.521***	-0.422***	0.071	0.239*
Chinese	0.040	0.046	0.547***	0.344***	0.082	0.108	0.446***	0.316***
Hispanic	—	—	-0.241***	-0.082**	—	—	-0.095***	0.058**
Mexican	—	—	-0.359***	-0.164***	—	—	-0.208***	-0.016
No tertiary education		-1.363***		-1.100***		-1.072***		-0.885***
Age		0.428***		0.030		0.672***		0.090***
Age squared		-0.050***		0.008*		-0.076***		0.003
Having dependent children		-0.048*		-0.115***		-0.046*		-0.110***
Unpartnered		-0.282***		-0.150***		-0.245***		-0.059***
Selection (LM participation)								
White (ref)	0	0	0	0	0	0	0	0
Black Caribbean	0.282***	-0.207**	0.087	0.051	-0.026	-0.192***	-0.051	-0.056
Black A/A American	0.314	-0.146	-0.529***	-0.492***	0.052	-0.181**	-0.541***	-0.490***
Indian	0.550***	-0.010	-0.209	-0.297*	0.289***	-0.058	0.108	-0.130*
Pakistani/Bangladeshi	0.289**	-0.254*	0.018	-0.035	-0.150***	-0.466***	0.330*	0.084
Chinese	0.138	-0.314	0.127*	-0.004	0.173	-0.095	0.224***	-0.004
Hispanic	—	—	-0.370***	-0.395***	—	—	-0.401***	-0.423***
Mexican	—	—	-0.176	-0.203**	—	—	-0.284***	-0.295***

Table 3. (*Continued*)

	1990/1				2000/1			
	Britain		United States		Britain		United States	
	Model 1	Model 2	Model 1	Model 2	Model 1	Model 2	Model 1	Model 2
Having long-term limiting illness	-2.138***	-2.036***	-1.574***	-1.441***	-1.686***	-1.560***	-0.398***	-0.294***
No tertiary education		0.048		-0.504***		-0.340***		-0.602***
Age		0.592**		0.505***		0.536***		0.064*
Age squared		-0.133***		-0.098***		-0.102***		-0.037***
Having dependent children		-0.031		0.453***		0.149***		0.447***
Unpartnered		-0.319***		-0.223***		-0.225***		0.029
Constant	1.859***	2.131***	1.576***	1.639***	1.481***	1.532***	1.181***	1.852***
Rho	-0.379***	-0.380***	-0.374***	-0.366***	-0.447***	-0.455***	-1.502***	-1.304***
Intercept 1	-1.081***	-1.647***	-1.623***	-2.381***	-1.361***	-1.146***	-1.580***	-1.952***
Intercept 2	-0.182***	-0.674***	-0.366***	-1.043***	-0.629***	-0.320***	-0.517***	-0.829***
Intercept 3	0.478***	0.100	0.369***	-0.193***	0.104***	0.543***	0.117***	-0.082*
N	12,899	12,899	77,089	77,089	19,233	19,233	95,151	95,151

Notes: In the section model, active = 1, inactive = 0; in the regression model, 1 = unemployed, 2 = working class; 3 = intermediate class and 4 = salariat.
* P<0.5; ** P<0.1; *** P<0.001.

Table 4. Conditional Mixture-Process Models on Female Labour Market Position in Britain and the United States (1990/1).

	1990/1				2000/1			
	Britain		United States		Britain		United States	
	Model 1	Model 2	Model 1	Model 2	Model 1	Model 2	Model 1	Model 2
Regression (LM position)								
White (ref)	0	0	0	0	0	0	0	0
Black Caribbean	-0.315***	-0.187***	0.116**	-0.053	-0.044	-0.035	-0.090*	-0.018
Black A/A American	-0.532***	-0.628***	-0.430***	-0.296***	-0.020	-0.260***	-0.310***	-0.173***
Indian	-0.425***	-0.258***	0.078	0.198**	0.054***	-0.022	-0.057	0.038
Pakistani/Bangladeshi	-0.676***	-0.279***	-0.203	0.011	-0.320***	-0.063	-0.018	0.189
Chinese	-0.074	-0.103	0.362***	0.162***	0.005	-0.188**	0.176***	0.086**
Hispanic	—	—	-0.246***	-0.087**	—	—	-0.170***	-0.024
Mexican	—	—	-0.278***	-0.090***	—	—	-0.207***	-0.004
No tertiary education		-1.198***		-0.851***		-0.890***		-0.716***
Age		0.727***		0.256***		0.894***		0.316***
Age squared		-0.097***		-0.022***		-0.111***		-0.027***
Having dependent children		0.093***		-0.077***		-0.092***		-0.006
Unpartnered		-0.150***		-0.207***		-0.105***		-0.155***
Selection (LM participation)								
White (ref)	0	0	0	0	0	0	0	0
Black Caribbean	0.190***	0.081*	0.009	0.022	0.020	0.004	0.013	0.016
Black A/A American	0.148	0.021	-0.011	-0.027	0.121*	0.012	-0.073***	-0.057**
Indian	0.201***	0.161**	0.054	-0.181	0.114***	0.014	0.253***	-0.065
Pakistani/Bangladeshi	-0.419***	-0.373***	-0.225	-0.408	-0.637***	-0.641***	0.140	-0.204
Chinese	0.188	-0.080	0.413***	0.159***	0.412***	0.099	0.322***	0.081**
Hispanic	—	—	-0.251***	-0.246***	—	—	-0.207***	-0.193***
Mexican	—	—	-0.193***	-0.121***	—	—	-0.114***	-0.109***

Table 4. (*Continued*)

| | 1990/1 | | | | 2000/1 | | | |
| | Britain | | United States | | Britain | | United States | |
	Model 1	Model 2	Model 1	Model 2	Model 1	Model 2	Model 1	Model 2
Having long-term limiting illness	-1.040^{***}	-1.093^{***}	-1.179^{***}	-1.117^{***}	-1.150^{***}	-1.137^{***}	-0.238^{***}	-0.144^{***}
No tertiary education		-0.686^{***}		-0.590^{***}		-0.560^{***}		-0.571^{***}
Age		-0.096		0.200^{***}		0.058		-0.090^{**}
Age squared		-0.006		-0.038^{***}		-0.023^{**}		-0.006
Having dependent children		-0.803^{***}		-0.339^{***}		-0.531^{***}		-0.085^{***}
Unpartnered		0.271^{***}		0.255^{***}		0.108^{***}		0.184^{***}
Constant	0.667^{***}	2.074^{***}	0.816^{***}	1.204^{***}	0.876^{***}	1.692^{***}	0.772^{***}	1.576^{***}
Rho	-0.438^{***}	-0.893^{***}	-0.397^{***}	-0.749^{***}	-0.372^{***}	-0.660^{***}	-1.102^{***}	-1.527^{***}
Intercept 1	-1.381^{***}	-1.334^{***}	-1.708^{***}	-1.955^{***}	-1.474^{***}	-0.773^{***}	-1.687^{***}	-1.550^{***}
Intercept 2	-0.851^{***}	-0.804^{***}	-0.722^{***}	-0.954^{***}	-0.629^{***}	0.134	-0.827^{***}	-0.647^{***}
Intercept 3	0.377^{***}	0.491^{***}	0.177^{***}	0.004	0.129^{***}	0.982^{***}	-0.134^{***}	0.086
N	12,589	12,589	78,317	78,317	19,451	19,451	95,278	95,278

Notes: In the section model, active $= 1$, inactive $= 0$; in the regression model, $1 =$ unemployed, $2 =$ working class; $3 =$ intermediate class and $4 =$ salariat.

$^{*}P<0.5$; $^{**}P<0.1$; $^{***}P<0.001$.

Our main interest is in the ethnic differences as shown in the regression part. Looking firstly at the data on men in Britain, we find grave instances of ethnic penalty. At both time points, second-generation men were, with the sole exception of Chinese, found holding significantly less desirable positions than White men did. Even though controlling for socio-demographic factors reduced the impact of ethnic penalty in most cases, the penalty actually increased for Black Africans and Indians in 2001, from $-.195$ to $-.401$ in the former, and from $-.027$ to $-.091$ in the latter, cases. The penalty for the two groups was brought into greater relief mainly because they were so much better qualified (45% and 40% having tertiary education, respectively) than White men (21%). Similar penalty was found in the case of Chinese men in 2001, with the coefficients changing from .082 to $-.108$ from model 1 to model 2, albeit failing to reach the conventional significance level.

With respect to US men, we find much weaker effects of ethnic penalty compared with the British case. After controlling for socio-demographic factors, some groups were found to hold more desirable positions than Whites did, especially in 2000. African American, Hispanic and Mexican men were markedly disadvantaged in 1990 even controlling for human capital and demographic attributes, but their penalty was much reduced a decade later.

Turning to women (Table 4), we find a notable and yet much expected difference to men's profile, namely, that having dependent children has a detrimental effect on women's participation in the labour market (the selection part). The other features are essentially the same as for men with the sole exception that, controlling for socio-demographic attributes, Black African women's labour market position worsened from model 1 to model 2 in both years, while the deterioration only occurred in 2001 for their male counterpart. Ethnic penalty was also found for Chinese women in Britain in 2001: without controlling for education and other factors, they were having a similar position to that of White women but after controlling for these factors (50% of them having tertiary education), they were significantly behind ($e^{-.188} = .829$) White women among whom only 21% had tertiary education, a net disadvantage of 17% in the odds of gaining desirable and avoiding undesirable positions in labour market hierarchy. The net disadvantages encountered by American second-generation women were much weaker in comparison with those in Britain.

The data on net ethnic disadvantages are not easy to grasp. To get an intuitive feel at changing fortunes over time or the differences between countries, we show, in Table 5, the results of Wald tests based on regression coefficients in model 2 of Tables 3 and 4. The part under 'Over Time' is aimed at testing the straight-line assimilation theory. If most second-generation

Table 5.   Changes Over Time and between Countries in Labour Market Positions by Second-Generation Minority Ethnic Groups in Britain and the United States in 1990/1–2000/1.

	Over Time (1990/1–2000/1)		Between countries (United States–Great Britain)	
	Great Britain	United States	1990/1	2000/1
Men				
Black Caribbean	↑***	ns	US***	US***
Black African/African American	ns	↑***	US***	US***
Indian	ns	↓*	US***	US***
Pakistani/Bangladeshi	ns	ns	ns	US***
Chinese	ns	ns	ns	US***
Hispanic	–	↑***	–	–
Mexican	–	↑***	–	–
Women				
Black Caribbean	↑***	ns	US*	Ns
Black African/African American	↑***	↑***	US***	Ns
Indian	↑***	↓*	US***	Ns
Pakistani/Bangladeshi	↑**	ns	ns	US*
Chinese	ns	↓*	US*	US***
Hispanic	–	↑*	–	–
Mexican	–	↑***	–	–

Notes:
1. Based on the regression coefficients for ethnicity in model 2, Tables 3 and 4, controlling for age, age squared and long-term illness.
2. In the within-country comparisons, ↑ means significant improvement and ↓ significant deterioration overtime. In the between-country comparison, US means the group was significantly more likely to have a better labour market position in the United States than in Britain, vice versa for Great Britain. In both types of comparison, ns indicates no significant difference either over time or between countries.

groups experience deteriorating labour market positions over time, then one would reject the hypothesis. What emerges from the test is that the theory survived the test. In a total of 24 tests, 11 groups improved their situation over time, with 10 showing no change. The remaining 3 cases of negative change concern reduced advantages over Whites: from .31 to .124 for men, and .198 to .038 for women, of Indian origins, and from .162 to .086 for Chinese women, in the United States. Thus, the overall picture (14 out of

24 tests) is one of convergence with the Whites as predicted by the straight-line theory, and no evidence of devastating contradiction was found.

The between-country comparisons were aimed at the applicability of the theories in the British context. That is, does American society provide an overwhelmingly more favourable situation for second-generation integration than Britain? Here we find that in a majority of tests (14 out of 20), it is indeed the case. The most surprising finding is that Blacks were doing better in the United States than in Britain.[13] Black Caribbean and African American men in the United States were outperforming Black Caribbean and Black African men in Britain at both time points, and the two groups of Black women were doing better in the United States than their British peers in 1991. The Black women were making good progress in 2001 and had no difference with their US counterparts in 2001. Thus at least for Black and Indian women, the gaps between the two countries were closed.

The modelling tables above concern the overall desirability in the labour market and it is hard to discern the specific position of the second-generation groups. To see this, we present the predicted probabilities in the different labour market positions for the economic active. The data, shown in Fig. 1, are the net effects based on the regression part of model 2 in Tables 3 and 4 taking the covariates at their mean values, which would also allow us to test some of the claims of the segmented assimilation theory. Of course, the census data do not allow us to conduct a systematic test of all the claims in the theory. Yet the thesis of dissonant acculturation would predict deteriorating labour market positions for groups from particularly disadvantaged origins. Since demographic factors and education have been controlled for (with the latter being the most powerful channel to labour market position over which parental resources would find the clearest influence), it could, we believe, be fairly safely assumed that the mechanism for dissonant acculturation would manifest itself in an overtime comparison just as it would in intergenerational analysis in the original enunciation of the theory. If there is clear evidence pointing to deterioration in the labour market position for certain groups, the hypothesis would be regarded as being substantiated.

Fig. 1 shows that most second-generation men (except Chinese) were much behind than White men in gaining access to the salariat and more likely to be unemployed in Britain in 1991, yet had improved situations in 2001, with only Pakistani/Bangladeshi men being some way behind White men in gaining access to the salariat in 2001. The improvement in the US case was even more salient. The situation for women largely mirrored that for men in both countries. Further analysis, using the difference of differences method, shows that out of all scenarios, only Pakistani/

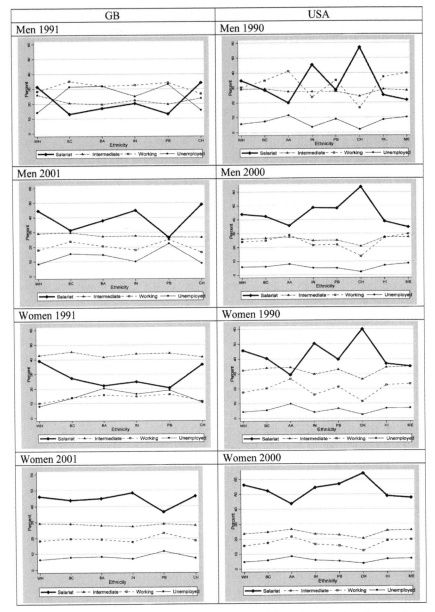

Fig. 1. Net Effects (%) of Labour Market Position Among the Economically
Active.

Bangladeshi men in Britain 'fit the bill' in terms of salariat access and avoidance of working-class positions. They were 18 percentage points behind White men in salarait access in 1991 (31–13) and the differences enlarged by only one point (45–26 = 19). And the same was true of working-class occupancy: they had a 'lead' of 6 points over White men in 1991 (34–28), which became 7 points in 2001 (25–18). Overall, then, only Pakistani/Bangladeshi men had a very slightly deteriorating situation in their fortunes and all other groups, for men and women and in both countries alike, showed improvement by differing degrees. In other words, the expectations of the segmented assimilation theory found no strong support.

DISCUSSION AND CONCLUSION

Both Britain and the United States hold, in principle and enshrined in the laws, the ideal of social justice and equal opportunity. To the extent that this is manifested in ethnic (as in gender and class) terms, the second-generation occupational attainment would provide a unique basis for testing the competing theses on racial assimilation. As the new second generation on both sides of the Atlantic now constitutes an increasingly important force in the labour market and the democratic process, their integration is of paramount interest.

Although academic interest in relative social fluidity in the two countries has a long standing and is still relevant, the current debate is more focused on the fortunes of the 'new second generation'. Here, the revised straight-line and the segmented assimilation theories envision different scenarios, with the former predicting overall progress, and the latter foreseeing a growing divergence between those achieving rapid upward mobility into the upper middle class typically occupied by the Whites and others facing downward spiral into the underclass of permanent poverty and social exclusion. The segmented assimilation theory has enjoyed considerable popularity in the United States and is finding its way into the European context (Portes, Vickstrom, & Aparicio, 2011; Thomson & Crul, 2007). Yet, there has been, to the best of our knowledge, no systematic research using national representative data to test the claims for the new second generation.

This study uses micro-data from the censuses in the two countries to examine the labour market situation of the second generation over the decade. Our main findings show both ethnic penalties/diversities and some notable progress. Thus, most second-generation men in both countries and at both time points, and most women in 1990/1 in both countries were found as being penalised. The variations concern people of Chinese and Indian origins outperforming Whites in the two countries with Black Africans, Black Caribbeans and Pakistanis/Bangladeshis in Britain, and African Americans, Black Caribbeans, Hispanics and Mexicans in the United States, doing much worse. While such penalties and variations as shown in our two modelling tables are not ostensibly denied by either theory, the evidence of most second-generation groups doing better in 2001 than 1991 as shown in Fig. 1 would, on most reasonable grounds, lend greater support for the revised straight-line theory than for the segmented assimilation theory.

The between-country analysis (Table 5) shows the United States as having more favourable chances for the second generation than Britain. Yet, there is also evidence of Britain catching up with the United States. Second-generation women in Britain were doing equally well as their American counterparts in 2001. In both countries, progress is visible, albeit slow.

The main limitation of the present study is the lack of information on parental class and community support in the Census data, which prevents a detailed analysis of the assumptions underlying the segmented assimilation theory (see Li, 2011 for analysis of ethnic social mobility in the two countries). However, it could also be said that whatever the presumed processes, it is still the outcomes that have the most crucial bearing on the validity of theories. In this sense, we believe that the present study has made a unique contribution to understanding the patterns and trends of second-generation integration in the two countries. We await the new data from the 2011 Census in Britain to see whether the momentum has been maintained so that the second and third generation in Britain are a step closer to the dream as promised by the Queen (2008) that everyone in the land shall have 'a fair chance in life'.

NOTES

1. In US literature, the children of the visible (non-white) minority ethnic groups who came to the United States in recent decades are called 'new second generation' to differentiate them from the descendants of those who came from Europe in the earlier period (Alba, 2005).

2. 'Until we summon up the courage to distinguish between the problems of poverty and the problems of race, we shall have to reckon with the consequences of our lack of candor' (Duncan, 1968, p. 109). It is noted here that all non-Black respondents are included in the White category in Duncan's analysis.

3. Black Africans in Britain and African Americans in the United StatesA are not comparable in a strict sense: the former are children of (mostly) voluntary

immigrants (some of their parents were refugees and asylum seekers, though), while the latter are the descendants of involuntary migrants who, for generations, suffered the worst kind of discrimination in American history.

4. In both the SARs and the IPUMS, we also coded two other categories: Black Other (those from places other than the West Indies and Africa in Britain, or from Cape Verde and Haiti in the United States) and Other ('Other Asia' and 'Other Other' in Britain; and those from South Korea, Japan, the Philippines, Vietnam, Laos and Cambodia in the United States). The Black Other and Other categories in the two countries are not included in the analysis as their compositions are too diverse to yield meaningful interpretation. Bangladeshis (only 15 in 1990 and 84 in 2000 being second-generation) were combined with Pakistanis in the US data.

5. With regard to ethnic coding, it is reassuring to report that our results (combining first and second generations, available on request) almost exactly match the official figures (http://www.census.gov/prod/cen2000/dp1/2khus.pdf), to the second decimal of the percentages. It is further noted here that there are concerns over the quality of data on Hispanics in the 2001 IPUMS. But since over 98% of them identified themselves with one or another of the source countries/communities, they are nearly all captured in our non-Mexican Hispanic category (see Citro, Cork, & Narwood, 2004, ch. 8).

6. While the inactive may be out of the labour market for different reasons, there is little doubt about inherent desirability in the first four categories.

7. The age bands are: $1 = 16/19$, $2 = 20/24$, $3 = 25/29$, $4 = 30/44$, $5 = 45/59$ and $6 = 60/64$. Age squared is coded in a similar way. Following standard practice, we exclude visitors in analysing the 1991 SARs (http://www.ccsr.ac.uk/sars/1991/indiv/variables/residsta/). Information on residential status is not available in the 2001 SARs or the IPUMS.

8. Weighted data are used in all analyses with unweighted Ns reported. All data sources used in this study contain weight variables except the 2001 SARs in which case we created a weight of 1.

9. The Wald test is written as $t = (b_1-b_2)/(s_1^2 + s_2^2)^{1/2}$.

10. Following Model (2005), we took a random sample of bigger groups and kept smaller groups intact. For the SARs, we sampled 2% Whites and kept all other groups intact. For the IPUMs, we sampled 1% Whites, 5% African Americans and 10% Hispanics and Mexicans while keeping the remaining groups intact.

11. An exceptional case here pertains to Indian women in 2000 having the highest unemployment rate (10.4%). Further analysis shows this to be significantly higher than that for White women with or without controlling for other socio-demographic factors. Yet they also had markedly lower inactivity rate (16.6% as compared with 24.2% for all). Combining unemployment and inactivity, we find their worklessness rate (27%) similar to that of White women (26%).

12. As class and earnings are closely related (Goldthorpe & McKnight, 2006), there is no disagreement between our findings and those from Chun and Lee (2001).

13. We also conducted loglinear and UNIDIFF models on the labour market position with or without the economically inactive, with basically the same pattern. For both men and women in 1990/1 and for men in 2000/1, the United States was found more open. There was no difference between women in the two countries in 2000/1. The data are available upon request.

REFERENCES

Alba, R. (2005). Bright versus blurred boundaries: Second-generation assimilation and exclusion in France, Germany and the United States. *Ethnic and Racial Studies, 28*, 20–49.

Alba, R., Kasinitz, P., & Waters, M. (2011). The kids are (mostly) alright: Second-generation assimilation: Comments on Haller, Portes and Lynch. *Social Forces, 89*(3), 763–774.

Alba, R., Lutz, A., & Vesselinov, E. (2001). How enduring were the inequalities among European immigrant groups in the U.S.? *Demography, 38*, 349–356.

Alba, R., & Nee, V. (2003). *Remaking the American mainstream: Assimilation and contemporary immigration.* Cambridge, MA: Harvard University Press.

Bell, D. (1972). On meritocracy and equality. *The Public Interest, 29*, 29–68.

Berthoud, R. (2000). Ethnic employment penalties in Britain. *Journal of Ethnic and Migration Studies, 26*, 389–416.

Blau, P., & Duncan, O. (1967). *The American occupational structure.* New York, NY: Wiley.

Cheng, Y. (1994). Education and class: Chinese in Britain and the United States. Aldershot: Avebury.

Chun, H., & Lee, I. (2001). Why do married men earn more: Productivity or marriage selection? *Economic Inquiry, 39*(2), 307–319.

Citro, C., Cork, D., & Narwood, J. (Eds.). (2004). *The 2000 census: Counting under adversity.* Washington D.C: The National Academic Press.

Daniel, W. (1968). *Racial discrimination in England.* London: Penguin.

Darity, W., Jr., & Mason, P. (1998). Evidence on discrimination in employment: Codes of color, codes of gender. *Journal of Economic Perspectives, 12*, 63–90.

Devine, F. (1997). *Social class in America and Britain.* Edinburgh: Edinburgh University Press.

Duncan, O. D. (1968). Inheritance of poverty or inheritance of race. In D. Moynihan (Ed.), *On understanding poverty: Perspectives from the social sciences* (pp. 85–110). New York: Basic Books.

Erikson, R., & Goldthorpe, J. (1985). Are American rates of social mobility exceptionally high? New evidence on an old issue. *European Sociological Review, 1*(1), 1–22.

Farley, R., & Alba, R. (2002). The new second generation in the United States. *International Migration Review, 36*, 669–701.

Goldthorpe, J., Llewellyn, C., & Payne, C. (1987). *Social mobility and class structure in modern Britain.* Oxford: Clarendon Press.

Goldthorpe, J., & McKnight, A. (2006). The economic basis of social class. In S. Morgan, D. Grusky & G. Fields (Eds.), *Mobility and inequality: Frontiers of research in sociology and economics* (pp. 109–136). Stanford, CA: Stanford University Press.

Gordon, M. (1964). *Assimilation in American life: The role of race, religion and national origins.* New York, NY: Oxford University Press.

Haller, W., Portes, A., & Lynch, S. (2011). Dreams fulfilled, dreams shattered: Determinants of segmented assimilation in the second generation. *Social Forces, 89*(3), 733–762.

Heath, A. (2007). Crossnational patterns and processes of ethnic minority disadvantage. In A. Heath & S. Cheung (Eds.), *Unequal chances: Ethnic minorities in western labour market* (pp. 639–695). Oxford: Oxford University Press.

Heath, A., & Li, Y. (2008). Period, life-cycle and generational effects on ethnic minority success in the labour market. *Kölner Zeitschrift für Soziologie und Sozialpsychologie, 48*, 277–306.

Heath, A., & Li, Y. (2010). *The feasibility of constructing a race equality index*, consultation report for the department of work and pensions, London: Research Report No 695. http://research.dwp.gov.uk/asd/asd5/rports2009-2010/rrep695.pdf

Heath, A., & McDonald, S. (1987). Social change and the future of the left. *The Political Quarterly, 58*, 364–377.

Heath, A., Rothon, C., & Kilpi, E. (2008). The second generation in Western Europe: Education, unemployment and occupational attainment. *Annual Review of Sociology, 34*, 211–235.

Hirschman, C. (2005). Immigration and the American century. *Demography, 42*(4), 595–620.

Hout, M. (2006). Economic change and social mobility. In G. Therborn (Ed.), *Inequalities of the world* (pp. 119–135). London: Verso.

Jowell, R., & Prescott-Clarke, P. (1970). Racial discrimination and white-collar workers in Britain. *Race, 11*, 397–417.

Kasinitz, P., Mollenkopf, J., Waters, M., & Holdaway, J. (2008). *Inheriting the city: The children of immigrants come of age.* New York, NY: Russell Sage Foundation.

Kerckhoff, A., Campbell, R., & Winfield-Laird, I. (1985). Social mobility in Great Britain and the United States. *American Journal of Sociology, 90*(2), 281–308.

Li, Y. (2009). Tertiary education and labour market position of the second generation minority ethnic groups in Britain and the US (1990/1–2000/1). Conference proceeding on *Adult education and labour market among the second generation immigrants.* http://doku.iab.de/veranstaltungen/2009/Educ2009_Li%20Yaojun.pdf

Li, Y. (2010). The labour market situation of minority ethnic groups in Britain and the USA. *EurAmerica: A Journal of European and American Studies, 40*(2), 259–309.

Li, Y. (2011, 13 September). Persisting distinction? The intergenerational social mobility of Whites and Blacks in Britain and the USA (1972–2006). Presentation at the Social Stratification Conference, Stirling University, UK.

Li, Y. (2012). Ethnic wage gaps in Britain and the US. In R. Connelly, P. Lambert, R. Blackburn & V. Gayle (Eds.), *Social stratification: Trends and processes* (pp. 167–179). Avebury: Ashgate.

Li, Y., & Heath, A. (2008). Ethnic minority men in British labour market (1972–2005). *International Journal of Sociology and Social Policy, 28*(5/6), 231–244.

Li, Y., & Heath, A. (2010). Struggling onto the ladder, climbing the rungs: Employment status and class position by minority ethnic groups in Britain (1972–2005). In J. Stillwell, P. Norman, C. Thomas & P. Surridge (Eds.), *Population, employment, health and well-being* (pp. 83–97). London: Springer.

Lipset, S. (1991). American exceptionalim reaffirmed. In B. E. Shafer (Ed.), *Is America different?* (pp. 1–45). Oxford: Clarendon Press.

Massey, D. (1995). The new immigration and ethnicity in the United States. *Population and Development Review, 21*(3), 631–652.

Menjívar, C. (2000). *Fragmented ties: Salvadoran immigrant networks in America.* Berkeley, CA: University of California Press.

Model, S. (2005). Non-white origins, Anglo destinations: Immigrants in the US and Britain. In G. Loury, T. Modood & S. M. Teles (Eds.), *Ethnicity, social mobility and public policy in the US and UK* (pp. 363–392). Cambridge: Cambridge University Press.

Olson, M. (1982). *The rise and decline of nations.* New Haven, CT: Yale University Press.

Park, R., & Burgess, E. (1921). *Introduction to the science of sociology.* Chicago, IL: University of Chicago Press.

Perlmann, J., & Waldinger, R. (1997). Second-generation decline? Immigrant children past and present: A reconsideration. *International Migration Review*, *31*(4), 893–922.

Portes, A. (1997). Immigration theory for a new century: Some problems and opportunities. *International Migration Research*, *31*(4), 0799–0825.

Portes, A., Fernandez-Kelly, P., & Haller, W. (2005). Segmented assimilation on the ground: The new second generation in early adulthood. Ethnic and Racial Studies, *28*(6), 1000–1040.

Portes, A., Fernandez-Kelly, P., & Haller, W. (2009). The adaptation of the immigrant second generation: Theoretical overview and recent evidence. *Journal of Ethnic and Migration Studies*, *35*(7), 1077–1104.

Portes, A., & Rumbaut, R. (2001). *Legacies: The story of the immigrant second generation.* Berkeley, CA: University of California Press.

Portes, A., Vickstrom, E., & Aparicio, R. (2011). Coming of age in Spain: The self-identification, beliefs and self-esteem of the second generation. *British Journal of Sociology*, *62*(3), 387–417.

Portes, A., & Zhou, M. (1993). The new second generation: Segmented assimilation and its variants among post-1965 immigrant youth. *Annals of the American Academy of Political and Social Science*, *530*, 74–96.

Queen's Speech. (2008). Retrieved December 3, 2008, from http://www.telegraph.co.uk/news/newstopics/politics/3545177/Queens-speech-in-full.html

Quillian, L. (1995). Prejudice as a response to perceived group threat: Population composition and anti-immigrant and racial prejudice in Europe. *American Sociological Review*, *60*, 586–611.

Roodman, D. (2009). Estimating fully observed recursive mixed-process models with cmp. Working Paper 168. Center for Global Development. Washington, DC

Rose, D., & O'Reilly, K. (1998). *Final report of the ESRC review of government social classifications.* Swindon: ESRC/ONS.

Ruggles, S., Sobek, M., Alexander, T., Fitch, C., Goeken, R., Hall, P., … Ronnander, C. (2008). *Integrated public use microdata series: Version 4.0 [Machine-readable database].* Minneapolis, MN: Minnesota Population Center [producer and distributor].

Stewart, M. (1983). Racial discrimination and occupational attainment in Britain. *The Economic Journal*, *93*, 521–541.

Telles, E., & Murguia, E. (1990). Phenotypic discrimination and income differences among Mexican Americans. *Social Science Quarterly*, *71*, 682–696.

Thomson, M., & Crul, M. (2007). The second generation in Europe and the United States: How is the transatlantic debate relevant for further research on the European second generation? *Journal of Ethnic and Migration Studies*, *33*(7), 1025–1047.

Tocqueville, A. (1835, 1968). De la démocratie en Amérique, J.-P. Mayer (Ed.). Paris: Gallimard.

Vermulen, H. (2012). Segmented assimilation and cross-national comparative research on the integration of immigrants and their children. *Ethnic and Racial Studies*, *33*(7), 1214–1230.

Vickerman, M. (1999). *Crosscurrents: West Indian immigrants and race.* New York, NY: Oxford University Press.

Waldinger, R. (2007). Did manufacturing matter? The experience of yesterday's second generation: A reassessment. *International Migration Review*, *41*(1), 3–39.

Waldinger, R., & Perlmann, J. (1998). Second generations: Past, present, future. *Journal of Ethnic and Migration Studies, 24*(1), 5–24.

Warner, W., & Srole, L. (1945). *The social systems of American ethnic groups.* New Haven, CT: Yale University Press.

Waters, M. (2008). Counting and classifying by race: The American debate. *The Tocqueville Review/La Revue Tocqueville, 24*(1), 1–21.

Waters, M., & Jiménez, T. (2005). Assessing immigrant assimilation: New empirical and theoretical challenges. *Annual Review of Sociology, 31*, 16.1–16.21.

Waters, M., Tran, V., Kasinitz, P., & Mollenkopf, J. (2012). Segmented assimilation revisited: Types of acculturation and socioeconomic mobility in young adulthood. *Ethnic and Racial Studies, 33*(7), 1168–1193.

Waters, M., Ueda, R., & Marrow, H. (2007). *The new Americans: A guide to immigration since 1965.* Cambridge, MA: Harvard University Press.

Zhou, M., & Bankson, C. L. (2001). Family pressure and the educational experience of the daughters of Vietnames refugees. *International Migration Review, 39*(4), 133–151.

LIFESTYLES AND SOCIAL STRATIFICATION: AN EXPLORATIVE STUDY OF FRANCE AND NORWAY

Gunn Elisabeth Birkelund and Yannick Lemel

ABSTRACT

To compare France and Germany, we will take a new approach to the discussion on lifestyles and social stratification. Instead of anchoring our definition of social stratification in predefined concepts, such as social class and status, we will empirically explore the latent patterns of social stratification and lifestyles. Our strategy allows us to investigate whether social stratification is best measured by one, two, or more dimensions; and then to map the associated patterns of lifestyles onto this/these dimension(s).

As indicators of social stratification, we use education, household income, and occupational status; and to measure lifestyles, we use data from two surveys on lifestyles and cultural consumption (Media og kulturforbruksundersøkelsen 2004, Norway; and module Pratiques culturelles et sportives, Enquête Permanente sur les Conditions de Vie 2003, France). We limit our analysis to occupationally active respondents, 20–64 years of age.

Class and Stratification Analysis
Comparative Social Research, Volume 30, 189–220
Copyright © 2013 by Emerald Group Publishing Limited
All rights of reproduction in any form reserved
ISSN: 0195-6310/doi:10.1108/S0195-6310(2013)0000030011

We would expect our findings to differ somewhat between the two countries; but given that social stratification is a pervasive element of all modern societies, we would also expect to find common empirical patterns that may be of relevance to the way we conceptualize lifestyles and social stratification.

Keywords: Social stratification; social space; lifestyle groups; latent dimensions

INTRODUCTION

Sociological research on lifestyles and cultural consumption usually builds on theoretically predefined concepts of social stratification, be it social class or social status, and then empirically correlates this/these concepts with lifestyle patterns. Different patterns have been identified: Bourdieu argues in favor of the so-called homology-thesis by correlating distinctions based on lifestyles and cultural consumption with economic and cultural capital (Bourdieu,1979/1984). According to this thesis, the higher class individuals distinguish themselves by consuming high-brow culture, such as opera, classical music, and theater, whereas the lower class individuals prefer watching movie on the TV and listening to pop music.

By contrast, recent Weberian-inspired studies across several countries have found a more differentiated lifestyle pattern, supporting the omnivore thesis, as advocated by Petersen (1992) (see also Chan, 2010). According to this thesis, people interested in culture are omnivores, that is they go both to the cinema and to the opera/theater.

Whereas the patterns of *lifestyles* in these studies *are explored empirically*, these approaches rely on *theoretical definitions of social stratification*, be it social class or status. Social structure is conceptualized in a number of ways, and within the literature on social class and stratification, there are (at least) two schools of thought: One emphasizing the unidimensionality of social stratification, such as the socioeconomic occupational scale (Blau & Duncan, 1967), the international scale of occupational prestige (Ganzeboom, de Graaf, & Treiman, 1992), and the social status scale recently developed by Chan and Goldthorpe (2007). Other schools of thoughts emphasize the multidimensionality of social stratification: For Bourdieu, the social space comprises two dimensions, one on capital volume, and the other on capital composition (Bourdieu, 1979). The class schemes of Wright

(1985) and Eriksen and Goldthorpe (1992) are theoretically different, yet also these schemes conceptualize social stratification as multidimensional.

In this chapter, we take a different approach. Instead of relying on theoretically predefined concepts, we will *empirically* explore the latent patterns of *lifestyles* and *social stratification*. By doing so, we take a pragmatic view on the dimensionality of social stratification, that is we are open to include more than one dimension, if necessary. Lifestyles can be defined in many ways; we will here refer to lifestyles and cultural activities interchangeably, using information on cultural activities as our basis for defining lifestyle groups. Thereafter, we will merge these patterns to visualize the association between lifestyle groups and social stratification.

Our study is based on two countries: France and Norway, including only economically active citizens between 20 and 64 years of age. Norway, a social-democratic country outside the European Union, with a more compressed income distribution than France, now one of the wealthiest countries in the world, has traditionally been poorer than France. France, a continental country with an old European history, has traditionally been more marked by aristocracy and bourgeois habits and cultures. Looking at lifestyle patterns and social stratification, we will explore what is common, what is unique, and what covaries between these countries (cf. Birkelund, 2006; Coulangeon & Lemel, 2009). Our methodology is explorative, yet our research questions can be summarized as follows:

Social Stratification

Our research design allows us to explore empirically, for France and Norway separately, if social stratification is best measured by one, two, or more dimensions. We would expect our findings to differ somewhat between the two countries, but given that social stratification is a pervasive element of all modern societies, we would also expect to find common empirical patterns that may be of relevance to the way we could theoretically conceptualize social stratification. Without theoretically predefined concepts of social stratification, what patterns of social stratification are found in the two countries?

Lifestyles

Are lifestyle groups easier to differentiate in France than in Norway? There is a long-standing discussion in sociology about how best one should measure cultural consumption and lifestyles. Should one study "tastes" or "activities?" Obviously, what people do might not reflect what they would do if they were free from various types of constraints. Without denying the interest in studying *tastes*, we may underline that their assessment requires complex and costly observation protocols – very seldom implemented in practice. *Our focus of interest is in what people say they do.* As such, we will use activities as our starting point and try to single out groups of people who appear to engage in similar activities and share the same sort of lifestyle.

These are questions we may begin to answer in this chapter, using data from two national representative surveys (2003/2004).

Why Compare France and Norway?

We are comparing two European countries, with some similarities and some differences. Both countries have relatively low levels of economic inequality, with a Gini index of 25.8 for Norway and 32.7 for France.[1] Whereas France is located at the center of the EU, and one of the first countries to initiate European collaboration, Norway is not a member of the EU (yet an active member of the European Economic Agreement), and located at the northern periphery of Europe. The two countries belong to different welfare state regimes, one continental and one social democratic (Esping-Andersen, 1990). Looking at cultural dimensions developed by Hofstede,[2] France and Norway have about the same scores on a scale that measures individualism versus collectivism, yet the two countries differ on other dimensions, in particular an index measuring power distance, an index measuring masculinity, and an index measuring uncertainty. Given the economic, political and cultural differences between Norway and France, we find it interesting exploring the patterns of social stratification and people's lifestyles in these countries.

A Twofold Explorative Design

Our analytic strategy is first constructing empirically the dimension(s) of social stratification in France and Norway separately, and then comparing them. Second, we construct the latent patterns of lifestyles in France and Norway separately, and then compare similarities and differences. Third, we will map lifestyles onto social spaces, for France and Norway separately.

SOME THEORETICAL POINTS

Weber identified social stratification as a multidimensional concept, including social class, status, and power as vital dimensions in modern societies (Weber, 1978[1925]). At the most general level, following Peter Blau's discussion on social structure (Blau, 1977), in order to explore social inequality, we should include the whole set of usual socio-demographic characteristics, such as age, generation, gender, ethnicity, education, income and wealth, occupation, and urbanization of the place of residence (McPherson & Ranger-Moore, 1991; Péli & Nooteboom, 1999). However, our interest here lies with the main variables that underlie the usual sociological representations of the structure of social stratification, and, as there are several ways to measure social stratification, our explorative approach is open to more than one dimension.

The Dimensions of Social Stratification

In *The Distinction*, Bourdieu determines social positions through their place in a bidimensional social space defined by the volume of global capital and the composition of capital, using economic and cultural capital as the main determinants of the social space. Actually, the social space thus developed is a particular variant of Blau's social spaces, which are made of homogeneous cells of various sociodemographic characteristics (McPherson, Miller, & Ranger-Moore, 1991), and the number of dimensions initially generated to define the space reflects the number of variables included in the analysis. For analytic purposes, however, one usually decides including only a reduced set of dimensions, in order to detect the most important dimensions of the social space.[3]

The Bourdieusian model relies on a social space essentially based on the combination of two individuals characteristics: the educational level and the resource level. Thus it could be argued that theoretically the Bourdieusian social space is a two-dimensional social space. Given the complexities in measuring cultural and economic capital, however, it is often necessary including several variables, thereby generating initially more than two dimensions. In this chapter, we limit ourselves to include education, income, and occupational status as measures of stratification. Ideally, we would also have wanted to include more variables. In particular, if we were to follow a usual interpretation of Bourdieus' design, which was never clearly defined by himself (Prieur, Rosenlund, & Skjøtt-Larsen, 2008, p. 49), we should have included a larger number of other variables. We will later include gender, age, and residence (rural/urban) to identify the most common profile of lifestyle groups.

Cultural Activities and Lifestyles

It seems clear by now that a strict version of the homology thesis associated with Bourdieus' work does not receive empirical support in modern analysis of lifestyles and social stratification. Admittedly, it would most likely be possible; using qualitative data, identifying a group attending only high-brow cultural events, yet this group is too small to be detected in survey data representing a sample of the population in a country. In addition, there is no convincing argument that this group has the power to define what constitutes high-brow culture.

The omnivore thesis is still being discussed, and though most empirically oriented research using representative surveys of the populations do find support for this thesis, there are still many questions about its validity and content (Chan, 2010; Peterson, 2005; Nyhammer, 2008; Skarpenes, 2007). Bluntly put, the thesis, first advocated by Richard Petersen (1992), argues there is a group of active consumers in modern societies who are open to various sorts of cultural expressions, including both mass cultural events (such as going to the cinema) and elitist high-brow culture (such as going to the opera). Certainly, more people go to the cinema than to the opera, but the findings support the omnivore thesis: those who do go to the opera (who are relatively fewer) also go to the cinema, and not only that, they also go more frequently to the cinema than others do. Thus, they are omnivores.

Cultural Niches

Lifestyle could work as an identity marker, and we will also be interested in the composition of lifestyle groups, are they on average old or younger, female or male dominated, etc. One may argue that modern societies are filled with small niches of subcultural groups, identifying with, interested in, and particularly also trying to develop specific types of subcultural lifestyles. In particular, young people are often actively engaged in what we may call cultural subgroups, such as the rock and rollers in the 1950s, and the Internet nerds in the 1990s. Some of these groups may also have a political agenda, which would usually be changing the establishment; as when the green activists practice a modest lifestyle to make modern consumer society more environmental friendly. The existence of these niches is an interesting phenomenon, yet exploring them is beyond the scope of this chapter. Lifestyle groups thus identified would probably be too small to be detected in survey data. Our data allows us to distinguish people who are interested in for instance music from people who are not, yet not what kinds of music they listen to.

In a nearby vein, the literature on lifestyle is not always clear on the following point: are lifestyles the prerogative of a limited number of persons or could everyone be characterized by their lifestyle? Surely Bourdieu examined population data (for a recent example, see Benett, 2009). This is not the case with all researchers, though. Like Bourdieu, we adopt here an approach which deals with the whole population, thus we will statistically classify *all* respondents into lifestyle clusters. Whether these clusters also are "cultural groups" in the sense of comprising members with subcultural group awareness is beyond the scope of this chapter to explore.[4]

DATA AND METHODS

Surveys

We use two surveys, one from each country, on lifestyle and cultural activities. For France, we use the survey on *Cultural and Sports Participation* which is part of the May 2003 issue of the *The Continuous Survey of Living Conditions* carried out three times a year by the French statistical office (INSEE). The random sample is representative of individuals aged 15 years or older who live in households in metropolitan France. The response rate is 67%.

For Norway, we use the survey *Kultur og mediebruksundersøkelsen 2004* (the 2004 survey on Cultural and Media Consumption), which was carried out by Statistics Norway. The random sample is representative for the Norwegian population aged 9–79 years.[5] The response rate is 70%.

Variables

Social Stratification Variables

In order to construct social structure, we need valid information on education, income, and occupation. The Norwegian data contains occupational information only on occupationally active respondents; thus for comparative purposes, we have limited both the French and the Norwegian samples to including only occupationally active individuals between 20 and 64 years, excluding students, housewives, unemployed, and retired people. Thus, our French sample comprises 3,744 individuals and the Norwegian sample 993. We will discuss the consequences of this selection at the end of the chapter.

Education will be measured as the number of years necessary to get the highest diploma people have. Given our interest in cultural activities, not tastes, we are interested in economic opportunities to undertake cultural activities. We therefore have constructed a measure of household income (per capita), and given the skewed distribution, we use the *Log of household income per capita*.[6] *Occupational status* is measured according to Chan and Goldthorpe's social status scale (Chan, Birkelund, Aas, & Wiborg, 2011; Chan & Goldthorpe, 2007; Lemel, 2006).

Cultural Activities Variables
The questionnaires in both surveys include items on a variety of cultural practices, such as reading, listening to music, attending festivals and other cultural outings, television viewing, artistic hobbies, going to the cinema, and watching sports activities. Generally, the questions are retrospective in nature, asking about the practice of an activity over the past 12 months (professional and school obligations excluded). The questionnaires used in the two surveys are, however, not identical. In particular, the French survey includes a large number of questions on sports activities, partly due to the French political authorities wanting to map the distribution of sports activities in the French population. By contrast, the Norwegian survey includes questions about time spent on the Internet, video and DVD; questions not included in the French questionnaire. Mainly for this reason, we will perform two sets of analysis for cultural activities; one using a small set of variables that are common in both questionnaires (as similar as obtainable in these surveys; there are still differences in the way some of these variables are worded and the framing of answers).[7] Second, in addition to the common variables, we add country-specific variables, thus obtaining measurements of a larger set of cultural activities (more in the French survey than in the Norwegian survey).

For the first set, we include 11 variables, some measuring cultural activities taking place outside the home: going to the opera, theater, ballet, concert, art exhibition, museum, sports events, movies, and visiting a library, while others (usually) taking place inside the home: reading books, watching TV, and reading newspapers. These variables measure the time the respondents spent on the cultural activity the last time they performed it, or the number of times they have undertaken a particular cultural activity in the last 12 months. We therefore can utilize metric strategies of analysis.

For the second set, we include 44 variables for France, and 21 variables for Norway. Again, the variables measure a number of different cultural activities, in particular related to sports for France.[8] The inclusion of more variables allows us to identify more precise lifestyle clusters in the French data which we will demonstrate later.

Omitted Variable Bias?
The limitations in the questionnaires have unfortunate consequences for our analysis. Our results are limited to the variables included, thereby possibly being unable to identify important lifestyle clusters defined around other cultural activities than measured here. We run the risk of identifying latent lifestyle clusters particular to each country that are an artifact of different, country-specific, variables. How precisely should the activities be defined? We might have chosen to limit the scope of investigation to a few domains, but, in this way, we could not have a more general view, which is precisely our goal. We have therefore tried to cover the various domains examined in the survey. We cannot exclude the possibility that the conclusions we will draw are partly an artifact of the activities we have chosen.

Methods

Various methods can be considered to group individuals presumably having similar lifestyles. One can choose certain practices characterized to be typical of a lifestyle. Thus, for instance, activities like visiting museums and going to classical music concerts are thought to be the distinctive mark of a highbrow lifestyle. This method allows the definition of lifestyle clusters through their *predefined* construction, but its drawbacks are its arbitrariness and the risk of giving too much importance to marginal phenomena. In this chapter, we favor an alternative approach. We have first performed separately *principal component analysis* (PCA) to identify the latent dimensions of social stratification. Second, looking at lifestyle patterns, we have used the K-means method.[9] Our results could be dependant of the specific clustering method implemented. Some sensitivity analyses were done in the French case (Coulangeon & Lemel, 2009). In this case, it appears that a three cluster solution on lifestyle groups is a stable one, rather independent from the clustering techniques used. The results are almost the same no matter if we proceed by describing the observations through the 44 detailed practice indicators or through the 2 or 3 synthetic indicators built up by a main component analysis. Results are also the same if we use other clustering techniques than the K-means method. So, the K-means method was implemented systematically for creating three groups in each case.[10]

The rest of the chapter is organized in the following way: In the first part, we apply PCA on social structure variables for France and Norway. We then continue using PCA and cluster analysis on cultural activity variables, again for France and Norway separately. We then merge the two analyses to map lifestyle clusters onto social structure.

SOCIAL STRATIFICATION – FRANCE AND NORWAY COMPARED

In both countries, we find a latent pattern describing the manifest variables education (log) household income, and occupational status. The pattern is very similar for the two countries, see Tables 1 and 2, and Figs. 1 and 2, and, we argue, mainly bi-dimensional. In both countries, all three variables have positive loadings on the first dimension: education, occupational status, and household income, and, in both countries, the second dimension is mainly defined by differentiation – or substitution – in composition, that is, between (log) household income on the one hand, and education and occupational status on the other. In the third dimension, education status and occupational status are opposing each other, yet this dimension is less important statistically (lower *eigenvalues*). Thus, the social structure/social space in France and Norway is mainly bidimensional.[11]

Looking at the loadings of each variable onto the latent dimension, the first dimension may be interpreted as a proxy for a socioeconomic dimension. Positive values on this dimension are associated with high education, social status, and income, whereas negative values are associated with low education, social status, and income. This dimension resembles in many ways what Bourdieu named the *global capital* dimension.

The second dimension is orthogonally related to the first dimension (i.e. the two dimensions are statistically independent). The second dimension is positively related to household income, whereas education and status have negative loadings on it, in both countries. This dimension resembles what Bourdieu called *capital composition*.

Table 1. Social Space – France – CA (Loadings). (Economically Active 20–65 Years).

Loadings	Components		
	1	2	3
Education	0.61	−0.41	0.68
Occupational status score	0.62	−0.30	−0.73
Log(Income/Head)	0.50	0.86	0.07
% explained	0.67	0.22	0.11

Table 2. Social Space – Norway – CA (Loadings). (Economically Active 20–65 Years).

Loadings	Components		
	1	2	3
Education	0.64	−0.34	0.69
Occupational status score	0.66	−0.20	−0.72
Log (income/head)	0.39	0.92	0.09
% explained	0.56	0.29	0.14

Our findings are not really surprising, given the initial positive correlation between the three manifest variables. In fact, it is precisely this positive correlation between the social stratification variables that leads to the first dimension being a "capital" volume dimension: high values on the first latent dimension means high values on each of the three manifest variables; low values on the first latent dimension means low values on each of the three manifest variables. In all societies where the social stratification variables are positively correlated (and we know of none where this is not the case), the first dimension would pick up this correlation. Thus, obviously a Bourdieusan capital volume dimension must be the first dimension of social spaces.

For the second dimension, the actual patterns between the manifest variables may be less obvious. The second dimension is generated as a dimension orthogonal on the first. This is the fact of the methodological strategy. It is therefore constructed on the association between the manifest variables that are *not* related to their positive correlations, but rather to the deviations from these correlations (off-diagonal patterns, if one compares with cross-tabulations). Which of the manifest variables that oppose the

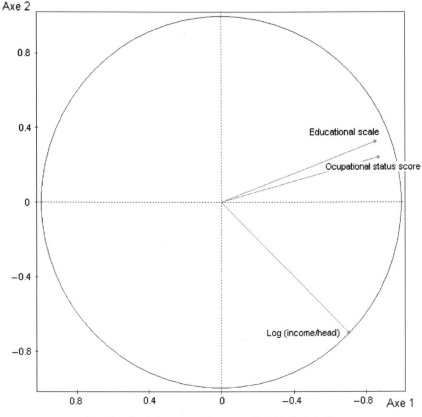

Fig. 1.   Social space – France – CA (Axis 1 & 2).

other(s) is an open question. Empirically, it appears that the occupational status variable is close to education, so that the two variables are therefore opposed to the economic variable. This proximity between occupational status and education deserves reflection and development, but they are outside the scope of this chapter.

We have therefore generated a social space, using only three manifest stratification variables, and we will expect that such a social space will appear in all countries where the stratification variables are positively associated. We do not need any theoretical justification for this "space," the main relevant information would be to find the criterion for deciding what variables go as stratification variables, of which, we would argue, education and income are the most important (cf. the close affinity of education and occupational status).

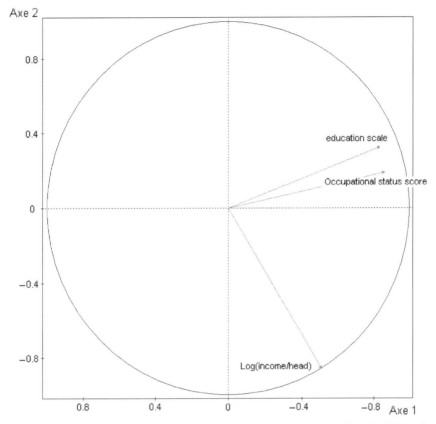

Fig. 2. Social space – Norway – CA (Axis 1 & 2). (Economically Active 20–65 Years)

There is an important conclusion of our results, in a comparative perspective. Even if the social structure of both countries looks very similar, the degree of status crystallization, as measured by our data, is weaker in Norway than in France: The first Eigen vector explains 56% of the variance in Norway and 67% in France (but slightly different measures of variables). This could imply a slightly less open social stratification system in France than in Norway.

LIFESTYLES – FRANCE AND NORWAY COMPARED

We will now proceed to explore lifestyles in the two countries. As discussed, we have some problems of measurements related to the fact that some of these questions are not identical. Further, we are able to use more questions in the French data than in the Norwegian case (simply because the French questionnaire is larger). We have therefore decided to perform two analyses for each country, one including the full set of variables for each country, second, we include only common variables for the two countries. In both cases, we use the K-means method, doing first PCA for smoothing the data and then creating clusters.

France

The Full Set of Activities – France
Looking at France first, we do not succeed finding identity markers that could clearly identify cultural clusters (Coulangeon & Lemel, 2009). Two reasons why: one, the data or the methods used are not good enough. Second, the data and methods are fine, but the reality is not as well-organized as we expect, that is the correlations between the activity variables are rather small in the French dataset. It therefore seems difficult to define social markers in such a way that a person practicing them (for instance going to the opera) with certainty belongs to a specific group (i.e., operalovers).[12]

As discussed earlier, we nevertheless find that a three cluster solution on lifestyle groups is a stable one, rather independent from the clustering techniques used. The first dimension in the activity "space" is a volume dimension, with high loadings from nearly all activities. We could call this dimension an omnivore dimension. The second component refers to sports, and especially "passive" sports, such as reading sports magazine. The exact meaning of the third component is less easy to define. For a three-cluster solution, we observe that whatever the activity, the indicators are weaker in cluster 1 than in clusters 2 and 3, except for TV watching and regional daily newspapers. The indicators are higher in cluster 2 for almost all sports activities (especially the "passive" ones), and higher in cluster 3 for all the other activities. It would thus be tempting to describe cluster 1 as *homebodies* (or TV addicts), cluster 2 as *sports enthusiasts*, and cluster 3 as *cultured*. The size of these groups is 1,708, 1,603, and 382 (see Figs. 3 and 4).

The Reduced Set of Activities – France
We proceed by including only a limited set of 12 variables, common to both countries.[13] We find, as with the full set, the first dimension which is more or less a "volume/diversity" dimension, that is, an omnivore component. The exact meaning of the other dimensions is less easy to define. Perhaps, the

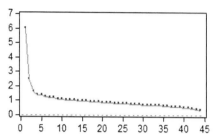

Fig. 3.   Lifestyles – France – CA (% Eigenvalues). (Economically Active 20–65 Years)

second one could be interpreted as an opposition between live spectacles (i.e., watching performances with live actors/players) compared with virtual entertainment (watching TV and movies, reading books, etc.). However, attending sports events is not confirming to this pattern.

The clusters are primarily identified by the volume of activities that people undertake (i.e., the first dimension). The number of clusters to be generated seems less evident than in the previous case, where we used the "full-set" of activity variables, since any cutting along the first dimension of CA is roughly satisfactory. For comparision purposes, we selected the three-clusters solution (respective size: 2,535, 1,063, and 146 people), the interpretation of which seems more straightforward: the first cluster is that of the *homebodies*. The last is that of the *cultured* and the second can be called the *middle-cultured*.

The *cultured* and *middle-cultured* clusters are distinguished by the mean level activity of each activity separately, lower for the "middle cultured" cluster with two exceptions. They are not going to the opera at all, but they go to libraries more frequently and read books more often than the "cultured" cluster. It would be advisable to check the residences of these two groups, access to the opera being obviously easier for people in very large cities, etc. We will get back to the composition of the lifestyle clusters later.

Comparing the Full Set Analysis with the Reduced Set in France
The French survey includes many questions about sports activities. Thus, it may not come as a surprise that, in addition to a home-centered cluster and a "culturally" active cluster, we find a cluster of sports enthusiasts in the full set analysis of cultural activities. Only including common variables for the two countries implies throwing out most of these sports variables. Then, we are unable to identify a cluster of sports enthusiasts, and the dominant lifestyle clusters in our data become the home-centerd cluster and two

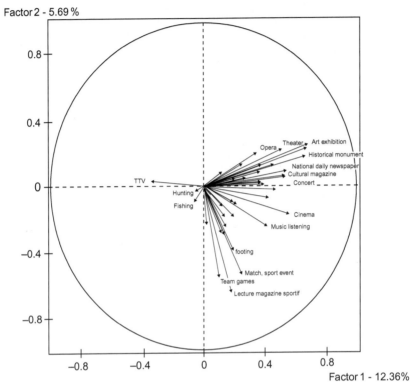

Fig. 4. Lifestyles – France – CA (Axis 1 & 2). (Economically active 20–65 years)

culturally oriented clusters, reflecting a more traditional definition of culture, based only on variables measuring theater, opera, concerts, art exhibitions, reading, etc.

These results demonstrate the importance of the definition of "culture," and accordingly which variables are selected for the analysis of cultural activities.

Norway

The Full Set of Activities – Norway

We now move to the full set of variables (21) for Norway. As in the French data, the variables are weakly correlated (in fact, weaker in Norway than in

France); thus, it is difficult to define social markers in such a way that a person practicing them (for instance going to the cinema) with certainty belongs to a specific group (i.e., cinema-lovers). We nevertheless have generated latent components, and the first component generated by PCA is also here a volume component, measuring most of the included cultural activities, TV apart. Thus, we can call it an omnivore component. The second component is about *video, the Internet, and music consumption,* in contrast to *reading* and attending some high-brow events.

We decided also here to perform clustering analysis based on the two most dominant dimensions, and to generate three lifestyle groups through the clustering technique: One group can be called the *nerds* (101 persons), because it is mainly composed of people who are actively using the Internet, etc. The second group is the *readers* (219 persons), and the last one is the *inactive* (home centered) (674 persons). Thus, the characteristics of Norwegian lifestyle clusters differ from the clusters generated in France. Also, as discussed, the pattern is weaker in Norway than in France (see Figs. 5 and 6).

The Reduced Set of Activities – Norway
We proceed by including only a limited set of variables, common to both countries (see footnote 10). Again, the first component is more or less a volume component, which could be called an omnivore component (TV apart). The exact meaning of the other components is less easy to define. Perhaps, the second one could be interpreted (in the Norwegian context) as an opposition between activities symbolically centered on activities at home and activities away from home.

For the pupose of comparision, we selected a three-clusters solution (respective size: 838, 105, and 41 people).[14] The first cluster is that of the *homebodies*. The two others are two types of *omnivores* and *cultured* people,

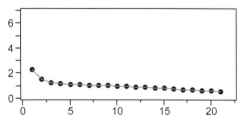

Fig. 5. Lifestyles – Norway – CA (% Eigenvalues). (Economically Active 20–65 Years)

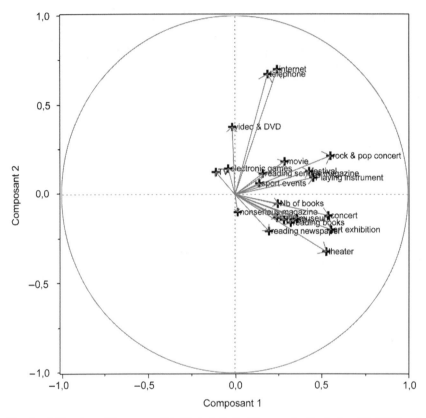

Fig. 6.   Lifestyles – Norway – CA (Axis 1 & 2). (Economically Active 20–65 Years)

one group being more involved in reading (books and newspapers), the
other more involved in going out for concerts and theaters.

Comparing the Full Set Analysis with the Reduced Set in Norway
In addition to media use and cultural activities, the Norwegian survey was
set up to measure young people's cultural activities, therefore including
questions on the use of the Internet, video, DVDs, etc. In 2004 many people
did not have access to the Internet, thus the mapping of this would seem
of interest. Again we see an example of analyses generating lifestyle
clusters dependent on our inclusion of different variables. In the full set
analysis, we find a cluster of *nerds*, who spend an inordinate time on the
Internet. Skipping these (and other specific variables in the Norwegian

questionnaire), we find, in the reduced set, clusters more as expected: one home-centered cluster, and two "cultural" clusters, differing in the time they use for reading or going out for concerts, etc.

Comparing Lifestyle Clusters – France and Norway
Looking at the full set of variables, we need more components to describe patterns of activities in Norway than in France. This is so despite the fact that there are fewer variables in the Norwegian full set than in the French full set. This implies that the cultural activities of Norwegian people are less structured, that is more individualistic, than that of the French people. Of course, we must be cautious because our data are not completely comparable; the samples are small; and so on. Nevertheless, this is the conclusion with the data we have.

Using only the reduced set of variables, we – again – see that the patterns are stronger in France than in Norway. Nevertheless, we are able to identify clusters in both countries, and we find rather similar lifestyle clusters in France and Norway: two clusters that are "cultural" in their activities, and one cluster of home sitters. In both countries, the largest cluster is the home sitters.

We will now proceed by mapping the lifestyle clusters onto the social space we have constructed, for France and Norway separately.

MAPPING LIFESTYLE CLUSTERS ONTO SOCIAL STRUCTURE

Building on the previous analysis, we have saved the scores of each individual on the two latent dimensions, capital volume and capital composition, defining the social space in France and Norway, respectively.[15] Using these dimensions, we have rotated them 90 degrees so that the "global capital" dimension is vertical, and the "capital composition" dimension horizontal (to obtain a similar picture of social space as Bourdieu used). We will first use the activity clusters as defined by the full set variables in each country. Figures 7–8 show the mapping of the French activity groups as defined by the full and then reduced set of cultural activity variables on the social space, whereas Figs. 9–10 show the mapping of the Norwegian activity groups as defined by the full and then reduced set of cultural activity variables in the Norwegian survey on the social space. The left part in each figure shows the distribution of respondents in the social space, and we see that the French sample is more dispersed along the "global capital" axis (the vertical axis) than the Norwegian sample. This finding is in line with established knowledge about an overall lower level of inequality in Norway than that of most OECD countries.

The right part of each figure shows the mapping of the lifestyle clusters onto the social space. If we had included all individuals, the groups would be

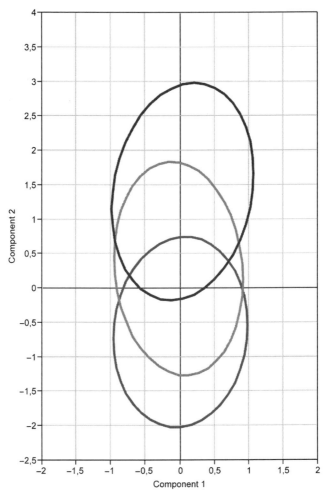

Fig. 7. Mapping Three Lifestyle Groups onto Social Structure – France – PCA – Full Set.

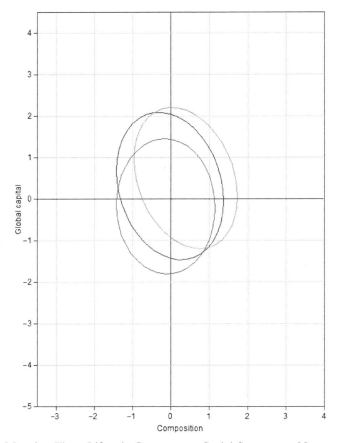

Fig. 8. Mapping Three Lifestyle Groups onto Social Structure – Norway – CA – Full Set.

more scattered in the social space and difficult to separate (cf. earlier comments about the fuzziness of the clusters and their boundaries). We have therefore drawn lines including 50% of the individuals in each cluster (see Figs. 7–10).

We note that in the French graphs, the lifestyle clusters are more dispersed along the "global capital" axis (the vertical axis). This is the case both for activity groups as defined by the full set of variables (Figs. 7 and 9) and activity groups as defined by the reduced set of variables (Figs. 8 and 10), implying that lifestyle is more strongly associated with "global capital" in France than in Norway. Also, we see no differences in lifestyles

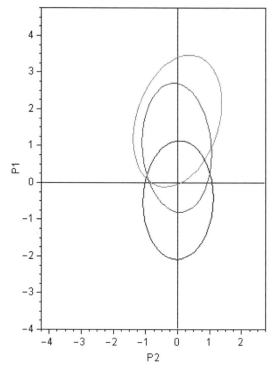

Fig. 9. Mapping Three Lifestyle Groups onto Social Structure – France – CA – Common Set.

associated with the composition of capital (the horizontal axis), and this is the case for both countries.

We also note that the degree of overlap of these ellipses within the social space is great. This means social positions are not corresponding directly with the lifestyle groups (a strong correspondence would be in line with the homology thesis). In addition, the degree of overlapping seems to be stronger in the Norwegian data than in the French data.

As argued earlier, in a Blau space, we would ideally include a number of relevant variables that are left out here. Particularly, three characteristics seem important for a better understanding of the activity groups: who they are in terms of gender and age, and what access they have to cultural events, such as opera, etc.

For instance, analysis not shown here tells us that the clusters are gendered: in the Norwegian data, looking at average figures we find that the

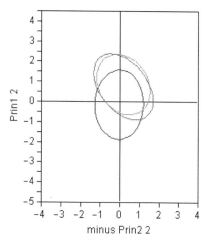

Fig. 10. Mapping Lifestyle Groups onto Social Structure – Norway – CA –
Common Set.

clusters we have called the *nerds* are mainly men (70% male) and slightly
younger (36 years) than the others. The clusters we called the *readers* are
mainly women (60% women) at nearly 40 years of age. The clusters we
called the *home sitters* are a bit older (41 years of age) and 50–50% men and
women. There are no differences between the clusters in their occupational
status and household income, and small differences in their average
educational level, again a reflection of the lack of association between the
social stratification variables and lifestyle clusters. In the French case, the
clusters are gendered too; for instance, we find that the clusters we have
called the *sports enthusiasts* are mainly men (61% male) and slightly younger
(41 years) than the others. As in Norway, there are no differences between
the clusters in their occupational status and household income, but
differences in their average educational level are a bit higher.

The heterogeneity of the lifestyle clusters adds more complexity to our
understanding of the association between social stratification and cultural
activities. Certainly, gender and age are important for people's lifestyles.

CONCLUSION

Using an explorative approach to social stratification and lifestyle patterns,
we have compared two countries. We cannot exclude the possibility that

the conclusions we draw are partly artifacts of the activities we have chosen to examine. Let us summarize our findings: We were interested in lifestyles and social stratification – what is learnt by this explorative exercise?

In both France and Norway, we found common patterns of social stratification – two dimensions in each country, as constructed by the stratification variables – education, occupational status, and household income. We have argued that the main dimension of this social space, often called the volume of capital, or "global capital," is simply a natural product of the positive correlation between these stratification variables, and the method used to generate the first latent dimension. For the second dimension, the actual patterns between the manifest variables may be less obvious. Empirically, it appears that the occupational status variable is close to education, so that the two variables are therefore opposed to the economic variable. Thus, for both countries, we are able to generate a social space that resembles Bourdieu's proposal.

Second, looking at the cultural activities of the respondents in our surveys, we find, depending on how many activity variables we include, important similarities and differences. Using all country-specific variables, we identify different lifestyle clusters in the two countries, reflecting differences in the questionnaires. For France, a cluster of sports enthusiasts reflects the large section with questions about sports; for Norway, a cluster of nerds reflects the large section with questions about Internet use. When we use only the questions that are common to both countries, we are left with the more traditional measures of cultural activities, such as going to the opera, theater, and concerts. Using only these questions, we are able to define three rather similar lifestyle clusters in each country, one cluster of home bodies, and two clusters of culturally active people (differences between them are related to the degree of activity in France, and home-centered versus outgoing activities in Norway).

Despite the fact that we are able to generate these lifestyle clusters, their boundaries are fuzzy when they are mapped onto the social space. Thus, in both countries, we find important overlapping cultural activity groups. For France, "global capital" is associated with lifestyle, but weakly so (overlapping groups), and "capital composition" is not at all important for distinguishing between different lifestyle groups. For Norway, the activity groups are distributed so that the social space is even less important than in France. Therefore, in both countries, the second dimension of the social space seems unimportant and not associated with lifestyle groups.

We did not find a strong association between the social space and cultural activity groups as expected from the homology thesis. The lack of support for this thesis (in its strong interpretation) could be due to changes in France over time (nearly 50 years have passed). With a growing middle class, differences in class structures may be part of the explanation for the lack of support for the homology thesis. Another explanation, of course, is that the thesis actually never was empirically supported, except, perhaps, in Bourdieus' data, which were oversampled in the urban area, thus not representative for the whole French population.

When we looked at the activity variables, we found a first latent dimension that supports the omnivore thesis, yet we would like to suggest a slightly different interpretation of this thesis. Usually, this thesis is taken to mean that a group in the society "eats everything," that is, enjoy different sorts of cultural expressions, be it paintings, literature, or art exhibitions. Consistent across all four sets of activity variables, the full and reduced set in France, and the full and reduced set in Norway, we find the first latent dimension to be a volume component. Thus, in line with Tally Katz-Gerro (2004), we would interpret the volume dimension as an omnivorousness axis, which turns out to be – as we also saw in the analysis of the social space – the first latent dimension extracting most of the (positive) correlations between the variables.

Our findings of course need to be validated by other methods of analysis and other data. It does, however, seem as if only one dimension is necessary to capture social stratification in modern societies, at least when looking at lifestyle groups. The first dimension of the social space, the volume of capital, or the "global capital" reflects the positive correlation between the social stratification variables, as measured here by education, occupational status, and income. We have seen that there is a weak association between stratification and lifestyles, but if stratification matters for lifestyles, it is the first dimension, not the "capital composition" dimension that is important. The Norwegian case is interesting, since we find no clear evidence of any social structuring of the activity groups, be it nerds, readers, or home sitters (as defined by the full set of activity variables), or home sitters, cultural actives (outgoing), or cultural actives (home centered), as defined by the reduced set of activity variables. The main conclusion, for both France and Norway, is the *overlapping of lifestyle groups in the social space;* a finding not in line with the Boudieusian homology thesis.

We have limited our analysis to occupationally active respondents between 20 and 64 years old, thereby excluding large fractions of the populations, such as the retired, students, and women outside the labour force. The students could perhaps form a lifestyle group on their own, if they had been included. Also, the average retirement age differs between the two countries, and in both countries we would expect respondents older than 60 years still in the labour market to be positively selected in terms of education. The consequences of this selection would most likely be that we – for the older age groups – mainly include the most active individuals, thus probably underestimating the number of home sitters in this group. By contrast, many retired persons are in good health, and the fact that they have retired could imply that they have more time to be culturally active. Certainly, this topic should be investigated later.

Our analytical strategy has been explorative. We have not tried to delineate the social mechanisms generating cultural activities. This is unfortunate, since, despite ambitious theoretical elaborations on the linkages between social stratification and cultural consumption/lifestyles, there is little empirical knowledge of the social mechanisms involved in these (potential) processes.

So, what is common, what is unique, and what co-varies between countries? We find a *similar* social space, and for both countries we find important overlapping of lifestyles, and no differences in lifestyles associated with the composition of capital, that is, the second stratification dimension is not relevant for differentiating between lifestyle clusters. Looking at what is *unique*, we find different lifestyle groups in the two countries (French sports enthusiasts and Norwegian nerds), related to different questionnaires. We do not think this is due to different definitions of culture in the two countries, because in both countries, sports are now part of the so-called extended culture concept. The inclusion of different questions in these surveys reminds us that we should be alert to the set-up of the questionnaires since they are formative for the data we generate. We have seen that using a traditional and limited definition of culture generates different lifestyle clusters than including a wider definition of cultural activities, that is, we get what we look for.

Finally, looking at issues that *co-vary*, the population is more dispersed along capital volume in France than in Norway, and the lifestyles groups are more dependent on capital volume in France than in Norway. The overlapping of the lifestyle groups therefore is greater in Norway, thus the mapping of lifestyle groups in the social space is less well-designed in Norway than in France.

These findings strongly indicate that status crystallization is lower in Norway; that is, Norwayy's stratification system is more open than France's.

ACKNOWLEDGMENTS

An earlier version of this chapter was presented at a meeting of the International Sociological Association's Research Committee on Social Stratification and Mobility, Yale University, August 4–6, 2009, at the SOCCULT seminar, Centre Maurice Halbwacks, October 26, 2009, and at the Monday Seminar at GEMASS, December 5, 2011, and at the AKS seminar, Lysebu, 4–5 January 2012. We thank the participants at these meetings for their valuable comments.

NOTES

1. http://en.wikipedia.org/wiki/List_of_countries_by_income_equality (read 17.03. 2009)

2. http://www.geert-hofstede.com/geert_hofstede_resources.shtml (read 17.03.2009).

3. This usually means dropping the dimensions generated last, with the lowest Eigenvalue/variance.

4. Lifestyles could also be a product of people's opportunities, as when rural citizens lack access to opera performances. However, in both countries, the authorities have implemented an active policy for culture dissemination. In Norway, *Riksteateret* and *Rikskonsertene* are established by Norwegian Parliament to provide live theater and music to rural citizens. In France, an active policy for "Culture" dissemination through the country was pursued by all the successive governments since that of the General de Gaulle and his culture minister, André Malraux.

5. The young age of some respondents in the Norwegian survey is related to a special part of the survey asking children and teenagers about their use of media, computers, the Internet, etc.

6. One Norwegian household with annual income higher than NOK 8 million is excluded. Thereafter, Norwegian households where information on income is missing ($N = 65$) are imputed with the average income value. In the French data, the French statistical office (INSEE) has preliminary edited the data before they are issued for research purposes. This also means imputing income for households without information on income, using an imputation formula for income.

7. Generally, in the French questionnaire, the respondents are asked about a specific activity and are allowed to answer that they engaged in this activity never, seldom, from time to time, or regularly over given period of time (last 12 months, or last week). The same question in the Norwegian questionnaire allows respondents to report how many times they were engaged in this activity over a given period of time (last 12 months, or last week). We have used these metrics as they are.

8. Table A1 (Appendix) shows the frequencies of respondents attending these activities, separately for France and Norway.

9. In this method, the three groups are created by an iterative procedure on the basis of randomly selected "seeds." Observations are described by synthetic indicators

built up by PCA. As usual, PCA is based on the correlations matrix of the variables included.

10. Factor analysis and principal component analysis are robust to different variable measurements and distributions (Rao, 1964; Kim & Mueller, 1978; Lebart, Piron, & Morineau, 2006).

11. See Rosenlund 2000; Hjellbrekke & Korsnes, 2006; for other constructions of social space, using correspondence analysis based on Norwegian data.

12. This fact is another reason for introducing the two-step procedure we use here, first PCA, then clustering.

13. These are: time watching TV, reading books, newspapers, number of times visiting libraries, movies, theatre, ballet, concert, opera, art exhibition, museum, and attending sport events, all measured for the last 12 months.

14. We deleted nine outliers in this procedure.

15. Another way would be to construct the social space using indicators of the two dimensions. Since the first part of our analysis has shown the two dimensions to be very similar in the two countries, we can construct the indicators of "capital volume" and "composition of capital" in similar ways for both countries: *Capital volume* would then be defined as [(occupational status indicator + indicator of educational level)/2] + indicator of economic level). *Composition of capital* could be defined as (occupational status indicator + indicator of educational level)/2 – indicator of economic level. We have tried both, and the correlation between the two indicators of the first dimension, as well as the two indicators of the second dimension, is in both cases approximately 0.8 and 0.9.

REFERENCES

Birkelund, G. E. (2006). Welfare states and social inequality. Key issues in contemporary cross-national research on social stratification and mobility. *Research in Social Stratification and Mobility*, 24, 333–351.

Blau, P. M. (1977). *Inequality and heterogeneity: A primitive theory of social structure.* New York, NY: Free Press.

Blau, P. M., & Duncan, O. D. (1967). *The American occupational structure.* New York, NY: Wiley.

Bourdieu, P. (1979/1984). *Distinction: A social critique of the judgement of taste.* London: Routledge & Keagan Paul.

Chan, T. W. (2010). *Social status and cultural consumption.* Cambridge: Cambridge University Press.

Chan, T. W., Birkelund, G. E., Aas, A. K., & Wiborg, Ø. (2011). Social status in Norway. *European Sociological Review*, 27, 451–468.

Chan, T. W., & Goldthorpe, J. H. (2007). Class and status: The conceptual distinction and its empirical relevance. *American Sociological Review*, 72, 512–532.

Coulangeon, P., & Lemel, Y. (2009). The homology thesis: Distinction revisited. In K. Robson & C. Sanders (Eds.), *Quantifying theory: Pierre Bourdieu* (pp. 47–60). Toronto: Springer.

Erikson, R., & Goldthorpe, J. (1992). *The constant flux: A study of class mobility in industrial societies.* Oxford: Clarendon Press.

Esping-Andersen, G. (1990). *Three worlds of welfare capitalism.* Cambridge: Polity Press.

Ganzeboom, H., de Graaf, P., & Treiman, D. (1992). A standardized international socio-economic index for occupational status. *Social Science Research*, 21, 1–56.

Hjellbrekke, J., & Korsnes, O. (2006). *Sosial mobilitet*. Oslo: Samlaget.

Katz-Gerro, T. (2004). Cultural consumption research: Review of methodology, theory, and consequence. *International Review of Sociology*, *14*, 11–29.

Kim, J. O., & Mueller, C. W. (1978). *Factor analysis. Statistical methods and practical issues*. Beverly Hills: Sage.

Lebart, L., Piron, M., & Morineau, A. (2006). Statistique Exploratoire Multidimensionnelle, [Visualisation et Inférence en Fouille de Données]. Dunod. (4kme edition), 480 p.

Lemel, Y. (2006). *The social positioning of the French according to the EPCV survey*. CREST Working Paper n° 2006–14.

McPherson, J. M., Miller, J., & Ranger-Moore, J. R. (1991). Evolution on a dancing landscape: Organizations and networks in dynamic Blau space. *Social Forces*, *70*, 19–42.

Nyhammer, E. (2008). *Mellom habitus of frihet. En kvantitativ studie av kulturelle forbruksmønstre i Norge*. Master Thesis. Department of Sociology and Human Geography, University of Oslo.

Péli, G., & Nooteboom, B. (1999). Market partitioning and geometry of the resource space. *Americal Journal of Sociology*, 104, 1123–1153.

Petersen, R. A. (1992). Understanding audience segmentation: From elite and mass to omnivore and univore. *Poetics*, 21, 243–258.

Prieur, A., Rosenlund, L., & Skjøtt-Larsen, J. (2008). Cultural capital today. A case study from Denmark. *Poetics*, 36, 45–71.

Rao, C. R. (1964). The use and interpretation of principal component analysis in applied research. *Sankhya Serie A*, *26*, 329–357.

Rosenlund, L. (2000). Social structures and change in Norway. *International Journal of Sociology*, *37*, 245–276.

Skarpenes, O. (2007). Den legitime kulturens moralske forankring. *Tidsskrift for samfunns-forskning*, 48, 265–275.

Weber, M. (1978[1925]). Status groups and classes. In G. Roth, & C. Wittich (Eds.), *Economy and society*. Berkeley, CA: University of California Press.

Wright, E. O. (1985). *Classes*. London: Verso.

APPENDIX

Table A.1.   Sample Characteristics.

	France	Norway
No. Obs	3,744	993
Age	42.4	39,8
% Female	0.49	0,48
Mean(education scale)	10.7	13,2
Mean (status score)	0.0	0,0

Common Set Results

France

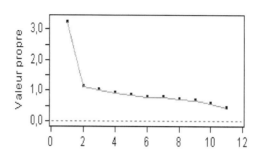

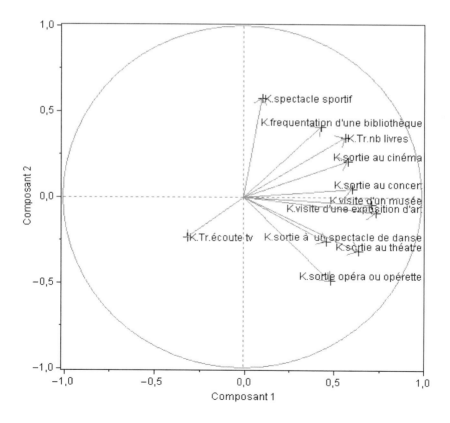

Norway

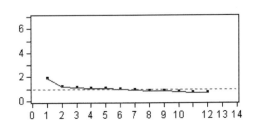

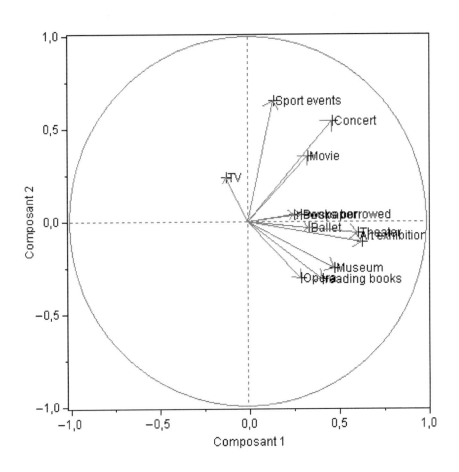

PART III
OPENING BLACK BOXES

FROM ABSTRACT TO CONCRETE: THE PRACTICAL RELEVANCE OF PARENTS' ECONOMIC AND CULTURAL CAPITAL FOR PERSISTENCE IN HIGHER EDUCATION

Liza Reisel

ABSTRACT

On the theoretical level, this chapter examines the mechanisms through which cultural and financial capital affects educational outcomes in different institutional contexts. On the methodological level, the central question in this chapter is how to resolve concerns in comparative analyses of educational attainment, such as variations in enrolment rates and study program duration across institutional settings. On the empirical level, the chapter asks whether family background predicts educational attainment in similar ways in two diametrically opposed welfare states: the United States and Norway. Differences in dropout from higher education were compared using nationally representative longitudinal data from the United States and Norway and event history and multilevel modelling

Class and Stratification Analysis
Comparative Social Research, Volume 30, 223–254
Copyright © 2013 by Emerald Group Publishing Limited
All rights of reproduction in any form reserved
ISSN: 0195-6310/doi:10.1108/S0195-6310(2013)0000030012

techniques. The chapter also makes use of the standardized sheaf coefficient to summarize central background variables for more direct comparison of effect sizes. The findings show that whereas parents' education level has strikingly similar effects on students' dropout probabilities in the two countries, the effect of parents' income varies substantially according to the institutional context. The chapter concludes that in comparative analyses of inequality in education the value of different types of family resources must be understood in light of the concrete, practical constraints of the national institutional contexts.

Keywords: Social stratification; educational attainment; dropout; Norway; United States

INTRODUCTION

Over the course of the 20th century, higher education has become an essential building block for economic development and the most clearly established route to individual social mobility. At the same time, higher education systems in different countries vary with regard to expansion history, financing, governance and control. This has consequences for how social inequality is reproduced at various educational transition points in different countries (Reisel, 2011). In this chapter, I compare two countries with contrasting developments on these accounts: Norway and the United States. I focus on students' ability to stay in college once they have enrolled, an increasingly relevant issue as enrolment in higher education continues to grow. The United States and Norway have similar levels of educational attainment among young adults, similar per capita expenditures on elementary and secondary education, and similar levels of academic achievement in math and science as measured on international tests (OECD, 2009). At the same time, these countries differ tremendously in their welfare state arrangements and educational systems. Compared with Norway, the United States is a highly stratified society with large differences between rich and poor (Goldin & Katz, 2007; Pontusson, 2005). According to Phipps (2001, p. 87), poverty rates among families with young children were about five times higher in the United States than they were in Norway in the mid-1990s (29.3 vs. 6.1% in 1994/1995) despite the fact that both countries rank among the world's 10 richest countries measured in GDP per capita.

The U.S. education system is also much more diverse and complex than the Norwegian education system. It has been characterized as a highly differentiated, market-driven system that has expanded dramatically since the Second World War (Calhoun, 2000). U.S. colleges vary tremendously in cost, selectivity and prestige. The Norwegian system of higher education, by contrast, has expanded in a more controlled fashion and is highly regulated by the central government and almost entirely publically funded. It is dominated by two types of relatively uniform public institutions; universities and more vocationally oriented university colleges (*høyskoler*). One consequence of the expansive and differentiated education system in the United States is that dropout rates vary drastically among colleges, ranging from a few per cent at elite private universities to over 50% at many community colleges. In Norway, dropout rates are relatively similar across higher education institutions, even when comparing universities with university colleges (Hovdhaugen & Aamodt, 2005; Mastekaasa & Hansen, 2005; Reisel & Brekke, 2010). Nevertheless, the probability of dropping out varies systematically with students' socioeconomic background in both countries.

A number of large-scale comparative studies of inequality in education have been published over the past 25 years, including the often cited studies by Ganzeboom, Luijkx, and Treiman (1989), Erikson and Goldthorpe (1992), Shavit and Blossfeld (1993) and, more recently, Shavit, Arum, and Gamoran (2007). One of the most prominent frameworks for explaining educational differentials emerging from this literature – rational action theory (e.g. Breen & Goldthorpe, 1997) – posits that students from different social class backgrounds make different decisions regarding educational transitions, according to the relationship between costs, benefits and the probability to succeed. All these three elements vary systematically with social background because their relative values will depend on a person's initial social status position.

Another strand of research on social inequality in education is based on Pierre Bourdieu's conceptualization of the different forms of capital (Bourdieu, 1986). This literature tends to study home and school environments, and explains differences in educational achievement and attainment using measures of economic, social and cultural resources. These three main forms of capital are generally understood to be theoretically interlinked and unequally distributed across social classes.

However, there is also a body of literature that is critical to the idea of social class altogether, questioning the concept's usefulness for explaining contemporary social inequalities. Different types of social hierarchies may overlap and intersect, but according to this perspective they are better understood if we distinguish between them analytically (Kingston, 2000). Moreover, different types of social hierarchies do not necessarily operate in the same fashion across social contexts.

In the analyses below, I use parents' income and parents' level of education as socioeconomic background indicators, representing families' economic and cultural capital. This approach is not new, but the contribution of this chapter is to closely compare two national contexts where we may expect these basic measures of social background to operate differently. Methodologically, it means resolving some challenges of comparability across institutional settings. Theoretically, it means questioning the mechanisms through which cultural and financial capital affects educational outcomes. Two empirical research questions have guided this inquiry: firstly, whether social status advantage and disadvantage is similarly related to dropping out across different institutional environments, and secondly, how the magnitude of the relationship between the two basic background factors and dropping out from higher education compares within and between the two countries.

No system of higher education has been able to completely eradicate the ability of socioeconomically privileged families to increase the chances of success for their offspring (Buchmann, 2002). However, as this cross-national comparison will show, the two most fundamental components of socioeconomic background – family income and parental education level – do not matter in the same way or to the same extent in differently organized systems of higher education.

THEORETICAL PERSPECTIVES ON SOCIAL CLASS AND THE FORMS OF CAPITAL

In analyses of education outcomes, researchers have sometimes found it useful to disentangle the effects of the different components of the traditional socioeconomic status or class measures, to see if different resources work differently over time, for different parts of the population or in different countries (Conley, 1999, 2001; DiMaggio, 1982; Jæger & Holm, 2007; Oliver & Shapiro, 1995).

Theoretically, these resources are often conceptualized in terms of three separate, but interrelated, forms of capital: financial, social and cultural, following Pierre Bourdieu (1984, 1986). As a critique of mainstream economic theory, Bourdieu argued that capital must be understood within a broader context of power relations, not just as economic exchange. Capital is not only material in form and will under specific circumstances be converted to and from immaterial strategies towards distinction. Economic capital does not automatically ensure a high social position; it must be spent in a way that signals belonging to the upper class. Likewise, social capital is only valuable when it allows you to signal belonging to the 'right' circles, or when through those circles you are able to achieve something that is desired by the elite. Cultural capital is only valued as such when it is perceived as innate and genuine, and cannot be directly obtained from or converted to social or economic capital without the appropriate context for its exposure (Bourdieu, 1984).

The use of 'cultural capital' in theorizing the maintenance of social distinction (Bourdieu, 1984), presumes a certain level of boundedness into separate classes, even if class boundaries are much more permeable today than they have been in the past. This assumption of social class differences has been challenged, especially in the United States. Paul Kingston (2000) and others have argued that although there are prevailing patterns of social stratification in our post-industrial economies, they do not fit neatly into the social class framework and are better understood through a different theoretical lens. Rather than a bounded class structure, what we have are a number of status dimensions that interact in different ways. Kingston suggests conceptualizing social stratification as 'multirung ladders of continuous gradation' and shows that there is in fact much overlap in behaviour, opinions and parenting habits across socioeconomic positions in American society.

From an interactional perspective, Randall Collins (2000) argues that at the micro-level, social class differences are played out through a number of 'Zelizer circuits' of exchange. The concept of the Zelizer circuit comes from Viviana A. Zelizer's (1994) ethnographic work on the social meaning of money, where she shows that the meaning of money and related currencies (food stamps/valuables) vary from one social setting to another and change over time. Educational credentials and income can be viewed as particular kind of 'Zelizer currencies' that are valuable only in specific circuits of exchange. The relevance of this perspective to the question at hand is that in terms of persistence in the education system, parental education and income are the two resources or 'currencies' most likely to be utilized, regardless of perceived class position. This means that if financial resources matter much more for persistence in college than parents' education level, there would be little difference between the attainment of the daughter of a plumber and a daughter of a university professor with similar incomes. By contrast, if parental education matters most, the daughter of the university professor would be more likely to persist in the educational system than the daughter of the plumber even if their family incomes are the same.

These three theoretical perspectives – the forms of capital, the multirung ladders and the micro-level interaction perspective – provide useful insights into the relationship between social class background, particular family resources, and educational progress. While Bourdieu emphasizes the power dynamics inherent in the invisible transmission of cultural capital within the family, Kingston emphasizes how different social status dimensions sometimes operate separately and are not always interrelated. Finally, Collins' perspective emphasizes that the usefulness of different kinds of resources changes according to social context.

LITERATURE REVIEW

The Institutional Contexts

In the United States, socioeconomic background strongly affects which college a person applies to (McDonough, 1997). McDonough argues that parents' education influences college choice in several ways, but first and foremost by transmitting knowledge about what it takes to prepare for college. In addition, she emphasizes that the institutional context of the child's schooling helps structure her future opportunities. Different high school environments and high school practices with regard to curriculum and academic standards lead to different placements in the stratified structure of higher education in the United States.

In Norway, the emphasis on uniformity and integration in elementary and secondary school has led to little systematic variation in quality among high schools. Differences in performance (on national exams or mean grade point average (GPA)) among high schools in Norway are largely explained by the composition of pupils, roughly corresponding to the socioeconomic composition of neighbourhood feeder schools (Hægeland, Kirkebøen, & Raaum, 2006). Socioeconomic background does predict secondary school grades in Norway, but at the same time almost all high schools are publically funded and have the same guidelines, curriculum and final exams.

One consequence of the long-term investment in and regulation of public education in Norway is that the different universities and university colleges are not viewed as varying substantially in terms of quality or prestige

(Hovdhaugen &Aamodt, 2005). For better or for worse, this means that socioeconomically advantaged families in Norway have very little leverage with regard to their child's institutional trajectory over and above what they can provide of expectations, knowledge and inculcation of a privileged *habitus* (Bourdieu, 1977), to give their child an advantage over her fellow students. Getting a child prepared for, and accepted to, a prestigious college is viewed as an important step towards success in the United States; there is no equivalent to this in Norway.

The Relevance of Economic and Cultural Capital for Educational Outcomes

There is evidence from other countries indicating that the impact of a family's economic capital on educational attainment is reduced with increased public funding. DeGraaf (1986) compared educational attainment among cohorts before and after the policy changes that made education in the Netherlands free for all students through secondary school and for low-income students from secondary school and onwards. Using structural equation models he showed that the impact of family finances was reduced between the two cohorts, such that family income became insignificant in the later cohorts although the strong positive effect of socioeconomic status as measured by parental education and father's occupation remained unchanged. DeGraaf, DeGraaf, and Kraaykamp (2000) argue further that in countries like the Netherlands and the United States, where cultural codes are not as bound up with highbrow elite culture as perhaps in France and Germany, the development of verbal/linguistic and cognitive skills will be the aspect of cultural capital with the largest impact on educational achievement.

Cultural capital has been found to be particularly strongly related to educational achievement in the Nordic countries. Are Turmo (2004) found that the influence of economic capital is weak in the Nordic countries and that cultural capital, particularly the availability of books in the home, is surprisingly strong in predicting scientific literacy among 15 years olds. It has been suggested that it is a paradox that social class differences in educational outcomes remain large in all Scandinavian countries despite the countries' efforts equalize educational opportunity (Jæger & Holm, 2007). Jæger and Holm argue that 'in the Scandinavian mobility regime cultural capital (or other non-monetary background factors) explains the majority of the social class effects on educational attainment, whereas in the liberal mobility regime parents' economic capital explains most of the social class effect' (*ibid.* p. 740). In their study, they use rich Danish data to operationalize cultural capital as parents' level of education, number of foreign languages spoken, number of newspaper subscriptions, whether they read fictional books, and whether they are interested in the visual arts. Since their analysis is a single-country analysis of Denmark, their conclusion about the relevance of the two forms of capital has only partially been confirmed by their empirical evidence, and will be explored further in this chapter.

Little has been written comparatively about the role played by the different forms of capital for outcomes among college level students. One of the reasons for the focus on earlier educational transitions is that the impact of family background is expected to be reduced as students become more and more selected over time. At each transition point, the more academically able students are more likely to go on to higher levels of education compared with the less academically able students. Also, socioeconomically advantaged students are more likely to remain in the school system longer than socioeconomically disadvantaged students (Hansen & Mastekaasa, 2006). This implies that there is a stronger positive selection among the less advantaged students, which in turn reduces the impact of family background on educational outcomes within higher education.

Contrary to Jæger and Holm's claim, there is reason to believe that cultural capital influences success in higher education just as much, if not more, in liberal mobility regimes as it does in Scandinavia. In the United States, secondary schools differ tremendously in quality, and what type of high school a student attends has a strong impact on their likelihood of enrolling in selective institutions of higher education (Persell, Catsambis, & Cookson Jr., 1992). Elite private high schools have well-equipped libraries, varied and challenging course offerings and extracurricular activities, adding to the social advantage the students who attend these schools tend to have before entry. Indeed, parents with graduate or professional degrees are much more likely than parents with lower degrees to send their children to these elite private high schools. Persell and her colleagues (*ibid.*) argue that the effect of high school type contributes to what they call a 'conjoint system of cultural capital transmission', where the cultural capital of the parents and the school interact to better prepare the students for elite higher education.

Dropping Out from College

Much has been written about persistence in and dropout from institutions of higher education in the United States. The classic theoretical approach is referred to as the 'student integration model' and is attributed to Vincent Tinto, starting with his article 'Dropout from Higher Education: A theoretical Synthesis of Recent Research' (Tinto, 1975). Tinto's main thesis revolves around the role that college plays in the lives of young students who attend college full time. He argues that college is a rite of passage to adulthood involving separation from family environments and integration into a new social context at college (Tinto, 1988). Those who do not successfully reintegrate are at risk of dropping out.

For less traditional college students who live with their families and work part time or full time while in college, these processes do not necessarily apply (Bean & Metzner, 1985). In what is often referred to as the 'student attrition model', Bean and Metzner argue that external pressures such as ability to finance one's education and family responsibilities interfere with student–institution integration, increasing attrition among nontraditional students. Several studies (e.g. Braxton, 2000; Cabrera, Nora, & Castaneda, 1993; Seidman, 2005) have elaborated on these obstacles and presented useful evidence for institutional administrators to organize their undergraduate programs in ways that improve institutional retention.

Even though the emphasis on student–institution relationships has remained central in American researchers' conceptualization of college persistence, a more systemic approach has emerged in recent years. Bozick (2007) argues that there is a systematic difference between higher income and lower income students in their ability to rely on their parents for help to pay for college, their knowledge about availability of financial aid, their attitude towards accruing debt through student loans and their need to prioritize working while in school in order to pay for college or living expenses. Using national data, he also shows that the combination of working while living at home impedes the prospect of lower income students to persist to the second year of college. Scott and Kennedy (2005) use national data and event history modelling techniques to show that characteristics such as delayed enrolment in higher education, disruptions in enrolment and working while in college, characteristics that are much more common among socioeconomically disadvantaged students, are associated with higher dropout rates over time.

The reasons for student dropout from higher education have been less systematically analysed in Norway. In a study of the relationship between parental background and different forms of student departure, researchers found that when students with more highly educated parents leave their program of study, it is often in favour of professional degree programs (e.g. medicine), whereas students whose parents have lower levels of education are more likely to leave higher education altogether or transfer to shorter, lower level vocational programs (Mastekaasa & Hansen, 2005). Mastekaasa and Hansen point out that they have excluded any measures of parental income in their presentation of the analyses because they did not find any statistically significant relationship between economic resources and dropout. In a report on reasons for departure among students at three of Norway's universities, Hovdhaugen and Aamodt (2005) also emphasize parental education rather than income.

In a broader analysis of persistence and attainment in Norway, Roedelé and Aamodt (2001) found that issues related to financing one's education or working while enrolled mattered much less for the outcomes than how the coursework was organized. They found that the more loosely the courses were structured, the more likely it was for students to leave. In many study programs at Norwegian universities, especially traditional disciplines in the humanities and social sciences, the responsibility of obtaining relevant knowledge lies with the student, who is obligated to take exams at the end of the semester or academic year but not required to follow classes or participate in other ways.[1]

This is different from the more clearly organized study structure of some of the hard sciences and most courses at the university colleges. In these latter study programs, students have less freedom to organize their time, but are also followed up more closely and have more contact with faculty. Roedele and Aamodt's study also lacks measures of parental income, presumably because income is viewed as largely irrelevant in the Norwegian higher education context. This stands in stark contrast to the literature from the United States, which focuses more often than not on economic disadvantages (e.g. Chen & DesJardins, 2008; Paulsen & St. John, 2002).

DATA AND METHODS

It has been a central goal in this chapter to make use of data and methods that are as comparable as possible across the two country settings. I use nationally representative datasets from both countries that contain information about college and university enrolment, attendance, graduation and some basic background measures. The Norwegian dataset was created through a combination of information from several public registers from Statistics Norway and from register data from the universities and university colleges. The dataset was assembled for the project 'Educational

Careers: Attainment, Qualification and Transition to Work', financed by the Norwegian Research Council and managed by the Department of Sociology and Human Geography at the University of Oslo. The dataset used for this chapter is a subset of this larger dataset and follows a cohort of students who started high school (*videregående skole*) in 1994 and began their undergraduate studies in Norway between 1997 and 1999. For the analyses of the United States, I use the National Education Longitudinal Study (NELS:88), which is a longitudinal dataset that follows a cohort of 8th grade students from 1988 until the spring of 2001. In this chapter I use a subset of this sample restricted to respondents who were in 10th grade in 1990 and started higher education between 1991 and 1993. I arranged both datasets in a person–period format that follow students for up to eight years.[2]

Because the community college sector in the United States may be more realistically compared with Norwegian vocational secondary schools rather than Norwegian higher education, I leave the two-year sector in the United States out of the analyses in this chapter. This provides a more conservative comparison of the mechanisms of inequality in the two countries, since the U.S. system of higher education is highly unselective at the community college level. According to my cohort data, 38.5% of high school graduates in Norway enter higher education (university colleges or universities[3]) within a few years. Comparatively, 42% of U.S. 10th graders enter four-year colleges within a couple of years after high school graduation. This confirms that in terms of selectivity it is more appropriate to compare the combined university/university college sector in Norway with the various types of four-year colleges in the United States. The 3.5% gap in enrolment across the two countries is small, but statistically significant. On the one hand, this means that the Norwegian students in this sample may be a slightly more selected group than the U.S. sample. On the other hand the Norwegian data is more complete than the U.S. data, because it is taken from public registries and the U.S. data is a random sample surveyed over time. Although survey weights help alleviate some of the challenges of random sampling and survey attrition, the more marginal students are still represented with relatively few data points in the U.S. data.

Taking the differences between the two education systems regarding selection into college into account, I measure the effect of socioeconomic background on the risk of dropping out from college across the two countries. The reason for the choice of outcome measure is twofold. Firstly, the act of leaving college without a degree is most often a sign of hardship – academic, financial or motivational. Some of the students who drop out of college for a period of time eventually return and complete their degree. This does not mean that going to college has been the same for them as for a student who went through the 'normal' trajectory of college without substantial interference. It is therefore a measure that is more sensitive to disadvantage than relying solely on graduation rates. Secondly, in order to control for the differences in enrolment rates in higher education in the two countries, the Norwegian sample includes degree programs of different durations. Using graduation rates would therefore be problematic. Also in general, when comparing two different education systems, there may be variation in the average time to graduation. For example, in the United States, it is not uncommon to go to college part time, which delays time to graduation substantially. Thus, a student enrolled part time may make good progress towards a degree, but will nonetheless be counted as a 'failure' (i.e. not graduated) if graduation rates are measured before he completes the degree. Using dropping out as the outcome measure, this student would be counted as a 'success' (i.e. not having dropped out), along with those who graduate without substantial delay.

I use discrete time event history analysis and multilevel models to predict dropping out from four-year colleges in the United States and universities and university colleges in Norway. Some of the students who were enrolled at the end of the observation period will graduate or drop out at some later (unobserved) time, which implies that the data is right censored. Event history analysis estimates event occurrence over time, which reduces some of the problems associated with right censored data (Singer & Willett, 2003). Within the person–period data structure (i.e. one record per person per year of attendance), both dropping out and graduating are events that remove students from the risk pool. In other words, a student can only drop out if he is actually attending without having graduated in a particular year. I conduct the analyses using maximum likelihood logit estimation with discrete time periods for each individual treated as separate observations (cf. Allison, 1982, p. 75). Discrete time indicators are entered into the models as a set of dummies representing year of enrolment. This means that the estimates of the other covariates in the model should be interpreted as the effect of the variable on the probability of dropping out in any given year of enrolment.

The dependent variable used in the analyses is a categorical variable with two values: 1 if a student has dropped out in a given year and 0 every year the student was enrolled without dropping out prior to that or every year for the duration of the observation period if a student never dropped out. I define *dropping out* as leaving higher education prior to graduation, and not returning within the next two years or more (cf. Scott & Kennedy, 2005). This way of defining dropout is useful when comparing two countries with different practices and trends regarding on-time graduation or timing of events such as dropping out. If, for example, students in the United States are more likely to drop out early in their college going career and Norwegian students are more likely to drop out later in their career, the comparative results would vary depending on when dropout is counted. Also, if students from more disadvantaged homes drop out earlier while more socio-economically advantaged students drop out later, one might inflate the numbers of disadvantaged dropouts due to an arbitrary cut-off time point by which to count dropping out. To avoid over- or under-counting dropout towards the end of the observation period, I only analyse dropping out in the first seven years of enrolment.

In order to directly compare the effect of the two elements of family background in the two countries, I make use of the 'standardized sheaf coefficient' in the event history analyses. The standardized sheaf coefficient was introduced by D. R. Heise in 1972 (Heise, 1972) and later generalized by Hugh P. Whitt (1986). One of its features is that it provides a summary term for the combined effect of a set of dummy variables (one or more categories that are that are coded 0-1) on an outcome variable. Because I estimate parental income and education as sets of dummies, the standardized sheaf coefficient helps determine the relative *overall* effect of parental education and family income on dropping out. The sheaf coefficient has largely been used in ordinary least squares regression situations, where the standardized beta coefficient is used to evaluate the impact of the composite on the outcome variable. The sheaf coefficient is a composite of regression weights optimally estimated to predict the outcome. Therefore the unstandardized sheaf coefficient will always sum to 1.00. In the following analyses I obtain estimates of the magnitude of the sheaf coefficient by fully standardizing the variables in the logistic regression framework (cf. Menard, 2004). In practice this means standardizing the coefficients using an estimation of the latent distribution of the dichotomous outcome variable (produced by the *listcoef* command in Stata) and standardizing the sheaf variables and the other predictors in the model to have a mean of zero and a standard deviation of one (for more details on the sheaf coefficient see Attewell, Heil, & Reisel, 2011). Because the unstandardized sheaf coefficient always sums to 1.00, it will also always be a positive number once it is standardized. This means that it represents the absolute size of the combined effect a group of coefficients, regardless of the direction of the effect.

Finally, I estimate variation in dropout across colleges in a multilevel framework. The basic structure of the analysis is still discrete time event history analysis. However, to evaluate whether stratification across institutions also contribute to differences in dropping out in the two countries, I add college random effects using multilevel modelling with the logit link function in HLM6. I use the HLM6 software because it allows me to use sample weights in the U.S. analyses. Because the U.S. sample includes a large number of colleges, and many colleges have few students represented in the sample, college random effects are estimated, rather than college fixed effects. This allows me to capitalize on the colleges that have enough cases to estimate reliable effects, without losing the cases that are enrolled in weakly represented colleges in the sample. It also gives me an estimate of the variability in dropout among college types, before and after controlling for individual level predictors. Moreover, the multilevel framework corrects for the nested structure of the data, providing an estimate of the basic background variables as they operate *within* institutions, which controls for the fact that students are clustered within institutions of different kinds.

Ideally I would also have presented the sheaf coefficients in the multilevel framework. Unfortunately, I have not been able to estimate the latent distribution of the outcome variable after running a multilevel model, which is a necessary step in order to produce the standardized sheaf coefficient in analyses where the outcome variable is dichotomous. For this reason I present the two analyses separately, first the event history analyses with sheaf coefficients, controlling for college types, and then the multilevel analyses with college random effects, without the sheaf coefficients. Together the two approaches provide a more complete picture of the relevance of cultural and economic capital for the probability of dropping out from college in the two countries.

Independent Variables in the Model

The independent predictors in the models are age, gender, parents' education level, family income in the students' early youth, high school grades and type of college. *Age* is measured at college entry and is restricted to 18–21 in both datasets. *Gender* is coded 1 for female and 0 for male.

Parents' education is the education level of the parent with the highest education, or of the only parent who is present. Parents' education has four values: In the Norwegian data these are (1) compulsory school or less,

(2) high school, (3) short higher education (any undergraduate degree) and (4) long higher education (master's or professional degree). In the U.S. data the categories are (1) less than high school education, (2) GED, high school degree or some college but no bachelor's degree, (3) bachelor's degree and (4) master's degree or higher.[4]

Family income was recorded as a continuous measure representing the value of both parents' combined incomes averaged over the years that the persons in the sample were 11–15 years of age in the Norwegian data. In the U.S. data it was recorded as a categorical variable representing intervals of combined parental income from the year the sample members were 7th graders. These measures include salary, income from self-employment and some state support benefits such as unemployment benefits, sickness benefits and maternity benefits. To make the income measures as comparable as possible I divided them into percentiles that align with the categories defined in the NELS:88, based on the relevant 10th grade cohort sample. The result is five dummies representing the lowest 19%, lower middle 17% (reference category), middle 24%, higher middle 24% and highest 16% of the income distribution in the two samples.

High School GPA ranges from 2 to 6 in Norway and 0 to 4 in the United States. Both are centred at their mean values within the population analysed in the chapter. Unfortunately there are substantial amounts of missing data on this variable in both countries. In the analyses below missing values were mean substituted and a dummy was added to account for the missing values.[5] This method of handling missing data is not ideal. One alternative would be to exclude from the sample those students with missing values on high school grades. This would restrict the data to a limited and possibly problematically selected sample and is therefore not preferable. Another alternative is not to use the variable at all. This may be the best solution when the variable is as incomplete as it is. However, I believe it adds an important control on the main independent variables of interest in these analyses (i.e. parental income and parental education level). Thus, I have made the choice to include it in the final models, but I would like to underscore that the inclusion of this variable is associated with some challenges.

Type of college is entered as a dummy variable representing selective or highly selective colleges in the United States. The reference category is unselective or unrated colleges. In the Norwegian analyses I use a dummy variable for whether the institution is a university. The more vocationally oriented university college (*høyskole*) is the reference category.

FINDINGS

Distribution of the Samples

A brief look at the descriptive statistics for the samples reveals that the two national samples are somewhat differently distributed on the independent variables (Table 1). The respondents in the Norwegian sample are older on average, and slightly more female than in the U.S. sample.

The distribution of parental education level differs in that the U.S. four-year college sample has more highly educated parents than the Norwegian students. Table 1 shows that the proportion of students in four-year colleges in the United States whose parents have MA or higher degrees is 10 percentage points higher than that of undergraduate students in Norway (26% vs. 16%). The proportion of students with the lowest educated parents is twice as large in Norway as in the United States, although in both cases this category is quite small (2.2% vs. 4.6%) As explained above, income is categorized into groups of equal percentiles across the two countries by design. This overview of the samples indicates that even if a slightly larger proportion of high school graduates enter into four-year colleges in the U.S. than start higher education in Norway, this does not mean that the Norwegian students are a more selected group according to their background variables.

Dropping Out by Parental Income and Education – Bivariate Relationships

When we look at the average dropout rates across the first seven years of enrolment by parental income category, we clearly see a much wider distribution in the United States (Fig.1)[6] than in Norway (Fig. 2). This gives us the first indication that dropout rates vary considerably less by family income in Norway than in the United States. However, because family income and parental education level are related, some of the effect we see in the income graphs may be attributable to parental education rather than to income. Comparing the per cent that drop out each year across parental education categories we see a wider distribution in Norway (Fig. 3) than we did in the Norwegian income graph (Fig. 2). In fact, the graph displaying the relationship between parental education and dropout in Norway (Fig. 3) looks much more, as dispersion is concerned, like either of the U.S. graphs (Figs. 1 and 4) than like the Norwegian parental income graph (Fig. 2). The seemingly extreme variation over time displayed for the students with

Table 1. Descriptive Statistics.

Variables	United States (NELS:88 weighted)					Norway (Educational Careers)				
	NA	Mean	SD	Min	Max	N	Mean	SD	Min	Max
Female	3470	0.526	0.499	0	1	16431	0.612	0.487	0	1
Age at entry	3470	18.298	0.524	18	21	16431	20.107	0.724	18	21
Parents' income (combined)										
Lowest 19% income	3470	0.191	0.393	0	1	16431	0.190	0.392	0	1
Lower middle 17% income	3470	0.171	0.376	0	1	16431	0.170	0.376	0	1
Middle 24% income	3470	0.240	0.427	0	1	16431	0.240	0.427	0	1
Upper middle 24% income	3470	0.238	0.426	0	1	16431	0.240	0.427	0	1
Highest 16% income	3470	0.160	0.367	0	1	16431	0.160	0.367	0	1
Parents' education (highest)										
Compulsory ed./Less than HS	3470	0.022	0.146	0	1	16431	0.046	0.210	0	1
HS diploma/less than BA	3470	0.460	0.498	0	1	16431	0.463	0.499	0	1
BA degree (US)/Undergraduate (NO)	3470	0.257	0.437	0	1	16431	0.330	0.470	0	1
MA/Professional or more	3470	0.262	0.440	0	1	16431	0.161	0.368	0	1
High school GPA	2540	3.124	0.577	0.3	4	15065	4.185	0.625	2	6
Missing high school grades	3470	0.286	0.452	0	1	16431	0.083	0.276	0	1
Unselective or unrated college U.S./University college Norway	3470	0.264	0.441	0	1	16431	0.398	0.490	0	1
Selective or highly selective college U.S./University Norway	3470	0.736	0.441	0	1	16431	0.602	0.490	0	1

[a] All U.S. sample sizes have been rounded to the nearest ten according to the U.S. Institute of Education Sciences, National Center for Education Statistics (2001, p. 20).

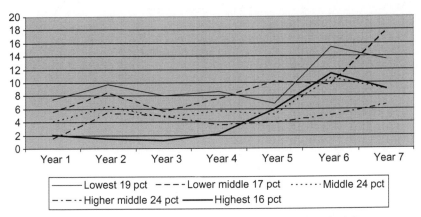

Fig. 1. Per Cent Dropout by Parental Income in the United States.

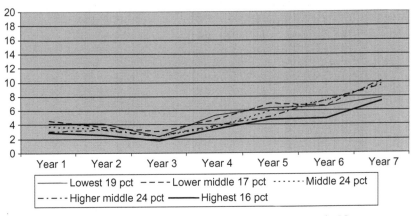

Fig. 2. Per Cent Dropout by Year and Parental Income in Norway.

the lowest educated parents in the U.S. is based on a small number of respondents and should be read with some caution.

Event History Analysis with Sheaf Coefficients

Table 2 displays the results of the event history analyses predicting dropping out for two years or more within the first seven years of attendance. Model One estimates the effect of parental income and education on this dropout

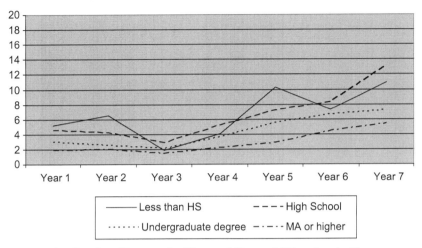

Fig. 3. Per Cent Dropout by Year and Parental Education in Norway.

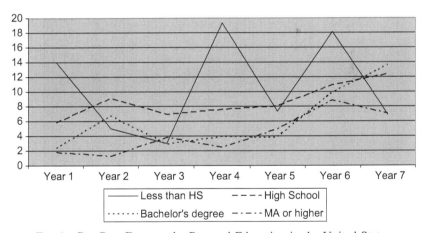

Fig. 4. Per Cent Dropout by Parental Education in the United States.

measure, and Model Two adds a control for high school grades and college type. Both models control for gender and age as well. In this analysis we see that when controlling for parental education, age and gender, being in the higher family income categories significantly reduces students' odds of dropping out of college in the United States relative to the reference

Table 2. Event History Models Predicting Dropping Out from College/University.

	United States (NELS:88)				Norway (Educational Careers)			
	Model One		Model Two		Model One		Model Two	
	e(b) (SE)	Std. xy	e(b) (SE)	Std. xy	e(b) (SE)	Std. xy	e(b) (SE)	Std. xy
Female	0.804*(0.073)	−0.093	0.882(0.082)	−0.050	0.786***(0.032)	−0.103	0.836***(0.034)	−0.070
Age at entry	1.476***(0.122)	0.169	1.357***(0.112)	0.124	1.413***(0.041)	0.219	1.259***(0.037)	0.132
Lowest 19% income	1.066ns(0.127)		1.082 ns(0.132)		0.948ns(0.061)		0.946ns(0.062)	
Middle 24% income	0.753*(0.094)		0.747*(0.094)		0.905ns(0.057)		0.900ns(0.057)	
Lower middle 17% income	(reference category)		(reference category)		(reference category)		(reference category)	
Upper middle 24% income	0.638**(0.107)		0.631**(0.108)		0.989 ns(0.063)		0.992ns(0.064)	
Highest 16% income	0.499***(0.091)		0.538**(0.096)		0.979ns(0.074)		0.987ns(0.075)	
Income sheaf		0.226***		0.201***		0.033ns		0.033ns
Parents have less than HS	1.071ns(0.248)		1.061ns(0.255)		1.154ns(0.104)		1.062ns(0.096)	
Parents have HS diploma	(reference category)		(reference category)		(reference category)		(reference category)	
Parents have BA degree	0.672**(0.086)		0.730*(0.096)		0.656***(0.031)		0.742***(0.036)	
Parents have MA or more	0.505***(0.076)		0.584**(0.088)		0.417***(0.030)		0.528***(0.039)	
Education sheaf		0.249***		0.184**		0.296***		0.192***
High school GPA			0.481***(0.034)	−0.283			0.497***(0.016)	−0.340
Missing HS GPA			1.111ns(0.123)	0.038			3.113***(0.168)	0.238
Selective college (US)/University (Norway)			0.628**(0.090)	−0.165			0.876**(0.039)	−0.053
N (Person–period)	16040		16040		68986		68986	
Estimated SD of latent Y	1.17		1.25		1.14		1.26	
Bayesian Information Criterion (BIC)	1566457		1527876		22040		21281.6	

ns = not statistically significant.

Notes: Dummies for year of enrolment were included in order to specify the models correctly, but they are not displayed in the table because their effect sizes are not relevant for the research questions. Wald tests were used to test the significance of the sheaf coefficients. The U.S. data were estimated using sample weights.

*p < .05; **p < .01; ***p < .001.

category. When controlling for high school GPA and college type in Model Two, the middle income category in the United States is associated with 25% lower odds of dropping out in an average year. Being in the upper middle income category in the United States is associated with 37% lower odds of dropping out and being in the highest income group is associated with 46% lower odds of dropping out, relative to students in the lower middle income group (Table 2, Model Two).

By contrast, none of the parental income categories have significantly higher or lower odds of dropping out compared with the lower middle income group in Norway (Table 2, Model One). This does not change when we control for high school GPA and college type (Table 2, Model Two).

Parents' highest education level is associated with lower dropout probabilities in both countries, and the pattern of the relationship is also similar; Relative to students with parents whose highest completed education is less than a B.A., students whose parents have B.A. degrees or graduate/professional degrees are significantly less likely to leave college for a substantial amount of time. The odds of dropping out are 27% and 42% lower for these two categories respectively in the United States, while they are 26% and 47% lower in Norway (Table 2, Model Two). There is no statistically significant difference in odds of having dropped out from college between students whose parents don't have a high school diploma and students whose parents do.

The range of odds ratios for different categories of parental income and education do not directly address how the overall relationships between the socioeconomic status indicators and dropout compare between the two countries. Therefore, Table 2 also reports the standardized sheaf coefficient for each of the groups of dummies representing parental income and education. The standardized sheaf coefficient is a summary measure that can be interpreted as the total effect of the latent construct to which the underlying dummy variables refer. In other words, the sheaf coefficients in Table 2 represent the same effect sizes as the odds ratios in the adjacent columns, just standardized according to the distribution of x and the estimated latent distribution of y. In addition, instead of presenting one effect size for each of the dummy variables for parents' income and education level, the sheaf coefficients represent the combined effect sizes of parental income and education respectively, as a group.

When we compare the standardized sheaf coefficient for parents' income in the two countries, we see that a standard deviation change in the group of dummies representing income categories in the United States is associated with a much larger change in dropout than the equivalent in Norway.

Whereas the standardized sheaf coefficient for income is .23 in the U.S. model, it is only .03 in the Norwegian model. Moreover, these summary measures show that parental education matters much more than income for dropping out Norway (.30), even more than parental education matters in the United States (.25) (Table 2, Model One). Because these are fully standardized coefficients, the numbers are directly comparable as indicators of the net effect of income and education on dropout in the two countries. Consequently, what we see is that whereas parental income and parental education matters to a similar extent in the United States, only parental education level has a substantial impact on students' probability of leaving college in Norway.

Model Two of Table 2 shows the sheaf coefficients for parental income and education level after controlling for high school GPA and college type. In both countries, controlling for prior academic achievement reduces the education sheaves more than the income sheaves. Whereas the income sheaves remain roughly the same size in Model Two, the standardized sheaf coefficient for parental education is reduced to .18 in the United States and to .19 in Norway. Thus, when controlling for academic performance in high school, and the type of college the students have enrolled in, the effect of parental education level on the probability of dropping out is nearly identical across the two countries.

The indicator for missing data on high school GPA warrants a comment here. The indicator is not significant in the U.S. analysis. This means that having missing information on high school GPA is not independently associated with the outcome variable in the U.S. sample. In the Norwegian data, on the other hand, the indicator is large and highly significant. This means that there is something about the students who do not have high school GPAs registered in the data that is non-randomly related to dropping out. Because of the way the Norwegian data was collected, students who enrolled in one of the few private colleges in Norway (the biggest one being BI School of Management) have more poorly represented high school data. These schools also have higher dropout rates on average than public colleges and universities. Yet this is not the only explanation for missing data on this variable. Students who apply with alternative credentials or who applied before high school grade point information was collected for statistical purposes (it only started in 1997) also are more likely to have missing information on this variable. This relationship complicates the interpretation of the high school GPA estimate in the Norwegian analysis.

Multilevel Models

Table 3 displays the results from the multilevel analyses. The table shows two models; the unconditional model and a conditional model. The unconditional model includes only the time indicators (year of enrolment), but no other independent variables. The conditional model includes all the same predictors as the final model in the event history analysis. The reported estimates are based on the unit-specific model, which means that they control for random effects. The unit-specific model should be interpreted as the average 'within-institution' effect of the predictors, controlling for variations across colleges (cf. Raudenbush & Bryk, 2002).

The unconditional model shows that the average yearly probability of dropping out in a 'typical' college is .06 in the United States and .03 in Norway. Note that schools are defined as first college of entry, but attendance is tracked regardless of whether the student transfers to a different college. The lower panel of Table 3 also shows the estimated random variance among institutions and the estimated variability in dropout rates across colleges. These measures from the unconditional model show that even though we are comparing a specific segment of the U.S. higher education system with the entirety of the Norwegian higher education system, there is more variability in dropout across colleges in the United States in a given year than in Norway. The probability of dropout varies from almost nothing in both countries to 39% in U.S. four-year colleges and 12% in Norwegian higher education institutions.

Turning to the conditional model and our main independent variables of interest; parents' income and parents' education level, we see that when dropout is estimated 'within institutions' rather than as an average probability across the population of students, the relationship between parents' income and dropout is strengthened in the Norwegian model. Two of the four income categories now emerge as significantly different from the reference category, albeit in a weak and somewhat nonlinear fashion. Being in the highest income category is associated with over 20% lower odds of dropping out than the reference category in Norway, when estimated this way. The U.S. estimates have not changed substantially compared with the final event history model – the highest income category is associated with 44% lower odds of dropping out than the reference category.

As we saw in the event history analysis, the parental education categories are more similar across the two countries than the income categories. These estimates remain similar in the multilevel framework. Having parents with

Table 3. Estimates of Dropout, Controlling for Random Variance Across Colleges of Entry.

| | United States (NELS:88 weighted) | | | | Norway (Educational Careers) | | | |
| | Unconditional Model | | Conditional Model | | Unconditional Model | | Conditional Model | |
Level One	B	Probability	b	e(b)	B	Probability	b	e(b)
Female			-0.172ns	0.842			-0.095ns	0.909
Age at entry			0.284**	1.329			0.168**	1.183
Lowest 19% income			0.088ns	1.092			-0.042ns	0.959
Middle 24% income			-0.318*	0.728			-0.140*	0.870
Upper middle 24% income			-0.484**	0.616			-0.122ns	0.885
Highest 16% income			-0.578**	0.561			-0.231**	0.793
Parents have less than HS			0.152ns	1.164			0.108ns	1.114
Parents have BA/Undergraduate degree			-0.434**	0.648			-0.262***	0.770
Parents have MA or more			-0.521***	0.594			-0.560***	0.572
High school GPA			-0.909***	0.403			-0.757***	0.469
Missing high school GPA			0.191ns	1.210			0.622***	1.862
Level Two	B	Probability	b	Probability	B	Probability	b	Probability
Nonselective or unrated (US)/University Colleges (Norway)			-2.898***	0.052			-3.964***	0.019
Selective colleges(US)/Universities (Norway)			-0.670**	0.027			0.542**	0.032
Intercept	-2.819***	0.056	-2.898***	0.052	-3.585***	0.027	-3.964***	0.019
Random variance level two	1.433		1.386		0.620		0.604	
Estimated variability in dropout across colleges (95%)	-5.17 – -0.46	0.01–0.39	-5.21 – -0.58	0.01–0.36	-4.85 – -1.76	0.01–0.12	-5.21 – -2.15	0–01–0.10
Number of institutions	980		980		52		52	

ns = not statistically significant (robust standard errors).

In Model 2, the probabilities are estimated students who are at the grand mean of all the level one variables (except the time-dummies, which were entered 'as is'). All coefficients in the table are reported from the unit-specific models. Dummies for years of enrolment are not shown.
*$p < .05$; **$p < .01$; ***$p < .001$.

an MA or higher degree is associated with 43% and 41% lower odds of dropping out in Norway and the United States respectively, relative to having high school graduated parents.

Figs. 5 and 6 display dropout probabilities based on the conditional unit-specific model from the multilevel analysis. Probabilities are estimated at the grand mean of all individual level variables in the model (except the time indicators), and for those who started at universities in Norway and selective colleges in the United States (these college types have most similar average dropout rates and are therefore more easily comparable). Fig. 5 shows that when we control for random variance across colleges, there is a weak but uneven income gradient in Norway. In the United States, the income gradient is much more linear and considerably steeper.

By contrast, the parental education level gradient is very similar across the two countries (Fig. 6). Thus, we see that parents' income and parents' education level are not necessarily associated with dropout in the same way in different institutional settings. Parental education plays a similar role in keeping students in college in Norway and the United States. When it comes to parents' income, the patterns are different across the two countries. When estimating average dropout probabilities over time for the student

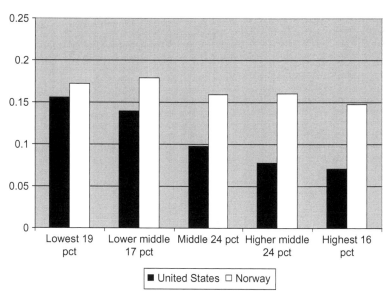

Fig. 5. Average Year to Year Probability of Dropout by Parent Income.

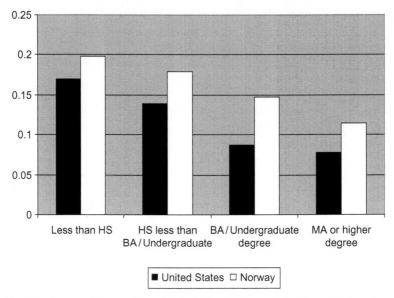

Fig. 6.   Average Year to Year Probability of Dropout by Parent Education.

population as a whole, income does not seem to make a difference in Norway. It clearly does in the United States. When estimating dropout probabilities within institutions, we see that parents' income does make some difference in keeping students in college in Norway as well, but not nearly as much as in the United States.

DISCUSSION AND CONCLUSION

In this chapter, I have compared the relationship between socioeconomic background and the risk of dropping out from college in two countries with quite different institutional contexts. I asked whether and to what extent financial and cultural resources matter in different ways in the two contexts. The purpose of this comparison has been threefold, comprising an empirical argument, a methodological argument and a theoretical argument. The empirical argument concerns the fact that socioeconomic indicators may have divergent effects on dropping out from higher education across national and institutional contexts. The methodological argument is that it is of central importance to define the data and analyses in the most comparable way. Finally, the theoretical argument concerns the interpretation of the forms of capital as concrete resources with different values in different national contexts.

Empirically, I found that in contrast to the United States, higher family income is not associated with lower risk of dropping out from universities and university colleges in Norway when estimated across the student population in the event history framework. On the other hand, according to the most comparable estimate – the standardized sheaf coefficient – parental education matters to the same extent in the United States and Norway. As expected, high family income predicts much lower odds of dropping out in the United States relative to the lower income reference group. Moreover, the U.S. estimates do not change substantially from the event history to the multilevel framework. By contrast, when dropout is estimated within institutions rather than for the student population as a whole, a relationship between parents' income and dropout emerges in Norway. This means that income matters for the risk of leaving college within the context of each institution in Norway, even though it matters substantially less than in the United States.

Methodologically, the suggestion put forward in this chapter is to use both event history models and multilevel models. Event history models estimate average effects of background variables over time, which alleviates some of the problems related to varying timing of events across institutional contexts. Also, I find it useful to predict breaks in enrolment rather than degree completion because of different practices and norms regarding part-time enrolment and degree duration across degree programs and college types. The sheaf coefficient is also useful, particularly when comparing groups of social background categories like different levels of parental education. The sheaf coefficient summarizes the effect of several elements of one latent construct (e.g. parents' education level) into one standardized effect size, which provides the opportunity to directly compare the latent constructs of interest. Multilevel modelling with random effects can add important information to the comparison, since the extent and pattern of random variation across colleges may vary with institutional structures.

Theoretically, the interpretation of these findings is quite straightforward. That is, I conceptualize financial and cultural capital as having a fundamentally practical relation to persistence in education in countries like Norway and the United States. They are resources that are relevant if they can be used *in practice,* to further a child's progress through the education system. If we concentrate on the differential value of economic capital in the two countries' education systems, we see that financial resources may be used by parents in the United States to obtain better primary and secondary schooling. Economic capital allows parents in the United States to send their children to private schools that have significantly more resources than public schools (Persell et al., 1992). Economic capital also makes it much easier to plan for college expenses and eventually pay for the child's college attendance, also when grants and scholarships are unpredictable or unavailable. Moreover, family finances likely have a direct effect on students' ability to make educational transitions and remain in school once the transitions are made.

By contrast, economic capital in Norway buys very little advantage in the education system because there are very few avenues to academic advancement based on finances. Also, the more compressed income distribution in Norway makes the general differences between rich and poor smaller than in the United States and therefore reduces the extent to which higher income families are advantaged relative to their lower income counterparts.

Nonetheless, inequality is maintained in the Norwegian system of higher education as well, in terms of lower dropout rates for students with more highly educated parents, and some effect of income within each institutional setting. In both countries, it is likely that the effect of parental education works both through the parents' ability to encourage and transmit academically relevant skills to their children and through their ability to directly guide and help their offspring through educational transitions, including persistence through college.

Social class differences are not synonymous with practical resources and cannot, as a general rule, be reduced to material inequality. There may be social and institutional contexts where more symbolic class differences are relevant for understanding the mechanisms of social inequality. However, in comparative analyses of inequality in education the value of different types of family resources must be interpreted in light of the concrete, practical constraints of the national institutional contexts.

ACKNOWLEDGEMENTS

I thank Paul Attewell, David E. Lavin, Philip Kasinitz, Arnfinn H. Midtbøen, Julia Orupabo and the two anonymous reviewers for their insightful comments on earlier drafts of this chapter. I would also like to thank Arne Mastekaasa and the Department of Sociology and Human Geography at the University of Oslo for facilitating my access to the Norwegian data. Any errors and omissions remain the responsibility of the author.

NOTES

1. This way of organizing studies at the university changed with a reform in 2003. Now courses are more tightly structured and the students are required to submit work over the course of the semester. The data used in this chapter is however taken from before the reform.
2. First-generation immigrants are excluded from the analyses because it is uncertain whether they went through the national educational systems relevant to the analysis.
3. Foreign institutions, military institutions and programs that do not qualify for a higher education degree are excluded. Only regular enrolment is counted as first enrolment, not registration for college preparatory tests (*forberedendeprøver*).
4. In both countries, the third category of parental education is the same as the types of degrees available at the college levels included in the respective country's sample.
5. Students in the sample with missing information about parental education or income were excluded from all the analyses.
6. Percentages in Figs. 1 and 4 are estimated using weights to adjust for survey attrition and design effects.

REFERENCES

Allison, P. D. (1982). Discrete-time methods for the analysis of event histories. *Sociological Methodology, 13,* 61–98.

Attewell, P., Heil, S., & Reisel, L. (2011). Competing explanations of undergraduate noncompletion. *American Educational Research Journal, 48*(3), 536–559.

Bean, J. P., & Metzner, B. S. (1985). A conceptual model of nontraditional undergraduate student attrition. *Review of Educational Research, 55*(4), 485–540.

Bourdieu, P. (1977). *Outline of a theory of practice.* Cambridge, MA: Cambridge University Press.

Bourdieu, P. (1984). *Distinction: A social critique of the judgment of taste.* Cambridge, MA: Harvard University Press.

Bourdieu, P. (1986). The forms of capital. In J. G. Richardson (Ed.), *Handbook of theory and research for the sociology of education* (pp. 241–258). New York, NY: Greenwood Press.

Bozick, R. (2007). Making it through the first year of college: The role of students' economic resources, employment, and living arrangements. *Sociology of Education, 80*(3), 261–285.

Braxton, J. M. (2000). *Reworking the student departure puzzle.* Nashville: Vanderbilt University Press.

Breen, R., & Goldthorpe, J. H. (1997). Explaining educational differentials: Towards a formal rational action theory. *Rationality and Society, 9*(3), 275–305.

Buchmann, C. (2002). Measuring family background in international studies of education: Conceptual issues and methodological challenges. In A. C. Porter & A. Gamoran (Eds.), *Methodological advances in cross-national surveys of educational achievement.* Washington, DC: National Academy Press.

Cabrera, A. F., Nora, A., & Castaneda, M. B. (1993). College persistence: Structural equations modeling test of an integrated model of student retention. *The Journal of Higher Education, 64*(2), 123–139.

Calhoun, C. (2000). The specificity of american higher education. In R. Kalleberg, F. Engelstad, G. Brochmann, A. Leira & L. Mjøset (Eds.), *Comparative perspectives on universities* (Vol. 19). Stamford, CT: JAI Press Inc.

Chen, R., & DesJardins, S. L. (2008). Exploring the effects of financial aid on the gap in student dropout risks by inciome level. *Research in Higher Education, 49*(1), 1–18.

Collins, R. (2000). Situational stratification: A micro-macro theory of inequality. *Sociological theory, 18*, 17–43.

Conley, D. (1999). *Being black, living in the red: Race, wealth and social policy in america.* Berkeley, CA: University of California Press.

Conley, D. (2001). Capital for college: Parental assets and educational attainment. *Sociology of Education, 74*, 59–73.

DeGraaf, P. M. (1986). The impact of financial and cultural resources on educational attainment in the Netherlands. *Sociology of Education, 59*, 237–246.

DeGraaf, N. D., DeGraaf, P. M., & Kraaykamp, G. (2000). Parental cultural capital and educational attainment in the Netherlands: A refinement of the cultural capital perspective. *Sociology of Education, 23*(2), 92–111.

DiMaggio, P. (1982). Cultural capital and school success: The impact of status culture participation on the grades of U.S. high school students. *American Sociological Review, 47*, 189–201.

Erikson, R., & Goldthorpe, J. H. (1992). *The constant flux: A study of class mobility in industrial societies.* Oxford: Clarendon.

Ganzeboom, H. B. G., Luijkx, R., & Treiman, D. J. (1989). Intergenerational class mobility in comparative perspective. *Research in Social Stratification and Mobility, 8*, 8–84.

Goldin, C., & Katz, L. F. (2007). Long-run changes in the U.S. wage structure: Narrowing, widening, polarizing. Paper presented at the the Brookings Panel on Economic Activity, Washington, DC.

Hansen, M. N., & Mastekaasa, A. (2006). Social origins and academic performance at University. *European Sociological Review, 22*(3), 277–291.

Heise, D. R. (1972). Employing nominal variables, induced variables, and block variables in path analysis. *Sociological Methods & Research, 1*(2), 147–173.

Hovdhaugen, E., & Aamodt, P. O. (2005). *Frafall fra universitetet.* Working paper 13/2005 NIFU STEP, Oslo.

Hægeland, T., Kirkebøen, L. J., & Raaum, O. (2006). *Resultatforskjeller mellom videregående skoler. En analyse basert på karakterdata fra skoleåret 2003–2004* (Vol. Report 2006/16). Oslo: Statistics Norway.

Institute of Education Sciences, National Center for Education Statistics. (2001). *Restricted-use data procedures manual* (p. 20). U.S. Department of Education. Retrieved from http://nces.ed.gov/pubs96/96860rev.pdf

Jæger, M. M., & Holm, A. (2007). Does parents' economic, cultural, and social capital explain the social class effect on educational attainment in the Scandinavian mobility regime? *Social Science Research, 36,* 719–744.

Kingston, P. W. (2000). *The classless society.* Stanford, CA: Stanford University Press.

Mastekaasa, A., & Hansen, M. N. (2005). *Frafall i høyere utdanning. Hvilken betydning har sosial bakgrunn? Utdanning 2005-deltakelse og kompetanse* (pp. 98–121). Oslo/Kongsvinger: Statistisk sentralbyrå.

McDonough, P. M. (1997). *Choosing colleges: How social class and schools structure opportunity.* New York, NY: SUNY Press.

Menard, S. (2004). Six approaches to calculating standardized logistic regression coefficients. *The American Statistician, 58,* 218–223.

OECD. (2009). *Factbook: Economic, Environmental and Social Statistics* (Vol. ISBN 92-64-05604-1). Retrieved from http://puck.sourceoecd.org/vl=5952342/cl=14/nw=1/rpsv/factbook2009/index.htm. Accessed on January 14, 2011.

Oliver, M. L., & Shapiro, T. M. (1995). *Black wealth/white wealth: A new perspective on racial inequality.* New York, NY: Rutledge.

Paulsen, M. B., & St. John, E. P. (2002). Social class and college costs: Examining the financial nexus between college choice and persistence. *The Journal of Higher Education, 73*(2), 189–236.

Persell, C. H., Catsambis, S., & Cookson, P. W., Jr. (1992). Family background, school type and college attendance: A conjoint system of cultural capital transmission. *Journal of Research on Adolescence, 2*(1), 1–23.

Phipps, S. (2001). Values, policies and the well-being of young children in Canada, Norway and the United States. In K. Vlemininckx & T. M. Smeeding (Eds.), *Child well-being, child poverty and child policy in modern nations: What do we know?* Bristol: Policy Press.

Pontusson, J. (2005). *Inequality and prosperity: Social Europe vs. liberal America.* Ithaca, NY: Cornell University Press.

Raudenbush, S. W., & Bryk, A. S. (2002). *Hierarchical linear models: Applications and data analysis methods* (2nd ed.). Thousand Oaks, CA: Sage Publications.

Reisel, L. (2011). Two paths to inequality in educational outcomes: Family background and educational selection in the united states and norway. *Sociology of Education, 84*(4), 261–280.

Reisel, L., & Brekke, I. (2010). Minority dropout in higher education: A comparison of the United States and Norway using competing risk event history analysis. *European Sociological Review, 26*(6), 691–712.

Roedelé, S. M., & Aamodt, P. O. (2001). *Studiemobilitet i norsk høyere utdanning* (Vol. rapport 9/2001). Oslo: NIFU.

Scott, M. A., & Kennedy, B. B. (2005). Pitfalls in pathways: Some perspectives on competing risk event history analysis in education research. *Journal of Educational and Behavioral Statistics, 30*(4), 413–442.

Seidman, A. (2005). *College student retention: Formula for student success.* Westport, CT: Praeger Publishers.

Shavit, Y., Arum, R., & Gamoran, A. (2007). *Stratification in higher education: A comparative study.* Stanford, CA: Stanford University Press.

Shavit, Y., & Blossfeld, H.-P. (Eds.). (1993). *Persistent inequalities: A comparative study of educational attainment in thirteen countries.* Boulder, CO: Westview Press.

Singer, J. D., & Willett, J. B. (2003). *Applied longitudinal data analysis: Modeling change and event occurence*. New York, NY: Oxford University Press.

Tinto, V. (1975). Dropout from higher education: A theoretical synthesis of recent research. *Review of Educational Research, 65*(Winter), 89–125.

Tinto, V. (1988). Stages of student departure: Reflections on the longitudinal character of student leaving. *The Journal of Higher Education, 59*(4), 438–455.

Turmo, A. (2004). Scientific literacy and socio-economic background among 15-year-olds – A nordic perspecitive. *Scandinavian Journal of Educational Research, 48*(3), 287–305.

Whitt, H. P. (1986). The Sheaf coefficient: A simplified and expanded approach. *Social Science Research, 15*(2), 174–189.

Zelizer, V. A. (1994). *The social meaning of money: Pin money, paychecks, poor relief, and other currencies*. New York, NY: Basic Books.

COMPLETION OF UPPER SECONDARY EDUCATION: WHAT MECHANISMS ARE AT STAKE?

Martin D. Munk

ABSTRACT

The purpose of this chapter is to reveal explanations for completing upper secondary education. Focus is on the mechanisms that drive attainment of upper secondary education. I analyze the relative contributions of different factors measured by the relative increases in the log likelihood function. I also investigate the importance of characteristics other than the traditional variables, such as fathers' and mothers' occupations, their education, and household income, often applied in studies of educational attainment. I used a recent 1984 cohort database with information about educational completion and an informative set of measurements on noncognitive capacities, parental cultural capital, cultural capital, reading score, several school-related variables, and a rich set of family background variables. Attainment of upper secondary education was analyzed by a multinomial logit model, showing that characteristics other than the traditional variables all have significant importance. The analysis clearly depicted that the social position and educational levels of both parents remain important in determining whether the child embarks on completing an upper secondary education. Additionally, noncognitive dispositions

Class and Stratification Analysis
Comparative Social Research, Volume 30, 255–291
ISSN: 0195-6310/doi:10.1108/S0195-6310(2013)0000030013

show to be very important in explaining educational attainment, even when controlling for family background and refined cultural capital variables. Therefore, society should direct more efforts towards establishing children's cognitive and noncognitive skills and their ability to focus on schoolwork along with building their beliefs. Parents should be involved in a more content-sensitive sense when raising their children.

Keywords: Educational completion; social origin; cultural capital; cognitive and noncognitive dispositions; and reproduction

INTRODUCTION AND PURPOSE

The fundamental question of what determines the intergenerational transmission of advantage and disadvantage remains somewhat open, as stated in various references: Bourdieu (2000); Borghans, Duckworth, Heckman, and Weel (2008); Beller (2009); Björklund, Lindahl, and Lindquist (2010b). In particular, the role a person's origin plays in determining life chances is not fully understood. Here, rather than concentrating on traditional family background variables to explain educational outcomes, I search for the explanation in characteristics, dispositions, and attributes. I believe that focusing on the details of what individuals were exposed to and experienced, in both the home and the school, when growing up will further our understanding of the role played by the traditional parental characteristics and will add new insight into what constitutes the carriers of characteristics from one generation to the next. I also assume that various forms of capital are accumulated and produced throughout a person's lifetime, especially during childhood, and that these forms of capital are mainly determined by the characteristics of the family in which the individual grows up (Dumais & Ward, 2010; Wildhagen, 2010).

First, I analyze whether cultural capital, school variables, cognitive skills and noncognitive skills (system of dispositions) simultaneously have a statistically significant impact on completion of upper secondary education after controlling for family background. Focus is on the degree to which noncognitive traits matter for educational success because soft skills are important for educational and other outcomes (Heckman, Stixrud, & Urzua, 2006). Therefore, I expect that items other than traditional family background characteristics matter. Influence could well be exerted by self-perception, locus of control, cultural orientation, taste for education or "educational affinity," teacher–student relationship and "school non-cognitive climate," which may sway the particular completion of an upper secondary school program (e.g., Goldthorpe, 2007, p. 13). In terms of the teacher–student relationship I introduce and use the item "Most of my teachers really listen to what I have to say" and capture some kind of recognition contributing to building up self-confidence and self-esteem (Bourdieu, 2000; DiMaggio, 1982; Dumais, 2006). It remains controversial whether cultural capital, in addition to social origin and other characteristics, is the driver of educational success (Kingston, 2001; Goldthorpe, 2007; Gaddis, 2013). Therefore, I use various measures of parental cultural capital and cultural capital variables to further test the degree to which cultural capital matters in educational attainment. The first dimension of cultural capital is usually missing in educational attainment studies, and I offer a measurement of this by introducing the formulation from the PISA study: "I cannot sit still and read for more than a few minutes." It is relevant to have such a category since it can capture a characteristic – not being able to sit still and read – that would probably make it unlikely that a high-school education was completed or even initiated. Goldthorpe (2007, p. 3) argues that for children from working-class or peasant origins, the school represents an alien environment, especially if the child is unable to meet the demands of school, including the ability to sit still and read for extended periods. Following Farkas (2003), I would argue that cultural capital is much broader than merely high-status culture signals.

Second and most importantly, the study aims to analyze the importance, or magnitude of effects, of these variables compared with the effects of family background. I use an idea from McIntosh and Munk (2007) where we look at the incremental increase in the likelihood function as each group of variables is included in the model of educational attainment. The objective is to determine the relative contributions of inherited and noninherited (acquired) attributes and characteristics in completing upper secondary education following the work of Breen and Goldthorpe (1997), Dustmann (2004), Erikson and Jonsson (1996), Erikson and Rudolphi (2010), Galindo-Rueda and Vignoles (2007), Gamoran and Mare (1989), Halsey, Heath, and Ridge (1980), Iannelli and Raffe (2007), Micklewright (1989), McIntosh and Munk (2007), Rudolphi (2011), and others. In particular, focus is on the explanation for completing different types of upper secondary education some eight years after leaving lower secondary education. I use a unique database of combined Danish administrative registers and survey information from PISA data 2000. The idea is to use information about the family background and school as being the places where a major part of the system of dispositions is created since this is assumed to have a marked influence on educational attainment.

The following section gives a literature review and elements of the theoretical foundation. I start by looking at social origin characteristics and then go on to give a thorough description of noncognitive and cognitive dispositions followed by a discussion of how to measure parental cultural capital and cultural capital; I end by formulating the two research hypotheses. This leads to the third section where I describe and discuss the applied data, variables and method. Findings and results from the statistical analysis of completion of upper secondary education are then presented and evaluated in the fourth section. In the final section, I discuss the results and conclude.

LITERATURE AND THEORETICAL BACKGROUND

The social and economic circumstances in which children grow up are crucial in determining children's outcomes as adults and play a major role in the attainment of education (Haveman & Wolfe, 1995). An early example of this research is Sewell, Haller, and Portes (1969), who looked beyond father's and mother's income and education and examined the roles of psychological and social psychological variables, such as measured mental ability and social capacity, as well as variables such as level of educational aspiration. Further, they discussed a possible mediator such as an individual's self-conception of ability. In their study, they explained 50% of the variation in the level of educational attainment. Micklewright's (1989) analysis of the National Child Development Study also supports the finding that social background has a major impact on educational completion, even when controlled for academic ability. Between half and two-thirds of educational success is explained by social background. Examples of educational attainment studies after 1995 are those of Dearden, Machin, and Reed (1997) and Dearden (1999). They found that father's years of education, mother's years of education, birth order, type of school, father's occupation, and the financial state of the household were significant in explaining completed years of school for both sexes. Like many other studies, they found that mother's education is more important than that of the father, even when scores from both verbal and mathematical ability tests are included as regressors. The possible effect of the mother's education was considered by Sewell and Shah as early as in 1968, despite the father's education being relatively more important at that time. Ermisch and

Francesconi (2001) found a strong relationship between parental educational attainment and the educational attainment of young cohorts and, in particular, individuals from the bottom income quartile showed to have much lower educational attainments. However, Behrman and Rosenzweig (2005) questioned whether there was a true causal relationship between mother's schooling and her child's schooling, which they found was not sufficiently robust to control for unmeasured, intergenerationally correlated endowments, while a positive effect of paternal schooling was robust. The intergenerational effects of changes in mother's education are rearticulated in Mare and Maralani (2006), who found a positive effect; however, the cost was a reduction in the overall number of children that a more educated population of women bears. A recent paper by Beller (2009) stresses the importance of including mother's social class (occupation) in explaining social mobility. It means that both mother's education and occupation should be part of the empirical model, and as Weeden and Grusky (2005) and McIntosh and Munk (2009) showed, it is better to use the actual occupations of the parents rather than a crude class measure.

Characteristics such as age, number of siblings and sex also play a possible role and other variables matter too, for example, school happiness (see Layard, 2005 for a definition of happiness). Girls are now doing much better in the educational system than boys are. Various international studies support this, and in a review of research in the area, Buchmann, DiPrete, and McDaniel (2008) overwhelmingly show that girls simply perform differently and are apparently better able to adapt to a world of academic education.

Without data on the details of time and expenditure allocations within the household, it is difficult to distinguish between the benefits that accrue to children through the actual investment process and those that depend on the quality of the parent as represented by his or her characteristics (Teachman, 1987) and applicable references (e.g., Leibowitz, 1974). Nevertheless, parents are involved as mentors and as providers of some of the resources required for the particular action chosen. I use information about how often the mother had helped with schoolwork during the time her child attended lower secondary school. Clearly, frequent help from the parents indicates that the child at age 15–16 has some difficulties with schoolwork or other areas; however, it is expected that some minimum time and involvement from the parents contributes positively to a better performance. I address this issue further when describing parental cultural capital. The fast growing literature on intergenerational causal effects is relevant (Holmlund, Lindahl, & Plug, 2011), and there is increasing focus on parental involvement. As an example, Björklund, Eriksson, and Jäntti (2010a) used the sibling correlation, rather than the parent–child correlation, as an estimate of the strength of the intergenerational association. They found that only about 13% of the variation in son's test score could be accounted for by father's test score, whereas the share was about 50% when using the sibling test score. This suggests that parental aspirations, attitudes and parenting practices may be important in accounting for the child's performance (Björklund et al., 2010a, p. 8; see also Björklund et al., 2010b), leaving open the role of parental genetic characteristics.[1] All in all it seems reasonable to look for additional family factors and characteristics.

Cognitive and Noncognitive Dispositions and Skills

As resources are clearly inherited, researchers have focused on the role of inheritance of parents' ability in this process, as suggested by Savage and Egerton (1997), for instance. While the dimension of ability is important because actual skills are determined to some degree by ability, concepts such as ability and intelligence quotient (IQ) are seen as controversial in the literature (Borghans et al., 2008; Loehlin, 2005 in Bowles, Gintis, & Osborne Groves, 2005; Nash, 2003; McIntosh & Munk, 2013). One of the results emerging from the debate between the psychologist Piaget and the linguist Chomsky was that they attributed both cultural and structural–biological dimensions to ability and concluded that ability was related to both experience and a generative IQ (see, e.g., Piattelli-Palmarini, 1980). Accordingly, it is important to address both cognitive and noncognitive elements. Both dimensions are relatively well articulated in recent sociological, economic and psychological literature. Introducing the sociological concept of habitus is useful because its definition as a system of dispositions[2] contains both cognitive and noncognitive elements. Bourdieu understands habitus as a generating principle of behavior and possibilities; and habitus affects individuals' estimations of the probability of the success of particular outcomes and represents an individual's disposition that stems from his or her standing in the game or his or her "feel for the game" (Bourdieu, 2000).

Although there is some criticism of the concept, for example, by Devine, who claims that Bourdieu's "account of the inculcation or internalization of the habitus is not well specified so that the processes by which cultural capital is mobilized across generations remains something of a black box" (Devine, 1998, p. 31), it is a reasonable concept to address the relationship between parents' investments, transmissions of cultural capital and other resources, and their children's future life chances (Bourdieu, 1984, 2000; Munk, 2003; Sayer, 2005; see also Breiger, 1995; Bennett et al., 2009; Wildhagen, 2010). How is this relationship constituted? In one of his last pieces, *Pascalien Meditations*, Bourdieu states that the principle of habitus is embedded in a complex process produced through a socialization motor, termed the search for recognition,[3] requiring an inculcation of the durable disposition to invest in the social game, which is one of the prerequisites of all learning, pedagogic work in its elementary form. It means that throughout childhood and adolescence every individual can obtain durable dispositions through a search for recognition, but with unequal starting points, and is then possibly able to investment in social arenas, such as education. It is claimed by Lizardo (2004, p. 395) that habitus consists of a sociologized version of Piaget's views of practical cognition, termed cognitive dispositions (p. 381). As Nash (2003, p. 446) puts it: "To speak of cognitive habitus is not to encode IQ theory in a radical discourse, but to draw attention to the relationship between classed environments and schemes of language, thought, and modes of specialized cognition."

The noncognitive part of the system of dispositions is often termed noncognitive dispositions or sometimes called noncognitive traits (Bowles, Gintis, & Osborne, 2001, Bowles et al., 2005; Farkas, 2003; esp. Osborne-Groves, 2005, p. 211). In three pieces, Borghans et al., (2008), Thiel and Thomsen (2011), and DiPrete and Jennings (2012) review early and new studies of noncognitive skills, now sometimes termed social and behavioral skills, and describe them at length. According to Borghans et al. (2008), Bowles and Gintis (1976) were the first to introduce the concept of noncognitive (personal) traits. In my view, Bourdieu was also trying to address similar or maybe even more profound items through his concept of system of dispositions or habitus, originally focusing on primary socialization, but later also on studying secondary socialization. To sum up these studies, we can expect that some of the variation in educational attainment, based on choices after lower secondary education, is due to noncognitive dispositions. Noncognitive elements include reliability, punctuality, drive, tolerance, belief structure, behavioral "traits," as Bowles et al. (2001) term them. A review by Farkas (2003) lists a number of items that could capture important aspects of noncognitive elements. He includes effort (industriousness and perseverance), spelling, capitalization, organization, discipline, attendance, participation, and enthusiasm; he also mentions leadership, sociability (extraversion), self-confidence, social sensitivity, impulsiveness, openness to experience, emotional stability (calmness), vigor, aggressiveness, disruptiveness, high culture, locus of control, and self-esteem. In a

MARTIN D. MUNK

262

sense, part of the noncognitive dispositions was already introduced in an early educational attainment study by applying the concept of educational aspirations, which focused on the desire to continue in the educational system (Sewell & Shah, 1968). However, Farkas (2003, p. 542) notes that: "Prior status-attainment models such as the Wisconsin model (Sewell & Hauser, 1975) incorporate social-psychological factors in addition to cognitive skills and yet completely ignore noncognitive behaviors." However, previous status-attainment studies did consider noncognitive behaviors when explaining educational outcomes, for example, Jencks et al. (1979, Chs. 4, 5) and especially Mueser (1979). Possibly, the literature is slightly ambiguous regarding the relationship between educational aspirations and noncognitive skills, but it seems that drive and ambition are part of both concepts. An empirical test of this idea is found in Dumais (2002) using the American National Educational Longitudinal Study. Her empirical notion of habitus is "occupational aspiration" (p. 50), which in my view, only partly measures habitus; a later use is "expectations of the parents" to measure parental habitus (Dumais, 2006). Although Farkas (2003, p. 547) suggests that the respondent's habitus may partly be influenced by parental habitus, these analyzes do not have a full measurement of parental habitus. In the analysis, I use information about parental cultural capital (see next paragraph).

To conclude, the combined cognitive and noncognitive habitus thus refers to capacities and capabilities of the body and mind to perform the kind of abstract problem-solving exercised in language-based and symbolic information processing. This is relevant for educational choice after lower secondary education and the completion of upper secondary education since most social science researchers assume that the production of noncognitive dispositions takes place before the age of 20 years (Borghans et al., 2008; Heckman, 2006).

Cultural Capital

I subscribe to the view that the capital accumulation process has a cultural dimension that can be understood only in the appropriate context, that is, both the household in which the child resided when the major possible investments in cultural capital were made and the educational setting, such as the school and surroundings. I am thus in line with Aschaffenburg and Maas (1997), Bourdieu (1986, 2000), Bourdieu and Passeron (1990), Bowles et al. (2001), De Graaf and Kalmijn (2000), Farkas (2003), Sullivan (2001),

Lareau and Weininger (2004), Wildhagen (2009, 2010), and Jæger (2009, 2011). Notions of cultural capital, as represented by household cultural activities, or parental involvement, are explored by De Graaf et al. (2000).

With reference to DiMaggio (1982), Teachman (1987, p. 548) argued that "cultural capital is only moderately related to conventional measures of family background (especially education of the parents)." Teachman proposes that "cultural capital is an element of status culture distinct from class position," but since he does not include other measurements of cultural capital, apart from parents' education, occupational status of the parents, and an index of educational resources, his analysis can give only a moderate measurement of the effect of parents' cultural capital on educational outcome. Kastillis and Rubinson (1990, p. 270) define cultural capital as "competence in a society's high status culture," but in their operationalization they limit parents' education to a traditional measurement of SES and instead employ an index of attendance to theaters and lectures and visits to museums. However, to omit parents' education from the notion and measurement of cultural capital, as these authors do, is inappropriate (see, e.g., Goldthorpe, 2007; Lareau & Weininger, 2004, p. 4). The problem in Kastillis and Rubinson's study (1990) is that there is too much emphasis on participation in high-status culture instead of viewing cultural capital as an encompassing set of resources that entrains a certain kind of habitus (see also Wildhagen, 2010). Note that Sullivan (2001) equates cultural capital with lifestyles, mirroring what DiMaggio had in mind some 30 years ago (1982, 1985 with Mohr). However, Sullivan (2007) later advocates that cultural capital is also educational capital, similar to the argument of Bourdieu (1986) and Lareau and Weininger (2004). Nevertheless, it should be underlined that cultural tastes and knowledge become capital only when these attributes become criteria for determining success within a particular field (Wildhagen, 2010, p. 521).

Although Jæger (2009) elaborates substantially on the specific levels and mechanisms encapsulated by the "black box" of cultural capital, he still measures parental cultural capital by possession of beaux arts items (classic literature, books of poetry, and works of art) and home educational resources (dictionary, a quiet place to study, a desk for study, and textbooks). Then Jæger measures child's cultural capital by participation in highbrow activities (visits to art museums and theatres and listening to classical music), distinguished from his or her academic abilities approximated by the same reading score as we use. Wildhagen (2009) casts doubt on the commonly accepted thesis, also found in Bourdieu, that cultural capital (as measured by cultural classes outside school and attending museums) improves the teacher–child relationship and thus academic performance (measured as grades and test scores). Although she finds an independent, significant effect of cultural capital and of teacher's perception of the respondent (measured as attentiveness in class, homework effort, and effort in class) on academic performance, she does not find an effect of cultural capital on teacher's perception. Instead, the indirect effect of cultural capital is related to self-selection through educational expectations.

Since these studies have had some success with cultural capital variables, our model's ability to explain the data would be improved if similar variables were included. We have information on household cultural activities – for instance, involving the child in discussions on politics and social issues, used to capture parental involvement – and number of books at home, and also on whether the child visits museums or art galleries. The first dimension of cultural capital, embodied dispositions, captures incorporated mindset and body knowledge, personalities, and mannerisms (Bourdieu, 1986; Wildhagen, 2010), usually missing in educational attainment studies, is introduced by a variable indicating whether the child cannot sit still and read. Since this dimension is an alias for a part of habitus, it reasonable to equate it with noncognitive dispositions.

Educational success is assumed to be related to how the teachers recognize and perceive the student. Farkas is precise when he understands cultural capital to be much broader than merely high-status culture signals. An early, classic contribution in this tradition was DiMaggio (1982, p. 190), who tried to operationalize cultural capital in explaining educational performance. He wrote that: "According to Bourdieu, schools reward students on the basis of their cultural capital, defined as: instruments for the appropriation of symbolic wealth socially designated as worthy of being sought and possessed. Teachers, it is argued, communicate more easily with students who participate in elite status cultures, give them more attention and special assistance, and perceive them as more intelligent or gifted than students who lack cultural capital." As a result of these studies, I used information about the recognition of the student (see also Bourdieu, 2000; Bourdieu & Passeron, 1990). Other related school features, such as discipline in the class room, are included to discover whether the students come from weak school environments, which ultimately matters. Bourdieu (1986) states that the initial accumulation of cultural capital, the precondition for the fast, easy accumulation of every kind of useful cultural capital, starts at the outset, without delay, without wasted time, only for the offspring of families endowed with strong cultural capital; in this case, the accumulation period covers the whole period of socialization.

Research Hypotheses and Assumptions

The research hypotheses are therefore that apart from dominant family background, other variables are important in explaining educational completion, and that measures of noncognitive and cognitive dispositions and cultural capital should also be included in the model to test whether cultural capital, school variables, cognitive skills, and noncognitive skills have a statistically significant effect on educational attainment after controlling for family background. In addition, I assume that these items differ in importance in such a way that cultural capital and school variables are less important and noncognitive and cognitive abilities are more important. Focus is on the degree to which noncognitive traits matter for educational success because various studies have shown that soft skills are important for both educational and labor market outcomes (Heckman, Stixrud, & Urzua, 2006). Accordingly, information about different self-concepts, locus of control, self-esteem and beliefs is used, all characteristics that indicate important features of habitus (Bourdieu, 2000). Even though some studies have found weak effects of cultural capital on educational attainment (Gaddis, 2013; Jæger, 2011; Wildhagen, 2010, p. 523), it is expected that including more refined variables will add to the explanation of educational success.

DATA, VARIABLES, AND METHOD

The dataset used in the empirical analysis is a combination of the Danish part of the 2000 OECD Program for International Student Assessment (PISA) survey and an extensive number of Danish register data from Statistics Denmark for the individuals in question, their parents, and siblings for the years 2000 and 2008.

I use a sample of 3,941 individuals born in 1984 who participated in the PISA survey. The sample is nationally representative of 15 years olds in education. PISA 2000 used a two-stage stratified sample design, where the first-stage sampling units are schools and the second-stage sampling units are students within the sampled schools, see OECD (2002a) and Jensen and Andersen (2006) for a detailed description of the PISA survey. Because of unobserved educational status in 2008, 120 observations were dropped.

To reduce the number of missing observations, categories for unknown/ missing values were included in the regression. The final sample consists of 3,821 observations.

The dependent variable in our study is a four-category variable for completed secondary education in 2008, that is, eight years after lower secondary education, focusing on a point in time when most young people have completed upper secondary education and not at different stages in time.[4] The four categories of the dependent variable are no youth education, academic high school,[5] technical or business high school, and vocational education. In Denmark, primary education or lower secondary education incorporating grade nine is compulsory; however, approximately 60% of children continue to grade ten at the age of 16 years. After grade nine or ten, there are two further educational choices at the upper secondary level in addition to not continuing at all.

The individual can elect to enroll in a vocational program – welding, carpentry, or hair dressing are typical options. Vocational programs can be lengthy and involve apprenticeships lasting up to four years. High schools, the other option for continuing at the upper secondary level, offer three types of curriculum: a general program with various theoretical programs in the humanities, natural, and social sciences; a technical program; and a business program. After grade nine or ten, students can enroll in these programs, which typically last three years and provide the qualifications required for university admission. Many short or intermediate tertiary educational programs also require a high-school diploma for entry. In the data set here, an individual is in the designated category provided he or she had completed the program associated with it.

The vast majority (94.5%) of the students had completed their secondary education by 2008.[6] Only 209 had still to complete upper secondary education, but since it was very few, it did not harm the estimates; most of those with unfinished upper secondary education were enrolled in the vocational program (185). I omitted the 209 individuals from the reference group to avoid heterogeneity. To test this choice of grouping, I ran a model with the 209 in the reference group so that the response variable was solely composed of those completing upper secondary education. The results gave the same overall view, except for minor changes in a few estimates. The distance between reference group and the completed group then decreased because those now inserted in the first group were de facto enrolled in upper secondary programs and were more alike the vocational outcome category.

Explanatory Variables

Two sets of explanatory variables are used in the analysis: register variables and PISA-survey variables. These are categorized according to the type of effect I attempted to capture. All variables were recoded on the basis of numerous preliminary, alternative model specifications.

The register variables are based on register data from 2000, unless otherwise specified. A series of dummy variables was used to control for family and individual background differences: female: specifying sex; urban: capturing all individuals living in either Copenhagen or Aarhus; nuclear family: all individuals living with both parents in 2000. A variable for number of siblings in 2000 was included from the PISA survey. All family background variables were measured when the respondent was 15–16 years old.

Some specifications of the household include parents' occupations and educations, and specifications of the capital of the individuals include cognitive functioning, other individual attributes and noncognitive dispositions. The latter soft attributes are believed to be very important for a person's capability.

Family income is measured as the combined gross income of parents divided by 100,000 DKK. To avoid extreme observations, the highest and lowest 1% observations are set equal to the 1% and 99% percentiles, respectively. Parental education is measured by categorical variables with 5 categories: primary school, high school, vocational education, short or intermediate college education, university education, and a final category is used for unknown. A categorical variable for occupational position is used for each parent. Fathers' occupations are measured by 11 categories[7]: (i) unskilled workers; (ii) skilled craft workers and machine operators; (iii) skilled agricultural/fishery workers; (iv) clerks and sales, service and care work; sales, finance and business administration; (v) technicians and intermediate professionals; (vi) professionals – arts and social sciences; (vii) teaching professionals; (viii) science professionals; (ix) managers; (x) legislators, senior officials; and (xi) unknown. Mothers' occupations are measured by 10 categories: (i) unskilled workers; (ii) skilled craft workers and machine operators; skilled agricultural/fishery workers; sales, service, and care work; (iii) clerks; (iv) sales, finance, and business administration; (v) technicians and intermediate professionals; (vi) professionals – arts and social sciences; (vii) teaching professionals; (viii) science professionals; (ix) managers, legislators, senior officials; and (x) unknown.

The PISA survey explanatory variables are split into four groups according to the effects they are to capture (see Appendix Table A.1 for the complete list of PISA explanatory variables): Group 1: parental cultural capital and cultural capital; Group 2: school; Group 3: noncognitive skills; and Group 4: cognitive skills. Parental involvement (parental cultural capital) is partly captured by the variable how often the parents discuss politics and social issues with the child.[8] This item is included in the analysis to indicate whether the child benefits from discussions with his or her parents. It is likely that this type of parental involvement will positively influence the likelihood of obtaining a high-school diploma. The number of books at home in 2000 (99% of the students live at home) is also included as a measurement of parental cultural capital. Yet another parental involvement variable is used to encapsulate the degree to which a mother spent time on schoolwork with her child.

Cultural capital is measured by the two variables: Whether the student had visited museums or art galleries several times in the past year and whether the student cannot sit still and read for more than a few minutes. The latter important first dimension of cultural capital, embodied individual dispositions and competencies, is taken into account to capture a possible negative feature. Normally, an accumulative positive variable would be applied. However, it is relevant to have such a category since it captures a characteristic that would probably make it unlikely that a high-school education was completed or even initiated. Goldthorpe (2007, p. 3) argues that for children from working-class or peasant origins the school represents an alien, and indeed a hostile, environment, especially if the child is unable to meet the demands of school, including the ability to sit still and read for extended periods. Two school-related variables are used: "Students don't start working for a long time after the lesson begins" is a dummy variable measuring the student's own impression of class discipline. The other dummy variable: "Most of my teachers really listen to what I have to say" captures whether the student feels the teachers listens to what he or she has to say, thereby resembling some kind of recognition contributing to building up self-confidence and even self-esteem.

The noncognitive dispositions are captured by a number of variables: "If I decide not to get any bad grades, I can really do it." This variable captures one component of locus of control. Locus of control individuals with a high internal locus of control believe that events result primarily from their own behavior and actions (Borghans et al., 2008; Piatek & Pinger, 2010). Those with a high external locus of control believe that powerful others, fate, or chance primarily determine events. Yet another item is when studying: "When studying, I keep working even if the material is difficult," entailing some aspects of effort (and self-efficacy), which we know plays an important role, recently confirmed in a British-Italian study (Fraja, Oliveira, & Zanchi, 2010). Self-efficacy corresponds to an individual's belief in his or her own competence and is usually defined as the belief that one is capable of performing in a certain manner to attain certain goals. Also, we included: "I like to try to be better than other students," which measures competiveness and sociability (extraversion).

More variables include: "I'm hopeless in Danish language classes," aiming for a negative self-esteem item in order to have a negative evaluation of the self, measuring how the student feels about herself or himself and underlining what Bourdieu conceptualizes as a negative lingual self-devaluation of students from nonacademic homes. Less-privileged students are influenced by a "cooling out" process in which they view their failures in school as their own fault and thus select themselves out of the competition for educational success (Bourdieu, 1984; Wildhagen, 2010, p. 525). Other variables are: "I have always done well in mathematics," which is a way to include a self-concept – what an individual thinks about the self; and: "When I study, I try to figure out which concepts I still haven't really understood," which captures control strategies (self-regulation cf. Borghans et al., 2008).

As suggested in the literature (Boudon, 1974), I focus on the effects of educational attainment, net of cognitive achievement (i.e., primary effects). A measurement of a reading score is therefore included to deal with cognitive dispositions.[9] The reading score has been normalized to mean 0 and standard deviation 1. The math and science tests were not included because both were answered by only one-third of the selected PISA students in Denmark.

Statistical Method

Completion of upper secondary education is modeled with a multinomial logit model, see, for example, Wooldridge (2010). Let y_i denote a random variable taking on values $j \in \{0,1,2,3\}$ and let x_i denote the set of conditioning variables containing variables such as sex and parental education. I want to estimate the response probabilities for each alternative conditional on a number of characteristics x_i. The response probabilities are

$$P(y_i = j|x_i) = P_{ij} = \frac{\exp(x_i\beta_j)}{1 + \sum_{k=1}^{J} \exp(x_i\beta_k)}, \, j = 1, 2, 3$$

where β_j is a $K \times 1$ vector of parameters related to the j'th alternative. The parameters are estimated by maximum likelihood. The ratio of the choice probabilities for alternatives j and l, relative risk ratios (RRR), is

$$\frac{P_{ij}}{P_{il}} = \exp(x_i(\beta_j - \beta_l))$$

We see that the RRR of alternatives j and l does not depend on any alternatives other than j and l. This property, also known as the Independence of Irrelevant Alternatives, is usually considered restrictive. However, the IIA assumption cannot be rejected by the Hausman–McFadden test and Small-Hsiao test, as implemented in Stata. The two-stage sampling design is taken into account by employing the final student weights provided by the OECD, see OECD (2002a) for details, and the clustering of students within schools is dealt with by computing cluster-adjusted robust standard errors, as implemented in Stata version 10.5.

FINDINGS

Descriptive Statistics

Using Tables 1 and 2 we can summarize the upper secondary education completion choice difference between two generations. The difference in intergenerational education choice shows that all four categories (no youth education, academic high school, business/technical high school, vocational education) are different. The percentage of no youth education after finishing basic education has dropped in the children's generation to 18%. Fewer children attend vocational school compared with their parents. Of those not attending vocational schools, there is an increase in the percentage completing high school.

In total, almost 60% of children pursue high school. This pattern probably stems from a high-school diploma being a prerequisite for admission to tertiary education. Both tables show similar figures in terms of how parents' educational level affects their children's. When I compare the percentages of each column in both Tables 1 and 2, academic high school is the highest for all the categories of parental education, except no youth education. While about 25% of children whose father or mother had no further education also had no further education, around 40–50% of children whose parents attended high school also attended high school.

Table 1. Completion of Upper Secondary Education by Father's Highest Completed Education.

Father's Highest Completed Education (Row Pct.)	No Youth Education	Academic High School	Business/Technical High School	Vocational Education	No. of Observations	Total Percentile
No further education	28	24	15	32	904	24
High school	15	50	27	8	116	3
Vocational education	16	31	23	30	1,503	39
Short/intermediate higher education	11	53	21	16	659	17
Long higher education	7	76	12	5	342	9
Unknown	30	34	14	21	297	8
No. of observations	698	1,457	732	934	3,821	
Total percentile	18	38	19	24		100

Table 2. Completion of Upper Secondary Education by Mother's Highest Completed Education.

Mother's Highest Completed Education (Row Percentile.)	No Youth Education	Academic High School	Business/Technical High School	Vocational Education	No. of Observations	Total Percentile
No further education	25	23	17	35	1,182	31
High school	19	41	25	15	150	4
Vocational education	18	31	24	27	1,162	30
Short/intermediate higher education	10	58	18	14	992	26
Long higher education	6	85	5	4	154	4
Unknown	29	34	13	24	180	5
No. of observations	698	1,457	732	934	3,821	
Total percentile	18	38	19	24		100

Parents' highest education has a different effect on children's completion of education.

To compare the children's completion of high school among parents' different backgrounds, the highest rate is parents' with long higher education. More specifically, when the mothers' final education is a long higher education, then 85% of their children choose to complete high school, which is in line with other researchers finding (Buchmann et al., 2008; Legewie & DiPrete, 2012). The rate decreases as the level of mother's education changes to short intermediate higher education and high-school graduates. Children's attainment of vocational education tends to be strongly influenced by their parents.

A comparison of the different influences of parent's highest attained education on children's educational completion shows that the mother's short/intermediate and long academic education has a slightly bigger impact on children's completion of high school than does the father's level of education.

Multinomial Logit Analysis

Table 3 shows the regression results with completion of upper secondary education as the dependent variable. The baseline group used for comparison is the "no youth education" group. For each covariate a RRR is shown.

The results were more significant for the high school and business/ technical high-school outcomes than for the vocational education outcome. This suggests that the distance to the reference group is larger for the high-school group than for the group of vocational education. Noncognitive dispositions have significant effects on students' attainment of upper secondary educational programs, especially high-school tracks, even after controlling for traditional family background. The magnitudes of these variables are discussed further in the analysis of Table 4. The item: "If I decide not to get any bad grades, I can really do it" matters a great deal for completing high school and shows that some students have a high locus of control and self-confidence in academic and other skills required to deal with challenges encountered in school. Another item: "I have always done well in mathematics," stands out, especially for technical high school, which is not surprising since people who perceive themselves as being skilled in mathematics tend to favor high schools offering natural and technical science programs. Having a strong belief about competencies in

Table 3. Completion of Upper Secondary Education – Multinomial
Logit (Ref.: No Youth Education).

	Relative Risk Ratios (*p*-values)		
	Academic High School	Business/ Technical High School	Vocational Education
Female	3.03 (0.00)***	1.39 (0.01)*	0.69 (0.00)**
Urban (Copenhagen and Aarhus)	0.71 (0.03)*	0.53 (0.00)**	0.65 (0.00)***
Nonwestern immigrant	2.10 (0.02)*	1.47 (0.25)	0.46 (0.00)**
Nuclear family	1.35 (0.12)	1.48 (0.05)*	1.51 (0.01)*
Number of siblings	0.98 (0.67)	0.91 (0.08)	0.98 (0.55)
Father's age	1.01 (0.43)	1.01 (0.38)	1.00 (0.84)
Mother's age	1.06 (0.00)***	1.03 (0.12)	1.02 (0.17)
Family income (1,00,000 DKK)	1.12 (0.00)***	1.12 (0.00)**	1.05 (0.18)
Father's occupation (ref: unskilled workers)			
Machine workers and skilled craft workers	1.22 (0.32)	1.23 (0.30)	1.00 (0.99)
Skilled agricultural and fishery workers	1.05 (0.88)	1.02 (0.95)	1.41 (0.31)
Sales, service and care work and clerks, sales, finance and business administration	1.66 (0.05)*	1.44 (0.19)	1.13 (0.61)
Technicians and associate professionals	2.02 (0.03)*	1.08 (0.84)	0.73 (0.35)
Professionals – arts and social sciences	6.03 (0.00)**	3.25 (0.05)*	1.26 (0.69)
Teaching professionals	1.49 (0.32)	0.58 (0.22)	0.46 (0.09)
Science professionals	1.23 (0.61)	0.80 (0.63)	0.77 (0.50)
Managers	2.03 (0.10)	2.02 (0.06)	2.00 (0.06)
Legislators and senior officials	1.97 (0.10)	1.72 (0.18)	1.06 (0.89)
Mother's occupation (ref: unskilled workers)			
Machine workers, skilled craft workers, skilled agricultural/fishery workers, sales, service, and care work	0.92 (0.70)	0.84 (0.46)	0.98 (0.90)
Clerks	1.45 (0.17)	1.41 (0.22)	0.98 (0.93)
Sales, finance, and business administration	1.74 (0.11)	1.39 (0.40)	0.84 (0.61)
Technicians and associate professionals	1.68 (0.09)	1.35 (0.39)	0.91 (0.74)
Professionals – arts and social sciences	1.71 (0.26)	1.46 (0.43)	0.94 (0.88)
Teaching professionals	3.70 (0.00)**	2.61 (0.03)*	0.97 (0.94)
Science professionals	1.19 (0.77)	0.74 (0.63)	0.71 (0.56)
Managers, legislators and senior officials	1.12 (0.78)	1.20 (0.70)	0.96 (0.94)
Father's education (ref: Elementary school)			
High school education	1.82 (0.14)	2.76 (0.02)*	0.54 (0.18)
Vocational education	1.57 (0.00)**	1.88 (0.00)***	1.55 (0.00)**

Table 3. (*Continued*)

	Academic High School	Business/ Technical High School	Vocational Education
		Relative Risk Ratios (*p*-values)	
Short/medium higher education	1.75 (0.01)*	2.05 (0.00)**	1.45 (0.09)
Long higher education	2.10 (0.05)*	1.36 (0.47)	0.79 (0.60)
Mother's education (ref: Elementary school)			
High school education	1.33 (0.42)	1.21 (0.61)	0.66 (0.23)
Vocational education	1.63 (0.00)**	1.68 (0.00)***	0.99 (0.92)
Short/medium higher education	1.69 (0.03)*	1.11 (0.71)	0.93 (0.72)
Long higher education	3.04 (0.03)*	0.56 (0.39)	0.54 (0.31)
Parents discuss politics or social issues with the child	1.73 (0.00)***	1.44 (0.01)*	1.11 (0.48)
Number of books at home (ref: Less than 50)			
Between 50 and 250	1.21 (0.20)	0.80 (0.15)	0.76 (0.04)*
More than 250	1.18 (0.40)	0.77 (0.17)	0.73 (0.07)
Mother helps with schoolwork (ref: never or hardly ever)			
A few times a year	1.33 (0.13)	1.10 (0.63)	0.90 (0.58)
Once a month	1.97 (0.03)*	1.46 (0.25)	1.23 (0.47)
Several times a month	0.90 (0.55)	0.88 (0.48)	0.89 (0.49)
Several times a week	0.63 (0.04)*	0.62 (0.05)	1.16 (0.50)
Visited a museum or art gallery several times in the past year	1.65 (0.00)***	1.00 (0.98)	1.07 (0.58)
I cannot sit still and read for more than a few minutes	0.67 (0.00)**	0.59 (0.00)***	1.07 (0.59)
Students don't start work for a long time after the Danish lessons begins	0.75 (0.06)	0.71 (0.02)*	0.76 (0.03)*
Most of my teachers really listen to what I have to say	1.49 (0.00)**	1.23 (0.12)	1.08 (0.57)
If I decide not to get bad grades, I can really do it	1.58 (0.00)***	1.55 (0.00)**	1.09 (0.45)
I am hopeless in Danish classes	0.66 (0.02)*	0.63 (0.01)**	1.00 (1.00)
I have always done well in mathematics	1.42 (0.01)**	2.29 (0.00)***	1.28 (0.06)
When I study, I try to figure out which concepts I still haven't really understood	1.24 (0.10)	1.24 (0.13)	0.99 (0.93)
I like to try to be better than other students	1.14 (0.39)	1.35 (0.07)	0.85 (0.24)
When studying I keep working even if the material difficult	1.04 (0.73)	0.86 (0.26)	0.96 (0.78)
Reading score	3.34 (0.00)***	2.64 (0.00)***	0.96 (0.60)
Observations	3821		
McFadden's R^2	0.25		
Log Likelihood	-3843		

Categories for missing observations and missing occupation included.

*$p<0.05$; **$p<0.01$; ***$p<0.001$.

Table 4. Types of Variables and Relative Contribution to the
Likelihood Function.

	# Parameters	Log- Likelihood	AIC	McFadden's R^2	Likelihood	
					ΔCum. %	Cum. %
Type of variable added (block)						
None (intercept only)	3	−5117	10240	0.00	0.0	0.0
Sex, ethnicity, and urbanization	12	−4981	9985	0.03	10.7	10.7
Family background	39	−4744	9566	0.07	18.6	29.3
Family background (+ parents' occupation)	101	−4504	9210	0.12	18.8	48.1
Family background (+ parents' education)	131	−4412	9085	0.14	7.2	55.4
Cultural capital	173	−4190	8727	0.18	17.4	72.7
School variables	185	−4156	8683	0.19	2.7	75.4
Noncognitive dispositions	221	−4036	8514	0.21	9.5	84.9
Cognitive dispositions	224	−3843	8134	0.25	15.1	100.0

Note: # Observations 3821. All the incremental increases to the likelihood function are significant on a 1% level. AIC takes the number of parameters into account.

mathematics will probably increase the likelihood of completing any high-school program. There is probably a high correlation between this type of noncognitive disposition and the ability to do well in math tests, but self-perception also plays an independent role.

Yet another noncognitive feature is revealed: negative self-esteem about being hopeless at the Danish language is detrimental for obtaining a high-school diploma. Hopeless is a strong expression; it adds to what Bourdieu and Passeron (1990) and Goldthorpe (2007) demonstrated, namely that some children, especially those from lower class backgrounds, tend to have negative self-images related to performances awarded in school. Even if this item is correlated with reading and writing ability, which is what I tested, it adds more than merely the reading score; accordingly, self-perception regarding language is important for educational success. "Keep working even when the material is difficult" did not prove to be statistically significant when having the self-esteem candidates onboard in the model, opposing the findings of some other studies (see Kingston 2001, p. 95; Farkas, 2003; Fraja et al., 2010); however, it does not prove that students should not participate in school life and social events, or should not do homework (Wildhagen, 2010, p. 523).

Cultural capital in the form of embodiment: "I cannot sit still and read" negatively influences the likelihood of completing any form of high-school education. In other words, individuals with less cultural capital at the deepest level are more likely to attend vocational schools or to not complete any education. Probably, negative experiences and dispositions lessen the probability of attending academic-oriented programs. This, together with a lack of recognition, leads to a number of young people tending not to favor demanding sit-still competences. However, this particular finding has received little attention.

At the school level it is also apparent that a positive relation with the teacher helps the student to pursue academic high-school programs. Early on, Bourdieu and Passeron (1990) and DiMaggio (1982) stressed that teachers treat academically oriented students more favorably and often perceive them as more gifted than those who lack cultural capital. Inability to sit still and read will strengthen this impression. What the variable: "Most of my teachers listen to what I have to say" actually measures are debatable. I consider it a measure of how well the student fulfills the expectations of the teacher, and it addresses whether the student devotes sufficient energy to school life to experience recognition from most teachers.

Students who reported that students do not start their schoolwork after the lesson begins show to have lower odds of attending high school than those not reporting it. This indicates that the disciplinary (or effort) climate in ninth grade has an effect on the likelihood of attaining an upper secondary education. Activities such as visiting museums or art galleries also increase the likelihood of a student entering an academic high-school program – this confirms what others have found. I also attempted to include listening to classical music and theater visits but neither was significant. For parents, we also included classic literature, books of poetry, and works of art, but none was significant. So beaux arts activities matter but perhaps not that much. Educational resources was also tried (as Teachman, 1987) but showed not to be significant.

Parental involvement seems to matter a great deal. However, mothers' help with schoolwork is divided into two so that children who receive help once a month are more likely to complete an academic high-school program than are children who receive help several times a week. Those requiring substantial help when they are 15 years old are probably less able and seemingly have difficulties with schoolwork. Often discussing politics and social issues with parents helps the student obtain a high-school diploma, especially from an academic program. These results are in line with a number of studies reported in the literature review in which a favorable reading climate and associated skills are argued to compensate for even low levels of parental education and little or no highbrow cultural capital (cf. de Graaf et al., 2000). More fundamentally, increased intergenerational education mobility in a number of European countries, including Denmark (McIntosh & Munk, 2012), has shown that even more disadvantaged classes with little access to high culture but favoring education still have chances in the educational system, but perhaps not in the most elitists places (see also Bourdieu and Passeron, 1990; Goldthorpe, 2007; Halsey et al., 1980, pp. 13–14).

As expected, we observe that a higher reading score is statistically significant, and this is associated with a much higher likelihood of completing either of the two high-school educations. The score is probably not a pure exogenous variable. However, there is a trade off in the statistical analysis. When the reading score is included in the model, most of the effect of number of books then disappears. Number of books becomes fully significant when the reading score is not included in the analysis and possibly indicates a higher reading ability because it is a proxy for parents focusing on fundamental skills such as literacy.

Overall, social origin, sex and reading score show the largest estimates and are more important than other characteristics. More specifically, the father's and mother's occupation and education both have significant effects on the student's completion of academic and business/technical high school. In particular, occupations such as social science and teaching professionals influence the completion of high school, but having fathers in intermediate, technical, sales and administration occupations, providing relevant resources, also increases the odds of completing a high-school education. Those with a father who has a vocational degree are likely to complete any kind of upper secondary education, while a mother with a vocational education will increase the likelihood of attaining a high-school diploma. Individuals coming from a family background with a father as a director or manager have more mixed choices. Some directors have less cultural capital and tend to come from a self-employed origin. However, the almost equal three estimates ($RRR = 2.0$) reflect that some students from these backgrounds experience a high degree of reproduction, while others experience educational mobility, either downward or upward. Lastly, the odds for children of mothers working as sales, service, and care workers imply an increased likelihood of completing high school (not statistically significant in the final model).

Additionally, the results suggest that children living with both parents are more likely to complete upper secondary education than those who do not live in a nuclear family setting. The number of siblings seems unimportant for attaining upper secondary education; however, mother's age improves the probability of completing academic high school. The estimated effect of family income is statistically significant and suggests that higher family income is associated with a higher probability of completing high school. Recently, it has been debated and argued that cultural capital is now much more important than income, especially in the Scandinavian countries (Jæger & Holm, 2007). However, our results indicate that income remains important. Not surprisingly, it is observed that girls are much more likely to complete academic high school than boys are but are less likely to complete vocational education school.

In line with McIntosh and Munk (2007), Table 4 shows the logarithm of the likelihood functions, the Akaike information criteria, McFadden's R^2 and the incremental increase in the likelihood function as each group of explanatory variables from the regression in Table 3 is added. The aim is to demonstrate the relative importance of different independent variables in explaining the variation in educational attainment.

Here, the order is important, for example, reading score depends on family background variables. Notably, models that explain test score results perform better than those designed to explain educational attainment (McIntosh & Munk, 2007). As a result, the net impact on educational attainment of a group of variables is measured by the reduction in log-likelihood function by including a particular group of variables. As an example, the increase in the log-likelihood function from rows eight to nine measures the net impact of test scores on educational completion. The variation explained by the model is captured by the difference between the baseline and final log-likelihood function values. The cumulative percentage increases and the differences are shown in columns five and six. Adding all the individual groups of variables incrementally leads to significant increases in the log-likelihood function.

First, we have a baseline model that contains no explanatory variables, and these occupy the first row of the table. The next row uses the dummies for basic demographic information. The third row includes family background such as income, siblings, parents' ages, and nuclear family structure. The fourth row includes parental occupation along with family background.

The fifth row uses parental educational variables together with all the family variables. The sixth row adds all the cultural capital variables. The seventh row lists school variables. The eighth row entails the noncognitive skills. Lastly, the reading score is added to the list.

The full model explains a significant part of the variation in educational attainment, and McFadden's R^2 equals 25%. We look at the incremental increase in the likelihood function as each group of variables is included in the model. Table 4 shows that sex, urban, and ethnicity variables account for 10.7% of the explained variation in completion of education. The measured family background accounts for almost 45% more of the contribution to the likelihood function when controlled for sex, urbanity and ethnicity. This is composed of 18.6% coming from the basic family variables, then 18.8% more when including parental occupations, and 7% more with parental education. It means that occupational status of the parents also influences the attainment of educational success, probably by improving skills and dispositions of the students. Then, somewhat unexpected, cultural capital gives another 17.4%, composed of 7.7% parental cultural capital, comprising "number of books at home," "discussions on politics and social issues" (supporting Björklund et al., 2010b); then 3.5% comes from the mother supporting the child, and lastly own cultural capital accounts for an additional 6.2%, also covering an embodiment variable: "I cannot sit still and read for more than a few minutes." It is here that cultural capital, habitus, and noncognitive dispositions meet. The school variables account for less than 3%. We cannot conclude that school does not matter. There could be an additional peer effect as well as a teacher effect; nevertheless, several studies show that school effects are smaller than social origin variables. After having controlled for most sets of variables, I found that the net effect of noncognitive variables accounts for almost 10% of the increased log-likelihood function. Those with high self-esteem and high internal locus of control have strong beliefs that the results they obtain originate from their own behavior and actions (Borghans et al., 2008). It is striking that the magnitude of noncognitive skills remains large even after controlling for a number of other background and cultural capital variables. This finding adds to the literature. Some of the variation in the reading score is likely to be influenced by the other variables in the model; therefore, including this variable as the last shows that the net effect of the reading score accounts for 15% of the explained variation.

The results support the findings of McIntosh and Munk (2007). For example, the present study shows that three sets of indicators, measuring cultural capital, school variables, and noncognitive dispositions, as a whole, account for almost 30% of the explained variation in the completion of upper secondary education, while family background alone accounts for nearly half of the explained variation. In addition to McIntosh and Munk's (2007) findings, there are now more candidates, for example, parental involvement and noncognitive dispositions. To conclude, Table 4 demonstrates the relative importance of different independent variables in explaining the variation in educational attainment.

DISCUSSION AND CONCLUSION

The results describe an asymmetry between families with many resources, much capital and many noncognitive capacities and those with fewer resources, less capital, and fewer noncognitive capacities. That a higher parental occupation clearly has the biggest effect on the model reflects the importance of the social position of the father and the mother when comparing parents with highly skilled jobs and parents with little education and semi- or unskilled jobs and will, to a great extent, still structure choices and attainments within a family. Many studies have found that parental occupational position structures educational and occupational attainment. Among employed parents, for instance, both parents' occupations independently shape children's educational outcomes (Kalmijn, 1994). Our results also show that mothers' and fathers' education matters for the offspring's attainment and, according to the definition from Bourdieu (1986), captures elements of parental cultural capital (see also Downey, 1995). Notably, there is a group of young people from vocational backgrounds who wish to complete high-school programs, potentially leading to an increase in educational mobility. The two types of high-school track create opportunities for children with little cultural capital but who realize that future labor markets demand people with applicable skills. Consequently, much has happened since Kandel and Lesser (1970, p. 285) wrote "Despite its intellectual climate, the Danish School does not appear to support social mobility to the extent observed for the United States." Educational mobility is perhaps due to a cumulative effect of improved social and educational conditions (DiPrete & Eirich, 2006). The remaining large social difference is still between families with extensive qualifications and those without or with very few qualifications. Gender matters too. The results confirm that girls are now doing much better in the educational system than boys are.

However, this is not the full picture. Those children who have more cognitive skills and more noncognitive skills will do better, supporting recent research highlighting that other variables play important roles in educational attainment. The reading score stands out and is associated with a much bigger chance of completing either of the two high-school streams of education. Accordingly, reading abilities influence the completion of upper secondary education and then a good predictor of choosing academic tracks. It is striking that the magnitude of noncognitive capacities stands out even after controlling for other kinds of variables. Having strong beliefs and the capability to carry out relevant actions in mathematics, language and other activities, in order to deal with demands in the school, makes a difference. Most likely, there is a high correlation between these types of noncognitive dispositions and the ability to do well in math tests; nonetheless, self-perception plays an independent role. It is important to underline that the noncognitive and cognitive dispositions are not created only in early childhood but throughout the entire childhood: "The evidence does not support the theses that educational achievement is determined by abilities fixed in early childhood, that family resources other than cultural capital are unimportant or that school processes are irrelevant" (Nash, 2003, p. 446; see also Bourdieu, 2000; Heckman, 2006, 2008).

I also found that those who reported that most teachers listened to them in ninth grade have a higher probability of completing high school. Although this variable is somewhat ambiguous, I consider it an indicator of how well the child fulfills the expectations of the teacher. Wildhagen (2009, p. 192f.) also finds an effect of respondent's adaptation to prevailing conduct and norms on teacher's perception. Parental involvement, measured by how often parents discuss politics and social issues with the child, and whether the mother helps with schoolwork, show to be important for completing any high-school program. It could be that middle- and upper-class parents intentionally cultivate children's social skills, such as addressing and negotiating with figures of authority (Lareau, 2003). The impact of cultural resources is likely to add up.

I believe the hypotheses are confirmed to some degree. Most of the noncognitive dispositions turned out to be important, while other items were not important, for example, the keep working category, so there is some support for the research hypothesis. Even after having controlled for different forms of family background and cultural capital variables, noncognitive skills show to contribute to almost 10% of the explained variation. It is surprising that the statistical effect is so big. However, it underlines the necessity of including more of these variables in future studies on educational attainment. Instead of focusing on forms of cultural capital, more noncognitive skills variables should be used. Much noncognitive skills-based literature does not relate to sociological literature about the parents' social position (an exception is DiPrete & Jennings, 2012). In other words, working-class students who in their neighborhood and school experience that their dispositions are less valuable than the class-based dispositions of their privileged peers will further realize that high educational attainment and superior academic achievements are simply not for them. Conversely, privileged students' confirmation of the legitimacy of their dispositions will serve to cement their sense of entitlement to educational rewards (Wildhagen, 2010, p. 525).

When both parental cultural capital and cultural capital are included in the model, I found that cultural capital is somewhat more important than expected, but some of the highbrow variables included (not shown in Table 3) showed not to be important. The fact that cultural capital still matters could be due to inclusion of more sophisticated cultural endowment variables rather than highbrow variables, even when compared with the dominant effect of family background. It could be that familiarity with legitimate culture incorporated at a deeper level related to the habitus of the family is more important than superficial status signals. Many studies focus on verbal and mental skills, and too few on the interconnected body skills and abilities (Dumais, 2006, p. 85, referring to David Swartz). The evidence in my study supports a point made by Wildhagen (2010), who contends that cultural capital and habitus work together to affect educational outcomes for students. In my view, they are per definition interrelated through the first dimension of cultural capital. This would also explain why so many studies have found that high aspirations or high self-esteem are important for determining educational and labor outcomes, where students with lower expectations are less likely to complete formal education. Kingston (2001) argued for better measures of cultural capital, which would facilitate a better condition for investigating the process from inherited and acquired cultural capital to the conversion into academic achievements and diplomas. Even if Kingston also pointed out the problem of omitted variables and stressed a number of important variables, for instance, parenting style, encouragement of academic engagement – omitted, for example, in Aschaffenburg and Maas (1997) – family income and occupational status of the parents, the importance of which my studies confirm, he still lacked the concept of habitus and possibly omitted to link his findings to the literature on noncognitive skills. Finally, most researchers of educational attainment have not looked into the strategic part of investments in education from different families with different positions.

ACKNOWLEDGMENTS

I thank the Danish Strategic Research Council for financial support. Special thanks to Gunnar Bjarnason and Nikita Baklanov for excellent research assistance. Thanks also to James McIntosh and Stefan Andrade for comments; and Volker Stocké, Richard Arum, and Amy Hsin for comments at the RC28 Essex Conference in April 2011. I benefited greatly from the comments of two anonymous referees, and I thank the editor for a helpful editorial process.

NOTES

1. Another important reference related to this issue is Black, Devereux, and Salvanes (2005), who ask whether parental education actually changes the outcome of children, suggesting an important spillover of education policies, or whether it is merely that more able individuals who have higher education also have more able children? They use the reform of the education system implemented in different municipalities at different times throughout the 1960s as an instrument for parental education. Their findings suggest that the high correlations between parents' and children's education are due primarily to family characteristics and inherited ability and not to education spillovers.

2. The individual's system of dispositions is thought to correspond with the system of social positions (Bourdieu, 1981, p. 309ff.).

3. "One may suppose that, to obtain the sacrifice of 'self-love' in favor of a quite other object of investment and so to in calculate the durable disposition to invest in the social game which is one of prerequisites of all learning, pedagogic work in its elementary form relies on of the motors which will be at the origin of all subsequent investments: the search for recognition" (Bourdieu, 2000, p. 166).

4. See for example Breen and Jonsson (2000) who developed a multinomial transition model and showed that the passage through the educational system influences the probability of making subsequent educational transitions. Advances in computational methods have made it possible to estimate dynamic structural models of the full sequence of educational decisions (Belzil & Hansen, 2003; Keane & Wolpin, 2001). While these models are considerably more complicated than those used here, conclusions are very much in line with what others have found.

5. This category also includes Higher Preparatory Examination (HF). Additionally, students who successfully completed both a vocational and high-school (or gymnasium in Danish) education are categorized with high-school graduates.

6. Some individuals may wait some time before continuing their studies after their primary education, that is, data is right-censored, but we assume this to be a limited problem here.

7. Unemployed, outside the labor market, and employed without further specification are also included in the analysis.

8. This five-category ordinal variable is included in the statistical model as a binary variable because of an unfortunate error in the Danish version of the Student Questionnaire. The third category is "once a year" instead "once a month". In an attempt to mitigate this, we have coded variable 0 = Not more than about once a month, 1 = more than several times a month, see Appendix Table A.1.

9. Weighted likelihood estimate provided by the OECD with the PISA data set (see OECD 2002a for a detailed description).

REFERENCES

Aschaffenburg, K., & Maas, I. (1997). Cultural and educational careers: The dynamics of social reproduction. *American Sociological Review, 62*(4), 573–587. doi:10.2307/2657427

Behrman, J. R., & Rosenzweig, M. R. (2005). Does increasing women's schooling raise the schooling of the next generation? Reply. *American Economic Review, 95*(5), 1745–1751. doi:10.1257/000282805775014263

Beller, E. (2009). Bringing intergenerational social mobility research into the twenty-first century: Why mothers matter. *American Sociological Review, 74*(4), 507–528. doi:10.1177/000312240907400401

Belzil, C., & Hansen, J. (2003). Structural estimates of the intergenerational education correlation. *Journal of Applied Econometrics, 18*(6), 679–696. doi:10.1002/jae.716

Bennett, T., Savage, M., Silva, E. B., Warde, A., Gayo-Cal, M., & Wright, D. (2009). *Culture, class, distinction.* New York, NY: Routledge.

Björklund, A., Eriksson, K. H., & Jäntti, M. (2010a). IQ and family background: Are associations strong or weak? *The B.E. Journal of Economic Analysis & Policy, 10*(1), art. 2. doi:10.2202/1935-1682.2349

Björklund, A., Lindahl, L., & Lindquist, M. J. (2010b). What more than parental income, education and occupation? An exploration of what swedish siblings get from their parents. *The B.E. Journal of Economic Analysis & Policy, 10*(1), art 102. doi:10.2202/1935-1682.2449

Black, S. E., Devereux, P. J., & Salvanes, K. G. (2005). Why the apple doesn't fall far: Understanding intergenerational transmission of human capital. *American Economic Review, 95*(1), 437–449. doi:10.1257/0002828053828635

Borghans, L., Duckworth, A. L., Heckman, J. J., & ter Weel, B. (2008). The economics and psychology of personality traits. *Journal of Human Resources, 43*, 972–1059. doi:10.3368/jhr.43.4.972

Boudon, R. (1974). *Education, opportunity, and social inequality.* New York, NY: Wiley.

Bourdieu, P. (1981). Men and machines. In A. V. Cicourel & K. Knorr-Cetina (Eds.), *Advances in social theory and methodology toward an integration of micro- and macro-sociologies* (pp. 304–317). London: Routledge.

Bourdieu, P. (1984[1979]). *La distinction, critique social du jugement.* Paris: Les Editions de Minuit, 1982/*Distinction: A Social Critique of the Judgement of Taste* (2nd ed.), London: Routledge and Kegan Paul.

Bourdieu, P. (1986). The forms of capital. In J. G. Richardson (Ed.), *Handbook of theory and research for the sociology of education* (pp. 241–258). New York, NY: Greenwood Press.

Bourdieu, P. (2000). *Pascalian meditations.* Cambridge: Policy Press.

Bourdieu, P., & Passeron, J. C. (1990[1977]). *Reproduction in education, society, and culture* (2nd ed.). London: SAGE.

Bowles, S., & Gintis, H. (1976). *Schooling in capitalist America: Educational reform and the contradictions of economic life.* New York, NY: Basic Books.

Bowles, S., Gintis, H., & Osborne Grooves, M. (2001). The determinants of earnings: A behavioral approach. *Journal of Economic Literature, 39*(4), 1137–1176. doi:10.1257/jel.39.4.1137

Bowles, S., Gintis, H., & Osborne Groves, M. (Eds.). (2005). *Unequal chances: Family background and economic success.* Princeton, NJ: Princeton University Press.

Breen, R., & Goldthorpe, J. H. (1997). Explaining educational differentials: Towards a formal rational action theory. *Rationality and Society, 9*(3), 275–305. doi:10.1177/104346397009003002

Breen, R., & Jonsson, J. O. (2000). Analyzing educational careers: A multinomial transition model. *American Sociological Review, 65*(5), 754–772. doi:10.2307/2657545

Breiger, R. L. (1995). Social structure and the phenomenology of attainment. *Annual Review of Sociology, 21*(1), 115–136. doi:10.1146/annurev.so.21.080195.000555

Buchmann, C., DiPrete, T. A., & McDaniel, A. (2008). Gender inequalities in education. *Annual Review of Sociology, 34*(1), 319–337. doi:10.1146/annurev.soc.34.040507.134719

Dearden, L. (1999). The effects of families and ability on men's education and earnings in Britain. *Labour Economics, 6*(4), 551–567. doi:10.1016/S0927-5371(98)00015-3

Dearden, L., Machin, S., & Reed, H. (1997). Intergenerational mobility in Britain. *The Economic Journal, 107*(440), 47–66. doi:10.1111/1468-0297.00141

Devine, F. (1998). Class analysis and the stability of class relations. *Sociology, 32*(1), 23–42.

DiMaggio, P. (1982). Cultural capital and school success: The impact of status culture participation on the grades of U.S. High school students. *American Sociological Review, 47*(2), 189–201. doi:10.2307/2094962

DiMaggio, P., & Mohr, J. (1985). Cultural capital, educational attainment, and marital selection. *American Journal of Sociology, 90*(6), 1231–1261. doi:10.1086/228209

DiPrete, T. A., & Eirich, G. M. (2006). Cumulative advantage as a mechanism for inequality: A review of theoretical and empirical developments. *Annual Review of Sociology, 32*(1), 271–297. doi:10.1146/annurev.soc.32.061604.123127

DiPrete, T. A., & Jennings, J. L. (2012). Social and behavioral skills and the gender gap in early educational achievement. *Social Science Research, 41*(1), 1–15. doi:10.1016/j.ssresearch.2011.09.001

Downey, D. B. (1995). When bigger is not better: Family size, parental resources, and children's educational performance. *American Sociological Review, 60*(5), 746–761. doi:10.2307/2096320

Dumais, S. A. (2002). Cultural capital, gender, and school success: The role of habitus. *Sociology of Education, 75*(1), 44–68. doi:10.2307/3090253

Dumais, S. A. (2006). Early childhood cultural capital, parental habitus, and teachers' perceptions. *Poetics, 34*(2), 83–107. doi:10.1016/j.poetic.2005.09.003

Dumais, S. A., & Ward, A. (2010). Cultural capital and first-generation college success. *Poetics*, *38*(3), 245–265. doi:10.1016/j.poetic.2009.11.011

Dustmann, C. (2004). Parental background, secondary school track choice, and wages. *Oxford Economic Papers*, *56*(2), 209–230. doi:10.1093/oep/gpf048

Erikson, R., & Jonsson, J. O. (1996). Explaining class inequality in education: The swedish test case. In R. Erikson & J. O. Jonsson (Eds.), *Can education be equalized? The swedish case in comparative perspective*. Boulder, CO: Westview Press.

Erikson, R., & Rudolphi, F. (2010). Change in social selection to upper secondary school – primary and secondary effects in Sweden. *European Sociological Review*, *26*(3), 291–305. doi:10.1093/esr/jcp022

Ermisch, J., & Francesconi, M. (2001). Family matters: Impacts of family background on educational attainments. *Economica*, *68*(270), 137–156. doi:10.1111/1468-0335.00239

Farkas, G. (2003). Cognitive skills and noncognitive traits and behaviors in stratification processes. *Annual Review of Sociology*, *29*(1), 541–562. doi:10.1146/annurev.soc.29.010202.100023

De Fraja, G., Oliveira, T., & Zanchi, L. (2010). Must try harder: Evaluating the role of effort in educational attainment. *Review of Economics and Statistics*, *92*(3), 577–597. doi:10.1162/REST_a_00013

Gaddis, S. M. (2013). The influence of habitus in the relationship between cultural capital and academic success. *Social Science Research*, *42*(1), 1–13. doi: 10.1016/j.ssresearch.2012.08.002

Galindo-Rueda, F., & Vignoles, A. (2007). The heterogeous effect of selection in UK secondary schools. In P. E. Peterson & L. Woessmann (Eds.), *Schools and the equal opportunity problem*. Cambridge, MA: The MIT Press.

Gamoran, A., & Mare, R. D. (1989). Secondary school tracking and educational inequality: Compensation, reinforcement, or neutrality? *American Journal of Sociology*, *94*(5), 1146–1183. doi:10.1086/229114

Goldthorpe, J. H. (2007). "Cultural capital": Some critical observations. *Sociologica*, *2*, 1–27. doi:10.2383/24755

de Graaf, N. D., de Graaf, P. M., & Kraaykamp, G. (2000). Parental cultural capital and educational attainment in the Netherlands: A refinement of the cultural capital perspective. *Sociology of Education*, *73*(2), 92–111. doi:10.2307/2673239

Halsey, A. H., Heath, A. F., & Ridge, J. M. (1980). *Origins and destinations: Family, class and education in modern Britain*. Oxford: Oxford University Press.

Haveman, R., & Wolfe, B. (1995). The determinants of children's attainments: A review of methods and findings. *Journal of Economic Literature*, *33*, 1829–1878.

Heckman, J. J. (2006). Skill formation and the economics of investing in disadvantaged children. *Science (New York, N.Y.)*, *312*(5782), 1900–1902. doi:10.1126/science.1128898

Heckman, J. J. (2008). Schools, skills, and synapses. *Economic Inquiry*, *46*(3), 289–324. doi:10.1111/j.1465-7295.2008.00163.x

Heckman, J. J., Stixrud, J., & Urzua, S. (2006). The effects of cognitive and noncognitive abilities on labor market outcomes and social behavior. *Journal of Labor Economics*, *24*(3), 411–482. doi:10.1086/504455

Holmlund, H., Lindahl, M., & Plug, E. (2011). The causal effect of parents' schooling on children's schooling: A comparison of estimation methods. *Journal of Economic Literature*, *49*(3), 615–651. doi:10.1257/jel.49.3.615

Iannelli, C., & Raffe, D. (2007). Vocational upper-secondary education and the transition from school. *European Sociological Review*, *23*(1), 49–63. doi:10.1093/esr/jcl019

Jæger, M. M. (2009). Equal access but unequal outcomes: Cultural capital and educational choice in a meritocratic society. *Social Forces*, *87*(4), 1943–1971. doi:10.1353/sof.0.0192

Jæger, M. M. (2011). Does cultural capital really affect academic achievement? New evidence from combined sibling and panel data. *Sociology of Education*, *84*(4), 281–298. doi:10.1177/0038040711417010

Jæger, M. M., & Holm, A. (2007). Does parents' economic, cultural, and social capital explain the social class effect on educational attainment in the scandinavian mobility Regime? *Social Science Research*, *36*(2), 719–744. doi:10.1016/j.ssresearch.2006.11.003

Jencks, C., Bartlett, S., Corcoran, M., Crouse, J., Eaglesfield, D., Jackson, G., McClelland, K., et al. (1979). *Who gets ahead? The determinants of economic success in America*. New York, NY: Basic Books.

Jensen, T. P., & Andersen, D. (2006). Participants in PISA 2000 – four years later. In J. Mejding & A. Roe (Eds.), *Northern Lights on PISA 2000: A reflection from the Nordic countries*. Copenhagen: Nordic Council of Ministers.

Kalmijn, M. (1994). Mother's occupational status and children's schooling. *American Sociological Review*, *59*(2), 257–275. doi:10.2307/2096230

Kandel, D., & Lesser, G. S. (1970). School, family, and peer influences on educational plans of adolescents in the United States and Denmark. *Sociology of Education*, *43*(3), 270–287. doi:10.2307/2112067

Kastillis, J., & Rubinson, R. (1990). Cultural capital, student achievement, and educational reproduction: The case of Greece. *American Sociological Review*, *55*(2), 270–279.

Keane, M. P., & Wolpin, K. I. (2001). The effect of parental transfers and borrowing constraints on educational attainment. *International Economic Review*, *42*(4), 1051–1103. doi:10.1111/1468-2354.00146

Kingston, P. W. (2001). The unfulfilled promise of cultural capital theory. *Sociology of Education*, *74*, 88–99. doi:10.2307/2673255

Lareau, A. (2003). *Unequal childhoods: Class, race, and family life*. Berkeley, CA: University of California Press.

Lareau, A., & Weininger, E. B. (2004). Cultural capital in educational research. In D. L Swartz & V. L. Zolberg (Eds.), *After Bourdieu: Influence, critique, elaboration* (pp. 105–144). Dordrecht: Kluwer Academic Publishers.

Layard, R. (2005). *Happiness: Lessons from a new science*. London: Penguin.

Legewie, J., & DiPrete, T. A. (2012). School context and the gender gap in educational achievement. *American Sociological Review*, *77*(3), 463–485. doi:10.1177/00031224124 40802

Leibowitz, A. (1974). Home investments in children. *Journal of Political Economy*, *82*(2), 111–131.

Lizardo, O. (2004). The cognitive origins of bourdieu's habitus. *Journal for the Theory of Social Behaviour*, *34*(4), 375–401. doi:10.1111/j.1468-5914.2004.00255.x

Loehlin, J. C. (2005). Resemblance in personality and attitudes between parents and their children: Genetic and environmental contributions. In S. Bowles, H. Gintis & M. Osborne Groves (Eds.), *Unequal chances: Family background and economic success* (pp. 192–207). Princeton, NJ: Princeton University Press.

Mare, R. D., & Maralani, V. (2006). The intergenerational effects of changes in women's educational attainments. *American Sociological Review*, *71*(4), 542–564. doi:10.1177/000312240607100402

McIntosh, J., & Munk, M. D. (2007). Scholastic ability vs. family background in educational success: Evidence from danish sample survey data. *Journal of Population Economics*, *20*(1), 101–120. doi:10.1007/s00148-006-0061-3

McIntosh, J., & Munk, M. D. (2009). Social class, family background, and intergenerational mobility. *European Economic Review*, *53*(1), 107–117. doi:10.1016/j.euroecorev.2007.10.006

McIntosh, J., & Munk, M. D. (2012). An explanation of intergenerational educational mobility using the correlated mare model: A Danish test case (Earlier presented as Family Background and Changing Educational Choices in Denmark at the RC28 Conference in April 2011: Longitudinal Approaches to Stratification Research: International and Comparative Perspectives).

McIntosh, J., & Munk, M. D. (2013). What do test scores really mean? A latent class analysis of Danish test score performance. *Scandinavian Journal of Educational Research*.

Micklewright, J. (1989). Choice at sixteen. *Economica*, *56*(221), 25–39. doi:10.2307/2554492

Mueser, P. R. (1979). The effects of noncognitive traits. In C. Jencks, S. Bartlett, M. Corcoran, J. Crouse, D. Eaglesfield, G. Jackson & K. McClelland (Eds.), *Who gets ahead? The determinants of economic success in America* (pp. 122–158). New York, NY: Basic Books.

Munk, M. D. (2003). Institutionalized legitimate informational capital in the welfare state. Has policy failed? In C. Torres (Ed.), *The international handbook on the sociology of education: An assessment of new research theory* (pp. 285–302). Boulder: Rowman and Littlefield Publisher.

Nash, R. (2003). Inequality/difference in education: Is a real explanation of primary and secondary effects possible? *The British Journal of Sociology*, *54*(4), 433–451. doi:10.1080/0007131032000143537

OECD. (2002a). Programme for International Student Assessment (Pisa): Pisa 2000 Technical Report R. Adams & M. Wu (Eds.), Paris: OECD Publishing.

OECD. (2002b). *Manual for the PISA 2000 Database*. Paris: OECD Publishing.

Osborne Groves, M. (2005). Personality and the intergenerational transmission of economic status. In S. Bowles, H. Gintis & M. Osborne Groves (Eds.), *Unequal chances: Family background and economic success* (pp. 208–231). Princeton, NJ: Princeton University Press.

Piatek, R., & Pinger, P. (2010). Maintaining (Locus of) control? Assessing the impact of locus of control on education decisions and wages. IZA Discussion Paper 5289. The Institute for the Study of Labor (IZA), Bonn. (Revise and resubmit to JAE)

Piattelli-Palmarini, M. (Ed.). (1980). *Language and learning: The debate between Jean Piaget and Noam Chomsky*. Cambridge, MA: Harvard University Press.

Rudolphi, F. (2011). Inequality in educational outcomes: How aspirations, performance, and choice shape school careers in Sweden. (Doctoral dissertation). Stockholm: Department of Sociology, Stockholm University.

Savage, M., & Egerton, M. (1997). Social mobility, individual ability and the inheritance of class inequality. *Sociology*, *31*(4), 645–672. doi:10.1177/0038038597031004002

Sayer, A. (2005). *The moral significance of class*. Cambridge: Cambridge University Press.

Sewell, W. H., Haller, A. O., & Portes, A. (1969). The educational and early occupational attainment process. *American Sociological Review*, *34*(1), 82–92. doi:10.2307/2092789

Sewell, W. H., & Hauser, R. M. (1975). *Education, occupation, and earnings. Achievement in the early career*. New York, NY: Academic Press Inc.

Sewell, W. H., & Shah, V. P. (1968). Parents' education and children's educational aspirations and achievements. *American Sociological Review, 33*(2), 191–209. doi:10.2307/2092387

Sullivan, A. (2001). Cultural capital and educational attainment. *Sociology, 35*(04), 893–912. doi:10.1017/S0038038501008938

Sullivan, A. (2007). Cultural capital, cultural knowledge and ability. *Sociological Research Online, 12*(6). doi:10.5153/sro.1596

Teachman, J. D. (1987). Family background, educational resources, and educational attainment. *American Sociological Review, 52*(4), 548–557. doi:10.2307/2095300

Theil, H., & Thomsen, S. L. (2011). Noncognitive skills in economics: Models, measurement, and empirical evidence, revised version, Centre for European economic research. ZEW Discussion Paper No. 09-076. Retrieved from http://ftp.zew.de/pub/zew-docs/dp/dp09076.pdf

Weeden, K. A., & Grusky, D. B. (2005). The case for a new class map. *American Journal of Sociology, 111*(1), 141–212. doi:10.1086/428815

Wildhagen, T. (2009). Why does cultural capital matter for high school academic performance? An empirical assessment of teacher-selection and self-selection mechanisms as explanations of the cultural capital effect. *Sociological Quarterly, 50*(1), 173–200. doi:10.1111/j.1533-8525.2008.01137.x

Wildhagen, T. (2010). Capitalizing on culture: How cultural capital shapes educational experiences and outcomes. *Sociology Compass, 4*(7), 519–531. doi:10.1111/j.1751-9020.2010.00296.x

Wooldridge, J. M. (2010). *Econometric analysis of cross section and panel data* (2nd ed.). Cambridge, MA: The MIT Press.

APPENDIX

Table A.1. Recoded PISA Survey Variables.

Questions/Items in Survey	Recoded Values
How many books are there in your home (st37q01)?	0. Less than 50, 1. Between 50 and 250, 2. More than 250
"In general, how often do your parents: Discuss political or social issues with you? (st19q01)?	0. Never or hardly ever- about once a month, 1. Several times a month – several times a week
"How often do the following people work with you on your <schoolwork>?" Your mother (st20q01).	0. Never or hardly ever, 1. A few times a year, 2. About once a month, 3. Several times a year, 4. Several times a month
"During the past year, how often have you participated in these activities?" Visited a museum or art gallery (st18q02)?	0. Never or hardly ever-once or twice a year, 1. More than twice a year
"How often do these things happen in your Danish lessons?" Students don't start working for a long time after the lesson begins	0. Never- some lessons, 1. Most lessons – Every lesson
"How much do you disagree or agree with each of the following statements about teachers at your school?" Most of my teachers really listen to what I have to say (st30q03)?	0. Strongly Disagree-Disagree, 1. Agree- Strongly agree
"How often do these things apply to you?" If I decide not to get any bad grades, I can really do it (cc01q11)	0. Almost never- Sometimes, 1. Often – Almost always
"How often do these things apply to you?" When studying, I keep working even if the material is difficult(cc01q12)?	0. Almost never- Sometimes, 1. Often – Almost always
"How much do you disagree or agree with each of the following?" I'm hopeless in Danish classes (cc02q05).	0. Disagree-Disagree somewhat, 1. Agree somewhat- Agree
"How much do you disagree or agree with each of the following?" I have always done well in mathematics (cc02q18).	0. Disagree-Disagree somewhat, 1. Agree somewhat- Agree
"How often do these things apply to you?" When I study, I try to figure out which concepts I still haven't really understood (cc01q19)?	0. Almost never- Sometimes, 1. Often – Almost always
"How often do these things apply to you?" I like to try to be better than other students. (cc02q04)	0. Disagree-Disagree somewhat, 1. Agree somewhat- Agree
How much do you disagree or agree with these statements about reading?" I cannot sit still and read for more than a few minutes (st35q09)?	0. Disagree-Disagree somewhat, 1. Agree somewhat- Agree

Note: Variable name in the PISA 2000 Questionnaire in parentheses, see OECD (2002b).

IDENTIFYING AND EXPLAINING HIDDEN DISADVANTAGE WITHIN THE NON-MANUAL GROUP IN HIGHER EDUCATION ACCESS

Delma Byrne and Selina McCoy

ABSTRACT

In an examination of class inequality in education in the Republic of Ireland over the period from the late 1990s to the mid 2000s, this chapter reveals class inequality in educational outcomes within social groups as well as across social groups, and places particular attention on the non-manual group. Within this group, a clear distinction can be made between those classified as having an 'intermediate non-manual' position and those classified as holding an 'other (lower) non-manual' position in terms of their educational performance at secondary education and subsequent access to higher education, which persists over the period. This finding has been revealed by disaggregating the non-manual group into the 'intermediate non-manual' and 'other (lower) non-manual' groups, a practice that has not been used by analysts in the past in the Irish context. In this chapter, we engage with theories of class which offer a framework

Class and Stratification Analysis
Comparative Social Research, Volume 30, 293–315
ISSN: 0195-6310/doi:10.1108/S0195-6310(2013)0000030014

for understanding educational inequality and in particular, why members
of the same social class groups experience different educational outcomes.

Keywords: Educational inequality; non-manual class; intra-class
differentials

INTRODUCTION

In this chapter, we engage with theories of class which offer a framework for
understanding educational inequality and in particular, why members of the
same social class groups experience different educational outcomes. This
chapter reports on a wider study which sought to explain declining higher
education entry rates among the non-manual socio-economic group in the
Republic of Ireland over time (see McCoy, Byrne, O'Connell, Kelly, &
Doherty, 2010). Earlier research had identified that young people from the
non-manual socio-economic group are poorly placed in terms of higher
education participation and are also the only group to have seen a fall in
levels of entry over the 10-year period between the late 1990s and the late
2000s (O'Connell, Clancy, and McCoy, 2006). In seeking to explain their
low rates of higher education participation, we identify a pattern of
differential educational attainment and achievement within the non-manual
group, differentiating between the intermediate non-manual group and
the other non-manual group. Using the nationally representative School
Leavers' Surveys between the late 1990s and early 2000s, we find that over
time at both secondary level and at higher education, the intermediate non-
manual group fares considerably better than the other non-manual group
which comprises lower-level service workers and accounts for just under 10
per cent of the Irish population (further details are provided in a subsequent
section). Based on these findings, we argue that the existence of varying
theoretical approaches to the class structure has implications for research
into the examination of educational inequality, and for education policy.
Given changes in the measurement of socio-economic and social class
position and their constituent categories over time, we provide evidence that
a classification that groups together the other non-manual and the intermediate non-manual groups serves to disguise important variations in the
life chances of the other non-manual socio-economic group. In understanding this disparity in educational outcomes among the non-manual
group, we engage with current theories of class which offer a framework
for understanding educational inequality and in particular, why members
of the same social class groups experience different educational outcomes.

CHANGING APPROACHES TO THE CLASS STRUCTURE

Central to this chapter is the examination of educational differentials over time in a larger context of changing approaches to the class structure in the Irish context. Defining parental social class background or parental socio-economic status has previously been documented to be problematic for studies that seek to examine educational differentials over time (see O'Hare, Whelan, & Commins, 1991; Drudy, 1991; Clancy, 1988; Clancy & Wall, 2000; O'Connell, Clancy, & McCoy, 2006). Such a task presents a range of problems, not only due to differences in the timing and adoption of social class and socio-economic grouping schemas used by the Census of Population but also due to fundamental changes introduced in the classification schemes for both social class and socio-economic group over time. Since 1951 the Irish Central Statistics Office (CSO) has employed a socio-economic group classification as part of its data output services, based on a nominal grouping of occupations. The socio-economic group classification has been a useful discriminator of socio-economic differences in many areas of research, and has been used extensively (but not exclusively) in Irish educational research, particularly in terms of monitoring changes over time in the socio-economic profile of higher education entrants (e.g. Clancy, 2001; O'Connell, Clancy, & McCoy, 2006; Byrne, McCoy, & Watson, 2008; McCoy et al., 2010). As a result of social and economic change,[1] the CSO introduced a revised system of classification of occupations to socio-economic groups for the 1996 Census. Up until the change, the socio-economic groupings of the Irish Census had been based on an assessment of the level of skill or educational attainment required by each occupation (Central Statistics Office, 1986). In contrast, the classification scheme adopted in 1996 is based on the UK Standard Occupational Classification (SOC) and is determined by occupation and additionally in some cases by employment status. The new classification scheme differs substantially from the previous occupational coding in a number of respects, but most importantly in that the new classification aggregates the 'intermediate non-manual' group and the 'other non-manual' group into a single non-manual socio-economic group.

Examination of educational inequality has not, of course, been confined to the use of socio-economic position, with others adopting the more discrete social class measurement. In 1991, the Irish Census of Population included a classification of occupations for the first time based on the work of Goldthorpe, but adjusted to the Irish occupational structure. This seven-class version of the Goldthorpe schema has also been used extensively in examination of educational inequality (see, e.g., Whelan & Hannan, 1999) with amendments that farmers are considered as a separate group (see, e.g., Smyth, 1999). As with the SOC classification outlined above, the 1991 social class schema confines the intermediate and lower non-manual group to a single non-manual group. The theoretical basis of this classification is to combine occupational categories which are typically comparable in terms of their market situation (source and levels of income, degree of economic security and chances of economic advancement) and their work situation (authority, control, degree of autonomy in performing work tasks). Other studies have adopted the classification employed in the CASMIN study (König, Lüttinger, and Müller, 1988) which typically separates 'higher grade' and 'lower grade' non-manual categories, but have aggregated the routine non-manual class (see Whelan & Layte, 2002, 2006).

In order to make comparisons of the distribution of school leavers to higher education over time, the older socio-economic status classification scheme has been adopted. Thus, in this chapter, we use the socio-economic classification scheme adopted in the 1986 Census of Population. Using this measure, household socio-economic position is conceptualised on the basis that the life chances (and thus educational chances) of individuals and their families are largely determined by their position in relation to the market and occupation is taken to be a central indicator, that is, the occupational structure is viewed as the backbone of the stratification system. The conceptual basis of the scheme assigns occupations to socio-economic groups based on similarity in terms of level of skill or educational attainment required. That is, the socio-economic position of persons aged 15 years or older who were at work is determined by their occupation or in some cases by a combination of occupation and employment status. Further, Drudy (1991) notes that in the case of socio-economic groups used by the Census, it is intended that each should contain people whose 'social, cultural and recreational standards and behaviour are similar'.

IRISH EDUCATION SYSTEM

How the Irish educational system is organised is highly relevant for understanding the experience of young people from different socio-economic groups, and how they navigate the system. In Ireland, young people enter secondary education at 12 or 13 years of age. Students complete three years of lower secondary education leading up to the Junior Certificate examination, and participation in full-time education is compulsory until the age of 16, or until lower secondary has been comp-leted, whichever is later. At present there are three types of school sectors: voluntary secondary schools, vocational schools and community/compre-hensive schools, each following a national standardised curriculum leading to standardised examinations at the end of compulsory education ('Junior Certificate') and at the end of post-compulsory secondary education ('Leaving Certificate'). In addition to ownership, the three school types also differ in their student composition with a greater concentration of working-class and lower achieving students in vocational schools (Byrne & Smyth, 2010; Smyth, 1999). Upper secondary education in Ireland follows a relatively formal tracking model which is hierarchical, as students study either a largely academic programme which offers direct entry to higher education (LCE, LCVP) or a distinct pre-vocational programme (LCA) which offers a mix of academic and vocational elements and is aimed at preparation for the labour market and participation in post-school education (e.g. further education sector) but does not offer direct access to higher education. Ireland differs from other tracked systems, however, in that the vast majority of students (93%) take academic programmes (Banks, Byrne, McCoy, & Smyth, 2010). Because the academic pro-grammes allow direct access to higher education, these tracks typically absorb students who have performed 'better' in their Junior Certificate (lower secondary) examinations while the pre-vocational programme is generally orientated towards young people at risk of leaving school and students who have learning difficulties. The higher education system operates on the basis of *numerus clausus,* whereby the highest ranking candidates are offered a college place. That is, the vast majority of places at higher education institutions are awarded on the basis of 'points' (grades) achieved in the Leaving Certificate examination and entry to more prestigious courses demands particularly high performance levels.[2]

SOCIAL POSITION AND EDUCATIONAL ATTAINMENT IN IRELAND

Ireland can be characterised as a country with substantial persistent inequalities in educational attainment. Numerous studies have demon-strated that rapidly rising participation and retention in education has been accompanied by remarkable stability and persistence in inequality in educational attainment (Smyth, 1999; Breen & Whelan, 1993; Whelan &

Layte, 2002; Whelan & Hannan, 1999; Byrne & Smyth, 2010; McCoy & Smyth, 2011). Among both school leavers and new entrants, progression and participation in higher education have increased over the period from the late 1990s to the late 2000s (see O'Connell, Clancy, & McCoy, 2006; Byrne et al., 2008; McCoy et al., 2010). Among new entrants, overall participation rates have increased from 44 to 55 per cent (O'Connell, Clancy, & McCoy, 2006), while among school leavers, progression to any higher education has increased to 60 per cent (Byrne et al., 2008). Furthermore, in highlighting social inequalities at the transition to higher education, a number of these studies have documented changes in the effect of social background on the transition, concluding that educational expansion has not resulted in any significant reduction in social class inequality over the period from the 1980s to the early 1990s (Breen & Whelan, 1993; Smyth, 1999; Whelan & Layte, 2002; McCoy & Smyth, 2011). In spite of the overall increase in the proportion of young people completing secondary education, the relativities between social classes have been maintained, in line with many other European countries (e.g. Shavit & Muller, 1998).[3] That is, the effects of social class background on higher education participation do not appear to have changed substantially over the period, with in fact a widening gap between the higher professional and other groups, with a reduction in the gap only emerging after the early 1990s (McCoy & Smyth, 2011).

In this context, persistent has been the finding that the children of non-manual workers, semi-and unskilled manual workers and agricultural workers are under-represented among new entrants to higher education, relative to their share of the population. Furthermore, between 1998 and 2004 the non-manual group has not shared at all in the general trend towards increased higher education participation (O'Connell, Clancy & McCoy, 2006). Furthermore, the relative disadvantage experienced by members of the lower non-manual group went undiscovered by earlier studies of inequality in higher education access. This we now know was due to the variability across studies of higher education participation in terms of the social class/socio-economic classifications used but also due to variation over time in the coding of social class/socio-economic position. Post 1986, the theoretical approach to the class structure commonly aggregated the lower non-manual group with the intermediate non-manual group, thus typically positioning the lower non-manual group outside categories that education policy defines as 'disadvantaged students' or 'under-represented' groups. Such disadvantaged or under-represented groups have typically been defined by academics and policy makers as young people from working class backgrounds and non-employed households. As a result, policy makers and academics have failed to take into account important differences across the social spectrum and within groups.

In all, the non-manual group accounts for approximately 20 per cent of the population, with little change since the mid 1990s, and is largely comprised of the intermediate non-manual group, with a ratio of approximately 60:40 between the intermediate and lower non-manual groups. Despite being categorised as a single non-manual group post 1986 in socio-economic group and social class classifications, we find that the two non-manual groups have distinct occupational profiles, with the intermediate group comprising relatively high status occupational positions such as Garda sergeants and lower ranks and government executive officials as well as proprietors of small business in the service industry. In contrast, the lower non-manual group is more homogenous, dominated by lower-level service workers including bus drivers, barbers/hairdressers, air stewards and waiters/waitresses, and where occupationalisation may be more weakly developed. Furthermore, across a range of educational and economic characteristics, occupants of the lower non-manual group share many similarities with lower manual groups rather than with the intermediate non-manual group. The lower non-manual group is also much more similar in profile to the semi- and unskilled manual groups in terms of their educational attainment and representation of higher education graduates among the group. The parent(s) of occupants of the intermediate non-manual group are themselves much more likely to have attended higher education, which one would expect to have implications for the numbers of children of such workers who similarly progress to higher education. There are also differences between these two groups in terms of the types of schools attended among their children. Furthermore, based on an analysis of the 2007 EU-SILC,[4] lower white collar groups (which overlap considerably with the lower non-manual group) display income patterns and state grant eligibility (financial aid for higher education) levels largely comparable to semi-and unskilled manual groups.

RELATION TO THEORIES OF CLASS

In explaining heterogeneity in terms of differential educational outcomes within a socio-economic group or social class group, we draw on two contrasting perspectives which offer explanations as to why a pattern of differential educational attainment and achievement may be evident *within* a social class/socio-economic group, and in particular, the non-manual group. We begin with the work of Goldthorpe (2000, 2007) who offers an explanation for educational inequality *within* social class groupings as occupational variation within classes rather than class variation as such. Goldthorpe adopts a neo-Weberian perspective of class analysis in that class analysis is viewed as beginning with a structure of positions associated with a specific historical form of the social division of labour, which is usually seen as being constituted in two ways; employment relationships (employers/self-employed) and varying employment functions and conditions which differentiate employees. Goldthorpe argues against a theory of class-based collective action, whereby individuals holding similar positions within the class structure will automatically develop a shared consciousness of their situation, and will, in turn, be prompted to act together in the pursuit of their common class interests (Goldthorpe & Marshall, 1992). That is, his version of class stays away from an explanation of class formation at a level at which 'a capacity for socialisation' is present, avoiding reference to distinctive class values, norms and 'forms of consciousness'. The persistence of class differentials between classes is then accounted for by reference not to continuing sub-cultural variations among classes, but, primarily, to the stability of patterns of relative risk aversion that can be understood as rational, given prevailing differences in class situations and given that a high priority in educational decision making is to avoid downward mobility. The argument is that children from less advantaged backgrounds will, on average, need to have a higher subjective probability of succeeding than will children from more advantaged backgrounds before they are ready to take up more rather than less ambitious educational options to the point at which safer or less 'risky' options appear to give them good chances of at least maintaining their parents' class position. Goldthorpe argues that occupational subcultures (and social networks) can also co-exist with similarities in economic circumstances deriving from similar employment relations. That is, if particular occupations seem to have distinctive economic features (employment stability, promotional opportunities, and variable pay) such features do not represent occupational variations on strong class themes. Rather, they can be explained as occupational variation within classes. Hence, educational inequality within social class groups can be explained through patterns of relative risk aversion.

Alternatively, we can hypothesise from the work of Grusky and colleagues (Grusky & Weeden, 2001a, 2001b; Grusky & Sørensen, 1998) that evidence of educational inequality within traditional social class groupings may represent underlying 'occupational communities' rather than occupational variation within classes. Unlike the work of Goldthorpe, Grusky and colleagues adopt a Marxist perspective of class, and wish to see a theory of class based action remain at the core of class analysis. Accordingly, it is the social processes that produce sub-cultural variation – processes of social selection, socialisation, and institutionalisation – that are essential to class analysis. Their focus echoes that of Lockwood (1966) in that they emphasise the class significance of *gemeinschaftlich* or 'real' occupational communities which have both meaning and consequences for their members (Crompton, 2010).[5] In particular, they place emphasis on class identity and formal and informal (e.g. interactional) mechanisms of social closure that generate *gemeinschaftlich* at the site of production when explaining class formation through the use of disaggregated occupations. According to Grusky, occupations tend to be economic and sociocultural entities and occupational groupings far more readily provide social contexts that can serve as the source of shared values and normative codes and in turn, distinctive lifestyles. While conventional class analysis typically aggregates occupations into social class positions, Grusky and colleagues put forward an argument for extreme disaggregation of occupational groups (Grusky & Sørensen, 1998, 2001; Grusky & Weeden, 2001, 2002).[6] In doing so, they stress the importance of the site of production for individual-level behaviour arguing that a 'big class assumption' dismisses the smaller social groups that emerge around functional niches in the division of labour.[7] Furthermore, Grusky and colleagues argue that the approach of disaggregation has a number of advantages over aggregate class analysis in relation to class identification, social closure, collective action and outcomes (Weeden & Grusky, 2005a, 2005b; Grusky & Weeden, 2001a, 2001b). In terms of identity, they argue that occupational identities and occupation-specific consciousness[8] are stronger than class identities at the aggregate level. Furthermore, it is put forward that patterns of social closure also operate at the occupational level and are represented by associations and organisations. The resulting restriction of social interaction generates and maintains occupational subcultures that are correspondingly disaggregate. Grusky and colleagues explain the social processes by which class membership occurs which has a bearing on intergenerational reproduction and thus, the educational choices that young people make. Workers choose occupations that are receptive to their personal values, and employers choose workers with values that are compatible with occupational demands. Occupations in turn require some form of training which inculcates explicit codes of behaviour (Caplow, 1954) or 'occupational habitus'. As a result, we may expect to find real subcultures through processes of work identification and boundaries and social closure the more we disaggregate social groups. Parental resources that result from the occupational positions of parents are both hierarchically and horizontally structured (van de Werfhorst & Luijkx, 2010; Jonsson, Grusky, Di Carlo, Pollak, & Brinton, 2009) and so the social conditioning mechanisms of class formation are partly mediated through the educational choices that children and young people make. Furthermore, the structure of educational systems encourages occupation-specific investments and commitments through practices such as tracking and attending schools that provide known access to certain occupations or occupational pathways.

DATA AND MEASURES

The analyses in this chapter are based on a regular survey of those exiting the secondary education system in Ireland. The School Leavers' Surveys have been conducted on a regular basis by the Economic and Social Research Institute since 1980. As well as information on educational level reached and qualifications attained, the survey collects information on parental employment and parental socio-economic background. The surveys come from two-stage stratified random samples of students who left secondary education in the late 1990s (in the academic year 1995/1996 and 1996/1997), early 2000s (2000/2001, 2002/2003) and late 2000s (2004/2005, 2005/2006), thus representing three time points over a 10-year period. The surveys are cross sectional: school leavers were interviewed at one time point, typically two years after leaving school. The full sample accounts for 15,009 pupils in 1,075 schools. In order to illustrate differential achievement at secondary level and entry to higher education within the non-manual group, for the purpose of this chapter we consider two dependent variables. Firstly, we consider whether the school leaver (1) completed second-level education and (2) whether the school leaver was in full-time higher education at the time of the survey. For each dependent variable, we estimate binary logistic regression models with robust standard errors to correct for the effect of the natural clustering of the data (students within schools). This method allows for within-cluster correlation of errors, and results in much more conservative standard errors and smaller t-statistics than those in an un-clustered model. In the case of the models pertaining to participation in higher education, three models are presented. Model 1 reports the influence of socio-economic position on higher education participation without a measure of educational attainment in the Leaving Certificate. Model 2 then reports the influence of socio-economic position on higher education participation this time including a measure of educational attainment in the Leaving Certificate. Finally, Model 3 reports the influence of socio-economic position on higher education participation including a measure of educational attainment in the Leaving Certificate but this time restricting the analysis to those have achieved eligibility in terms of 'points' for higher education entry.

In this chapter, the eight-category household socio-economic position is used on the basis that the life chances of individuals and families are largely determined by their position in the market, and occupation is taken to be a central indicator; that is, the occupational structure is viewed as the backbone of the stratification system. All occupations are coded based on the Census Classification of Occupations 1986. The socio-economic groupings of the Irish Census have been based on an assessment of the level of skill or educational attainment required by each occupation. Using this classification, the allocation of occupied persons to socio-economic groups is determined by considering occupation and for some, employment status. The entire population was classified to one of eleven socio-economic groups plus a residual 'unknown' group. A 'dominance approach' is used in the definition of socio-economic position (as developed by Erikson 1984). Thus, the socio-economic position of the household is based on the socio-economic position of the parent with the highest occupation, or the occupation requiring the highest level of skill or educational attainment.[9] For the purpose of this chapter, those from families where both parents were unemployed or one parent was unemployed and a second parent is on 'home duties' or whose occupation is unknown, the dominant situation of the household was classified as 'unemployed'. An 'unknown' category includes those from families where no information on parental/ guardian occupation was given.

The measure of academic attainment is restricted to those who have completed the academic track Leaving Certificate.[10] Thus, our measure of academic attainment is based on self-reported grades in the examination. In terms of measures of the school attended, we also include the type of school attended (secondary, vocational or community/comprehensive) and a dummy identifying whether the school attended is designated disadvantaged (and hence in receipt of additional state funding), thus reflecting the student intake to the school. Time period dummies are also included, distinguishing between the late 1990s, the early 2000s and the late 2000s. The reference case is standard across each set of analysis: a male from an 'lower non-manual' background, who attended a vocational school and a school that has been designated 'disadvantaged' in the late 1990s.[11]

FINDINGS

Completion of Secondary-Level Education

The period since the early 1980s has been one of rapid change in levels of educational attainment, that is, in the stage at which young people complete their secondary-level education (Smyth, 1999). However, since the mid 1990s, rates of Leaving Certificate completion have remained relatively stable (Byrne & Smyth, 2010). Table 1 shows the pattern of Leaving Certificate completion according to parental socio-economic group over the period 1997–2007. While retention levels have remained largely constant over this 10-year period, completion rates are significantly higher among young people from professional and employer/manager and farming groups. Considerable variation is also evident in retention patterns between those from intermediate non-manual and lower non-manual backgrounds. While the retention rates of young people from intermediate non-manual backgrounds remain relatively persistent at around 85 per cent over time, they are substantially higher than corresponding rates of young people from the lower non-manual group. This results from an raw odds ratio

Table 1.   Leaving Certificate Completion Rates by Parental
Socio-Economic Group.

	Late 1990s		Early 2000s		Late 2000s	
	%	N	%	N	%	N
Farmer/other agricultural	85.8	707	87.3	535	88.6	727
Professional	92.3	693	91.5	773	93.0	334
Employer/manager	89.1	505	88.7	513	88.9	291
Intermediate non-manual	84.1	862	85.7	922	85.1	808
Lower non-manual	72.1	960	75.2	990	76.6	699
Skilled manual	74.9	738	78.3	658	82.1	375
Semi- and unskilled manual	62.1	721	68.8	526	74.3	313
Non-employed	65.3	316	48.8	228	57.1	228
Unknown	76.9	119	63.0	143	74.2	249
Total	80.4	5,621	82.3	5,288	83.9	4,024

differential showing students from intermediate non-manual backgrounds as 1.9 times more likely to complete secondary level than students from lower non-manual backgrounds.[12] While young people from lower non-manual backgrounds have also experienced some increase in retention over time, clearly there is a pattern of differential educational achievement at the secondary-level completion stage.

In Table 2 multivariate analyses are used whereby completion of secondary-level education is contrasted against departure from secondary level at an earlier stage. The model estimates the relative influence of each of the observed variables on the likelihood that people complete secondary education. Significant socio-economic differences are evident as students from higher socio-economic backgrounds have higher odds of completing secondary education: over three times for a person from a professional

Table 2. Binary Logistic Regression of Completion of Secondary Level Education.

	Coefficient	Robust Standard Error	$P>z$	Exp(b)
Constant	−0.283	0.131	0.030	
Female	0.874	0.053	0.000	2.4
ref: male				
Professional	1.216	0.077	0.000	3.4
Employer/manager	0.859	0.079	0.000	2.4
Farmer	0.707	0.082	0.000	2.0
Intermediate non-manual	0.572	0.059	0.000	1.8
Skilled manual	0.159	0.066	0.017	1.2
Semi-unskilled manual	−0.272	0.070	0.000	0.8
Unemployed	−0.972	0.095	0.000	0.4
Unknown	−0.351	0.092	0.000	0.7
ref: lower non-manual				
Secondary school	−0.015	0.110	0.894	1.0
Community/comprehensive school	−0.264	0.102	0.010	0.8
ref: vocational school				
Disadvantaged school	−0.710	0.107	0.000	0.5
ref: non disadvantaged				
Early 2000s	0.257	0.098	0.009	1.3
Late 2000s	0.268	0.111	0.016	1.3
ref: Late 1990s				
15,009 students in 1,075 schools				
$\chi^2(14) = 1167.18$***				
Pseudo $R^2 = .1146$				

***$p<0.000$.

background, twofold for a person from an employer/manager background and (almost) two times for a person from a farming or intermediate non-manual background. Those from semi-skilled manual, unemployed or unknown backgrounds are less likely to complete secondary education than the lower non-manual group. These findings have important implications for the pool of young people eligible for higher education, with the intermediate non-manual rather than the lower non-manual group most likely to succeed in making the trajectory towards eligibility for higher education.

Participation in Full-Time Higher Education

Table 3 indicates that participation in higher education has remained relatively stable across each of the socio-economic groups over the 10-year period from the late 1990s to the late 2000s. Furthermore, the percentage of young people who have completed secondary education and are in higher education at the time of the survey has also remained relatively stable across time. Further examination of the non-manual groups shows that while patterns of participation for school leavers from lower non-manual backgrounds are remarkably similar to those from semi-skilled and unskilled manual backgrounds, patterns of participation of the intermediate non-manual group more closely resemble those of the employer/manager group. Table 3 indicates that levels of participation among those from lower non-manual backgrounds are among the lowest, and that participation

Table 3. Participation in Higher Education Among Senior Cycle Leavers by Parental Socio-Economic Background.

	Late 1990s		Early 2000s		Late 2000s	
	%	N	%	N	%	N
Farmer/other agricultural	47.0	441	46.5	369	44.0	197
Professional	64.7	542	62.6	594	63.4	576
Employer/manager	57.5	357	53.0	356	52.7	234
Intermediate non-manual	46.2	516	47.9	593	57.6	522
Lower non-manual	41.7	421	34.8	493	31.3	350
Skilled manual	36.2	351	42.3	336	48.6	197
Semi-unskilled manual	38.2	231	32.9	239	37.9	136
Non-employed	31.7	110	28.6	54	38.1	55
Unknown	31.3	54	20.1	56	32.7	113
Total	45.9	3,023	51.2	3,090	45.6	2,380

rates have declined over time. The intermediate non-manual group have significantly higher levels of higher education participation and we see that their participation has increased over time.[13] These results are confirmed in the multivariate analyses (see Table 4).

In the case of Table 4, three models are presented. Model 1 reports the influence of socio-economic position on higher education participation without a measure of educational attainment in the Leaving Certificate. Model 2 then reports the influence of socio-economic position on higher education participation this time including a measure of educational attainment in the Leaving Certificate. Finally, Model 3 reports the influence of socio-economic position on higher education participation including a measure of educational attainment in the Leaving Certificate but this time restricting the analysis to those who are eligible for higher education entry. Across each of the three models, professional, employer/manager, farming and intermediate non-manual groups are more likely to enter higher education than the lower non-manual group. Indeed, the position of the lower non-manual group is similar to that of the semi-skilled and unskilled manual group and those from work poor households (households without parental employment). As well as the influence of socio-economic background, there are also clear effects of performance in the Leaving Certificate, with those who have performed highly in the examination displaying a higher probability of entry to higher education. From our study, we found that a higher proportion of the intermediate non-manual group achieve at least two honours in the examination than the lower non-manual group (24 per cent relative to 15 per cent), suggesting that a higher share of intermediate non-manual students are eligible for higher education than their lower non-manual counterparts, and this is evident in the multivariate analyses shown in Model 2 of Table 4. Thus, when educational attainment is included in the model, we find that some of the differences within the non-manual group can be accounted for by differences in academic performance. However, the effects of social background remain strong even when we take into account previous attainment in the Leaving Certificate. That is, even when we take into account previous educational attainment, the intermediate non-manual group continue to be 1.6 times more likely to participate in higher education than the lower non-manual group. The type of school that young people attend is also an important variable as school leavers who attended secondary or community/comprehensive schools are most likely to enter higher education relative to those who attend a vocational school. Model 3 of Table 4 restricts the analysis to those who are eligible to enter higher education (that is, those

Table 4. Binary Logistic Regression of Participation in Higher Education.

| | Model 1 | | | | Model 2 | | | | Model 3 | | | |
| | Robust | | | | Robust | | | | Robust | | | |
	Coefficient	Standard Error	P > z	Exp(b)	Coefficient	Standard Error	P > z	Exp(b)	Coefficient	Standard Error	P > z	Exp(b)
Constant	-1.533	0.117	0.000	0.2	-2.524	0.179	0.000	0.1	-0.874	0.149	0.000	0.4
Female	0.204	0.065	0.002	1.2	0.156	0.065	0.017	1.2	0.237	0.081	0.003	1.3
ref: male												
Professional	1.302	0.089	0.000	3.7	0.922	0.097	0.000	2.5	0.912	0.123	0.000	2.5
Employer/manager	0.841	0.098	0.000	2.3	0.631	0.101	0.000	1.9	0.514	0.140	0.000	1.7
Farmer	0.737	0.104	0.000	2.1	0.639	0.110	0.000	1.9	0.517	0.145	0.000	1.7
Intermediate non-manual	0.589	0.081	0.000	1.8	0.467	0.085	0.000	1.6	0.442	0.121	0.000	1.6
Skilled manual	0.189	0.105	0.072	1.2	0.218	0.110	0.047	1.2	0.269	0.131	0.039	1.3
Semi-skilled manual	-0.086	0.128	0.502	0.9	0.035	0.133	0.794	1.0				
Unemployed and unknown	-0.113	0.180	0.531	0.9	-0.012	0.189	0.951	1.0				
Unknown	0.083	0.148	0.573	1.1	0.340	0.153	0.026	1.4				
ref: lower non-manual												
Secondary school	1.206	0.092	0.000	3.3	0.936	0.082	0.000	2.5	1.130	0.100	0.000	3.1
Community/comprehensive School	0.312	0.096	0.001	1.4	0.259	0.098	0.008	1.3	0.353	0.133	0.008	1.4
ref: vocational school												
Disadvantaged school	-0.432	0.100	0.000	0.6	-0.395	0.093	0.000	0.7	-0.367	0.110	0.001	0.7
ref: not disadvantaged school												
Early 2000s	0.071	0.084	0.396	1.1	0.584	0.084	0.000	1.8	0.594	0.098	0.000	1.8
Late 2000s	-0.020	0.094	0.831	1.0	0.256	0.089	0.004	1.3	0.402	0.106	0.000	1.5

ref: late 1990s			
5+ Honours	2.462	0.162	0.000	11.7
2–4 Honours	1.273	0.157	0.000	3.6
1 Honour	0.356	0.193	0.065	1.4
5+ Passes	0.249	0.160	0.120	1.3
Result unknown	−0.120	0.156	0.442	0.9

ref: less than 5 passes

8540 students in 1009 schools
$\chi^2(14) = 718.56$***

Pseudo $R^2 = .1166$

8540 students in 1009 schools
$\chi^2(19) = 1400.08$***

Pseudo $R^2 = .2363$

4118 students in 848 schools
$\chi^2(11) = 331.07$***

Pseudo $R^2 = .0884$

who have achieved at least two 'honours' in the Leaving Certificate, i.e.
higher performing students) in an attempt to compare 'like-with-like'.
Again, we find that the professional, employer/manager, farming and
intermediate non-manual groups are more likely to enter higher education
relative to the lower non-manual group.

CONCLUSION

In this chapter, we engage with theories of class which offer a framework for
understanding educational inequality and in particular, why members of the
same social class groups experience different educational outcomes, using
the educational experiences of the intermediate non-manual and lower non-
manual groups in the Republic of Ireland as an example. Central to this
chapter is also the examination of educational differentials over time in a
larger context of changing approaches to the class structure in Ireland. As a
result of such changes, we argue that policy makers and academics have
failed to take into account the ongoing disadvantage of the lower non-
manual group. This chapter highlights the need to question how best to
measure the class structure in an examination of educational inequality.

This chapter highlights the consequences of aggregating the intermediate
non-manual and lower non-manual socio-economic groups. We identify
clear patterns of underperformance among the lower non-manual group in
terms of participation in higher education but also in terms of secondary
education. This group clearly is at a disadvantage in terms of secondary-
level completion, and the wider study from which this chapter is based also
shows that the lower non-manual group is at a disadvantage in terms of
making the transition from lower secondary to upper secondary, in terms of
the tracks (academic versus vocational) they pursue at upper secondary
level, but also in terms of their educational attainment in the Leaving
Certificate examination which is central to achieving entry to higher
education. Moreover, divergent patterns of educational attainment evident
between the intermediate non-manual group and the lower non-manual
groups have remained stable in each of these aspects over the 10-year period
considered here (see McCoy et al., 2010).

In addressing explanations for within group inequality, we set out
conflicting positions by Goldthorpe and Grusky (and colleagues) as to why
educational inequality should occur within social class/socio-economic
groups. Goldthorpe argues that such variation can be attributed to occupational variation within classes, and primarily be explained through patterns

of relative risk aversion. Alternatively, Grusky and colleagues argue that within social class/socio-economic variation is likely to represent the existence of occupational communities (which serve as the source of shared values, normative codes and distinctive lifestyles) and subcultures which are formed through processes of work identification, boundaries and social closure. Thus, such membership has a bearing on intergenerational repro-duction and the educational choices that people make. While our findings support those of Grusky and Weeden (2001a, 2001b) who argue that the costs of aggregation may be especially high for some social class groupings, and although we do not further disaggregate social class groups in this chapter due to the issue of small numbers, we question whether such differentiation in outcomes can be explained as a result of specific 'occu-pational communities'. That is, while the findings presented in this chapter suggest that the occupations that comprise the lower non-manual group may indeed represent a specific 'occupational habitus', they do not fully support Gruskys' claim given that much of this group display 'primary effects' as articulated by Boudon (1974), that is, differences in educational attainment at earlier stages of education, as well as clear differences in educational decision making or 'secondary effects' once eligibility for entry to higher education has been achieved. However, this is not to dismiss the social closure mechanisms evident at secondary-level education, for example, the tracking system, which has the potential to reinforce educational disadvan-tage among less advantaged groups (see Banks et al., 2010). Likewise, the theory of 'relative risk aversion' avoids the issue of the role of the school in reducing or exacerbating educational inequality. An essential part of the wider study reported here (qualitative interviews with a diverse sample of young people from the two non-manual backgrounds)[14] revealed that information and the role of the school in disseminating information play a central role in the educational decision making of young people and their parents. A lack of information about the college application process, a lack of assistance with the range of subject choice on offer in schools and a lack of information about the financial aspects of higher education and financial supports available each represented perceived barriers for the children of lower non-manual backgrounds (McCoy & Byrne, 2011).

NOTES

1. Such change includes changes in the occupational structure, the need to facilitate computer automated coding and to meet the requirements to adhere to the international occupational classifications.

2. Two honours in the Leaving Certificate accrues the necessary minimum points to be eligible for entry to higher education.

3. These findings have been seriously challenged by a body of recent research evidence (Shavit, Arum, & Gamoran, 2007; Breen & Jonsson, 2005).

4. Higher and lower white collar groups which overlap considerably with the intermediate and other non-manual groups respectively can be identified using the European Socio-Economic Classification schema (ESeC). Information required to create ESeC includes occupation (3-digit), employment status, number of employees at workplace and supervisory status for workers (Harrison & Rose, 2006).

5. One of the rationales for moving to an occupationally defined social class definition is to identify local boundaries that have come to be institutionalised and are therefore salient to workers themselves. Grusky and Weeden (2001a, 2001b) argue that although conventional occupational classification schemes provide a useful basis for such research, it should not be assumed that their constituent detailed categories are in all cases socially meaningful.

6. In this work, they argue that the preference for analytically derived groupings increases the vulnerability of class analysis to the post-modern critique (Weeden & Grusky, 2005a, 2005b).

7. This work also has its roots in the work of Durkheim (1933) and Bourdieu (1984). In the view of Durkheim (1933) occupational associations come to serve as important mediators between the state and the individual, actively discouraging processes of inequality while Bourdieu (1984) places emphasis on characterising habitus and lifestyles, because the conditions of existence are assumed to be unacceptably heterogeneous (Grusky & Sorensen, 2001).

8. Some argue that contemporary class identities are strongly shaped by aggregate affiliations (e.g. Marshall, Rose, Newby, & Vogler, 1988) but the prevailing position is that conventional classes now only have a weak hold over workers. For Goldthorpe (2002), 'classes' can be identified independently from 'consciousnesses' and the absence of class consciousness does not imply the end of class. Sociologists may be using the same word (class) but they are talking about different things (Crompton, 2010).

9. There are problems associated with using a 'dominance approach' when using class measurements based on the very nature (nominal) of socio-economic groupings. However, we argue that father's socio-economic background insufficiently represents family socio-economic position and thus, it is deemed important to also consider the mother's socio-economic status. For a more detailed discussion of varying approaches to measuring family socio-economic resources, see Korupp, Ganzeboom, and Van Der Lippe (2002).

10. A measure of previous academic attainment is not collected in the surveys.

11. Further controls were included in previous models; however, the main results did not change considerably.

12. There was a significant association between completion of second-level education and parental socio-economic group $\chi^2(7) = 755.399$, $p < .001$. Furthermore, this association was evident across each of cohorts: Late 1990s $\chi^2(1) = 56.39$, $p < .001$; Early 2000s $\chi^2(1) = 42.23$, $p < .001$; Late 2000s $\chi^2(1) = 35.04$, $p < .001$. Based on the odds ratio, students from an intermediate non-manual background were 1.8 times more likely to complete second level than students from other non-manual

backgrounds in the early and late 2000s, and 1.9 times more likely to complete second level than students from other non-manual backgrounds in the early 1990s.

13. There was a significant association between participation in higher education and parental socio-economic group. Furthermore, this association was evident across each of cohorts: Late 1990s $\chi^2(1) = 124.970$, $p < .001$; Early 2000s $\chi^2(1) = 86.458$, $p < .001$; Late 2000s $\chi^2(1) = 79.865$, $p < .001$. Based on the odds ratio, students from an intermediate non-manual background were three times more likely to enter higher education than students from other non-manual backgrounds in the early and late 2000s, and five times more likely to enter higher education than students from other non-manual backgrounds in the early 1990s.

14. This sample included young people who made the transition to higher education as well as those who did not.

REFERENCES

Banks, J., Byrne, D., McCoy, S, & Smyth, E. (2010). *Engaging young people? Student experiences of the leaving certificate applied.* Dublin: ESRI.

Boudon, R. (1974). *Education, opportunity, and social inequality.* New York: Wiley.

Breen, R., & Jonsson, J. O. (2005). Inequality of opportunity in comparative perspective: Recent research on educational attainment and social mobility. *Annual Review of Sociology, 31*, 223–243.

Breen, R., & Whelan, C. T. (1993). From ascription to achievement? Origins, education and entry to the labour force in the Republic of Ireland during the Twentieth Century. *Acta Sociologica, 36*, 3–18.

Byrne, D., McCoy, S., & Watson, D. (2008). *School leavers' Survey Report 2007.* Dublin: ESRI.

Byrne, D., & Smyth, E. (2010). *No way back? The dynamics of early school leaving.* Dublin: The Economic and Social Research Institute in association with The Liffey Press.

Caplow, T. (1954). *The sociology of work.* Minneapolis: University of Minnesota Press.

Central Statistics Office. (1986). *Census 1986 Dublin.* The Stationery Office.

Clancy, P. (1988). *Who goes to college?* Dublin: Higher Education Authority.

Clancy, P. (2001). *College entry in focus: A Fourth National Survey of access to higher education.* Dublin: Higher Education Authority.

Clancy, P., & Wall, J. (2000). *Social background of higher education entrants.* Dublin: Higher Education Authority.

Crompton, R. (2010). Class and employment. *Work, Employment and Society, 24*(1), 9–26.

Drudy, S. (1991). The classification of social class in sociological research. *British Journal of Sociology, 42*(1), 21–41.

Erikson, R. (1984). Social class of men, women, and families. *Sociology, 18*, 500–514.

Goldthorpe, J. H (2000). *On sociology.* Oxford: Oxford University Press.

Goldthorpe, J. H. (2002). Globalisation and social class. *West European Politics, 25*(3), 1–28.

Goldthorpe, J. H. (2007). *On sociology. Volume Two: Illustration and retrospect.* Stanford: Stanford University Press.

Goldthorpe, J. H., & Marshall, G. (1992). The promising future of class analysis: A response to recent critics. *Sociology, 26*(3), 381–400.

Grusky, D. B., & Sørensen, J. B. (1998). Can class analysis be salvaged? *American Journal of Sociology, 103*, 1187–1234.

Grusky, D. B., & Sørensen, J. B. (2001). Are there big social classes? In D. B. Grusky (Ed.), *Social stratification: Class, race, and gender in sociological perspective* (2nd ed., pp. 183–194). Boulder, CO: Westview Press.

Grusky, D. B., & Weeden, K. A. (2001a). Class analysis and the heavy weight of convention. *Acta Sociologica, 45*(3), 229–236.

Grusky, D. B., & Weeden., K. A. (2001b). Decomposition without death: A research agenda for a new class analysis. *Acta Sociologica, 44*, 203–218.

Harrison, E., & Rose, D. (2006). *The European Socio-economic Classification User Guide.* Colchester: ISER, University of Essex.

Jonsson, J. O., Grusky, D. B., Di Carlo, M., Pollak, R., & Brinton, M. C. (2009). Microclass mobility: Social reproduction in four countries. *American Journal of Sociology, 114,* 977–1036.

Korupp, S. E., Ganzeboom, H. B. G., & Van Der Lippe, T. (2002). Do mothers matter? A comparison of models of the influence of mothers' and fathers' educational and occupational status on children's educational attainment'. *Quality and Quantity, 36,* 17–42.

König, W., Lüttinger, P., & Müller, W., (1988). *Comparative analysis of the development and structure of educational systems.* CASMIN working papers. Institut fur Sozialwissenschaften, Universitat: Mannheim.

Lockwood, D. (1966). Sources of variation in working class images of society. *Sociological Review, 14*(3), 244–267.

Marshall, G., Rose, D., Newby, H., & Vogler, C. (1988). *Social class in modern Britain.* London: Hutchinson.

McCoy, S., & Byrne, D. (2011). The sooner the better I could get out of there: Barriers to higher education access in Ireland. *Irish Educational Studies, 30*(2), 141–157.

McCoy, S., Byrne, D., O'Connell, P.J., Kelly, E., & Doherty, C. (2010). *Hidden disadvantage? A Study on the low participation in higher education by the non-manual group.* ESRI:HEA.

McCoy, S., & Smyth, E. (2011). Higher education expansion and differentiation in the Republic of Ireland. *Higher Education, 61*(3), 243–260.

O'Connell, P. J., Clancy, D., & McCoy, S. (2006a). *Who went to college in 2004? A National Survey of new entrants to higher education.* Dublin: HEA.

O'Hare, A., Whelan, C. T., & Commins, P. (1991). The development of an Irish census-based social class scale. *The Economic and Social Review, 22*(2), 135–156.

Shavit, Y., Arum, R., & Gamoran, A. (2007). *Stratification in higher education. A comparative study.* Palo Alto: Stanford University Press.

Shavit, Y., & Muller, W. (1998). *From school to work.* Oxford: Oxford University Press.

Smyth, E. (1999). Educational inequalities among school leavers in Ireland 1979–1994. *Economic and Social Review, 30*(3), 267–284.

Van de Werfhorst, H. G., & Luijkx, R. (2010). Educational fields of study and social mobility: Disaggregating social origin and education'. *Sociology, 44*(4), 695–715.

Weeden, K. A., & Grusky, D. B. (2005a). The case for a new class map. *American Journal of Sociology, 111*(1), 141–212.

Weeden, K. A., & Grusky, D. B. (2005b). Are there any big classes at all? *Research in Social Stratification and Mobility, 22*, 3–56.

Whelan, C. T., & Hannan, D. F. (1999). Class inequalities in educational attainment among the adult population in the Republic of Ireland. *Economic and Social Review*, *30*(3), 285–307.

Whelan, C. T., & Layte, R. (2002). Late Industrialisation and the increased Merit Selection Hypothesis: Ireland as a test case. *European Sociological Review*, *18*, 35–50.

Whelan, C. T., & Layte, R. (2006). Economic boom and social mobility: The Irish experience. *Research in Social Stratification and Mobility*, *24*, 193–208.

PART IV
MODELING TECHNIQUES
AND MEASUREMENTS

MEASURING SOCIAL INEQUALITY IN EDUCATIONAL ATTAINMENT

Ottar Hellevik

ABSTRACT

In the literature on the relationship between class of origin and educational attainment, the typical conclusion is that class inequality was stable over the last century, and the attempts at egalitarian reform thus proven ineffective. The conclusion turns out to depend on the choice of statistical measure, in this case loglinear measures of association. Also linear measures of association give similar results. If instead, measures of inequality are used, the contrasting conclusion of a strong reduction in the class bias in recruitment to higher education emerges.

As the provision of higher education has increased over time, the trends in the results of these three measures differ. It is argued that it is measures of inequality that capture inequality in the allocation of higher education or bias in the allocation mechanisms. The argument in favor of using loglinear measures has been the special property of "margin insensitivity" attributed to them. It has also been suggested that they capture bias in the allocation mechanism, which may develop in a way different from the trend in the inequality of the allocation outcome. It is argued that neither claim is tenable.

Keywords: Inequality; margin insensitivity; linear; loglinear; inequality measures

Class and Stratification Analysis
Comparative Social Research, Volume 30, 319–339
Copyright © 2013 by Emerald Group Publishing Limited
All rights of reproduction in any form reserved
ISSN: 0195-6310/doi:10.1108/S0195-6310(2013)0000030015

INTRODUCTION

Systematic differences between social groups in their access to privileged positions and attractive goods are found in all societies. Such differences are passed on from generation to generation through biases in the processes of allocation that favor the offspring of privileged parents. The educational system plays a key role in the allocation of attractive positions and goods in modern society. At the beginning of the 20th century, higher education was mainly available to children from the upper class. But with the expansion of higher education in the second half of the century, an increasing number of children from less-privileged social groups were given access to institutions of higher learning. What this means for the reproduction of social inequality has been a matter of dispute, springing from a disagreement concerning how to measure social inequality in educational attainment.

The study of recruitment to higher education is characterized by methodologically sophisticated analyses of large high-quality datasets. The extensive number of scientific publications makes this one of the most thoroughly researched and well-documented social processes. An outsider cannot fail to be impressed by the active and well-integrated international mileu of researchers within the *Research Committee on Social Stratification and Mobility (RC28)* of the International Sociological Association (here-after referred to as SSM). Equally impressive is the high degree of consensus within this milieu regarding how the research should be carried out.

It may be argued, however, that some of the choices central to this methodological consensus have been unfortunate, leading to incorrect conclusions regarding important empirical realities. This concerns the choice between three kinds of statistical measures that may be used to study social differences in recruitment to higher education: loglinear and linear measures of association and measures of inequality. Loglinear analysis has been the preferred technique within SSM, but there are compelling reasons for instead using one of the other two, the choice depending on the research question. When studying inequality in the distribution of higher education across classes or bias in the allocation mechanisms, measures of inequality are the appropriate ones. When interested in a causal decomposition of the association between class of origin and education, occupation or income, linear measures should be used.

This view has previous work on related statistical problems within political science as its point of departure (Hellevik, 1983a, 1983b, 1984). The arguments against the reliance on loglinear analysis have been presented in several articles (Hellevik, 1997, 2000, 2002, 2007, 2009). Others have made similar points (Lampard, 2000; Logan, 1996; Marks, 2004; Ringen,1997, 2000, 2005, 2006), or based their conclusions on measures of inequality (Glennerster & Low,1990; Saunders, 1996). So far, however, the critique seems mostly to have been ignored. For instance, when Breen and Jonsson (2005) reviewed recent developments in the field, they did not mention alternative approaches to measuring inequality and the resulting divergence in results. In the few instances where the critique has been explicitly addressed, it has been rejected (Kivinen, Ahola, & Hedman, 2001; Kivinen, Hedman, & Ahola, 2002; Marshall & Swift,1999, 2000).

At the spring meeting of RC28 in Brno, Czech Republic in 2007, Stein Ringen and I were invited to present papers, and there was a panel debate. This was a welcome opportunity for discussion, and there were indications that a reconsideration of positions may be under way. The *Czech Sociological Review* had invited the panel participants and other central SSM researchers to contribute to a special issue.[1] Regrettably, the only presentation submitted was my paper (Hellevik, 2007), thus putting an end to the debate started at the meeting.[2]

The chapter starts with a brief review of the literature on the class–education relationship, where the typical conclusion is one of stable class inequality and ineffective egalitarian reform. This is based on results from analyses using loglinear measures of association. If instead measures of inequality are used, the contrasting conclusion of a strong reduction in the class bias in the recruitment to higher education emerges.

To better understand this discrepancy in results, the properties of the three kinds of statistical measures are compared. In a situation where the provision of higher education increases over time, the trends in the results of these three measures differ. The justification for using loglinear measures rather than measures of inequality has been the special property of "margin insensitivity" attributed to them. It has also been suggested that the loglinear measures capture bias in the allocation *mechanism*, which may develop in a way different from the trend in the inequality of the allocation *outcome*. It is argued that neither claim is tenable.

STABLE INEQUALITY AND INEFFECTIVE EDUCATIONAL REFORMS

In a series of studies of class differences in recruitment to higher educational or occupational positions in Britain, class inequality has been described as essentially unchanging, also during periods of energetic policy reform. From this, it has been concluded that reformist policies are inadequate in relation to egalitarian goals. A few quotes illustrate the unequivocal conclusions drawn.[3]

The empirical results mean that "... no significant reduction in class inequalities was in fact achieved" (Goldthorpe, Llewellyn, & Payne et al., 1987, p. 328), and that "... the terms of the competition between the classes has shown little sign of change" (Heath & Clifford, 1990, p. 15).

The implication is that the egalitarian reforms have failed: "Neither the meritocratic reforms of the 1944 Act nor comprehensive reorganization can, in this respect at least, be said to have succeeded" (Heath & Clifford, 1990, p. 15). "The implications of the findings ... have therefore to count as rather grave ones for the general strategy of egalitarian reform that was pursued during the post-war period" (Goldthorpe et al., 1987, p. 328). "The post-war project of creating in Britain a more open society, through economic expansion, educational reform and egalitarian social policies, has signally failed to secure its objectives" (Marshall, Newby, Rose, & Vogler, 1988, p. 138).

This failure is all the more conspicuous since the post-war period of economic growth should have offered exceptionally favorable conditions for egalitarian reform. The consequence, however, "... of post-war economic growth was not that it facilitated egalitarian reform but rather that it obscured its failure" (Goldthorpe et al., 1987, p. 328). The reformers underestimated "... the resistance that the class structure can offer to attempts to change it; or, to speak less figuratively, the flexibility and effectiveness with which the more powerful and advantaged groupings in society can use the resources at their disposal to preserve their privileged positions" (Goldthorpe et al., 1987, p. 328). "... the advantaged social classes have been able to outmanoeuvre the social reformers" (Heath, Mills, & Roberts, 1992, p. 219).

Describing the pattern of class inequality in educational attainment as stable and reforms as ineffective is not restricted to British studies. In their introduction to the impressive volume of comparative analyses of the educational systems of 13 different countries, titled *Persistent inequality*, Blossfeld and Shavit sum up the results as follows: "... despite the marked expansion of all the educational systems under study, in most countries there has been little change in socioeconomic inequality of educational opportunity." (1993, p. 19). "Finally, the impact of educational reforms on changes in educational stratification seems to be negligible. Nowhere have

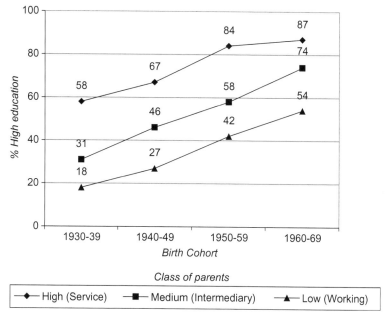

Fig. 1. Birth Cohort, Class of Origin and Educational Attainment in Britain (Percentage of High Education. Data: see note 4).

they reduced inequalities of educational opportunity between socioeconomic strata." (1993, p. 21).

Fig. 1 based on data used in an article by Heath and Clifford (1990) shows the proportion with a high level of education for three classes of origin within different birth cohorts in Britain.[4] The overall increase in the provision of an O-level education is remarkable, from 28% in the oldest to 68% in the youngest cohort, which are just 30 years apart.

The absolute increase in percentage points is approximately the same for the three classes, preserving the pattern of marked class differences in educational attainment during this period of rapid educational expansion. Results like these constitute the empirical basis for the conclusions of no reduction in inequality and ineffective educational reforms. But how the trend in social differences is described turns out to depend very much on the choice of statistical measure.

THREE KINDS OF MEASURES

We shall start by comparing the general properties of the three kinds of statistical measures used to analyze the class-by-education table: linear measures of association, loglinear measures of association, and measures of inequality. Fig. 2 shows how these measures behave in a hypothetical scenario. It reflects the actual empirical tendencies, where the provision of higher education increases, while the linear association between class and education remains stable. The PD (the absolute difference in proportions) is kept constant at 0.20 in the figure. The interpretation is straightforward, as it shows the absolute difference or gap between two classes in the probability of obtaining higher education.

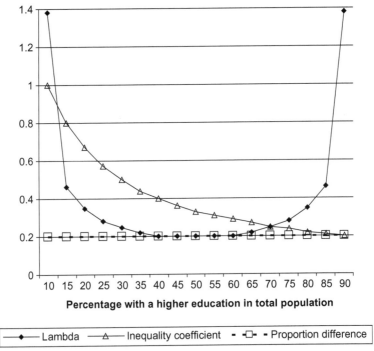

Fig. 2. Results for the Lambda Coefficient (Loglinear Association), the Proportion Difference (Linear Association), and the Inequality Coefficient for Comparisons of Two Groups of Equal Size, with Different Levels of Provision of Higher Education (Proportions for High Education in the Two Groups Lying, Respectively, 0.10 Above and 0.10 Below the Total Population Level).

The loglinear measures, here represented by the lambda coefficient, cannot be given such a simple and intuitively meaningful explanation. Lambda equals one-quarter of the logistic regression coefficient, which in turn is the natural logarithm of the odds ratio (OR), which is the ratio between two odds, each being a ratio between the proportion having and the proportion not having obtained a higher education. The reason for using the lambda coefficient in the figure is that its results are usually identical to or just slightly higher than those of the PD for the same empirical data.[5]

The "inequality coefficient" (IC) used in Fig. 1. is defined as 1 – PR. The "participation ratio" (PR) is the ratio between the proportions obtaining a higher education within two classes. (PR may accordingly also stand for the proportion or probability ratio.) It has also been called the disparity ratio (Saunders, 1996), but is perhaps best-known as relative risk (Hosmer & Lemeshow, 1989). The PR is identical to another measure of inequality, the ratio of advantage ratios.[6]

When the lowest proportion is used as the denominator of the fraction, the PR varies between 0 (minimum equality where none of the good goes to the less fortunate group) and 1 (maximum equality where the two proportions are equal). The IC accordingly acquires the value 0, where there is no inequality, and 1, where inequality is at its maximum.

The horizontal axis in Fig. 2 may be interpreted as a time axis, with an increasing provision of higher education over time. The linear PD and the loglinear lambda are identical or close in value when the proportions compared lie within the range between 0.25 and 0.75, but show divergent results when the proportions approach the extreme values of 0 or 1, where the loglinear effects are much stronger than the linear ones.

Starting out from proportions with a higher education near 0, the loglinear measures behave similarly to the inequality measures as the provision increases.[7] The lambda shows a decreasing association, and the inequality coefficient shows decreasing inequality. However, this parallel in the trends ceases when we move past the midpoint of 50% of the population with a higher education and approach 100%. There, according to the lambda, the association rises, while the IC continues to drop. When, 80% and 100% of the population in the two classes, respectively, obtain a higher education, the lambda exceeds 1, while the IC with a value of 0.2 reaches its minimum value, given that the gap between the two groups is fixed at 20 percentage points.[8]

The reason for the difference in results is that the loglinear measures, in contrast to the inequality measures, treat the two extremes of the dependent variable as identical. For the lambda, it is of no consequence whether the level for higher education in the population is 10% or 90%. For measures of inequality, however, there is a fundamental difference in meaning between 10% and 90% having obtained the good in question. Or, to put it another way, the values of the dependent variable, high and low education, are treated symmetrically by the loglinear and asymmetrically by the inequality measures.

A DIFFERENT STORY

Returning to the British data in Fig. 1, the conclusion of stable inequality is based on using measures of association, whether linear or loglinear, to describe the trends (Table 1). But a very different story emerges when the same data are analyzed with a measure designed to capture inequality in the distribution of a good.

Table 1 shows the results for the IC. They indicate that instead of being stable, class inequality in the last cohort is reduced to nearly half of what it was in the first cohort.

Also shown in the table is a more complex measure of inequality, the bivariate version of the Gini coefficient – the so-called coefficient of concentration – which measures the degree to which a good (higher education) is concentrated across a population grouped according to a different variable (social class).[9] The coefficient is calculated by comparing the

Table 1.   Class of Origin and Educational Attainment: Measures of Association and Inequality (Comparing Service and Working Class, Data from Fig. 1).

	Birth Cohort			
	1930–39	1940–49	1950–59	1960–69
Linear association				
Proportion difference ($= P_s - P_w =$ linear b)	0.40	0.40	0.42	0.33
1930–39 = 100	100	100	105	83
Loglinear association				
Lambda ($=\frac{1}{4}$ logistic b or $\frac{1}{4}$ ln $OR_{s/w}$)	0.46	0.43	0.49	0.42
1930–39 = 100	100	93	107	91
Inequality				
Inequality coefficient IC $= 1 -$ PR	0.69	0.60	0.50	0.38
1930–39 = 100	100	87	72	55
Gini-coefficient (comparing all three classes)	0.24	0.20	0.15	0.10
1930–39 = 100	100	80	60	44

cumulative distribution of places in higher education across the three classes with the classes' cumulative share of the population. If every group gets a share of positions in higher education in direct proportion to its share of the population, the Gini-coefficient is 0. The reduction shown in Table 1, as we move from older to younger cohorts, indicates that the distribution of places of higher education across classes over time comes closer and closer to the class distribution of the population. Or to put it another way, the social composition of those members of the population attaining a higher education becomes steadily more representative for (similar to) the entire population.[10]

An alternative interpretation of what has taken place in the educational system in the past century is that the importance of class of origin for the probability of attaining a higher education remains strong throughout the period. In a path-analytic framework, this would be interpreted as a strong and stable causal effect of class on education. But the decrease in inequality measures tells us that a rising level of education in the population, in combination with a stable association between class and education, has produced a steady reduction in the degree of inequality in the distribution of higher education across classes.

New research on the relationship between class and education has found, according to a recent review, that there in several countries now are trends of a decreasing association between class and educational attainment (Breen & Jonsson, 2005). This further weakens the persistent inequality thesis, and implies an even steeper reduction in inequality according to inequality measures.

ARE LOGLINEAR MEASURES "MARGIN INSENSITIVE"?

Considering how central the concept of inequality is to the study of class differences in educational attainment, it is surprising that the statistics called "measures of inequality" have more or less been overlooked in the SSM literature. One possible reason may be that such measures are not so much used in sociology. They are rarely mentioned in statistical textbooks for sociologists, in contrast to textbooks for political scientists.[11]

Pointing out the divergent results for the different kinds of measures, has not been sufficient to find acceptance for the view that measures of inequality, rather than loglinear measures of association, should be used to analyze class inequality. One reason for this may have been the widespread belief that loglinear measures have special properties that take care of the objections discussed above.

When either the provision of higher education or the class composition of society changes, this supposedly does not affect the association shown by the loglinear measures. These measures are said to capture the effect "net of" such changes in the marginals of the class-by-education table, thus reflecting the "true nature" of the allocation mechanism. The pattern of stable association and decreasing inequality is accordingly interpreted as a result of a stable allocation mechanism working within a changing framework of increasing provision.

In his seminal article presenting the idea of *margin insensitivity* in the analysis of class and educational attainment, Mare writes, "Under the logistic response model, differences in background effects, either over school transitions or over cohorts, cannot result from changing marginal distributions of either independent or dependent variables because such changes do not affect the [loglinear measure]." Since the loglinear measures are "invariant under changes in the marginal distributions of the variables," they give "true effects" (Mare, 1981, p. 75).

We find similar statements in later contributions to the educational attainment literature, as for instance, "In addition because the Mare model is based on the odds ratio, which is insensitive to marginal distributions, the parameters of the model are unaffected by aggregate expansion or contraction of the educational system" (Breen & Jonsson, 2000, p. 758). "This [logit analysis] will ensure that we focus on measuring the mechanism behind the distribution of education across class backgrounds – our estimates will not be confounded if there is an overall increase (or decrease) in the general transition probabilities" (Erikson & Jonsson, 1996, p. 75). The loglinear measures are described as "margin free" (Grusky & Tienda, 1993, p. vii), and as "revealing the 'pure' association between origin characteristics and educational attainment" (Breen & Jonsson, 2005, p. 225). The use of the loglinear model is hailed as a methodological breakthrough, making it "… possible to specify the intrinsic association between variables after purging out nuisance variability in marginal distributions" (Grusky & Tienda,1993, p. vii).

The idea of margin insensitivity seems to have been inspired by a statistics textbook (Bishop, Fienberg, & Holland,1975), which is the only reference given in central texts such as Mare (1981, p. 74) and Erikson and Goldthorpe (1992, p. 56). Other texts refer to Mare (1981) or give no references at all. Bishop et al. (1975, p. 14) say that the odds ratio (called the cross-product ratio) is "invariant under row and column multiplications." If we multiply columns and/or rows with constants (different from 0), this does not change the OR, even though the marginals of the table will change.

Table 2 illustrates what this means. In the cells of the left column, frequencies *a* and *c* have been multiplied by *X*, and in the cells of the upper row, *a* and *b* have been multiplied by *Y*. This produces a change in the marginals; for instance, an increase in the proportion with a higher education in the population, and in the proportion with an upper class background. The formula for the OR shows why this measure and other measures derived from it such as lambda are unaffected by row/column multiplication with constants. The constants appear in the nominator as well as the denominator of the fraction and are thus cancelled out. Further, the proportion difference is unaffected by multiplication by *X* in cells with the same value on the independent variable (i.e. columns in Table 2). Changes in the distribution of the independent variable from multiplication by a constant do not alter the result for the PD. But row multiplication in Table 2, which changes the distribution on the dependent variable, affects the linear measure of association, but only slightly unless the distribution on the dependent variable (education) becomes very skewed.

What is the implication of all this? What the statisticians say is precise and clear – no change in OR when columns and/or rows of the table are multiplied by a constant – an operation that also changes the marginal distributions. However, in the educational attainment literature, this statement has been given a much wider and unfounded interpretation. We have a logically untenable deduction, from *insensitivity in relation to one specific kind of change in the marginals* to the claim that the OR is *insensitive to marginal changes in general*. But if, for instance, we were to multiply the frequency in just one of the cells, then the marginal distributions and the OR

Table 2. Class and Education: Row and Column Multiplication by, Respectively, X and Y.

	Before Multiplication			After Multiplication		
	Upper class	Lower class	SUM	Upper class	Lower class	SUM
High education	a	b	a+b	XYa	Yb	Y(Xa + b)
Low education	c	d	c+d	Xc	D	Xc + d
SUM	a+c	b+d		X(Ya + c)	Yb + d	

Before: OR = (a/c)/(b/d) = ad/bc
After: OR = (XYa/Xc)/(Yb/d) = XYad/XYbc = ad/bc

Before: PD = a/(a + c)–b/(b + d)
After: PD = XYa/X(Ya + c)–Yb/(Yb + d) = Ya/(Ya + c)–Yb/(Yb + d)

would both be altered. For all kinds of marginal changes that are not the result of column and/or row multiplication with constants, it is difficult to see what could be the meaning of the concept of "margin insensitivity."

One might have thought that the above discussion would be sufficient to lay the notion of "margin insensitivity" to rest. However, the experience in the debate so far is that those who believe that there is such a thing as margin insensitivity are not easily persuaded otherwise. Therefore, further arguments against the use of loglinear measures as indicators of bias in allocation mechanisms will be presented in the next two sections.

A FUNDAMENTAL DIFFERENCE BETWEEN LOGLINEAR AND LINEAR MEASURES?

The belief that loglinear measures are margin insensitive manifests itself in descriptions of a fundamental difference in substantive meaning between loglinear and linear measures of association. In his influential 1981 article, Mare makes the following distinction between linear and loglinear measures:

> Simple differences in proportions continuing in school among background groups change over cohorts primarily in response to the average level of proportions, rather than in response to changes in the principles by which schooling is allocated. By contrast, statistical models that measure the association between school continuation and social background, net of the marginal distribution of schooling, [i.e. loglinear measures] are sensitive to changes in the principles by which schooling is allocated and not to changes in the dispersion of the schooling distribution. (Mare, 1981, p. 83)

However, the claim that loglinear and linear measures capture quite different aspects of the allocation process is undermined when we take into consideration how similar, in most instances, the results for the two kinds of measures are. There is no difference at all when the distribution of the independent variable (the class composition of society) changes. Also, if the distribution of the dependent variable (education) changes, there is little or no difference in results for loglinear and linear measures as long as the proportions compared lie within the interval of 0.25–0.75.

We may thus have a society undergoing all kinds of changes with regard to its class composition, and also have a dramatic increase in the level of higher education, for instance from 35% to 65% for the total population, without there being any noticeable difference in results between the linear proportion difference and the loglinear lambda. The suggestion that there is a fundamental difference in substantive meaning between the two kinds of statistical measures is thus not tenable within a "normal" range of variation for the level of higher education in a society. This means that in analyses of class inequality, the important distinction is *not* between linear and loglinear measures, but between the two kinds of measures of association on the one hand and the measures of inequality on the other.

When we move toward the extremes of the distribution on the dependent variable, however, there is an increasing gap between the results for linear and loglinear measures. This has implications for the choice of measure if we want to do a causal (or path) analysis, as is sometimes the case for SSM-studies: "The causes and consequences of social inequality have been hot issues among social scientists of various disciplines for several decades."[12] An example is analyses of the role of education as an intervening variable in the process linking class of origin and occupational destination (Heath et al., 1992).

When analyzing changes in the importance of direct versus indirect effect in this causal model, the linear regression coefficient guarantees a perfect decomposition of bivariate associations, in the sense that the sum of components will always add up to the bivariate association. This will not be the case with the loglinear measure lambda when it departs from the results for the linear regression coefficient. Accordingly, logistic regression is not suited for causal/path analyses (Davis & Schooler, 1974; Fienberg, 1977; Hellevik, 1984, 2009; Reynolds, 1977).[13]

A DIFFERENT TREND FOR MECHANISM AND OUTCOME?

Marshal and Swift (1999, 2000), judging from their replies in the debate in *Acta Sociologica*, were not convinced by the above arguments against the idea of margin insensitivity. They did accept, however, that the distribution of higher education among classes had become less unequal, as shown by the inequality measures. But according to them, the results of the loglinear measures are more interesting, since they capture something essential – namely, the bias in the allocation mechanism itself – which appears to be highly persistent over time.

Here one may ask whether it is possible to have a process where the bias in the allocation mechanism develops in a way that is different from the inequality in the allocation outcome. Owing to the extreme complexity of the process of recruitment to higher education, attempts to specify in any detail the concrete nature of the mechanisms involved in allocating educational positions are rarely made. Instead the mechanisms are treated as black boxes, and conclusions about their unknown contents are based on the outcome as shown in the class-by-education table.

If the "fairness" of the allocation mechanism is something that has to be inferred from the results it produces, a divergence with regard to bias/inequality in mechanism and outcome is by definition impossible. Inferences about stability or change in the unknown allocation mechanism would be based on information of stability or change in the inequality of the distributional outcome of the allocation process.

To be able to prove that mechanism and outcome may show divergent trends, one would have to "look inside" the black box, in order to find indicators of bias in the mechanism, which are independent of the outcome. I have suggested various sampling models as representations of the allocation process (Hellevik, 1997, p. 390, 2000, pp. 82–83; 2002, pp. 155–157). The models are extremely simple, and of course nowhere near a realistic representation of the actual recruitment processes. Nevertheless, they are realistic in the sense that they represent methods of selection that could have produced the results found in empirical studies of class differences in educational attainment.

Table 3 presents two such models, using as an illustration a situation where there is an increase of 40 percentage points in the level of higher education in both classes. The PD and lambda show a *stable association* between class and education, and the IC shows *decreasing inequality* over time. (To simplify calculations, the two classes are assumed to be of equal size.)

The question now is what the two sampling models, each representing a process of recruitment to higher education that would have produced the outcome shown in Table 3, will tell us about bias in the allocation mechanism. Is the bias stable, as Marshal and Swift (1999) would infer from the stable loglinear measures? Or is there less mechanism bias at Time 2, as the inequality measures suggest?

If we imagine that recruitment to higher education is done by means of quota sampling, the quotas are clearly biased at Time 1, since the upper class gets more than their share of the population (67% compared with 50%). The quotas at Time 2 are less biased since, to produce the results in the table, they must have been fixed so as to make the social composition of the sample more similar to the 50–50% distribution on classes in the population. The sample distribution has changed from 67–33% at Time 1 to 57–43% at Time 2. If we regard the additional positions of higher education allocated at Time 2 as a new quota sample, added to the original one with a 67–33 distribution, the 50–50 composition of the additional sample is

Table 3. Two Sampling Models for Recruitment to Higher Education (Classes of Equal Size).

Class	Time 1		Time 2		Conclusion with Regard to
	Lower	Upper	Lower	Upper	change from time 1 to 2
% Higher education	20	40	60	80	
Proportion difference U – L	0.20		0.20		Stable association
Odds	0.25	0.67	1.50	4.00	
Odds ratio U / L	2.67		2.67		Stable association
Lambda	0.25		0.25		Stable association
Participation ratio: L / U	0.50		0.75		Increased equality
Inequality coefficient (1– PR)	0.50		0.25		Reduced inequality
% quota of sample	33	67	43	57	Reduced selection bias
% additional quota at time 2	–	–	50	50	Reduced selection bias
Sampling fraction	0.2	0.4	0.6	0.8	
Difference in sampling fractions	0.2		0.2		
Ratio of sampling fractions	0.5		0.75		
Weights needed to make sample representative of population	1.52	0.75	1.16	0.88	Reduced selection bias

proportionate to the population distribution. The allocation of the "new" positions among classes is unbiased since it reflects the class composition of society.

Either way, the conclusion from the quota sampling model is clear: There is a change in the selection mechanism (the quota distribution) that makes it less biased at Time 2 than it was at Time 1. In other words, the trend of *mechanism bias* is the same as the trend of *outcome inequality* shown by inequality measures. Both indicate decreased inequality/bias, in contrast to the stable results shown by the loglinear and linear measures of association.

If we instead use stratified random sampling as a selection model, bias in the mechanism may be defined as disproportionality, which is indicated by the difference between the sampling fractions within the two classes. However, this difference may be described in two ways: as the absolute difference, or as the ratio between the fractions. The first is the same as the proportion difference (PD), the second the same as the proportion or participation ratio (PR). Thus, we are back where we started, forced to choose between measures of association and inequality to describe selection bias.

However, there is a criterion for determining the degree of bias in the sampling procedure that may solve the question of change or stability in the selection mechanism. With a disproportionate sample, weighting is used to restore representativity. The weights are calculated as the ratio between a group's share of the population and its share of the sample. The closer the weights are to the value 1, the less bias there is in the sampling procedure that needs to be corrected through weighting. Table 3 shows that the weights needed at time 1 to correct for sampling bias are further away from unity than the weights at time 2.[14]

What both models show is that when the outcome of the allocation process becomes less unequal according to measures of inequality, the selection mechanism is less biased, and not stable, according to the composition of the quotas and the sampling weights. It is thus measures of inequality, and not loglinear measures, that capture the trend for bias in the allocation mechanisms.[15]

Those who would still insist that loglinear measures reflect bias in the selection procedures, face the challenge of arguing against the relevance of the above models, and of establishing counterexamples in the form of models in which the distribution of higher education may become more equal at the same time as the bias in the allocation mechanism remains unchanged. This challenge was made early on in the debate (Hellevik, 2000, 2002), but so far no one has taken it up.

CONCLUSION

For anyone interested in the importance of methodological choices for substantive conclusions drawn in empirical social research, the debate on class inequality in educational attainment ought to be fascinating. No one can deny the great theoretical and practical implications of the question discussed. This makes it all the more remarkable that the views differ so sharply on what actually took place during the second half of the past century with regard to recruitment to higher education.

The prevailing view in the literature of educational attainment seems to be that reforms aimed at reducing bias in the allocation mechanisms have been without effect. Reforms expanding the provision of higher education, although increasing recruitment from the working class, have not contributed to reducing class inequality.

For some, the expansion is even seen as the culprit, responsible for the preservation of bias: "As long as the educational attainment of lower social strata is rapidly increasing, political attention can neglect any parallel increases among the privileged classes. Thus, educational expansion can alleviate political pressure to reduce inequalities. (...) the modernization theorists' hypothesis that educational expansion results in greater equality of educational opportunity must be turned on its head; expansion actually facilitates to a large extent the persistence of inequalities in educational opportunity" (Blossfeld & Shavit, 1993, p. 22).

The opposing view presented here is that there has in fact been a substantial reduction of inequality in educational opportunity. This is the trend for measures of inequality. Increasing the provision of higher education may have contributed to this result.

There are indications that the view on the consequences of increasing the provision of higher education may be changing. Yossi Shavit, in his presentation for the final plenary session at the RC28 Brno meeting, said that it has been a mistake to regard educational expansion as a "nuisance" to be adjusted for, and suggested that it be brought back into the recruitment models instead of being ignored.[16] One way of doing this, would be to use measures of inequality.

To reduce the association between class and educational attainment, one would have to accomplish a reversal of bias in the allocation of new positions/goods, favoring the underprivileged in order to compensate for the existing pattern of inequality. If the goal of the egalitarian reforms was to achieve such a radical change in allocation principles, the observed stability in association would indicate a lack of success.

With increasing provision of a good, however, egalitarian goals can be furthered also through more "moderate" reforms, aiming not at reversing, but at reducing or removing the bias for new allocations. The reduction of inequality in this case will be slower, and complete elimination of inequality impossible, since the original gap in educational level is allowed to persist. But the impact of this persisting difference on social inequality is gradually reduced as the framework of the allocation process changes. As the British experience proves, impressive egalitarian changes may still be accomplished, in ways that are less conflict-generating than radical reforms reversing the pattern of bias in the distribution of additional positions.

NOTES

1. "In the Summer issue of the *Czech Sociological Review*, we published an article by Stein Ringen on THE TRUTH ABOUT CLASS INEQUALITY. In it the autor challenges 'the stability thesis' of trends in class inequality, as was summarised by J.H. Goldthorpe, referring to the high degree of 'temporal constancy and cross-national communality' in social mobility. At a CSR board meeting held this spring in

Prague, the idea emerged to open a debate on this thesis and present the related discussion on the pages of the CSR. After consultation with Stein Ringen, Robert M. Hauser and PetrMateju, I have decided to invite contributions from the following leading scholars in social stratification: John H. Goldthorpe, Robert M. Hauser, Ottar Hellevik, Michael Hout, John Logan, Petr Mateju, Ray Pahl, Peter Saunders and Yu Xie." Excerpt from the letter "Invitation to a debate," sent by Editor-in-Chief Jiří Večerník October 10, 2006.

2. Based on the notes I took at the meeting, I have discussed some of the objections made by my opponents in the debate (Hellevik, 2007).

3. A more extensive list of similar quotes is found in Hellevik (1997).

4. The figure is based on the same data as Table 7, Heath and Clifford (1990, p. 12), but without differentiation according to gender, and classes categorized as follows: Service class: 1–2, Intermediary class: 3–5, Working class: 6–7. High education: O-level or higher. Anthony Heath kindly provided the data necessary to make these calculations.

5. If instead, the lambda coefficient is kept constant, this would produce a figure showing the values of lambda as a horizontal line and those of PD as a curve starting out from values close to 0 when the level of education is low, climbing to 0.20 for medium levels, and again sinking towards 0 as the provision of higher education approaches 100%.

6. The advantage ratio is the proportion of a good possessed by a group – here the proportion of positions in higher education obtained by a class – divided by its population share. A ratio of more than 1 indicates a privileged situation, a ratio below 1 correspondingly an underprivileged position. The closer to 1 the RAR – the ratio between these two ratios – is, the more equal the distribution of higher education.

7. The OR is in fact sometimes described as the ratio between probabilities, or the PR. However, this is not correct in general. What the OR shows is the ratio between odds, not between proportions. But when the proportions are small, the results for the OR are similar to the ratio of proportions. In epidemiological research, the OR is therefore sometimes referred to as relative risk (Hosmer & Lemeshow, 1989). In analyses of survey data, however, where the phenomena studied usually occur more frequently, this interpretation will be misleading.

8. To calculate the OR and the Lambda in the extreme case, the percentages 99.9 and 79.9 at the upper end of the axis and correspondingly 20.1 and 0.1 at the lower end are used, which gives a Lambda of 1.38.

9. The groups are ranked according to their advantage ratio (the proportion of the good divided by the proportion of the population). See Lambert (1993) for a formal exposition of the Gini-coefficient. The Lorenz curve and the calculation of the Gini coefficient for this table are shown in Hellevik (1997).

10. Also, changes in the class composition of society may affect inequality. Unlike both the linear and loglinear measures of association, as well as inequality measures such as the IC and the PR, the Gini coefficient is also sensitive to changes in the class marginal of the class-by-education table (Hellevik,1997).

11. Some early examples of statistics textbooks for political science that discuss measures of inequality such as the Gini Coefficient/Index are Alker (1965), Benson (1969), Hellevik (1971), and Leege and Francis (1974). In contrast, the Gini is not

mentioned in Blalock's classic sociology text (1960), nor in Galtung (1967), or Iversen (1979).

12. Quoted from: "Call for Papers: Social inequality and mobility in the life-course. Causes and consequences of social stratification. 7th July – 9th July 2011, Mannheim Centre for European Social Research, Mannheim, Germany."

13. Some would object that since obtaining a higher education or not is a dichotomy, linear regression cannot be used. The objections against linear analysis with a binary dependent variable are not as decisive as many seem to think (Hellevik, 2009). Two statistical arguments are given for the rejection of linear regression with a binary dependent variable. One is that linear coefficients may give meaningless results, since a predicted probability may fall outside the range 0–1. The risk for "impossible predictions" is not relevant in a causal analysis, however. What matters here is that the sum of causal components add up to the bivariate association, which they do with linear but not with logistic regression results.

The other objection is that the statistical tests from linear regression analyses are inappropriate with a binary dependent variable, since the assumption of homoscedastisity is violated. By means of simulations, it can be shown, however, that the significance probabilities from linear and logistic regression analyses turn out to be nearly identical, even with sample sizes unusually small for survey research and very skewed distributions on the dependent variable. The p values from the linear and logistic significance tests in 20% of the 320 cases were completely identical with four digit probabilities. In 43% of the comparisons, the difference was less than 0.001, in 90% less than 0.005 (Hellevik, 2009, p. 63). The theoretical objection against the linear test thus seems to be of little practical importance.

14. This is no surprise, since the ratio of the sampling weights in fact corresponds to the participation ratio.

15. In an article from 1996, John Logan developed another allocation model, a two-sided logit model (TSL), derived from a random matching model of opportunity, for the matching of individuals to jobs. He defined an explicit set of rules of access and was thereby able to test, through simulations, the effect of changes in demand (job offers) on loglinear measures. He concludes, "Margin insensitivity – the ability to multiply rows and columns without affecting odds ratios – does not guarantee demand insensitivity, the ability of parameters to measure the rules of access without being affected by shifts in demand. Loglinear models possess the former but not the latter property, while the situation is reversed for TSL models." (Logan, 1996, p. 176)

16. Quotes from the PowerPoint presentation by Yossi Shavit, Meir Yaish, and Eyal Bar Haim, posted at the conference website: "Despite the importance of educational expansion in the public and theoretical debate concerning IEO, it is usually ignored by empirical research. Rather, it is treated as a nuisance to be adjusted for." (From slide 5). "Effective egalitarian educational policy increases participation (expansion). However, much of our collective work ignores expansion and thus, misses an important beneficial outcome. Let's bring expansion back into our models" (From slide 26 – the final one). One way of doing this, would be to use measures of inequality, as suggested by Ringen and myself.

REFERENCES

Alker, H. R., Jr. (1965). *Mathematics and politics.* New York, NY: The Macmillan Co.
Benson, O. (1969). *Political science laboratory.* Columbus, Ohio: Charles E. Merrill Publishing Co.
Bishop, Y. M., Fienberg, S. E., & Holland, P. W. (1975). *Discrete multivariate analysis.* Cambridge: MIT Press.
Blalock, H. M. (1960). *Social statistics.* New York, NY: McGraw-Hill & Co.
Blossfeld, H. P., & Shavit, Y. (1993). Persisting barriers. Changes in educational opportunities in thirteen countries. In Y. Shavit & H.-P. Blossfeld (Eds.), *Persistent inequality. Changing educational attainment in thirteen countries* (pp. 1–23). Boulder: Westview Press.
Breen, R., & Jonsson, J. O. (2000). Analyzing educational careers: A multinomial transition model. *American Sociological Review*, 65, 754–772.
Breen, R., & Jonsson, J. O. (2005). Inequality of opportunity in comparative perspective: Recent research on educational attainment and social mobility. *Annual Review of Sociology, 31,* 223–243.
Davis, J. A., & Schooler, S. R. (1974). Nonparametric path analysis – The multivariate structure of dichotomous data when using the odds ratio or Yule's Q. *Social Science Research*, 3, 267–297.
Erikson, R., & Goldthorpe, J. H. (1992). *The constant flux. A study of class mobility in industrial societies.* Oxford: Clarendon Press.
Erikson, R., & Jonsson, J. O. (Eds.). (1996). Can education be equalized? . Boulder, CO: Westview.
Fienberg, S. M. (1977). *The analysis of cross-classified categorical data.* Cambridge: MIT Press.
Galtung, J. (1967). *Theory and methods of social research.* Oslo: Universitetsforlaget.
Glennerster, H., & Low, W. (1990). Education and the welfare state: Does it add up? In J. Hills (Ed.), *The state of welfare. The welfare state in Britain* since 1974, (pp. 28–87). Oxford: Clarendon Press.
Goldthorpe, J. H., Llewellyn, C., & Payne, C. (1987). *Social mobility and class structure in modern Britain* (2nd ed.). Oxford: Clarendon Press.
Grusky, D. B., & Tienda, M. (1993). Foreword. In Y. Shavit & H.-P. Blossfeld (Eds.), *Persistent inequality. Changing educational attainment in thirteen countries* (pp. vii–viii). Boulder, CO: Westview Press.
Heath, A. F., & Clifford, P. (1990). Class Inequalities in Education in the Twentieth Century. *Journal of the Royal Statistical Society, 153*(Series A), 1–16.
Heath, A. F., Mills, C., & Roberts, J. (1992). Towards meritocracy? Recent evidence on an old problem. In C. Crouch & A. Heath (Eds.), *Social research and social reform.* Oxford: Clarendon Press.
Hellevik, O. (1971). Forskningsmetode i sosiologi og statsvitenskap *(Research methods in sociology and political science).* (7th ed.). Oslo: Universitetsforlaget.
Hellevik, O. (1983a). Politisk deltakelse I Norge – begrenset og skjev? (Political participation in Norway – limited and skewed?). *Tidsskrift for samfunnsforskning*, 24, 3–30.
Hellevik, O. (1983b). Decomposing proportions and differences in proportions: Approaches to contingency table analysis. *Quality and Quantity*, 40, 79–111.
Hellevik, O. (1984). *Introduction to causal analysis.* London: George Allen & Unwin (1998). Oslo: Norwegian University Press.

Hellevik, O. (1997). Class inequality and egalitarian reform. *Acta Sociologica*, 40, 377–397.

Hellevik, O. (2000). A less biased allocation mechanism. *Acta Sociologica*, 43, 81–83.

Hellevik, O. (2002). Inequality versus association in educational attainment research: Comment on Kvininen Ahola and Hedman. *Acta Sociologica*, 45, 151–158.

Hellevik, O. (2007). Margin insensitivity and the analysis of educational inequality. *Czeck Sociological Review*, 43, 1095–1119.

Hellevik, O. (2009). Linear versus logistic regression when the dependent variable is a dichotomy. *Quality & Quantity*, 43, 50–74.

Hosmer, D. W., & Lemeshow, S. (1989). *Applied logistic regression*. New York, NY: Wiley.

Iversen, G. (1979). *Statistics for sociology*. Dubuque Iowa: C. Brown.

Kivinen, O., Ahola, S., & Hedman, J. (2001). Expanding education and improving odds. Participation in higher education in Finland in the 1980s and 1990s. *Acta Sociologica*, 44, 171–181.

Kivinen, O., Hedman, J., & Ahola, S. (2002). Changes to differences in expanding higher education: Reply to Hellevik. *Acta Sociologica*, 45, 159–162.

Lambert, P. J. (1993). *The distribution and redistribution of income. A mathematical analysis*. Manchester: Manchester University Press.

Lampard, R. (2000). Measuring inequality in a cross-tabulation with ordered categories: From the gini coefficient to the tog coefficient. *International Journal of Social Research Methodology*, 3, 1–14.

Leege, D. C., & Francis, W. L. (1974). *Political research. Design, measurement and analysis*. New York, NY: Basic Books.

Logan, J. A. (1996). Rules of access and shifts in demand: A comparison of log-linear and two-sided logit models. *Social Science Research*, 25, 174–199.

Mare, R. D. (1981). Change and stability in educational stratification. *American Sociological Review*, 46, 72–87.

Marks, G. N. (2004). The measurement of socio-economic inequalities in education: A further Comment. *Acta Sociologica*, 47, 91–93.

Marshall, G., Newby, H., Rose, D., & Vogler, C. (1988). *Social class in modern Britain*. London: Hutchinson.

Marshall, G., & Swift, A. (1999). On the meaning and measurement of inequality.. *Acta Sociologica*, 42, 241–250.

Marshall, G., & Swift, A. (2000). Reply to Ringen and Hellevik. *Acta Sociologica*, 43, 85–86.

Reynolds, H. T. (1977). *The analysis of cross-classifications*. New York, NY: Free Press.

Ringen, S. (1997). *Citizens, families and reform*. Oxford: Clarendon Press.

Ringen, S. (2000). Inequality and its measurement. *Acta Sociologica*, 43, 84.

Ringen, S. (2005). *Citizens, families and reform* (2nd ed.). New Brunswick: Transaction Publishers.

Ringen, S. (2006). The truth about class inequality. *Czech Sociological Review*, 42, 475–491.

Saunders, P. (1996). *Unequal but fair? A study of class barriers in Britain*. London: IEA.

REPRODUCTION OF ECONOMIC INEQUALITIES: ARE THE FIGURES FOR THE UNITED STATES AND UNITED KINGDOM TOO HIGH?

Gary N. Marks

ABSTRACT

Since the early 1990s there has been a growing body of research on intergenerational income elasticities and correlations. One of the most prominent findings is that these associations are much higher in the United States (and the United Kingdom) than in Canada, Australia and many European countries. This finding is often interpreted as America being much less fair than other industrialized societies since the reproduction of economic inequalities is substantially stronger. This chapter questions these conclusions on the following grounds: (i) inconsistencies with other outcomes, such as socio-economic inequalities in student achievement, educational attainment, occupation attainment and the patterning of intergenerational occupational mobility, (ii) family income having weaker effects on educational attainment (which has substantial effects on earnings and income) than other parental characteristics and (iii) methodological issues such as estimates based on the concept of 'permanent income' and the use of instrumental variables. Even if the consensus estimate of 0.4 for the intergenerational correlation in the

Class and Stratification Analysis
Comparative Social Research, Volume 30, 341–363
ISSN: 0195-6310/doi:10.1108/S0195-6310(2013)0000030016

United States is accepted, it may not mean that the United States is unusually unfair due to larger regional differences in labour market returns and/or stronger associations between parents' and their children's ability, ability and education attainment, and education and earnings.

Keywords: Intergenerational income correlations; social stratification; cross-national differences

BACKGROUND

Up until the early 1990s, the general consensus among both economists and sociologists was that the relationship between a person's income and that of their parents when they were growing up was weaker than that for other intergenerational relationships, for example, in students' test scores, educational attainment, occupational class and occupational status. Becker and Tomes (1986) report a widely cited correlation of 0.15 and conclude that in the United States, father's income has little influence on son's income. Weak correlations were also reported in the sociological literature, below and around 0.20 (Jencks et al., 1979, p. 327; Sewell & Hauser, 1975, p. 93). This lower correlation is consistent with the idea that the influence of socio-economic background on socio-economic outcomes weakens with age since earnings is typically measured in mid-adulthood whereas test scores and educational attainment are measured during adolescence or early adulthood.

The conclusion of a weak correspondence between parental and children's incomes in the United States was overturned by Solon (1992) and Zimmerman (1992) analyzing respectively the Panel Study in Income Dynamics (PSID) and several cohorts of the National Longitudinal Study (NLS). They concluded that the intergenerational correlation in income was much stronger than previously thought. They argued that measures of annual income or earnings attenuated the intergenerational correlation since earnings in one year are little indication of earnings over a longer period. Supposedly, income and earnings consist of permanent and transitory components. Averaging reduces the transitory component. Averaging incomes over a three or five year period increases the intergenerational correlation (or elasticity[1]) to around 0.40. The correlation is also attenuated because of substantial measurement error, and adjusting for measurement error with a fairly dubious instrument, father's education, increases the estimate for the elasticity to well above 0.50. Although the conclusion of substantial intergenerational correlations was based on small samples in only two data sets,[2] later work using social security records over a 15 year period shows even higher correlations of 0.60 or even higher (Mazumder, 2001, 2005). However, these estimates of correlations 0.60 or higher can be questioned since the calculations are based on the concept of permanent income and other assumptions. The high correlations are not actually observed.

The conclusion of substantially higher intergenerational correlations has become so established that in 2006 the British weekly *The Economist* ran feature articles endeavouring to answer why the reproduction of inequality in the United States is so high. The high intergenerational correlations in the United States have made odd bedfellows; Herrnstein and Murray (1994) cite them as evidence of the increasing importance of cognitive skills and the formation of a cognitive elite,[3] whereas Bowles and Ginitis (2002a, 2002b, 2005) understand them as further support for their radical critique of American society, especially its education system, which began in the early 1970s.

The work on intergenerational income correlations led Bowles and Gintis (2002b, p. 4) to make the extraordinary claim that 'Knowing the income or wealth of someone's parents is about as informative about the person's own economic status as is the person's own years of schooling attained, or score on a standardized cognitive test'. This statement is at odds with the bulk of research from economics, sociology and psychology which concludes that education is clearly the primary influence on adult occupational and economic outcomes and that cognitive ability (test scores) is a major influence on educational attainment (Duncan, Featherman, & Duncan, 1972; Jencks et al., 1972, 1979).[4] Within the ascription versus achievement paradigm, the general conclusion is that ascription is much less important than achieved characteristics (Blau & Duncan, 1967; Grusky & DiPrete, 1990). In the light of high intergenerational correlations for income and earnings such a conclusion would appear unwarranted. Theoretically, the focus would switch from a range of sociological influences to perhaps credit constraints arguing that poor and middle income families are unable to borrow the money necessary for a good education for their child (Becker, 1975; Carneiro & Heckman, 2002).

Sociologists have, in general, not contributed to this research literature. This is particularly surprising given the large body of sociological research on the reproduction of educational and occupational attainment, on occupational mobility and indeed on earnings. Economists in the intergenerational income field have almost completely ignored this extensive literature. Hauser (2010, p. 3) is particularly scathing:

> In 1997, when I first began to work on this chapter, my intent was mainly to question the naïve approaches and extreme conclusions of the several economists who had recently begun to measure intergenerational (income) mobility. Somewhat to my surprise, in the past decade the measurement of intergenerational economic mobility has become a minor industry, and its visibility – and the visible ignorance of scholars new to the field – has begun drive sociological studies of mobility off the map and to ignore the lessons of sound research and scholarship across the past half-century.

Hauser (2010) indirectly argues that the intergenerational income correlation is likely to be lower. He indexed occupations in two ways: by the typical education of occupations and typical income of occupations. The intergenerational correlations were much stronger for the education measure (at around 0.37) than for occupation income (at around 0.21). Earlier, Hauser and Warren (1997, pp. 222–224) found that income-derived measures of occupational standing showed much lower intergenerational correlations (between 0.21 and 0.25) than prestige-based (about 0.30), socio-economically based (about 0.35) or education-based measures (0.30–0.38).

CROSS-NATIONAL COMPARISONS

High intergenerational elasticities have been found for the United Kingdom. Using instrumental variable methods, Dearden, Machin and Reed (1997) report very high elasticities: 0.57 for father's and son's wages and an incredible 0.68 between father's and daughter's. Analysing data from the British Household Panel, Ermish and Francescionui (2004, p. 182) conclude that intergenerational correlations range from 0.45 to 0.75 for father-son pairs and from 0.30 to 0.50 for mother-daughter pairs. After reviewing several studies, Corak (2006, p. 63) offers a preferred estimate for the United Kingdom of 0.50 with lower and upper bounds of 0.42 and 0.55. An OECD (2009, p. 205) report places the United Kingdom at the top of the ranking for intergenerational income elasticities. The finding that income inequalities in Great Britain are strongly reproduced across generations is readily accepted given the pervasive and accepted wisdom that Britain is a highly stratified class-ridden society. The high intergenerational correlation in Britain led Corak (2005, p. 9) to conclude that reforms to the British education system dating back to the 1980s have actually decreased social mobility.

Cross-national comparisons in earnings and income suggest that the United Kingdom and the United States stand out as countries that strongly reproduce economic inequalities (Corak, 2005, p. 9; OECD, 2009). Although, it may be tempting to argue that the high elasticities in the United States and Great Britain have something to do with their liberal capitalist economies, their more limited social welfare provisions or Anglo-Saxon culture, the intergenerational correlations are much weaker in Australia and Canada. In the introduction to *Generational Income Mobility in North America and Europe*, the editor Miles Corak (2005, p. 9) summarizes: 'In the US and the UK at least 40% of the economic advantage high-income parents have over low-income parents is passed on to the next generation. The Nordic countries and Canada seem to be the most mobile societies, with less than 20% of an income advantage being passed on between parent and child'. The OECD's (2009) report *Growing Unequal?* concluded that earnings elasticities were lowest (meaning more mobility) in Denmark, Australia,[5] Norway, Finland and Canada (in that order) and highest in Great Britain, Italy, the United States and France.

The finding of high intergenerational income correlations in the United States turns the American exceptionalism argument on its head. The country was renowned (since at least Tocqueville) for being more 'open' than the old world countries of Europe with their supposedly more rigid class structures.[6] If the research on income correlations is to be believed, then the United States is much more closed than European countries, with the notable exception of Britain and possibly Italy and France.

INCONSISTENCIES WITH THE INTERGENERATIONAL ASSOCIATIONS FOR OTHER OUTCOMES

The conclusion of high intergenerational income correlations in the United Kingdom and United States, if correct, is not consistent with other (generally sociological) literatures. These include cross-national comparisons in cognitive test scores (Marks, 2005, 2011; Woessmann, 2008), educational attainment (Hertz et al., 2007; Treiman & Yip, 1989), occupational status (Beller & Hout, 2006; Björklund & Jäntti, 2000; Treiman & Yip, 1989) and occupational mobility (Eberharter, 2008; Erikson & Goldthorpe, 1992, pp. 308–337).[7] It certainly does not correspond with the high levels of occupational class mobility observed in the United States and Great Britain

(Kingston, 2000; Saunders, 1996). Also, it is not consistent with the general conclusion from the social stratification literature that the impact of socio-economic background is fairly modest (Blau & Duncan, 1967; Hauser & Carter, 1995).

There are several possibilities for the discrepancies between cross-national research in the intergenerational reproduction of educational and occupational inequalities and research on the intergeneration income or earnings elasticities and correlations: the estimates for the latter in the United States and the United Kingdom are too high; the estimates by sociologists and others for the reproduction of other aspects of socio-economic inequality are too low and finally there is no inconsistency. This chapter argues that the correlations reported for the United States (and the United Kingdom) are too high, that father's earnings/family income has weaker effects on student achievement, educational attainment and subsequent outcomes than other parental characteristics. Furthermore, if the correlation is around 0.4, the evidence suggests that the direct effect of the family's economic resources is small.

Although, it is plausible that a theory could be developed that somehow explains the high intergenerational correlations for earnings in the United States and United Kingdom compared to other countries together with their unexceptional intergenerational associations for test scores, education and occupation – for example, more flexible labour markets or stronger regional differences[8] – Occam's Razor would suggest otherwise.

There are large regional differences in earnings between metropolitan and non-metropolitan areas in the United States (Glaeser & Maré, 2001; Jencks & Tach, 2006). Jencks and Tach (2006, p. 40) cite personal communication with Bonggeum Kim who controlled for the size of the community and the region in which sons were raised, found that the father-son earnings elasticity in the PSID fell from 0.447 to 0.315. This adjustment suggests the relative high reproduction of economic inequality in the United States can be attributed somewhat to region. The same argument may apply to the United Kingdom where wages are higher in London than in other regions. However, regional disparities in earnings exist in most other countries with large urban centres, so regional labour markets in the United States may not help explain cross-national differences.

ECONOMIC RESOURCES AND EDUCATION

This literature on intergenerational income mobility implies that family or father's income is of paramount importance for children's education since education is by far the strongest influence on earnings and income. A strong influence educational attainment is ability or test scores. Only in the relatively rare case of family or small businesses could it be argued that the relationship between the family of origin's economic circumstances and adult earnings or income is direct. The indirect relationships between parental income and (adult) children's income are weak because of the weak effects of parental income on test scores, educational attainment and other mediating variables that link family and child's incomes.

Family Income and Test Scores

In the Wisconsin Longitudinal Study, less than 10% of the variation in test scores was accounted for by family income (obtained from tax records), father's occupation or father's or mother's education (Sewell, Hauser, & Wolf, 1980, p. 566). Fejgin (1995) reported a standardized effect of 0.07 for family income on mathematics score compared to 0.32 for parents' education. Furthermore, family income has only weak effects on social, cognitive and behavioural outcomes in young and very young children (Aughinbaugh & Gittleman, 2003; Blau, 1999). Mayer's (1997) analysis of the PSID and NLSY also concluded that the influence of family income on social and economic inequalities is, at best, modest when taking into account other family characteristics.

Family Income and Educational Attainment

Sewell, Haller and Ohlendorf's (1970) analysis of the 1958 Wisconsin Longitudinal Study concluded that of the three aspects of socio-economic background, father's occupation, father's education and family income, family income has the weakest relationship with educational attainment. This finding could not be attributed to measurement error, since family income data were derived from official tax returns. Olneck (1977) reports his own analysis of the same data where the addition of average family income over 3 years did not increase the explained variance in educational attainment beyond that provided by father's and mother's education and father's occupation. According to an early analysis of the PSID, family income had no effect on young men's educational attainment, net of a rough measure of ability and father's education (Kiker & Condon, 1981).

The weaker influence of family income on educational attainment has been observed in other more recent studies.[9] In a review article, Haverman and Wolff (1995, p. 1856) conclude that 'changes in economic resources are associated with only small changes in educational attainment'. They cite Hill and Duncan's (1987) analysis of the PSID where a 10% increase in family income (averaged over 3 years) was associated with an increase in educational attainment by only 1.4%, and less when controlling for other background factors. This is equivalent to a standardized effect of around 0.04. Similarly, Belzil and Hansen (2003) conclude that father's and mother's education have much stronger effects on educational attainment than that for family income. A 1 year increase in parental education is reflected by an increase of 0.3 of a year of schooling. To obtain a similar increase requires a difference of $30,000 in income, a large difference given the average income in that study (conducted in 1990) was $37,000. For school completion, Belley and Lochner (2007, pp. 51, 52) found modest effects of family income, with a 7 or 8 point difference (in the percentage completing school) between the top and bottom income quartiles, net of measured Armed Forces Qualification Test score quartile[10] and parental education.

Family Income and College Attendance

In the United States going to college is often expensive, so it is expected that income should have more noticeable effects on college than school completion. Belley and Lochner (2007, pp. 51, 52) found modest effects in the 1979 NLSY cohort, the difference in college attendance at age 21 between the top and bottom income quartiles, net of measured ability was 9 percentage points. For the NLSY97 study the effect had risen to 16 percentage points.[11] However, even in the United States the effect of family background on college entry is not economic but social. For enrolling in US graduate programmes, family income has only weak effects. Net of GPA and other factors, a $10,000 increase in income increases the probability of graduate school enrolment by only 0.37% (Zhang, 2005). Morgan and Kim (2005) also report small effects of family income on college enrolment. They (2005, p. 177) note an 'increase of $500 in monthly family income is associated with an increased probability of enrolling in college of between 0.006 and 0.010 (depending on the values at which other variables are set)'. Later in the chapter they concede that the effects of income and wealth are overestimates due to absence in cognitive ability in their models. Conley (2001) found statistically *insignificant* effects for parental income (averaged over 5 years), net of family wealth, on each postsecondary transition investigated. Cameron and Heckman (2001, p. 492) conclude that 'the importance of short-term credit constraints is greatly exaggerated'. Altonji and Dunn (1996) found the earnings returns to qualifications do not vary by the income of the family of origin. They argued that if the availability of short-term credit was an important factor then wealthy parents would be able to use their capital to buy the college courses that produce the greatest return. In addition, the social effects on college entry are considerably weaker than the influence of academic factors, primarily test scores (Alexander, Holupka, & Pallas, 1987; Belley & Lochner, 2007, p. 48; Korenman & Winship, 2000; Thomas, Alexander, & Eckland, 1979).

Family Wealth and Educational Attainment

If education and test scores are only weakly related to family income then a possible alternative explanation for the high intergenerational correlation is through family wealth. Rather than family income facilitating higher educational attainment, a plausible alternative explanation is direct transfer of income producing assets. Wealth could be understood as a reliable indicator of permanent income (Pfeffer, 2011). However, family wealth does not have particularly strong effects on test scores or education. Analysing data collected in 1966, Rumberger (1983) found no wealth effects on scores in a knowledge (of the working world) test. For years of education, the effect for wealth was significant, net of the ability measure, but quite small: a 100% increase in wealth was associated with an increase of only 0.1 of a year of schooling. Pfeffer (2011) presents correlations from the PSID of around 0.30 between wealth and educational attainment: comparable with the correlations for father's occupation and household income. However, his structural equation model reports only moderate effects of family wealth and income on educational attainment, net of family occupational status and education.[12] Ability was not included. There are reported effects of wealth on college enrolment and in accounting for the black-white differences in college enrolment (Conley, 2001; Orr, 2003). However, the effects of wealth are not strong: a *doubling* of parental assets increases years of education by 0.11 years and increased the probability of going to college from high school by 8%. A doubling of assets increased the chances of college completion by about 6% but this effect was not significant at the conventional $P<0.05$ level (Conley, 2001, p. 68). These models did not include cognitive ability which has a strong effect on college entry and completion.[13]

Since family wealth is a combination of the cumulative returns to human capital, monetary gifts, inheritance and luck, the intergenerational correlation for wealth should at least be comparable to that for income. Contrary to popular conceptions, the inheritance of wealth has little to do with income inequalities. Jencks et al. (1972, p. 214), citing the findings from a 1960 survey, point out that inheritance plays an extremely limited role: 80% of families inherited nothing, a further 14% inherited very little and only 1% of families inherited enough to substantially boost their income. Keister (2005) reports an intergenerational correlation of 0.5 for wealth. However, there is much variation in the estimates. Bowles and Gintis (2002b) report estimates ranging from 0.27 to 0.76 from nine studies. Charles and Hurst (2003) calculated the age-adjusted (pre-bequest) elasticity of child and parental wealth in the United States at 0.37. They note that less than 10% of the variation in child's wealth can be accounted for by parental wealth. Lillard (1977) found that a limited set of social background variables and schooling and ability account for about 12% of the variation in wealth (which is equivalent to a multiple correlation of 0.35). This is less than the variation in income explained solely by parental income in the economic intergenerational correlation literature. In a recent review article, Black and Devereux (2011, p. 1533) simply note that the intergenerational wealth elasticity appears to be lower than intergenerational earnings elasticity and suggest this raises questions for further work.

METHODOLOGICAL ISSUES

Consistency

Although the consensus estimate for the intergenerational elasticity for the United States is 0.4, there is great variation in the estimates. Mayer and Lopoo (2005) report that in 18 US studies the elasticity of son's and father's earnings range from 0.13 to 0.53. Corak (2006, p. 52) reports elasticities from the published literature ranging from 0.08 to 0.60. Similarly, Grawe (2006) lists six US studies with estimated elasticities ranging from 0.13 to 0.42. There is even a lack of consensus of the extent of the intergenerational correlations within the same data set. In the PSID least squares estimates (not using instrumental variable techniques), reported correlations range between 0.13 and 0.48, while in the NLS the correlations are generally lower but ranging between 0.14 and 0.54 (Solon, 1999). Such variation is not encountered for the corresponding relationships in adolescent achievement, educational attainment or occupational attainment. The raw correlation between father's and son's earnings in the PSID according to Björklund and Jäntti (1997) is between 0.26 and 0.31. This is about 25% less than the consensus estimate of 0.4.

Even the estimates calculated over long periods are lower than that expected from the literature on permanent income. Hertz (2005, p. 177) analysed up to 30 years for parental earnings (average 11.5 years) and 28 years for the second generations' earnings (average 11.9). He reports age-adjusted elasticities for parental family earnings on family earnings: 0.53 for the entire sample, 0.39 for whites, and 0.32 for blacks. These respective correlations are lower at 0.42, 0.32 and 0.21 which could be regarded as upper bounds given the long time periods involved.[14]

For the United Kingdom, there is also considerable variation in the estimates. Although the United Kingdom is supposed to show large intergenerational elasticities and correlations, those reported for the British Birth Cohort studies are quite low for sons with elasticities between 0.18 and 0.25 and unexpectedly higher for daughters, between 0.31 and 0.32 (Blanden, Goodman, Gregg, & Machin, 2004). The low elasticities can be attributed to only having one observation for family income in the 1958 cohort and only two in the 1970 cohort. Hobcraft (2001) reports elasticities ranging from 0.10 to 0.33 for the same data, the 1958 NCDS cohort.[15] Among males, perversely the elasticity is lower for family income than for father's income. However, the most challenging finding is that the elasticities between male incomes and their partner's family's income (or father's earnings) is comparable to that for their own parents' income or father's earnings suggesting that 'assortative mating' may play a substantial role in the intergenerational income correlation. The bizarre implication is that for the economic standing of men, 'assortative mating' is just as important as the family of origin's economic resources.

Unfortunately, different methods generate disparate estimates. Despite the prominence given to the purportedly high intergenerational correlations between parent's income and child's income in the United Kingdom, Erikson and Goldthorpe (2010) report correlations of only 0.18 between father's and son's income for the 1958 NCDS cohort and 0.29 for the 1970 BCS cohort. These estimates have not been adjusted for permanent versus transitory components. As mentioned earlier, the correlation for the 1958 is unusually low since it is based on only 1 year's measure of parents' income. It is only after making statistical adjustments for permanent and transitory income components and instrumental variables for measurement error that the intergenerational income correlation approaches 0.5 or higher.

Gorard (2008) makes the simple point that these correlations are not particularly high explaining less than 8% of the variation in income (3% for the older cohort). He also questions the reliability of the estimates noting that the analyses were based on just 13% and 12% of the original NCDS and BCS samples, the remainder lost through attrition.

Measurement Issues and Permanent Incomes

The estimation of elasticities and the intergenerational income and earnings correlations are not usually estimated with a single regression or correlation analysis with accurate data on both parents' and (adult) children's income or earnings. There are a number of measurement-related issues that affect the estimates.

Mazumder's (2005) estimates of 0.6 are obtained by estimating permanent income (which is not observed) from observed incomes over 15 years. The greater the number of instances (years) a variable is averaged, the greater the correlation it will have with other variables. The justification for this practice is that it minimizes measurement error since income has both permanent and transitory components. Beller and Hout (2006, p. 25) doubt the estimate of 0.6 for father-son earnings persistence. They argue that averaging earnings over a long period of time is a dubious practice since it is difficult to believe there is one true value. Muller (2010) makes the point that simply averaging the years will lead to over-estimates of the elasticity because there is serial correlation in the measures of annual income. In other words, if the serial correlation of earnings (or income) is low – that is, there is much year-to-year volatility in earnings – then averaging earnings will produce a higher estimate of the intergenerational associations than if the year-to-year correlations in earnings were close to 1.[16] Typically, the year-to-year correlations are about 0.8 for adjacent years declining to around 0.5 or less for observations 10 or more years apart. Muller (2010) also makes the substantive point that averaging parental income is based on the questionable assumption that family income is equally important no matter the child's age. He found family income is more important at younger ages and his estimates from the PSID are considerably lower than 0.4.[17]

Some estimates only use proxies for income. The estimate for Australian measure calculated by Leigh (2007) was not based on any measure of father's income but estimated from son's reports of his father's occupation and education. Son's income was based on quite unreliable questions that ask respondents the income band of their or their family's (son's generation) income. Such indirect and very questionable measures are not unknown in studies conducted in other countries. Solon (2002) notes that Dearden et al. (1997) estimate of an elasticity of 0.57 may be biased upward since father's income was not used but predicted by education and occupational class. An estimate for the intergenerational elasticity for Singapore was based on the weak association found for youths aged between 23 and 29 and then adjusted upwards by comparison with the PSID taking into account the sample's youth and the limitation of only 1 year of earnings data (Ng, Shen, & Ho, 2009). There must be much error associated with these quite substantial adjustments which nearly double the magnitude of the original estimates. The over-time analysis of Aaronson and Mazumder (2008) uses census data without any direct linkage between father's and son's earnings.

Most often low elasticities are found with reliable data. Their estimate of 0.2 for the intergenerational elasticity for Canada was based on longitudinal data from 400,000 father-son pairs (Corak & Heisz, 1999). Hansen's (2010) estimate of around 0.3 for Norway is based on very reliable registry data for incomes with hundreds of thousands of cases.[18] The estimates for Sweden are also usually based on registry data (Hirvonen, 2008). These reliable estimates are often included in summary tables with estimates from other countries based on a small number of respondents or in some cases proxies for income.

Instrumental Variables

Instrumental variables are commonly used in the estimation of intergenerational elasticities and correlations. The estimates from instrumental variables are almost invariably larger than conventional estimates. Sometimes, instrumental variables lead to extraordinary increases in the estimates of the elasticities. Normally, instrumental variables are used to counter 'endogeniety' or more sociologically speaking 'specification error'. In the context of intergenerational income elasticities and correlation, instruments are used to purge the dependent variable of measurement error. The greater the error variance in the exogenous variable the greater the downward bias in the estimate. The resulting purged regressor is uncorrelated with measurement error and error in prediction (Angrist & Krueger, 2001). An ideal instrument is strongly correlated with the exogenous variable but has no direct association with the endogenous variable. In the first stage the exogenous variable is regressed on the instrument or instrumental variables and the predicted values are obtained which are (of course) uncorrelated with the instrumental variable(s) and the error term. These predicted values are then used as the regressor for the second stage. The logic is that the predicted values represent the exogenous variable removed of its error. Instrumental variables do not work very well if the instruments are only weakly correlated with the exogenous variable (Bound & Baker, 1995) or are moderately correlated with the endogenous variable.

Solon (1992) used father's education as an instrumental variable, Zimmerman (1992) the Duncan SEI index. The problem with these instruments is that they tend to have non-trivial correlations with the child's (adult) income. That is why predicted values of family income typically have stronger relationships with child's income than the original observed measure of family income. Also parental education and occupational status have plausible causal relationships with child's income that do not involve family income. A well educated parent or a parent in a higher status job may have the 'know how', cultural resources, social connections or whatever to land their child a higher paying job. For estimating the returns (in earnings) to education, Card (1999, p. 1825) demonstrates that family background is not a legitimate instrument. Finally, instrumental techniques do not produce stable estimates. Blanden et al. (2004, p. 9) noted that 'limited experimentation here revealed that their use, especially in the cross cohort context, seemed rather dubious, both on the basis of Sargan tests and on the sensitivity of IV estimates to choice of instrument'.

Net Effects of Background Earnings or Income

The impact of father's earnings or family's income is much weaker when controlling for other background factors. Hertz (2006, p. 19) concludes that three-fifths of the effect of family income can be attributed to family characteristics other than income.[19] Jencks and Tach (2006) find that the weak impact of family income (elasticity $= 0.10$) on daughters' earnings was no longer statistically significant when controlling for father's education and occupation. For sons' earnings, the bivariate relationship was stronger (elasticity $= 0.21$) but declined substantially (elasticity $= 0.13$) with the addition of father's occupation and education, and declined again after controlling for ability (elasticity = 0.11).

Solon (1999, pp. 1763–1766) develops a theoretical model which shows that the relationship between parents' and their adult children's economic situation, for example intergenerational elasticities and correlations, is dependent on

1. parental investment in the child's human capital. This depends partly on parental earnings but also other background factors. Parents may prefer to consume than invest in their children's education. If there is a strong relationship between parental income and children's educational attainment then the intergenerational associations for earnings/income is likely to be larger.
2. the efficacy of the transformation of the child's human capital into earnings.
3. the intergeneration transmission of ability. If ability is strongly transmitted across generations, the intergenerational association in earnings/income will be higher.

There is substantial evidence that biology is more important than the family's environment for the intergenerational income correlations. This implies the intergenerational transmission of ability is important. Intergenerational income correlations are much lower for adopted children than biological children. Using the PSID, Liu and Zeng (2009) found that intergenerational elasticity for wages and earnings among adopted children were 0.113 and 0.096 compared to 0.345 and 0.369 for biological children. These differences even applied to adopted and non-adopted children in the same family. They conclude that a large proportion of the transmission of earnings inequality across generations can be attributed to genetic factors. For Sweden, Björklund, Lindahl, and Plug (2006, p. 1013) report earnings and income elasticities of 0.10 and 0.17 for adopted children (with non-biological fathers) compared to 0.24 for biological children.

The intra-class sibling correlations (in the United States) are much weaker for earnings than for other socio-economic outcomes, around 0.2 compared to 0.47 for test scores 0.55 for education (Olneck, 1977). Similarly, Jencks et al. (1979, p. 340) report sibling correlations for earnings between 0.13 and 0.21 from three studies. These sibling correlations for earnings are much weaker than those for test scores (0.47 and 0.48), education (0.53–0.55) and occupation (0.31–0.37), indicating that family background has a much weaker impact on earnings than on earlier outcomes. Olneck (1977) calculated that even if all family background differences in earnings were eliminated, the variation in earnings would be only slightly smaller: 87% of the original standard deviation. Jencks et al. (1972, p. 220) estimated that income differences between randomly chosen men averaged $6,200 (in 1968 dollars), but only $600 less between brothers brought up in the same family.

Taubman (1976) collected data on the 1973 earnings of white male twins who had both served in the American armed forces during World War II. Monozygotic twins' 1973 earnings correlated at 0.54, while dizygotic twins' earnings correlated at 0.30. Similarly, Ashfelter and Krueger (1994, p. 1160) report correlations for wage rates at 0.56 for identical twins and 0.36 for fraternal twins. A later study found correlations for hourly wage rates of 0.63 and 0.37, respectively (Jencks & Tach, 2006, p. 51, note 15). The correlations of identical twins' earnings in Australia and Sweden are even higher, approaching 0.7 with correlations for fraternal twins much lower (Solon, 1999, p. 1774). In a study of twins and other sibling types in Sweden, Björklund, Jäntti and Solon (2005, p. 161) initially estimated that about 80% of the intergenerational earnings correlations among twins and siblings could be accounted for by genetic factors. This estimate was based on the reasonable assumption that the importance of the environment is the same for identical twins and non-identical twins or siblings. When they relaxed this assumption and set the correlation for the environment among monozygotic twins reared together at 1.0 and the environmental correlation for dizygotic twins and siblings at less than 1.0 and had to be estimated, they concluded that about 60% of the intergenerational correlation was due to genetics (2005, p. 161). Here the environmental component includes the in *utero* environment, as well as their more similar treatment as infants and probably their similar schooling environments. These aspects are quite distinct from the family's socio-economic resources. In a different type of analysis, Jencks and Tach (2006, p. 24) conclude that approximately half of the correlation of earnings across generations can be attributed to genes and individual values. These studies imply that genes, including but not exclusively ability, are a major contributor to the intergenerational associations in earnings.

CONCLUSION

The purpose of this chapter was to document some of the inconsistencies and methodological issues relating to the relatively high intergenerational elasticities and correlations for the United States and less prominently the United Kingdom. There are several reasons to doubt the accuracy of the high-end estimates. These high intergenerational elasticity and correlations are not consistent with cross-national comparisons in the intergenerational relationships for test scores, educational attainment, occupational status and occupational mobility. Family income tends to have a much weaker relationship with test scores, educational attainment and other childhood outcomes than parental occupation and parental education. There are issues with the data, for some countries the number of cases is small and earnings and income are not accurately measured. In some countries the estimates do not involve actual data on income or the earnings of the older generation. There are doubts surrounding the concept of 'permanent income'; the higher the assumed transitory component, the higher the intergenerational correlation. Theoretical estimates obtained from assumptions about the permanent income are usually considerably higher than observed averages calculated over long periods. Instrumental variable approaches using social background variables are inappropriate, biasing the estimates upward. Finally, the net effect of family income on adult child's earnings or income is quite weak when taking into account other family background variables and cognitive ability. This indicates that the observed association does not really reflect the direct impact of the family of origin's economic resources on the subsequent generation's economic situation or even its indirect impact through education.

NOTES

1. Elasticity is the coefficient β_1 in the equation linking parents' and their (adult) child's income or earnings (both logged). $\text{Ln}(Y_c) = \alpha + \beta_1 \text{Ln}(Y_p)$. Where Y_p and Y_c are parents' and child's income or earnings, respectively, and β_1 is the elasticity. If $\beta_1 = 0.10$ then children who grow up in families where family income differs by 50% will typically have incomes that differ by 5%. If $\beta_1 = 0.50$ then their incomes will differ by 25 per cent. The correlation (ρ) is the elasticity standardized: $\rho = \beta_1 (\sigma_p/\sigma_c)$ where σ_p and σ_c are the standard deviations of the income distributions for parents and children, respectively. The correlation will be close to the elasticity if the distributions of income for both generations are much the same.

2. The well-cited estimates by Solon and Zimmerman are based on only 290 and 175 father-son pairs.

3. The cognitive elite comprise high income professionals and managers that attended the most prestigious universities. The cognitive elite are understood as self-perpetuating since they tend to inter-marry.

4. A meta-analysis of data from over 50 samples from mostly US studies estimates an average correlation of about 0.56 between cognitive ability and educational attainment measured by years of education (Strenze, 2007).

5. The low correlation for Australia, although not inconsistent with average or weaker than average effects for social background, is questionable since it is based on occupation rather than income.

6. There is little empirical support for the American Exceptionalism thesis for occupational mobility (Erikson & Goldthorpe, 1985, 1992, pp. 308–337; Lipset & Zetterberg, 1959; Wong, 1990).

7. Breen (2004, p. 401) in his edited book on occupational mobility in European countries cites personal communication with Mike Hout who has analysed the data from the General Social Survey comments that 'fluidity is high in the United States'.

8. If more flexible labour markets and stronger regional differences were the explanation, then Canada (and Australia) would exhibit similarly high intergenerational associations for earnings and income.

9. Teachman (1987) reports correlations of around 0.26 for family income and educational attainment. Ganzach (2000) reports a correlation of 0.3 between family income and educational attainment compared to correlations of around 0.45 for father's and mother's education and 0.62 with cognitive ability.

10. Quartile measures of ability are less powerful than continuous measures. The effect for family income is likely to be smaller if the ability measure had not been aggregated into quartiles.

11. The comparable effect for ability was 55 percentage points for the NSLY79 cohort and 52 percentage points for NSLY97 cohort (Belley & Lochner, 2007, p. 50).

12. For the NLSY, Pfeffer (2011) reported standardized effects on education of 0.13, 0.09, 0.16 and 0.16 for family of origin's wealth, income, occupational status and education. For the PSID, the comparable effects were 0.15, 0.02 (not significant), 0.12 and 0.35. The NLSY's AFQT ability measure was not included, nor was the abridged measure in the PSID.

13. According to both the 1979 and 1997 US National Longitudinal Studies of Youth, more than 80% of those in the highest ability quartile attended college, and nearly 70% of those in the highest achievement quartile and who were also from the lowest family income quartile (Belley & Lochner, 2007). Korenman and Winship (2000) found strong positive effects for ability on obtaining a BA degree, net of socio-economic background. A one standard deviation increase in ability increased the odds of obtaining a BA degree by about six times.

14. The elasticities are higher because of greater variance in earnings in the second generation.

15. The intergenerational correlation for men's income and that of their family of origin is 0.21 and for women 0.11. For father's and son's income the elasticity is higher at 0.30 but father's and daughter's lower at 0.15.

16. This implies that unreliable measures of earnings/income will produce higher estimates of the intergenerational associations than highly reliable measures.

17. According to Muller (2010):

> Applying these results to our estimates would put the range of the betas conservatively between 0.05 (in the late teens and early 20s) and 0.25 (in early childhood), so early childhood income may be four times as important as income in other periods.

18. The estimate of 0.3 is the highest based on family income including capital income limited to men. However, family income together with father's age and child's cohort explain little of the variation in sons' or daughters' income, 4.4 and 3.4%, respectively (Hansen, 2010, p. 144).

19. Parental characteristics with at least moderate effects include race, education and religion.

REFERENCES

Aaronson, D., & Mazumder, B. (2008). Intergenerational economic mobility in the United States, 1940 to 2000. *Journal of Human Resources, 43*(1), 139–172.

Alexander, K. L., Holupka, S., & Pallas, A. M. (1987). Social background and academic determinants of two-year versus four-year: College attendance: Evidence from two cohorts a decade apart. *American Journal of Education, 96*(1), 56–80.

Altonji, J., & Dunn, T. (1996). Returns to education and the family. *Review of Economics and Statistics, 78*(4), 692–704.

Angrist, J., & Krueger, A. B. (2001). Instrumental variables and the search for identification: From supply and demand to natural experiments. *Journal of Economic Perspectives, 15*(4), 69–85.

Ashenfelter, O., & Krueger, A. (1994). Estimates of the economic return to schooling from a new sample of twins. *American Economic Review, 84*(5), 1157–1172.

Aughinbaugh, A., & Gittleman, M. (2003). Does money matter? A comparison of the effect of income on child development in the United States and great Britain. *Journal of Human Resources, 38*(2), 416–440.

Becker, G. S. (1975). *Human capital* (2nd ed.). New York, NY: Columbia Uniersity Press.

Becker, G. S., & Tomes, N. (1986). Human capital and the rise and fall of families. *Journal of Labor Economics, 43*(3), S1–S39.

Beller, E., & Hout, M. (2006). Intergenerational social mobility: The United States in comparative perspective. *Future of Children, 16*(2), 19–36.

Belley, P., & Lochner, L. (2007). The changing role of family income and ability in determining educational achievement. *Journal of Human Capital, 1*(1), 37–89.

Belzil, C., & Hansen, J. (2003). Structural estimates of the intergenerational education correlation. *Journal of Applied Econometrics, 18*(6), 679–696.

Björklund, A., & Jäntti, M. (1997). Integenerational income mobility in sweden compared to the United States. *American Economic Review, 87*(5), 1009–1117.

Björklund, A., & Jäntti, M. (2000). Integenerational mobility of socio-economic status in comparative perspective. *Nordic Journal of Political Economy, 26*(1), 3–32.

Björklund, A., Jantti, M., & Solon, G. (2005). Influences of nature and nuture on earnings variation. In S. Bowles, H. Ginitis & M. O. Groves (Eds.), *Unequal chances: Family background and economic success princeton*. NJ: Russell Sage Foundation Press, Princeton University Press.

Björklund, A., Lindal, M., & Plug, E. (2006). The origins of intergenerational associations: Lessons from swedish adoption data. *Quarterly Journal of Economics, 121*(3), 999–1028.

Black, S. E., & Devereux, P. J. (2011). Recent developments in intergenerational mobility. *Handbook of Labour Economics, 4*(Part B), 1487–1541.

Blanden, J., Goodman, A., Gregg, P., & Machin, S. (2004). Changes in intergenerational mobility in Britain. In M. Corak (Ed.), *Generational income mobility in North America and Europe* (pp. 123–146). Cambridge: Cambridge University Press.

Blau, D. M. (1999). The effect of income on child development. *Review of Economics and Statistics, 81*(2), 261–276.

Blau, P. M., & Duncan, O. D. (1967). *The American occupational structure.* New York, NY: Wiley.

Bound, J., & Baker, D. A. J. R. M. (1995). Problems with instrumental variables estimation when the correlation between the instruments and the endogenous explanatory variable is weak. *Journal of the American Statistical Association, 90*(430), 443–450.

Bowles, S., & Gintis, H. (2002a). The inheritance of inequality. *Journal of Economic Perspectives, 16*(3), 3–30.

Bowles, S., & Gintis, H. (2002b). Schooling in capitalist America revisited. *Sociology of Education, 75*(January), 1–18.

Bowles, S., & Gintis, H. (2005). Introduction. In S. Bowles, H. Gintis, & M. Osbourne (Eds.), *Unequal chances: Family background and economic success.* Princeton, NJ: Russell Sage Foundation, Princeton University Press.

Breen, R. (2004). *Social mobility in Europe.* Oxford: Oxford University Press.

Cameron, S. V., & Heckman, J. J. (2001). The dynamics of educational attainments for black, hispanic, and white males. *Journal of Political Economy, 109*(3), 455–499.

Card, D. (1999). The causal effect of education on earnings. In D. Card & C. A. Orley (Eds.), *Handbook of labor economics* (Vol. 3, part 1, pp. 1801–1863). Amsterdam: Elsevier.

Carneiro, P., & Heckman, J. J. (2002). The evidence on credit constraints in post-secondary schooling. *Economic Journal, 112*(482), 705–734.

Charles, K. K., & Hurst, E. (2003). The correlation of wealth across generations. *Journal of Political Economy, 111*(6), 1155–1182.

Conley, D. (2001). Capital for college: Parental assets and postsecondary schooling. *Sociology of Education, 74*(1), 59–72.

Corak, M. (Ed.). (2005). *Generational income mobility in North America and Europe.* Cambridge: Cambridge University Press.

Corak, M. (2006). *Do poor children become poor adults? Lessons from a cross country comparison of generational earnings mobility* (No. 1993). Forschungsinstitut zur Zukunft der Arbeit, Institute for the Study of Labor.

Corak, M., & Heisz, A. (1999). The intergenerational earnings and income mobility of canadian men: Evidence from longitudinal income tax data. *Journal of Human Resources, 34*(3), 504–533.

Dearden, L., Machin, S., & Reed, H. (1997). Intergenerational mobility in Britain. *The Economic Journal, 107*(January), 47–66.

Duncan, O. D., Featherman, D. L., & Duncan, B. (1972). *Socioeconomic background and achievement.* New York, NY: Seminar Press.

Eberharter, V. (2008). Parental background and intergenerational occupational mobility – Germany and the United States compared. *Journal of Income Distribution, 17*(2), 74–94.

Erikson, R., & Goldthorpe, J. H. (1985). Are American rates of social mobility exceptionally high. New evidence on an old question. *European Sociological Review, 1*(1), 1–22.

Erikson, R., & Goldthorpe, J. H. (1992). *The constant flux. A study in class mobility in industrial nations.* Oxford: Clarendon Press.

Erikson, R., & Goldthorpe, J. H. (2010). Has social mobility in Britain decreased? Reconciling divergent findings on income and class mobility. *British Journal of Sociology, 61*(2), 211–230.

Ermisch, J., & Francesconi, M. (2004). Intergenerational mobility in Britain: New evidence from the Bhps. In M. Corak (Ed.), *Income mobility in North America and Europe*. Cambridge: Cambridge University Press.

Fejgin, N. (1995). Factors contributing to the academic excellence of American Jewish and Asian students. *Sociology of Education, 68*, 18–30.

Ganzach, Y. (2000). Parent's education, cognitive ability, educational expectations and educational attainment. *British Journal of Educational Psychology, 70*(3), 419–441.

Glaeser, E. L., & Maré, D. C. (2001). Cities and skills. *Journal of Labor Economics, 19*(2), 316–342.

Gorard, S. (2008). A re-consideration of rates of 'social mobility' in Britain: Or why research impact is not always a good thing. *British Journal of Sociology of Education, 29*(3), 317–324.

Grawe, N. D. (2006). Lifecycle bias in estimates of intergenerational earnings persistence. *Labour Economics, 13*(5), 551–570.

Grusky, D. B., & DiPrete, T. A. (1990). Recent trends in the process of stratification. *Demography, 27*(4), 617–637.

Hansen, M. (2010). Change in intergenerational economic mobility in norway: Conventional versus joint classifications of economic origin. *Journal of Economic Inequality, 8*(2), 133–151.

Hauser, R. M. (2010). *Intergenerational economic mobility in the United States: Measures, differentials, and trends*. Department of Sociology, Center for Demography and Ecology, The University of Wisconsin-Madison, Madison, WI.

Hauser, R. M., & Carter, W. Y. (1995). The bell curve: A perspective from sociology. *Focus, 17*, 2.

Hauser, R. M., & Warren, J. R. (1997). Socioeconomic indexes for occupations: A review, update, and critique. *Sociological Methodology, 27*(1), 177–298.

Haveman, R., & Wolfe, B. (1995). The determinants of children's attainments: A review of methods and findings [Review]. *Journal of Economic Literature, 33*(4), 1829–1878.

Herrnstein, R. J., & Murray, C. (1994). *The bell curve: Intelligence and class structure in American life*. New York, NY: The Free Press.

Hertz, T. (2005). Rags, riches and race: Intergenerational economic mobility of black and white families in the United States. In S. Bowles, H. Gintis, & M. Osbourne (Eds.), *Unequal chances: Family background and economic success*. Princeton, NJ: Russell Sage Foundation Press, Princeton University Press.

Hertz, T. (2006). *Understanding mobility in America*. Washington, DC: Center for American Progress.

Hertz, T., Jayasunderay, T., Pirainoz, P., Selcuk, S., Smithy, N., & Verashchaginaz, A. (2007). The inheritance of educational inequality: International comparisons and fifty-year trends. *The B.E. Journal of Economic Analysis & Policy, 7*(2), 10.

Hill, M., & Duncan, G. J. (1987). Parental family income and the socioeconomic attainment of children. *Social Science Research, 16*(1), 39–73.

Hirvonen, L. H. (2008). Intergenerational earnings mobility among daughters and sons: Evidence from sweden and a comparison with the United States. *American Journal of Economics and Sociology, 67*(5), 777–826.

Hobcraft, J. (2001). *Intergenerational transmission of inequality in a British birth cohort*. Paper presented at the Population Association of America Annual Meeting.

Jencks, C., Smith, M., Acland, H., Bane, M. J., Cohen, D., Gintis, H., ... Michelson, S. (1972). *Inequality: A reassessment of the effect of family and schooling in America.* New York, NY: Basic Books.

Jencks, C., Bartlett, S., Corcan, M., Crouse, J., Eaglesfield, D., Jackson, G., ... Williams, J. (1979). *Who gets ahead ahead? The determinants of economic success in America.* New York, NY: Basic Books.

Jencks, C., & Tach, L. (2006). Would equal opportunity mean more mobility? In S. L. Morgan, D. B. Grusky, & G. S. Fields (Eds.), *Mobility and inequality.* Stanford, CA: Stanford University Press.

Keister, L. A. (2005). *Getting rich: America's new rich and how they got that way.* Cambrige: Cambridge University Press.

Kiker, B. F., & Condon, C. M. (1981). The influence of socioeconomic background on the earnings of young men. *Journal of Human Resources, 16*(1), 94–105.

Kingston, P. W. (2000). *The classless society.* Stanford, CA: Stanford University Press.

Korenman, S., & Winship, C. (2000). A reanalysis of the bell curve: Intelligence, family, background and schools. In K. Arrow, S. Bowles, & S. Durlauf (Eds.), *Meritocracy and economic inequality* (pp. 137–178). Princeton, NJ: Princeton University Press.

Leigh, A. (2007). Intergenerational mobility in Australia. *The B.E. Journal of Economic Analysis and Policy, 7*(2), Article 6.

Lillard, L. A. (1977). Inequality: Earnings vs. human wealth. *American Economic Review, 67*(2), 42–53.

Lipset, S. M., & Zetterberg, H. (1959). Social mobility in industrial societies. In S. M. Lipset & R. Bendix (Eds.), *Social mobility in industrial society* (pp. 11–75). Berkeley, CA: University of California Press.

Liu, H., & Zeng, J. (2009). Genetic ability and intergenerational earnings mobility. *Journal of Population Economics, 22*(1), 75–95.

Marks, G. N. (2005). Cross-national differences and accounting for social class inequalities in education. *International Sociology, 20*(4), 483–505.

Marks, G. N. (2011). Issues in the conceptualisation and measurement of socioeconomic background: Do different measures generate different conclusions? *Social Indicators Research, 104*(2), 225–251.

Mayer, S. E. (1997). *What money can't buy: Family income and children's life chances.* Cambridge, MA: Harvard University Press.

Mayer, S. E., & Lopoo, L. M. (2005). Has the intergenerational transmission of economic status changed? *Journal of Human Resources, 40*(1), 169–185.

Mazumder, B. (2001). *Earnings mobility in the us: A new look at intergenerational mobility.* Chicago, IL: Federal Reserve Bank of Chicago.

Mazumder, B. (2005). Fortunate sons: New estimates of intergenerational mobility in the United States using social security earnings data. *Review of Economics and Statistics, 87*(2), 235–255.

Morgan, S. L., & Kim, Y.-M. (2005). Inequality of conditions and intergenerational mobility: Changing patterns of educational attainment in the United States. In S. L. Morgan, D. B. Grusky, & G. S. Fields (Eds.), *Mobility and inequality: Frontiers of research from sociology and economics.* Stanford, CA: Stanford University Press.

Muller, S. M. (2010). Another problem in the estimation of intergenerational income mobility. *Economics Letters, 108*(3), 291–295.

Ng, I. Y. H., Shen, X., & Ho, K. W. (2009). Intergenerational earnings mobility in Singapore and the United States. *Journal of Asian Economics, 20*(2), 110–119.

OECD. (2009). Growing unequal? Income distribution and poverty in oecd countries. *Paris Organization for Economic Co-operation and Development.*

Olneck, M. R. (1977). On the use of sibling data to estimate the effects of family background, cognitive skills and schooling. In P. Taubman (Ed.), *Kinometrics: Determinants of socio-economic success within and between families.* Amsterdam: North-Holland Publishing.

Orr, A. J. (2003). Black-white differences in achievement: The importance of wealth. *Sociology of Education, 76*(4), 281–304.

Pfeffer, F. (2011). Status attainment and wealth in the United States and Germany. In R. Erikson, M. Jäntti, & T. M. Smeeding (Eds.), *The comparative study of inter-generational mobility.* New York, NY: Russell Sage Foundation.

Rumberger, R. W. (1983). The influence of family background on education, earnings, and wealth. *Social Forces, 61*(3), 755–773.

Saunders, P. (1996). *Unequal but fair? A study of class barriers in Britain. Choice in welfare* (Vol. 28). London: IEA Health and Welfare Unit.

Sewell, W. H., Haller, A. O., & Ohlendorf, G. (1970). The educational and early occupational status attainment process: Replication and revision. *American Sociological Review, 35*(5), 1014–1027.

Sewell, W. H., & Hauser, R. M. (1975). *Education, occupation and earnings. Achievement in the Early Career.* New York, NY: Academic Press.

Sewell, W. H., Hauser, R. M., & Wolf, W. C. (1980). Sex, schooling, and occupational status. *American Journal of Sociology, 86*(3), 551–583.

Solon, G. (1992). Intergenerational income mobility in the United States. *American Economic Review, 82,* 393–408.

Solon, G. (1999). Intergenerational mobility in the labor market. In O. Ashenfelter & D. Card (Eds), *Handbook of labor economics* (pp. 1761–1800). Amsterdam: Elsevier.

Solon, G. (2002). Cross-country differences in intergenerational earnings mobility. *Journal of Economic Perspectives, 16*(3), 59–66.

Strenze, T. (2007). Intelligence and socioeconomic success: A meta-analytic review of longitudinal research. *Intelligence, 35*(5), 401–426.

Taubman, P. (1976). Earnings, education, genetics, and environment. *The Journal of Human Resources, 11*(4), 447–461.

Teachman, J. (1987). Family background, educational resources and educational attainment. *American Sociological Review, 52,* 548–557.

Thomas, G. E., Alexander, K. L., & Eckland, B. K. (1979). Access to higher education: The importance of race, sex, social class, and academic credentials. *The School Review, 87*(2), 133–156.

Treiman, D., & Yip, K.-B. (1989). Education and occupational attainment in 21 countries. In M. L. Kohn (Ed.), *Cross national research in sociology* (pp. 373–394). Newbury Park, CA: Sage.

Woessmann, L. (2008). How equal are educational opportunities? Family background and student achievement in Europe and the United States [CESifo Working Paper]. *Zeitschrift für Betriebswirtschaft, 78,* 45–70.

Wong, R. S.-K. (1990). Understanding cross-national variation in occupational mobility. *American Sociological Review, 55*(4), 560–573.

Zhang, L. (2005). Advance to graduate education: The effect of college quality and undergraduate majors. *Review of Higher Education, 28*(3), 313–333.

Zimmerman, D. J. (1992). Regression toward mediocrity in economic statue. *American Economic Review, 82*(3), 409–429.

THE INTERNATIONAL STANDARD CLASSIFICATION OF EDUCATION 2011

Silke L. Schneider

ABSTRACT

The International Standard Classification of Education (ISCED) is a tool for harmonising education-related information. It covers almost all countries in the world and is centrally maintained and documented by UNESCO Institute for Statistics. ISCED is commonly used in official statistics and surveys (e.g. by OECD and Eurostat), but it is also increasingly used for the measurement of educational attainment in academic cross-national surveys. ISCED has been revised between 2008 and 2011, and the new version was adopted by the UNESCO General Conference in November 2011. This research note describes ISCED 2011 and the most important changes as compared to the previous version, ISCED 1997, with a special focus on educational attainment. A brief discussion of strengths and weaknesses of the classification as well as future challenges conclude the note.

Keywords: Education; measurement; comparative research; classification

Class and Stratification Analysis
Comparative Social Research, Volume 30, 365–379
Copyright © 2013 by Emerald Group Publishing Limited
ISSN: 0195-6310/doi:10.1108/S0195-6310(2013)0000030017

INTRODUCTION

An individual's educational attainment, or often simply 'education', is one of the most used concepts and variables in sociological survey research (Smith, 1995). Education is meant to draw distinctions between people and thus implies inequality in education (Lucas & Beresford, 2010). In social stratification research, educational attainment is typically a substantive variable, whereas in other research areas, it functions often as a control variable. Of course, both substantive and control variables should be measured with a high degree of quality (i.e. reliability and validity).

A continuing challenge of comparative social research is the measurement of educational attainment in cross-national surveys and studies. In this context, measurement quality in addition to validity and reliability also entails cross-national *comparability*. A number of solutions to this problem have been proposed in the past, usually involving the harmonisation of country-specific educational attainment variables into cross-nationally comparable variables (Brauns, Scherer, & Steinmann, 2003; Hoffmeyer-Zlotnik & Warner, 2007; Treiman & Yip, 1989; Schneider, 2010).[1]

A classification to serve this purpose that is commonly used in official surveys and also increasingly so in academic surveys is the International Standard Classification of Education, ISCED. All official cross-national data already use ISCED for education-related variables. Academic surveys like the European Social Survey (ESS), the Survey of Health, Aging and Retirement in Europe (SHARE) and, more recently, the International Social Survey Programme (ISSP) also use educational attainment measures closely related to ISCED.

This research note describes ISCED 2011 and the most important changes as compared to the previous version, ISCED 1997. In the last part, strengths and weaknesses of the classification are discussed from a conceptual point of view.[2]

THE INTERNATIONAL STANDARD CLASSIFICATION OF EDUCATION

ISCED is an internationally agreed classification designed for the cross-nationally comparable coding, analysis and reporting of data related to educational programmes and qualifications. It was initially developed for policy planning and the promotion of education worldwide. Its first version was adopted in 1975 and then revised in 1997 (UNESCO, 2006[1997]). This revision was motivated by the OECD to improve economically relevant education indicators in order to promote the performance of educational systems and thereby economies. Its most recent version, ISCED 2011, was adopted in November 2011 (UNESCO, 2011). This revision was promoted by Eurostat because of the Bologna reforms and the importance of ISCED for the production of education-related indicators, e.g., in the Europe 2020 strategy.

ISCED has, since the 1970s, been used as the standard for international education statistics and indicators as published e.g. by UNESCO, the OECD or Eurostat (e.g. OECD, 2011). In line with its initial purpose, the technical means and data available, ISCED made use of administrative rather than survey data in the early phase. ISCED 1997 was still highly focused on concepts to be derived from administrative data. But slowly, the focus changed from enrolment, finance and personnel statistics (education inputs) to indicators related to educational attainment as well as knowledge, skills and competences (education outputs).[3] Sample surveys organised by official bodies such as OECD and Eurostat (e.g. PISA, PIAAC, EU-LFS or EU-SILC) have therefore started to use ISCED in the late 1990s for the coding of micro-data related to educational attainment. Given ISCED 1997 was not designed to be used for survey data and lacked the relevant concepts for this purpose, especially the concept of educational attainment, this development was another driver of the 2011 revision. Finally, ISCED 97 did not yet provide a standard coding system.

CENTRAL CONCEPTS AND COVERAGE OF ISCED

The units of classification of ISCED are educational programmes and qualifications.[4] The term 'educational qualification' was introduced to ISCED for the first time with ISCED 2011. Educational attainment is defined as the highest level of education successfully completed, as typically indicated by the highest educational qualification obtained. Statistical indicators related to entrants, enrolments, drop out and graduations are based on data referring to educational programmes, whereas indicators related to educational attainment are thus (mostly) based on data referring to formal educational qualifications.

ISCED classifies educational programmes and qualifications by level and field of education. In the terms of Sørensen (1970), the former reflects vertical and the latter horizontal distinctions. The sub-classification for field of education has not been reviewed for ISCED 2011. Fields of study are not covered in this research note.

Generally, only formal education is taken into account when measuring educational attainment. Formal and non-formal education are distinguished by the recognition (or not) of an educational programme as part of the country's educational system by the relevant authorities. Formal education is ultimately institutionalised by the state, whereas non-formal education is designed by its providers in order to complement the formal education system.

LEVELS OF EDUCATION IN ISCED 2011 AND COMPARISON WITH ISCED 1997

Levels of education group educational programmes and qualifications into an ordered series of categories, which represent gradations from foundational to complex and specialised educational content and learning outcomes. ISCED 2011 has nine levels of education, compared to seven levels in ISCED 1997.[5] This is due to the differentiation of tertiary education in accordance with the Bologna process. Table 1 shows the correspondence between ISCED levels in ISCED 2011 and ISCED 1997.

ISCED level 0 or early childhood education provides learning and educational activities with a holistic approach to support children's early cognitive, physical, social and emotional development. In contrast to ISCED 1997, ISCED 2011 also covers (and distinguishes, on the second digit) early childhood educational development, which refers to educational programmes targeting children under the age of 3. For educational attainment, ISCED level 0 is defined as not having completed primary education. For countries where this is common, the second digit can then be used to distinguish 'no education (at all)' from 'some primary education' also a new feature of ISCED 2011.

ISCED level 1 or primary education provides learning and educational activities typically designed to provide students with fundamental skills in reading, writing and mathematics (i.e. literacy and numeracy). The content of this level was not changed in ISCED 2011.

Secondary education is differentiated into ISCED levels 2 and 3. Broadly speaking, secondary education aims at learning at an intermediate level of complexity. It provides learning and educational activities building on primary education and preparing for both labour market entry as well as

Table 1.   Correspondence of ISCED Levels for 1997 and 2011 Versions.

ISCED 2011		ISCED 1997	
Level	Label	Level	Label
0	Early childhood education (attainment: less than primary education)	0	Pre-primary education
1	Primary education	1	Primary education
2	Lower secondary education	2	Lower secondary education
3	Upper secondary education	3	Upper secondary education
4	Post-secondary non-tertiary education	4	Post-secondary non-tertiary education
5	Short cycle tertiary education	5	First stage of tertiary education
6	Bachelor level education and equivalent		
7	Master level education and equivalent		
8	Doctoral level education	6	Second stage of tertiary education

post-secondary and tertiary education. Whereas ISCED level 2 or lower secondary education usually covers a broad range of fields of education and does not yet give access to tertiary education, ISCED level 3 or upper secondary education offers more specialisation and access to tertiary education.

ISCED level 4 or post-secondary non-tertiary education provides learning and educational activities building on secondary education preparing for both labour market entry as well as tertiary education. It aims at learning below the high level of complexity characteristic of tertiary education, e.g. in the form of vocational training after the completion of secondary education. Although there were intentions to abolish this level, it has in the end been kept to satisfy needs in a number of countries.

ISCED levels 5 to 8 or tertiary education builds on upper secondary education, providing learning opportunities in specialised fields of education at a high level of complexity. ISCED levels 5 to 7 are where most changes happened between ISCED 1997 and 2011. Tertiary education includes what is commonly understood as higher education, but is broader than that because it also includes advanced vocational or professional education below the level of a first university degree (ISCED level 5, which largely corresponds to the former ISCED 5B) that is not considered as part of higher education in all countries. ISCED level 6 or bachelor level education corresponds to the level of first university degrees to be obtained after 3 to 4 years of study. ISCED level 7 or master level education corresponds to the level of first university degrees to be obtained after more than 4 years of study, or second university degrees and post-graduate qualifications below the doctoral level. ISCED level 8 finally comprises only doctoral programmes and thus corresponds to ISCED level 6 in ISCED 1997.

COMPLEMENTARY DIMENSIONS IN ISCED

Given the differentiation of educational systems, ISCED offers further distinctions within levels relating to several complementary dimensions: programme orientation, level completion, and access to higher ISCED levels.[6]

The *orientation* of an educational programme refers to its specialisation and what kinds of tasks it prepares participants to perform upon successful completion. *Vocational education* is defined as 'Education that is designed for learners to acquire the knowledge, skills and competencies specific to a particular occupation or trade or class of occupations or trades' (UNESCO, 2011, p. 81). This definition largely corresponds to the respective concept in ISCED 97. *General education* in contrast is defined as 'Education that is designed to develop learners' general knowledge, skills and competencies and literacy and numeracy skills, often to prepare students for more advanced educational programmes at the same or higher ISCED levels and to lay the foundation for lifelong learning' (UNESCO, 2011, p. 80). ISCED 1997 had a third orientation category called 'pre-vocational education' comprising programmes preparing for vocational education. These are typically general programmes with introductory vocational elements and lower academic standards than other general programmes at the same level of education that do not yet provide a full vocational qualification. This category was dropped with ISCED 2011 in order to simplify the complementary dimensions.

Access to a higher ISCED level distinguishes educational programmes and qualifications that give access to the next higher ISCED level from those that don't. The latter are also referred to as *terminal* programmes, although some of them may lead to another programme at the same ISCED level. For ISCED level 3, the 'next higher' ISCED level is tertiary education, thus ISCED levels 5, 6 and 7, rather than level 4. In ISCED 1997, there were three *destination* categories, which were however inconsistent across levels. ISCED 2011 drops the 'access' dimension from tertiary education (5A vs. 5B) and for secondary education summarises the former destination categories A and B in 'access' and C in 'no access'.

Completion of an ISCED level is an important characteristic of an educational programme and qualification for determining an individuals' level of educational attainment. Some qualifications result from educational programmes that are too short to be considered as completing the level at which the programme is classified. They are thus regarded as attainment of the next lower ISCED level only. In ISCED 1997, the concept of level completion was only provided for in ISCED category 3C by distinguishing between short and long terminal programmes in ISCED 3C.

Access to a higher ISCED level and level completion partly overlap: Programmes that do not (fully) complete an ISCED level generally do not give access to the next higher ISCED level. Within programmes that *do* complete an ISCED level, a distinction is made between those that give access to the next higher ISCED level and those that don't. Orientation is in turn conceptually independent from both 'access' and 'completion', although empirically there will also be more and less common combinations (e.g. there are only very few general education qualifications completing a level but not providing access to a higher ISCED level).

THE ISCED 2011 CODING SCHEME

ISCED 1997 did not have a numeric coding scheme. Whenever data were presented with more detail than just the (numbered) ISCED levels, different users and organisations developed their own way of coding ISCED, substantially limiting the comparative potential of ISCED. ISCED 2011 offers two standard coding schemes with three digits, one for educational programmes (ISCED-P), and one for educational attainment (ISCED-A). This distinction is necessary because the completion of 'short' programmes at an ISCED level is not considered as leading to attainment of that level (see above) so that the programme and the corresponding qualification cannot be classified in the same way. Furthermore, some distinctions are only important for programme-based statistics, but not for attainment, like a programme's position in the national qualification structure. Beyond these points, both coding schemes are however fairly consistent.

The first digit of the classification refers to the ISCED level of the programme or qualification. The second and third digits of the classification refer to specific values on the complementary dimensions. Most of them only apply to specific levels and have only few different values, so that different complementary dimensions were combined in one digit. This may look strange at first, but was necessary because of stakeholders' reluctance

Table 2. ISCED Coding Scheme for Educational
Attainment ('ISCED-A').

First digit: level of education attained
0   Less than primary
1   Primary
2   Lower secondary
3   Upper secondary
4   Post-secondary non-tertiary
5   Short cycle tertiary
6   Bachelor or equivalent
7   Master or equivalent
8   Doctoral or equivalent
9   Not elsewhere classified

Second digit
0   Not further defined/not applicable
9   Not elsewhere classified
Sub-category within ISCED level 0
1   Never attended an educational   These codes do not apply to ISCED levels
       programme   1–8
2   Some early childhood education
3   Some primary education (without level
       completion)
Orientation of the qualification
4   General/Academic   These codes do not apply to ISCED levels
5   Vocational/Professional   0–1. Code 6 is only foreseen for ISCED
6   Orientation unspecified   levels 5–8.

Third digit
0   Not further defined/not applicable
9   Not elsewhere classified
Level completion and access to a higher ISCED level
2   Partial level completion, no access to   These codes do not apply to ISCED levels
       higher ISCED level (levels 5/6/7 for   0–1 and 5–8.
       ISCED level 3)
3   Level completion, no access to higher
       ISCED level (levels 5/6/7 for ISCED
       level 3)
4   Level completion, access to higher
       ISCED level (levels 5/6/7 for ISCED
       level 3)[a]

[a]Including successful completion of a programme or stage of a programme at a higher ISCED
level insufficient for (full or partial) level completion.

to use further digits. Since this paper focuses on educational attainment, Table 2 shows the coding structure for educational attainment only. Given not all differentiations apply at all ISCED levels, the total number of ISCED categories is much lower than a three-digit coding scheme may suggest. Table A.1 listing all combinations foreseen by ISCED-A is provided in the appendix.

As an example, an individual with completed general lower secondary education with access to upper secondary but without any higher qualification would be coded 244 (e.g. Hauptschulabschluss in Germany or Brevet de college in France). A respondent with a bachelor's degree would be coded 660, and one with a PhD 800.

DISCUSSION

There are three core strengths of ISCED 2011 for social science research. First, it permits increasing standardisation in the measurement of education by providing standard three-digit coding schemes for both educational programmes (ISCED-P) and educational attainment (ISCED-A). It could thus become much easier in the future to provide and apply coding routines for education-related information (comparable to what ISCO already provides for occupation). Second, ISCED covers almost all countries in the world and is thus widely applicable. Since 1997, mappings linking national educational programmes with detailed ISCED categories have been developed for a large number of countries,[7] and these will be extended in the future. Third, the concept of educational attainment that was added to ISCED 2011 closely corresponds to the typical proxy measures for human and cultural capital in the social sciences.

Although a lot of progress has been made between ISCED 1997 and ISCED 2011, ISCED 2011 is still unsatisfactory from the point of view of social science and especially social stratification research.

The most important dimension of educational systems that ISCED does not grasp is external differentiation, also referred to as 'tracking' (e.g. LeTendre et al., 2003). It means that pupils or students are sorted into different types of educational programmes (often even different types of schools) depending on their level of ability and achievement. If these different programmes do not differ on any of the other dimensions relevant to ISCED (e.g. orientation), this distinction disappears in data coded using ISCED. This, for example, happens with the different types of lower secondary schools in the Netherlands and German speaking countries. Why does ISCED omit this prominent feature of educational systems? First, it is only relevant to a rather small number of European countries. Second, the governments of those countries do not have any interest in this feature being traceable in ISCED.[8]

Furthermore, ISCED 2011 is supposed to clarify the boundary between ISCED levels 2 and 3, which is disputed in Britain and in countries inspired by the British educational system (see Schneider, 2008 and Steedman, 1996). I have strong doubts whether the introduction of the concept of 'partial level completion' achieves this clarification – on the contrary it legitimises the classification of GCSEs as 'not quite complete upper secondary education' as completed ISCED level 3 (even if only 'partially completed'). This is like saying that somebody who ran 80 instead of 100 m has 'successfully completed' a 100 m race, just because it was substantially more than what would have been necessary for a 50 m race.

A third weak point of ISCED is the boundary between post-secondary non-tertiary and tertiary education. This is important because the dimension 'access to a higher level' of an ISCED level 3 programme depends on where the 'accessible' programmes are classified – at level 4 (then: no access) or level 5 (then: access, even if there is no access to level 6). In consequence, quite incomparable national programmes and qualifications end up in the same ISCED categories. For example, an apprenticeship in Germany, giving access to master craft programmes at ISCED level 5, is classified as 354 despite the fact that these programmes do not give access to studies at the bachelor level. In most other countries, educational programmes in ISCED category 354 would give access to the bachelor level also, e.g. vocational matura in Eastern European countries.

Finally, the main weakness of ISCED is one that is implied by its origins: the classification is maintained by official bodies and needs to be adopted by the UNESCO general conference with every major revision. This makes the concepts building ISCED vulnerable to political interests, and the weaknesses described previously to a large degree arise from the agenda-setting of the political rather than research communities. Education remains a politically highly charged field, and governments do not like to see the effects of tracking exposed, and they want to look good in the 'league tables' produced by the OECD and in the Europe 2020 indicators. Basically, there is a lack of legitimacy in a statistical tool that is developed by the same community who has the strongest interests in avoiding certain aspects of the concept in question to be measured: it's like putting the fox in charge of the henhouse. The influence of scientific evidence or otherwise more disinterested expertise on the review and implementation process continues to be minimal. UNESCO Institute for Statistics, OECD and Eurostat seem to have only little leverage and enthusiasm to engage in conflict with individual countries as regards to recommending (or enforcing) a correct mapping of ISCED to national education systems.

The latest ISCED revision process was however more open and structured than the previous one, leading to a substantially higher input from around the world, including statisticians, (a few) researchers and practitioners, compared to the small panel of seven designing ISCED 1997. Over the last 10 years and with the current revision, documentation of ISCED has also improved considerably. These days, a fair number of governments and national statistical offices are also seriously committed to the goal of high-quality cross-nationally comparable data rather than just their own country's position on international education indicators, and the ISCED mappings can broadly be regarded as adequate for most (but certainly not all) countries.

Research using large-scale surveys will be increasingly *bound* to using ISCED because many large surveys are conducted by official bodies relying on ISCED. Given the weaknesses of ISCED continue to be substantial, the social science research community should better try to influence it in the future. The community should engage in a lasting debate with official statistics, and official bodies should invite researchers to do so. A stronger engagement of the scientific community with concepts from official statistics could improve the way ISCED will be implemented in official surveys like the EU-LFS, which will be determined in the next couple of years. In the long run, further improvements of ISCED itself could be aimed at: the next revision will be on its way 10 or 15 years down the road.

ACKNOWLEDGEMENTS

I would like to thank UNESCO Institute for Statistics (UIS) for the invitation to serve on the ISCED Technical Advisory Panel and the panel members for the fruitful discussions. I would also like to thank Michael Bruneforth at bifie, Austria, for his valuable contributions to the discussion of ISCED 2011 and have borrowed the illustration of 'partial completion' by an 80 m run in a 100 m race from him.

NOTES

1. Educationalists and psychometricians have in addition developed complex tests to measure individuals' competences and skills in a range of areas (e.g. literacy or

numeracy). These are not the subject of this paper because actual skills and educational attainment in terms of qualifications obtained are, although related, different concepts. Educational attainment reflects those elements of knowledge and skills that were officially recognised at some point in an individual's life.

2. For empirical evaluations of different harmonised educational attainment measures, see Braun and Müller (1997), Kerckhoff, Dylan, Ezell and Brown (1999, 2002) and Schneider (2010).

3. For detailed accounts of the historical development of ISCED, see Sauvageot (2008), Smyth (2008) and Tréhin-Lalanne (2011).

4. Definitions of those terms can be found in the main text as well as in the glossary which is annexed to the official ISCED document (UNESCO, 2011, pp. 77–85).

5. For a detailed description of ISCED 1997, see UNESCO (2006[1997]), Schneider and Kogan (2008) and Sauvageot (2008).

6. For ISCED levels 6 and 7, there is also a distinction by a qualification's *position in the national degree and qualification structure*. This is irrelevant for educational attainment and thus not further presented here.

7. See http://www.uis.unesco.org/Education/ISCEDMappings/ and http://circa.europa.eu/Public/irc/dsis/edtcs/library?l = /public/unesco_collection/programmes_isced97/

8. While tracking is most visible in secondary education, it also exists in tertiary education. Conceptually, this distinction is more difficult to make, but broadly speaking an upper and a lower tier of higher education can often be distinguished by referring to different entry requirements or qualifications and fields of study offered as well as focus on teaching for application or research. The external differentiation of the higher education sector continues to be regarded as an important social stratifier (Shavit et al., 2007).

REFERENCES

Braun, M., & Müller, W. (1997). Measurement of education in comparative research. *Comparative Social Research, 16*, 163–201.

Brauns, H., Scherer, S., & Steinmann, S. (2003). The CASMIN educational classification in international comparative research. In J. H. P. Hoffmeyer-Zlotnik & C. Wolf (Eds.), *Advances in cross-national comparison: A European working book for demographic and socio-economic variables* (pp. 221–244). New York: Kluwer Academic/Plenum.

Hoffmeyer-Zlotnik, J. H. P., & Warner, U. (2007). How to survey education for cross-national comparisons: The Hoffmeyer-Zlotnik/Warner-matrix of education. *Metodološki zvezki, 4*(2), 117–148.

Kerckhoff, A. C., & Dylan, M. (1999). Problems with international measures of education. *Journal of Socio-Economics, 28*(6), 759–775.

Kerckhoff, A. C., Ezell, E. D., & Brown, J. S. (2002). Toward an improved measure of educational attainment in social stratification research. *Social Science Research, 31*(1), 99–123.

LeTendre, G. K., Hofer, B. K., & Shimizu, H. (2003). What is tracking? Cultural expectations in the United States, Germany, and Japan. *American Educational Research Journal, 40*(1), 43–89.

Lucas, S. R., & Beresford, L. (2010). Naming and classifying: Theory, evidence, and equity in education. *Review of Research in Education, 34*(1), 25–84.

OECD. (2011). *Education at a glance: OECD indicators 2011 edition.* Paris: OECD.

Sauvageot, C. (2008). Un outil au service des comparaisons internationales: la Classification Internationale Type de l'Éducation. *Éducation & formations, 78*, 221–232.

Schneider, S. L. (2008). The application of the ISCED-97 to the UK's educational qualifications. In S. L. Schneider (Ed.), *The international standard classification of education (ISCED-97). An evaluation of content and criterion validity for 15 European countries* (pp. 281–300). Mannheim: MZES.

Schneider, S. L. (2010). Nominal comparability is not enough: (In-)equivalence of construct validity of cross-national measures of educational attainment in the European social survey. *Research in Social Stratification and Mobility, 28*(3), 343–357.

Schneider, S. L., & Kogan, I. (2008). The international standard classification of education 1997: Challenges in the application to national data and the implementation in cross-national surveys. In S. L. Schneider (Ed.), *The international standard classification of education (ISCED-97). An evaluation of content and criterion validity for 15 European countries* (pp. 13–46). Mannheim: MZES.

Shavit, Y., Arum, R., & Gamoran, A. (Eds.). (2007). *Stratification in higher education: A comparative study.* Stanford, CA: Stanford University Press.

Smith, T. W. (1995). Some aspects of measuring education. *Social Science Research, 24*(3), 215–242.

Smyth, J. A. (2008). The origins of the international standard classification of education. *Peabody Journal of Education, 83*(1), 5–40.

Sørensen, A. B. (1970). Organizational differentiation of students and educational opportunity. *Sociology of Education, 43*(4), 355–376.

Steedman, H. (1996). *Measuring the quality of educational outputs: A note.* London: Centre for Economic Performance, LSE.

Tréhin-Lalanne, R. (2011). Mesurer l'éducation à l'ère de la « société de la connaissance »: les usages de la Classification Internationale Type de l'Éducation. *Éducation & formations, 80*, 9–16.

Treiman, D. J., & Yip, K.-B. (1989). Educational and occupational attainment in 21 countries. In M. L. Kohn (Ed.), *Cross-national research in sociology* (pp. 373–394). Newbury Park: Sage.

UNESCO. (2006[1997]). *International Standard Classification of Education: ISCED 1997* (rev. ed.). Montreal: UNESCO Institute for Statistics.

UNESCO. (2011). *Revision of the international standard classification of education.* Paris: UNESCO Retrieved from http://www.uis.unesco.org/Education/Documents/UNESCO_GC_36C-19_ISCED_EN.pdf

APPENDIX

Table A.1. List of Codes of the Classification of Educational Attainment ('ISCED-A') in ISCED 2011 (UNESCO Institute for Statistics, 2011).

0 Less than primary
  01 Never attended an educational programme
    010 Not further defined
  02 Some early childhood education
    020 Not further defined
  03 Some primary education (without level completion)
    030 Not further defined
1 Primary
  10 Not further defined
    100 Not further defined
2 Lower secondary
  24 General
    242 Partial level completion and without access to upper secondary
    243 Level completion but without direct access to upper secondary
    244 Level completion with direct access to upper secondary[a]
  25 Vocational
    252 Partial level completion and without access to upper secondary
    253 Level completion but without direct access to upper secondary
    254 Level completion with direct access to upper secondary[a]
3 Upper secondary
  34 General
    342 Ppartial level completion and without access to tertiary
    343 Level completion but without direct access to tertiary
    344 Level completion with direct access to tertiary[a]
  35 Vocational
    352 Partial level completion and without access to tertiary
    353 Level completion but without direct access to tertiary
    354 Level completion with direct access to tertiary[a]
4 Post-secondary non-tertiary
  44 General
    443 Level completion but without direct access to tertiary education at ISCED 5, 6 or 7
    444 Level completion with direct access to tertiary education at ISCED 5, 6 or 7[a]
  45 Vocational
    453 Level completion but without direct access to tertiary education at ISCED 5, 6 or 7
    454 Level completion with direct access to tertiary education at ISCED 5, 6 or 7[a]
5 Short cycle tertiary
  54 General
    540 Not further defined
  55 Professional
    550 Not further defined

Table A.1. (*Continued*)

56 Orientation unspecified[a]
  560 Not further defined
6 Bachelor or equivalent
  64 Academic
    640 Not further defined
  65 Professional
    650 Not further defined
  66 Orientation unspecified[b]
    660 Not further defined
7 Master or equivalent
  74 Academic
    740 Not further defined
  75 Professional
    750 Not further defined
  76 Orientation unspecified[b]
    760 Not further defined
8 Doctoral or equivalent
  84 Academic
    840 Not further defined
  85 Professional
    850 Not further defined
  86 Orientation unspecified[b]
    860 Not further defined
9 Not elsewhere classified

[a]Including successful completion of a programme or stage of a programme at a higher ISCED level insufficient for level completion or partial completion.
[b]To be used in the absence of internationally agreed definitions of academic and professional orientations of qualifications (or intermediate qualifications) from the successful completion of programmes (or stages of programmes) at ISCED levels 6–8.